The Indian Princes and Their States

Although the princes of India have been caricatured as Oriental despots and British stooges, Barbara Ramusack's study argues that the British did not create the princes. On the contrary, many were consummate politicians who exercised considerable degrees of autonomy until the integration of the princely states after independence. Ramusack's synthesis has a broad temporal span, tracing the evolution of the Indian kings from their pre-colonial origins to their roles as clients in the British colonial system. The book breaks new ground in its integration of political and economic developments in the major princely states with the shifting relationships between the princes and the British. It represents a significant contribution, both to British imperial history in its analysis of the theory and practice of indirect rule, and to modern South Asian history, as a portrait of the princes as politicians and patrons of the arts.

BARBARA N. RAMUSACK is Charles Phelps Taft Professor of History at the University of Cincinnati. Her publications include *Women in Asia: Restoring Women to History* (1999), and *The Princes of India in the Twilight of Empire: The Dissolution of a Patron–Client System, 1914–1939* (1978).

THE NEW CAMBRIDGE HISTORY OF INDIA

General editor GORDON JOHNSON

President of Wolfson College, and Director, Centre of South Asian Studies,
University of Cambridge

Associate editors C. A. BAYLY

Vere Harmsworth Professor of Imperial and Naval History, University of Cambridge,
and Fellow of St Catharine's College

and JOHN F. RICHARDS

Professor of History, Duke University

Although the original *Cambridge History of India*, published between 1922 and 1937, did much to formulate a chronology for Indian history and describe the administrative structures of government in India, it has inevitably been overtaken by the mass of new research over the past sixty years.

Designed to take full account of recent scholarship and changing conceptions of South Asia's historical development, *The New Cambridge History of India* is published as a series of short, self-contained volumes, each dealing with a separate theme and written by one or two authors. Within an overall four-part structure, thirty-one complementary volumes in uniform format will be published. Each will conclude with a substantial bibliographical essay designed to lead non-specialists further into the literature.

The four parts planned are as follows:

I The Mughals and their Contemporaries

II Indian States and the Transition to Colonialism

III The Indian Empire and the Beginnings of Modern Society

IV The Evolution of Contemporary South Asia

*A list of individual titles in preparation will be found
at the end of the volume.*

THE NEW CAMBRIDGE HISTORY OF INDIA

III · 6

The Indian Princes and Their States

BARBARA N. RAMUSACK
University of Cincinnati

CAMBRIDGE
UNIVERSITY PRESS

For Margaret, Roberta, Jerry and George

PUBLISHED BY THE PRESS SYNDICATE OF THE UNIVERSITY OF CAMBRIDGE
The Pitt Building, Trumpington Street, Cambridge, United Kingdom

CAMBRIDGE UNIVERSITY PRESS
The Edinburgh Building, Cambridge CB2 2RU, UK
40 West 20th Street, New York, NY 10011–4211, USA
477 Williamstown Road, Port Melbourne, Vic 3207, Australia
Ruiz de Alarcón 13, 28014 Madrid, Spain
Dock House, The Waterfront, Cape Town 8001, South Africa

http://www.cambridge.org

First published 2004

Printed in China through Bookbuilders

Typeface Garamond 10.5/13 pt.   *System* LATEX 2_ε [TB]

A catalogue record for this book is available from the British Library

National Library of Australia Cataloguing in Publication data
Ramusack, Barbara N.
The Indian princes and their states.

Bibliography.
Includes index.
ISBN 0 521 26727 7.

1. Princes – India.   2. India – History – British
occupation, 1765–1947.   3. India – Kings and rulers.
4. India – Politics and government – 1765–1947.   I. Title.
(Series: New Cambridge history of India ; III, 6).
954.03

ISBN 0 521 26727 7 hardback

CONTENTS

v

ILLUSTRATIONS

GENERAL EDITOR'S PREFACE

The New Cambridge History of India covers the period from the beginning of the sixteenth century. In some respects it marks a radical change in the style of Cambridge Histories, but in others the editors feel that they are working firmly within an established academic tradition.

During the summer of 1896, F. W. Maitland and Lord Acton between them evolved the idea for a comprehensive modern history. By the end of the year the Syndics of the University Press had committed themselves to the *Cambridge Modern History*, and Lord Acton had been put in charge of it. It was hoped that publication would begin in 1899 and be completed by 1904, but the first volume in fact came out in 1902 and the last in 1910, with additional volumes of tables and maps in 1911 and 1912.

The *History* was a great success, and it was followed by a whole series of distinctive Cambridge Histories covering English Literature, the Ancient World, India, British Foreign Policy, Economic History, Medieval History, the British Empire, Africa, China and Latin America; and even now other new series are being prepared. Indeed, the various Histories have given the Press notable strength in the publication of general reference books in the arts and social sciences.

What has made the Cambridge Histories so distinctive is that they have never been simply dictionaries or encyclopaedias. The Histories have, in H. A. L. Fisher's words, always been 'written by an army of specialists concentrating the latest result of special study'. Yet as Acton agreed with the Syndics in 1896, they have not been mere compilations of existing material but original works. Undoubtedly many of the Histories are uneven in quality, some have become out of date very rapidly, but their virtue has been that they have consistently done more than simply record an existing state of knowledge: they have tended to focus interest on research and they have provided a massive stimulus to further work. This has made their publication doubly worthwhile and has distinguished them intellectually from other sorts of reference book. The editors of *The New Cambridge History of India* have acknowledged this in their work.

The original *Cambridge History of India* was published between 1922 and 1937. It was planned in six volumes, but of these, volume 2 dealing with the period between the first century AD and the Muslim invasion of India, never appeared. Some of the material is still of value, but in many respects it is now out of date. The past fifty years have seen a great deal of new research on India, and a striking feature of recent work has been to cast doubt on the validity of the quite arbitrary chronological and categorical way in which Indian history has been conventionally divided.

The editors decided that it would not be academically desirable to prepare a new *History of India* using the traditional format. The selective nature of research on Indian history over the past half-century would doom such a project from the start and the whole of Indian history could not be covered in an even or comprehensive manner. They concluded that the best scheme would be to have a *History* divided into four overlapping chronological volumes, each containing short books on individual themes or subjects. Although in extent the work will therefore be equivalent to a dozen massive tomes of the traditional sort, in form *The New Cambridge History of India* will appear as a shelf full of separate but complementary parts. Accordingly, the main divisions are between I. *The Mughals and their Contemporaries*, II. *Indian States and the Transition to Colonialism*, III. *The Indian Empire and the Beginnings of Modern Society*, and IV. *The Evolution of Contemporary South Asia*.

Just as the books within these volumes are complementary so too do they intersect with each other, both thematically and chronologically. As the books appear they are intended to give a view of the subject as it now stands and to act as a stimulus to further research. We do not expect the *New Cambridge History of India* to be the last word on the subject but an essential voice in the continuing discussion about it.

ACKNOWLEDGMENTS

A fellowship year at the National Humanities Center in North Carolina during 1986–87 (when the earth was young) gave the great gifts of time, intellectual companionship and a congenial environment for the initial stages of thinking, organising and writing this book. I greatly appreciate the support of Charles Blitzer, then the director, whose passion for India was inspiring; and Kent Mullikin, the ever accommodating and resourceful associate director. All the Center staff, but especially the bibliographical and electronic expertise of Allan Tuttle and Rebecca Vargas, were extraordinary and are much appreciated. My colleagues at the Center, especially in the seminar on 'The Other', and the Triangle Seminar on South Asia, particularly David Gilmartin and John Richards, enlarged my interdisciplinary horizons. That year enabled me to recharge my intellectual batteries and renew my historiographical capital.

The genealogy of this volume begins with the suggestion of John Broomfield and D. Anthony Low that my dissertation research might focus on the Chamber of Princes. They launched my continuing interest in the princes, a topic long on the margins of South Asian historiography. Richard and Donna Park offered crucial support and friendship while I wrote that dissertation and later revised it for publication. My debt is great to the directors and staffs of the numerous archives where I have worked over the past decades. They include the National Archives of India and the Nehru Memorial Museum and Library in New Delhi, the National Library of India in Calcutta, the Punjab State Archives in Patiala, the Karnataka State Archives in Bangalore, and the India Office Library in its many incarnations from King Charles Street to the British Library. My research was supported by fellowships and grants from the American Institute of Indian Studies, the Fulbright-Hays program of the US Department of Education, the Fulbright program of the US Department of State, the National Endowment for the Humanities, the Social Science Research Council, the Charles Phelps Taft Memorial Fund, and the University Research Council at the University of Cincinnati. As will be quickly evident, this volume is shaped by and also owes substantial debt to the uneven but recently enhanced historiography on the princes and princely states of India. The path-breaking work of Ian Copland, Edward Haynes, John Hurd II, Robin Jeffrey, Karen Leonard, James Manor, John McLeod, Mridula Mukherjee, William Richter, Lloyd Rudolph,

Susanne Hoeber Rudolph, and Robert Stern has crucially shaped my synthesis. The research of newer entrants to the still marginal arena of princely states, especially that of Manu Bhagavan, Shail Mayaram, Janaki Nair, Mridu Rai, Satadru Sen, Nandini Sundar, and Chitralekha Zutshi, has stimulated me to rethink older paradigms. I greatly appreciate the willingness of many scholars who provided offprints, pre-publication copies of articles, and abstracts of books. Kenneth and Joyce Robbins have been extraordinarily liberal in sharing their hospitality, their knowledge and their superb collection of art, artefacts, books, documents and medals from the princely states of India.

A synthetic overview of the Indian princes and their states emerged as a much more complex intellectual venture than I had initially thought it would be. Personal issues and administrative responsibilities further delayed the writing and revising processes. Marigold Acland was the most patient and encouraging editor an author could want, while John Richards, Christopher Bayly and Gordon Johnson sustained me when I wondered if this project was feasible. I am most grateful for their trust and gentle prodding. The generosity of Christopher Bayly, Ian Copland, John McLeod, John Richards, William Richter and Tanika Sarkar, who read draft chapters or the whole of the manuscript, substantially improved this book. They urged me to clarify arguments, cautioned me to correct errors, suggested pertinent sources and provided prompt answers to my queries. Although their research does not focus on the princes, Sanjam Ahluwalia, Richard Bingle, Judith Brown, Antoinette Burton, Geraldine Forbes, Doranne Jacobson, Carol Jean and Timothy Johnson, Sanjay Joshi, Mrinalini Sinha and Sylvia Vatuk tolerated my complaints and urged me to continue when I was most discouraged. In Cincinnati my colleagues and friends, but especially Roger Daniels, Katharina Gerstenberger, Sigrun Haude, Gene Lewis, Zane and Janet Miller, Maura O'Connor, Thomas Sakmyster, Willard Sunderland and Ann Twinam, sustained me during extended periods of administrative commitments. At crucial junctures Judith Daniels was an astute and sympathetic editor; John Waldrodt provided computer expertise and a beautiful map on exceedingly short notice; Doranne Jacobson responded quickly and generously to my requests for information and permission to use her photographs, and Venetia Somerset was a most helpful copyeditor whose eagle eye is much appreciated. I am grateful to the Charles Phelps Taft Memorial Fund for grants to undertake the research for the illustrations and to support the costs of their reproduction. This book is dedicated to my brothers and sisters for their love and support. In the end I, of course, remain responsible for any misinterpretations or errors in this volume.

ABBREVIATIONS

AGG   Agent to the Governor-General
AISPC   All-India States' People's Conference
AR   *Asian Review*
b.   born
BCAS   *Bulletin of Concerned Asian Scholars*
BHM   *Bulletin of the History of Medicine*
BJP   Bharatiya Janata Party
CSSH   *Comparative Studies in Society and History*
CE   *Cincinnati Enquirer*
CIS   *Contributions to Indian Sociology*
CR   Crown Representative Records at the Oriental and India Office Collection
d.   died
EPW   *Economic and Political Weekly*
F&P   Foreign and Political Department of the Government of India
GH   *Gender and History*
GIPR   Great Indian Peninsular Railway
GOI   Government of India
HJFRT   *Historical Journal of Film, Radio and Television*
IAR   *Indian Annual Register*
IBS   *Indo-British Review*
ICS   Indian Civil Service
IESHR   *Indian Economic and Society History Review*
ISPC   Indian States' People's Conference
JAMWI   *Journal of the Association of Medical Women in India*
JAOS   *Journal of the American Oriental Society*
JAS   *Journal of Asian Studies*
JASB   *Journal of the Asiatic Society of Bengal*
JCCH   *Journal of Colonialism and Colonial History*
JCCP   *Journal of Commonwealth and Comparative Politics*
JPC   Joint Political Congress
JPHS   *Journal of the Pakistan Historical Society*
JWH   *Journal of World History*

KSA	Karnataka State Archives, Bangalore
MAO	Muhammadan Anglo-Oriental College at Aligarh, United Provinces
MAS	*Modern Asian Studies*
NAI	National Archives of India, New Delhi
NGSR	Nizam's Guaranteed State Railway
NLI	National Library of India, Calcutta
NMML	Nehru Memorial Museum and Library, New Delhi
NSR	Nizam's State Railway
NSS	Nair Service Society
OIOC	Oriental and India Office Collections at the British Library, London
PA	*Pacific Affairs*
PEPSU	Patiala and East Punjab States Union
PSA	Punjab State Archives, Patiala
r.	ruled
RSS	Rashtriya Swayamsevak Sangh
RTC	Round Table Conference
s.	succeeded to the gaddi
SA	*South Asia*
SALNQ	*South Asia Library Notes & Queries*
SGPC	Shiromani Gurdwara Parbhandhak Committee
SH	*Studies in History*
SNDP	Sri Narayana Dharma Paripalana
TISCO	Tata Iron and Steel Company
TSC	Travancore State Congress
VHP	Vishwa Hindu Parishad

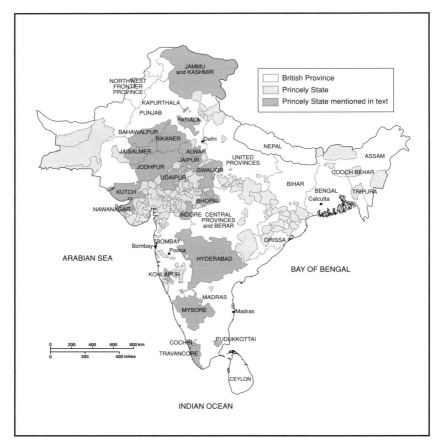

Princely States and British Indian Provinces in 1912

CHAPTER 1

INTRODUCTION: INDIAN PRINCES AND BRITISH IMPERIALISM

Air India, the overseas airline of the independent Government of India (GOI), chose a bowing, smiling, turbaned maharaja or prince as its mascot during the 1950s. Why did a democratic government choose this image as an icon for its most modern means of transportation when a decade earlier its prime minister had castigated the princes as rulers whose states were 'very backward and many of them . . . still in the feudal age'?[1] This rotund, red-coated figure epitomises the profoundly ambivalent attitudes towards the Indian princes among successive governments in India. British colonial officials had claimed them as faithful military allies, denounced them as autocrats, praised them as natural leaders of their subjects, chided them as profligate playboys, and taken advantage of their lavish hospitality. During the struggle for independence, Indian nationalists had initially cited the princes as evidence of the ability of Indians to govern effectively; they had occasionally sought their financial patronage of political organisations and collaboration during constitutional negotiations, but ultimately had assailed them as arbitrary autocrats. In independent India and Pakistan, governments have appointed them to positions ranging from state governors to ambassadors; political parties have co-opted erstwhile princes as candidates for the central and state legislatures and appointed them as ministers; public corporations and private entrepreneurs have promoted former princely capitals as destinations for international and domestic tourists; and popular media have represented them as an integral part of Indian culture. In the public sphere, princes were and are portrayed in newspapers, magazines, novels, newsreels and feature films as benevolent paternalists, remnants of feudalism ensconced in romantic forts, sexually ravenous predators, fierce hunters, audacious sportsmen, especially in cricket and polo, and extravagant clients of jewellers and luxury hotels in India and Europe. However, in the historiography of South Asia, the princes and their states have remained on the margins of the dominant narratives of Indian nationalism and its alter ego of religious communalism.

The synthetic overview presented in this book joins a growing effort to integrate the princes into the grand sweep of modern Indian history. Its underlying

---

[1] *What are the Indian States?* Foreword by Jawaharlal Nehru (Allahabad, n.d. 1939?), p. 5.

1

argument is that many princes represented a continuity of traditional state formation in India and remained autonomous rulers, exercising substantial authority and power within their states, until 1948. In other words, British imperialists did not create the princely states as states or reduce them to theatre states where ritual was dominant and governmental functions relegated to imperial surrogates. Indeed, British power gradually restrained sovereign princely authority, especially in defence, external affairs and communications. Indian princes nevertheless taxed their subjects, allocated state revenues, had full criminal and civil judicial powers, maintained internal law and order to varying degrees, patronised traditional and modern cultural activities and institutions, and synthesised elements of *rajadharma* or indigenous kingly behaviour with those of British models.

Much of the muddled tedium in histories of the princely states of India may be traced to the use of the label of princely states for diverse political entities. The development of an inclusive, reputedly rationalised list of princely states was a colonial venture. Beginning during the 1820s when the English East India Company was consolidating its territorial possessions, this endeavour was pursued more diligently once the British Crown formally assumed responsibility for the rule of India in 1858. The British categorisation of indirectly controlled areas as native states may be seen as one aspect of their project to understand the history, the extent and the present condition of the empire that they now formally acknowledged. Thus here as in their discussions of caste, indigenous legal systems and local customs, British administrators and scholars were creating a category of native or Indian states that did not necessarily correspond to Indian conceptions of what constituted viable political states. The *Imperial Gazetteer of India* listed 693 states, including the Shan states in Burma as well as Nepal, but the Report of the Indian States Committee in 1929 reduced the number to 562.[2]

During the 1960s Bernard Cohn articulated an influential typology useful for understanding different levels of statehood. He delineated four levels of political organisation during the eighteenth century:

1. the imperial, represented by the continuing authority but not power of the Mughal emperors, whose territory gradually contracted to Delhi;
2. the secondary states ruled by Mughal-appointed governors who extended their autonomous control over a historically or culturally defined area;

[2] Imperial Gazetteer of India, *The Indian Empire* vol. 4, *Administrative* (Oxford, 1909), pp. 92–103. East India (Indian States). *Report of the Indian States Committee 1928–1929* (London, 1929), pp. 10–11. The states were divided into three groups: 108 states had rulers in the Chamber of Princes, 127 states had rulers represented in the Chamber; and 327 were estates, jagirs and others.

3. the regional spheres, where leaders were granted the authority to rule from the imperial or secondary level after they had secured military control; and finally

4. the local level, which Cohn labelled 'little kingdoms'.

The founders of little kingdoms frequently started with one or more of three offices: *zamindar*, meaning a holder of *zamin* or land who acquired a right to a share of the produce of the land for fostering its cultivation; *jagirdar*, indicating the possessor of a *jagir* or the right to collect revenue from a tract of land granted by a superior power in return for service or acknowledgment of suzerainty; or *taluqdar*, the leader of a *taluqa* or area controlled by a male lineage. As these ambitious men extended their authority into administrative as well as military spheres, they took the title of raja, which means king in Sanskrit, even though British sources labelled them chiefs or princes.[3] Edward Haynes claims that this translation of raja was part of the British effort to create Indian rulers as a subordinated category.[4] But Indian rajas legitimated their ruling status by religious and social rituals and symbols of sovereignty, the latter being granted from any of the three superior levels of authority.

In subsequent scholarship Cohn's classification has been compressed to three levels: the imperial, the regional (which incorporates both the secondary and the regional), and the local or little kingdoms.[5] As the power of the Mughal Empire was dissipated through succession struggles, territorial overextension and economic limitations during the eighteenth century, the lower two levels augmented their power under the tattered imperial umbrella of Mughal suzerainty. The proportion of little kingdoms to regional states is impossible to quantify. Highlighting their regional concentration, Ian Copland pointed out that 361 out of the 620 claimed by Lee-Warner were located within the Bombay Presidency and comprised one-third of its territory excluding the area of Sind.[6] Several of these 'princely states' in western India were less than one square mile, with a population of fewer than 200 people that could be one large extended family and servants. A common joke was that houses here were constructed with the front door opening into one state and the back door

---

[3] Bernard S. Cohn, 'Political Systems in Eighteenth Century India: The Benares Region', *JAOS* 83 (1962), pp. 313–14.

[4] Edward Haynes, 'Rajput Ceremonial Interactions as a Mirror of a Dying Indian State System, 1820–1947', *MAS* 4 (1990), n. 1, p. 459.

[5] Cohn himself had previously set the pattern of discussing only three levels of political organisation in his 'The Initial British Impact on India: A Case Study of the Benares Region', *JAS* 19 (1960), pp. 418–24.

[6] Ian Copland, *The British Raj and the Indian Princes: Paramountcy in Western India 1857–1930* (Bombay, 1982), pp. 1–2.

into another. The anomaly of including these units in the category of princely states is put into sharper perspective when one remembers that some zamindars or estate-holders such as the maharaja of Darbhanga, who controlled 2400 square miles in Bihar and had magisterial powers, were excluded. This book concentrates on those princely states that survived after 1858, possessed some attributes, both indigenous and colonial, of sovereign status, and had their superior rank recognised in the twentieth century by their inclusion in the Chamber of Princes, a British-instituted advisory assembly. Thus most of the little kingdoms of western India as well as Bengal, Awadh (Oudh) and Punjab, although major Indian states during the eighteenth and early nineteenth centuries but British provinces by 1858, will receive only brief notice in this volume.

Chapter 2 traces the evolution of the major princely states before British officials articulated their goal of creating an imperial state in the early nineteenth century. States are grouped into three categories: the antique, the successor, and the warrior or conquest. Antique states are mostly Rajput-ruled entities that predated the Mughal Empire founded in 1526. They generally entered alliances with the Mughals, continued as internally autonomous units, began to act independently as Mughal power atrophied, and expanded territorially during the eighteenth century. *Subadars* or governors of Mughal provinces, principally those of Awadh, Bengal and Hyderabad, created the second category when they transformed themselves into autonomous rulers. Their states 'presided over a redistribution of agrarian resources which favoured local gentry and magnates . . . [and they] adapted more successfully to the cultural assumptions of their rural and Hindu subjects' than had the Mughals.[7] Although military force was essential to political dominance in most princely states, conquest states are deemed a third category to designate polities that warrior groups established by offering military protection to local populations against other competitors. This category ranges from the Maratha states in the west, to Travancore and Mysore in the south, to the Sikh-ruled states in Punjab. The chapter concludes with a delineation of patterns of state formation by which ambitious leaders asserted their autonomy, expanded their territory and legitimated their claims to sovereignty and kingship by performing rajadharma.

According to Hindu political treatises and religious texts, rajadharma included offering protection to prospective subjects; adjudicating disputes among

---

[7] C. A. Bayly, *Rulers, Townsmen and Bazaars: Northern Indian Society in the Age of British Expansion 1770–1870* (Cambridge, 1983), p. 12.

social groups including kinspeople, clans and castes; patronising religious leaders and institutions; and distributing gifts, or what Pamela Price has labelled 'dharmic largesse',[8] to other cultural activities and social groups claiming kingly support. Lloyd and Susanne Rudolph have elaborated the notion that a key responsibility of Indian rulers was to preserve and protect social formations that existed prior to the state, such as 'the customs, activities, and prerogatives of communities, castes, sects, status orders, and guilds (craft and commercial)'.[9] A king was also to manifest certain personal qualities. The relevance for both kings and gods of the Hindu concept of *darshan* (the auspiciousness of seeing and being seen by a superior being) indicated the overlap between secular and sacred spheres in Indian society. In a discussion of medieval Hindu kingship, Ronald Inden declared: 'A view of the king, handsome, in good health, bathed, anointed, crowned, decked with ornaments, and seated in state was believed to be auspicious and to please (rañj) the people.'[10]

Many historical empires from Pharaonic Egypt onward have employed indirect rule to extend their influence over disparate peoples with a minimum expenditure in material and human resources. When the English East India Company secured the *diwani* right to collect the revenues of Bengal in 1765, they embarked on a lengthy transformation from trading enterprise to imperial power. Chapter 3 traces how the British first devised and then sustained a system of indirect rule that enabled them to emerge by 1858 as the paramount power in control of approximately three-fifths of the territory and four-fifths of the population of the Indian subcontinent. The frequently asked questions about indirect rule are why did the Indian states first ally themselves with the British and then why did the British maintain these alliances with Indian regional states and even petty chieftains after British military and political superiority was clearly established? How much did British policies of indirect rule and annexation reflect individual agency, contemporary political, economic and social conditions, or institutional constraints? What motivated Indian rulers to enter alliances with the British? The answers are that dynamic tensions characterised British policies of indirect rule and annexation, imperial intervention and non-intervention in Indian state affairs, and princely collaboration and overt or covert non-cooperation with British policies and advice. The British

---

[8] Pamela G. Price, *Kingship and Political Practice in Colonial India* (Cambridge, 1996), p. 190.
[9] Lloyd I. Rudolph and Susanne Hoeber Rudolph, 'The Subcontinental Empire and the Regional Kingdom in Indian State Formation'. In Paul Wallace (ed.), *Region and Nation in India* (New Delhi, 1985), p. 46.
[10] Ronald Inden, 'Ritual, Authority, and Cyclic Time in Hindu Kingship'. In J. F. Richards (ed.), *Kingship and Authority in South Asia* (Madison, 1978), p. 54.

and the princes used each other to achieve their own objectives with varying degrees of success. While the British pursued imperial dominance, Indian princes sought greater control over their internal allies and challengers and a larger share of local revenues. Although British power could be both arbitrary and oppressive, shrewd Indian princes centralised their administrations and enlarged their share of local revenues.

After 1858, when Queen Victoria resolved that the British Empire would encompass both directly and indirectly ruled areas, British administrators in India set out to codify policies towards the princely states based on precedents, labelled political practices, that were reinforced with expediency. Chapter 4 analyses both the construction of British theories and operation of indirect rule and the diverse experiences of Indian princes as participants in that system. Officials in the foreign, later the foreign and political, department of the GOI emerged as authorities on doctrines, regulations and rituals that would govern British and princely relations into the twentieth century. Although significant annexation of territory no longer occurred, the British continued to intervene, most dramatically in the deposition or exile of recalcitrant princes, but more regularly in relation to succession and minority administrations and conflicts between a ruler and his kinspeople or nobility. As the nature of challenges to British imperial power changed, the British and the princes themselves evolved new roles for the princes in the public spheres both in India and the broader empire.

In her study of two zamindaris in south India, Pamela Price cogently argues for the agency 'of persons meeting historical contingencies with the use of both indigenous and colonial categories and concepts, with the manipulation of indigenous and colonial institutions and ideologies to achieve personally constructed goals'.[11] After exploring the life cycle of princes, Chapter 5 examines how many rulers synthesised and adapted the injunctions of rajadharma to changing British and Indian nationalist conventions of political authority and political and social reforms. Thus princes continued to patronise holy men and religious institutions but now sustained colleges that combined indigenous religious learning and western science. They extended dharmic largesse to underprivileged groups ranging from scholarships for untouchables (later called scheduled castes) to medical relief for Indian women. They nourished Indian music, dance and the visual arts in their *durbar*s (courts) and in the public sphere of local museums and all-India festivals. Simultaneously, princes

---

[11] Price, *Kingship*, p. 6.

assimilated elements of the British gospel of social improvement through disciplinary institutions such as schools, hospitals and prisons. This creative synthesis, which evolved in myriad formats, nourished the complex and sometimes conflicting perceptions of the princes mentioned earlier. It also reflects the fact that many princes were adroit politicians whom both British imperialists and Indian nationalists had to accommodate, and that colonial cultural forms and power structures did not efface indigenous ones.

Indian princely states were diverse in their administration, economic structure, social composition and politics. Chapter 6 focuses on three major aspects of the development of princely states as political and economic entities from the 1860s to the 1940s. First, the administrative frameworks that existed in the princely states provided the parameters in which other elements functioned. Examining the governmental structures first is not meant to imply that they were the dominant factor but merely reflects the available scholarship. Second, although the states were autocracies, the rulers had to rely on indigenous and 'foreign' collaborators to administer them. A scrutiny of the formation and activities of these elites underscores the bureaucratisation of the late nineteenth and early twentieth centuries in the princely states. This trend shifted the internal balance of power to princes who had greater control over paid bureaucrats than nobles with independent incomes and kinship ties. Third, the economic configuration of the princely states determined the resources available to the administration, the elites who contended for dominance, and the people at the base. But economic activities and development highlight the imperial restrictions on the autonomy of states and their rulers. Enterprising rulers and merchants nevertheless crafted opportunities for economic initiatives.

The ethnic origins, social structures and religious affiliations of the peoples in the Indian princely states were extraordinarily intricate and have attracted relatively little scholarly attention. Although much remains to be done, some historians are now studying popular politics. Chapter 7 begins with an analysis of how treaties, maps and physical markers constructed the territorial boundaries of the states that contained heterogeneous populations and goes on to delineate the efforts of elite and non-elite subjects to gain material benefits and legal rights. Simultaneously, princes used their social and religious status as well as autocratic power to buttress their internal political control as concepts of nationalism, communalism and political reform challenged their dominance. Although the borders of princely states were as porous to political ideas as to smuggled goods, it was local leaders rather than nationalists from British

India who actively organised informal campaigns and associations that sought a greater share of scarce resources such as education and government jobs for caste, religious and ethnic groups, the exercise of civil rights such as freedom of assembly, association and speech, and improved economic conditions. In states where rulers shared their religion with a minority of their subjects and favoured their co-religionists with generous patronage or protective legislation, popular political activity could quickly become communal, that is, seeking to enhance a particular religious or social community, rather than being more broad-based. However, there has been relatively little consideration of what constituted nationalist ideology or politics among either princes or their subjects within the internally autonomous states.

By the late 1920s, Indian princes as well as Indian nationalists were seeking dramatic revisions in their relationships with the British imperial structure. Chapter 8 examines the constitutional negotiations from 1930 to 1948 that led to the integration of the princely states into either India or the newly created state of Pakistan. It argues that their relatively quick and smooth integration was not foreseen. There have been various answers to the question of when the demise of the princes as autonomous rulers became inevitable. James Manor, who argues that 'the fate of the princely order was sealed long before 1935', represents one extreme.[12] In my own earlier work, I proposed a later date, namely the suspension of negotiations over federation in 1939, as the beginning of the end. However, subsequently opened government records, memoirs of participants, and research, most notably by Robin Moore, Michael Witmer and Ian Copland, indicate that until at least mid-1947 both British officials and Indian politicians were anxious about the future of the Indian princes and the possible balkanisation of the British Empire in India.

About sixty to ninety of the supposedly 600-odd princes of India exercised significant power in local, regional, all-India and imperial politics during the British colonial period. Some remained politically prominent during the initial decades of independence. The fact that in early 2003 Captain Amarindar Singh, the scion of the Patiala dynasty, and Virbhadra Singh of Bashahr are serving as chief ministers of Punjab and Himachal Pradesh illustrates the possible residual value of a princely heritage in electoral politics. Consequently an intellectual and cultural puzzle is why there is a historical lacuna when the princes themselves and their states, some of which were larger than many European countries, presented such an enticing array of images,

---

[12] James Manor, 'The Demise of the Princely Order: A Reassessment'. In Robin Jeffrey (ed.), *People, Princes and Paramount Power: Society and Politics in the Indian Princely States* (Delhi, 1978), p. 306.

controlled substantial wealth and power, and survived for so long. The following speculations are meant to stimulate more research and more cogent interpretations.

First, scholars and the general public frequently, though certainly not always, are interested in events and personalities, phenomena that seem relevant to their daily concerns. Before 1947 British historians, who were often officials or associated with imperial institutions, studied aspects of Indian politics and culture that provided legitimacy and perhaps guidance for British policies. When they noticed the princes, these scholars extolled them as faithful allies or castigated them for misgovernment that justified annexation or deposition. Indian historians produced either hagiographical accounts of the princes as astute political leaders and social reformers or acerbic censures of princely oppression. After 1947 British historians concentrated on the dilemmas that confronted colonial officials in the governance of India. Many Indian and some North American historians told the story of a triumphant Indian National Congress and the selfless ideological commitment of nationalist leaders, most notably Mahatma Gandhi and Jawaharlal Nehru, to the struggle for freedom. After the princely states were quickly integrated into the independent nation-states of India and Pakistan (with the fateful anomaly of Jammu and Kashmir), there was some interest in why the princely rule had collapsed so quickly. The usual explanations were princely political ineptness and personal degeneracy, the political shrewdness of Indian negotiators, and the lack of viable alternatives for the princes. In other words the princes were losers, and immediately after a contest winners attract more historians than the vanquished.

Second, because British administrators had reneged on earlier promises to protect them from external and internal opponents, their princely clients became an embarrassment to the departing imperialists and a disconcerting topic for historical analysis. Indian nationalist leaders were equally chagrined by the princes. Some Indian nationalist and communal leaders had sought princely patronage, but they directed their political activity and rhetoric against the British colonial administration. They neglected organising a political base in the princely states among their rulers or subjects until the final decades of colonial rule. The partition that accompanied independence for India and Pakistan made their leaders wary of further balkanisation. The reluctance of the rulers, especially of Hyderabad and more significantly of Jammu and Kashmir, to accede to India rendered the princes problematic for Indian politicians, who were now constructing new nation-states under the chaotic conditions of collapsing colonial structures and unprecedented internal migration marked by death and destruction. Since both imperial officials and South Asian nationalists, who were initially concentrated in colonial port cities, had struggled largely within British Indian territory, historians forging the dominant narratives of colonial benevolence or exploitation and nationalist triumphs or communal challenges relegated the princes to footnotes.

Third, primary sources, the bricks of historical scholarship, on the princes and their states were not easily available. The archives of most princely states were not as well catalogued and well preserved as colonial ones. In some cases officials in princely states had treated the documents they generated during their ministerial tenure as personal property and removed them when they left office.[13] What their descendants did not later sell as scrap paper, humidity and insects destroyed. Many princes were equally reluctant to place documents that they deemed personal or politically dangerous in any archive. Maharaja Yadavindra Singh of Patiala was a striking exception. The last Chancellor of the Chamber of Princes, he preserved the Chamber's records at his capital and supported the effort to gather available records from the erstwhile states in the Patiala and East Punjab States Union (PEPSU) created in 1948.[14] During the tumultuous years of integrating autonomous units into larger entities, officials in former princely state territory accorded a low priority to the establishment of archives. Consequently the records of the princely states were geographically scattered, often in locations difficult to reach and lacking facilities for researchers, and access could be difficult to obtain. On the imperial side, some British officials handling relations with the princes destroyed records that might prove politically or economically injurious to the princes in independent India.[15] Records deemed sensitive because they dealt with personal issues, political manipulations or communal politics were transferred to the India Office Library in London, where a fifty-year rule on when documents became open precluded early research. In the late 1960s a reduction to thirty years stimulated more research. Scholars began to portray princes as political leaders who assessed opportunities and choices; negotiated compromises with British officials, recalcitrant nobles and popular political leaders; initiated reforms; jailed critics; and survived as rulers. A few analysed particular groups or associations within the states and contributed to the complex mosaic of

---

[13] Daya Kishan Kaul, 'Care and Preservation of Old Records in Northern Indian States', *Indian Historical Records Commission, Proceedings*, 2 (January 1920).

[14] Barbara Ramusack, 'The Princely States of Punjab: A Bibliographic Essay'. In W. Eric Gustafson and Kenneth W. Jones (eds), *Sources on Punjab History* (New Delhi, 1975), pp. 374–449.

[15] Conrad Corfield, *The Princely India I Knew: From Reading to Mountbatten* (Madras, 1975), p. 155.

social history in South Asia. Their work undergirds this synthesis and will be acknowledged in subsequent chapters that plot the indigenous origins of the princely states, their fluctuating fortunes within the British imperial systems and the nature of their administrations, economies, societies and politics in order to restore the princes and their states to the history and the future of India.

CHAPTER 2

PRINCELY STATES PRIOR TO 1800

Political chaos disrupts the status of many, but for others it provides opportunities for political advancement, social mobility and economic gain. During the eighteenth century the Mughal Empire, the largest, most extensive political organisation to evolve in India, suffered an attenuation of its power and its territory. Even so, the Mughal emperor continued to be a source of legitimacy through the bestowal of offices and titles, and Mughal patterns of administration and elite culture persisted in emerging states. Until the 1980s, historians taking a bird's-eye view from European and Mughal sources have often lamented the political turmoil and economic disruption during the eighteenth century. Only the expanding political power of the British supposedly created stable conditions. During more recent decades scholars have taken a worm's-eye view from the ground of local and regional records in Indian languages, and the political landscape of eighteenth-century India has been significantly altered.

Current scholarship indicates that while the Mughals may have been losing their power to accumulate economic resources and control the actions of subordinate personnel, new political formations emerged and implemented, with varying success, centralising reforms that would enable them to control the resources of the countryside more effectively than the Mughals had. These robust challengers were the successor states to the Mughals, most importantly Awadh, Bengal and Hyderabad, and warrior states, the creations of military entrepreneurs, more specifically Maratha states in the west, Mysore in the south and the Sikhs in the north. Other beneficiaries were Hindu trading groups such as Jagat Seths in Bengal and Marwaris from Rajasthan, who were forging interregional trade networks; and Muslim revenue farmers with contracts to collect revenue who amassed capital that they lent to aspiring indigenous kings and encroaching foreign commercial ventures, most notably the English East India Company. Thus the eighteenth century, once shrouded in the gloom of Mughal decline and deemed too politically fragmented for coherent historical analysis, has now become an era of strong states and aggressive indigenous capitalists. This revisionism provides a dynamic background for the study of Indian political entities known as the native (the word 'native' meaning Indian) states during the nineteenth century and as the princely states during the twentieth century. In this book I will use the term 'princely' rather than 'native' state except where it would be anachronistic. Indian princely states that survived from 1858 to 1947 may be grouped into three categories: antique states, successor states, and warrior or conquest states.

GENRES OF PRINCELY STATES

Antique states: the Rajputs

Antique, archaic or vintage states originated from the thirteenth century onward and their judicious incorporation into the Mughal administrative and military system prefigured their subsequent accommodation within the British Empire. Rajput-ruled states dominated this category. The specific historical ancestors of the Rajputs (from the Sanskrit *rajaputra*, which means son of a raja or king) remain contested. An evolving consensus postulates that the Rajputs represent an integration of diverse elements ranging from Central Asian groups who accompanied the Scythians into the Indian subcontinent in the early centuries of the Christian era to indigenous, pastoral warrior groups.[1] A lively scholarly debate has ensued whether ascriptive, genealogical status or occupational activity as soldiers was the determining factor in constituting Rajput identity. In western scholarship the emphasis on genealogy begins with the bardic traditions of the Rajputs, which Lieutenant-Colonel James Tod (1782–1835), the first British political agent in Mewar and western Rajputana from 1818 to 1822, encoded in his frequently cited *Annals and Antiquities of Rajast'han* (1829–32). It continues in British official records and extends into modern anthropological analysis. But Dirk Kolff has argued that as pastoral bands achieved landed status from the thirteenth to fifteenth centuries and acquired a group identity, they took the name Rajput, which indicated warrior status and association with a king. Thus until at least the seventeenth century and perhaps into the eighteenth century, Rajput was an open-ended category based on a military career undertaken in alliance with a regional or imperial power through the agency of a *jama'dar* or military jobber-commander. According to Kolff, it was only during the sixteenth and seventeenth centuries that some Rajput rulers and their *charans* (bards) developed myths of origins that established their status as *kshatriyas* and legitimated their political power and social status 'exclusively in the language of descent and kinship' rather than

---

[1] B. D. Chattopadhyaya, 'The Emergence of the Rajputs as Historical Process in Early Medieval Rajasthan', in Karine Schomer et al. (eds), *The Idea of Rajasthan: Explorations in Regional Identity*, vol. 2 (New Delhi, 1994), pp. 161–91.

through occupational activity as warriors.[2] Under this genealogical formula, the most basic definition of Rajput is one to whom other Rajputs will give their sisters or daughters in marriage. My approach uses the typology of Tod while simultaneously recognising the contested nature of Rajput origins and hierarchy.

According to their charans, the Rajputs arose after Parashurama, an incarnation of the Hindu god Vishnu, and an alternative form of Rama, the hero of the pan-Indian epic of the *Ramayana*, nearly exterminated the kshatriya or warrior-ruler *varna* (division) of the caste order. After a few surviving kshatriyas emerged from hiding, brahmans questioned their kshatriya status and labelled them 'sons of kings' rather than 'kings'. These 'sons of kings' became the ancestors of the Suryavanshi and Chandravanshi Rajputs, claiming descent from the sun and the moon gods respectively. When disorder became endemic because of an absence of kshatriyas, the gods created four supernatural warriors from a fire-sacrifice. They were the ancestors of the Agnikula (Fire) Rajputs. Thus three *vams* or mythological units of inclusiveness for Rajputs emerged. This classification does not have a direct social function such as defining marriage boundaries but possibly serves to link the Rajputs to the ancient Vedic gods of Hinduism.

By the sixth century AD there are historical indications of groups calling themselves Rajputs settled in the Indo-Gangetic plain. Over the course of ten centuries they came to control land and people, working the land in an irregular crescent from Saurashtra on the edge of the Arabian Sea through the Thar or Great Desert of northwestern India. Skipping across the invasion route of Muslim armies from the Khyber Pass to Delhi, the Rajputs emerged again in the foothills of the Himalayas that bordered Punjab and finally curved down into the present states of eastern Uttar Pradesh and Bihar. By the sixteenth century Rajput conquests of waste land or underpopulated areas on the borders of larger political states had evolved into little kingdoms and regional states. Little kingdoms predominated in the Gangetic Plain, where Muslim conquest states functioned first as regional kingdoms and then as the Mughal imperial overlord, and in the Himalayas, where a restricted resource base could not sustain elaborate political organisations.

The geographically broad sweep of Rajput political and social prominence was reflected as late as 1931 in census statistics. Rajputs as a social group formed a higher percentage of the population in four British Indian provinces and the

---

[2] Dirk H. A. Kolff, *Naukar, Rajput and Sepoy: The Ethnohistory of the Military Labour Market in Hindustan, 1450–1850* (Cambridge, 1990), p. 72.

princely state of Jammu and Kashmir than in the area known in the British colonial period as Rajputana.[3] Deryck Lodrick argues that it was only during the sixteenth century that the Mughals defined the boundaries of the region that is the contemporary state of Rajasthan.[4] In their efforts to establish their political legitimacy, the Rajput rulers of Rajputana-Rajasthan, who sprawled from the Thar Desert across the Arvalli Mountains into the plains drifting into central India, became the exemplars of genealogical orthodoxy. Consequently they challenged the claims of rulers of regional states and little kingdoms in Saurashtra and in central India to Rajput status and became more reluctant to enter matrimonial alliances with them. The category of Rajput, however, remained elastic into the twentieth century.

Two broad groups of Rajput rulers existed on the eastern end of the crescent of Rajput settlement. First, there are those on the Gangetic Plain itself in eastern Uttar Pradesh and western Bihar. Richard Fox has emphasised the significance of kinship in the formation of Rajput states on the Gangetic Plain and has seen the rajas 'as a hinge linking the local stratified lineage with state authority'.[5] Here resilient Rajput zamindars and taluqdars who helped to populate their lands and acquired rights to a share in its products would survive as collaborators, first with the Mughal Empire, then with the nawabs of Awadh, and eventually with the British imperial power.[6]

The second cluster is situated on the jungly border between present-day Uttar Pradesh and Madhya Pradesh and extends into the Malwa Plateau of central India. It includes the princely states of Baghelkhand, where Rewa was most prominent, Bundelkhand, and Malwa. In his analysis of Bundelkhand, Dirk Kolff contends that the so-called 'spurious' Rajputs in the persons of the Bundela rulers of Orchha, Chanderi and Datia, who combined landowning status with military entrepreneurship, claimed Rajput identity because of their occupation as soldiers.[7] In the early 1600s Bir Singh Deo, who had displaced a brother as the ruler of Orchha, received a *jagir* and eventually the title of

[3] Deryck O. Lodrick, 'Rajasthan as a Region: Myth or Reality?' In Karine Schomer et al., *The Idea of Rajasthan: Explorations in Regional Identity*, vol. 1 (New Delhi, 1994), pp. 6–7 and note 7. Kashmir, Punjab, the United Provinces, Central India and Bihar had higher percentages of Rajputs than did Rajputana.

[4] Ibid., p. 9. Doris Kling has advised me that 'Rajasthan' was first used in 'Tarikh-i-Rajasthan,' a history of Jaipur, Mewar, Marwar, and Bundi/Kota commissioned by Maharaja Pratap Singh of Jaipur and written in 1794.

[5] Richard G. Fox, *Kin, Clan, Raja and Rule: State–Hinterland Relations in Preindustrial India* (Berkeley CA, 1971), p. 47.

[6] Thomas R. Metcalf, *Land, Landlords, and the British Raj: Northern India in the Nineteenth Century* (Berkeley CA, 1979).

[7] Kolff, *Naukar*, pp. 117–58.

maharaja (great king) from the Mughal emperor Jahangir, who also married one of his daughters. Bir Singh further justified his status as a ruler by the construction of palace-forts as physical symbols of power and by religious activities such as pilgrimages to Hindu temple sites located in major recruiting areas, the building of temples, and generous charitable donations. Despite these symbols of sovereignty and continuing activity as military labour contractors, the Orchha Rajput rulers were unable to achieve the transition to the genealogical orthodoxy linked to descent, and so western Rajputs denied them matrimonial alliances. The Orchha rulers, however, never ceased to claim Rajput status.

The Malwa Plateau in central India presented variations of Rajput identity. Perhaps the best known states in this region are Dewas Senior and Junior founded in 1730 by Tukoji Rao and Kiwaji Rao, two Maratha brothers who claimed Rajput ancestry.[8] Their situation provides evidence of some fluidity of ethnic categories and kinship ties among Marathas and Rajputs before the nineteenth century.[9] Ratlam and its two breakaway states of Sailana and Sitamau, whose rulers traced their descent from a younger branch of the Rathor ruling family in Jodhpur, illustrate how able men might experience rapid political mobility and gain symbolic legitimacy. As a young man of 23, Ratan Singh, the founder of Ratlam, armed only with a dagger, boldly attacked a mad elephant rampaging in the streets of Delhi. An impressed Shah Jahan, the Mughal builder of the Taj Mahal, inducted him into the *mansabdari* (imperial administrative system), where the Rathor Rajput served with distinction. In 1648 Ratan Singh received a jagir in Malwa, a *mansab* rank of 3000, the emblem of the Mahi Maratib (Order of Fish), and settled in Ratlam village as his capital.

Kolff challenges the intense weight assigned to kinship and descent as the basis for Rajput identity. Both the Mughals and the British fostered this genealogical focus since it enhanced the status of their Rajput collaborators and thereby undergirded their imperial authority.[10] The alliances between Mughal overlords and Rajput rulers waxed and waned according to material circumstances. André Wink has labelled this strategy *fitna*, a combination of conciliation and competition which a centralised empire viewed as rebellion, in the

---

[8] Manohar Malgonkar, *The Puars of Dewas Senior* (Bombay, 1963); E. M. Forster, *The Hill of Devi* (Harmondsworth, Middlesex, 1965, first published in 1953).
[9] Norbert Peabody, in 'Tod's Rajasth'an and the Boundaries of Imperial Rule in Nineteenth-Century India', *MAS* 30 (1996), note 54, pp. 208–9 argues that the 'precolonial divide between Maratha and Rajput . . . [was] labile and contextually contingent'.
[10] Kolff, *Naukar*, pp. 72–4.

context of Muslim and later Maratha state formation.[11] Rajput state formation in central India required military entrepreneurship – activities that reflected common ideas about rajadharma – and legitimating and mutually beneficial alliances with superior powers. Kinship was only one among several factors in this process.

Probably the most long-lived Rajput-ruled states were in the Punjab hills of the Himalayas.[12] Some of these states traced their establishment from either the sixth and seventh centuries when Rajputs initially reached India or the eleventh and twelfth centuries when Rajput ruling families fled from Turkish Muslim invaders. Rajput leaders from the more productive Indo-Gangetic plains moved into this less desirable area and established conquest states over the indigenous populations. There are three broad groupings of Rajput-ruled hill-states according to geographical locations: the western in the *doab* or land between the Indus and the Jhelam Rivers and centred on Kashmir, whose Rajput ruler was displaced by Muslims during the fourteenth century; the central between the Jhelam and Ravi focused on Jammu; and the eastern between the Ravi and the Sutlej ranging from the states of Kangra and Guler, later annexed by the British, to the more remote states such as Chamba, Suket and Mandi, which managed to retain their autonomy, as did Jammu and Kashmir, until 1948.

Jammu and Kashmir were the only remnants of once powerful states in the Himalayas to survive the British onslaught, but to the present day they remain a tragically contested site. These two entities were linked in 1846 because of British strategic needs. Kashmir is an ancient state whose history of Buddhist and Hindu rulers is recorded in the *Rajatarangini*, a Sanskrit chronicle. After 1339 Muslims ruled there as a regional kingdom until Akbar added Kashmir to the Mughal Empire in 1586. He and his successors used Srinagar as their summer capital. Kashmir regained its autonomy, as did Jammu, in 1762. Kashmir was then effectively under the control of Muslim governors until the Sikh ruler Ranjit Singh conquered it in 1819. Jammu's history is less well documented. Petty chiefs called *rana*s and *thakur*s are thought to have ruled it until Dogras, asserting Rajput status that was not acknowledged in the crucial test of marriage, established a regional state. By the early nineteenth century, the Dogra ruler of Jammu was in the service of Ranjit Singh.

---

[11] André Wink, *Land and Sovereignty in India: Agrarian Society and Politics Under the Eighteenth-century Maratha Svarajya* (Cambridge, 1986), pp. 23–41 and passim.

[12] J. Hutchison and J. P. Vogel, *History of the Panjab Hill States*, 2 vols (Lahore, 1933) is the basis for the following narrative.

Among the eastern Himalayan group of Rajput-ruled states, Chamba claimed to be founded about AD 550 and enjoyed an unusual historical source. Its thakurs, exercising rajadharma, supported brahmans and Hindu temples with land grants recorded on copper plate title deeds dated as early as AD 700. Suket asserted its descent from the Pandavas of the *Mahabharata*, the other pan-Indian epic, but more historically from the Sena dynasty of Bengal, a branch of which moved into the Himalayan foothills about the eighth century AD. Mandi state broke off from Suket during the eleventh century, and these two states fought a see-saw battle in an effort to define borders. Southwest of Delhi are five major states of Rajasthan deemed the core of Rajput political culture.

James Tod is probably as responsible as anyone for initiating the comparison of the Rajput polity to European feudalism. In the first volume of *Annals and Antiquities of Rajast'han*, published in 1829, Tod declared: 'there is a martial system peculiar to these Rajpoot states, so extensive in its operation as to embrace every object of society. This is so analogous to the ancient feudal system of Europe, that I have not hesitated to hazard a comparison between them.'[13] Tod became required reading for later generations of British political agents and for scholars whose research analysed documents produced by those officers. Some British administrators and later scholars have disputed his characterisation of Rajputs as feudal;[14] others castigated him for attributing essential qualities to Rajputs that justified British intervention;[15] and Indian nationalists used his ideas as 'a call for Indian resistance against the British'.[16] Tod was also instrumental in propagating the idea that Mewar was the premier Rajput state, despite declining territory and revenues, because its rulers followed most assiduously the Rajput chivalric code.

The ruling house of Mewar, which means central region, allegedly gained possession of the commanding plateau of Chitor by AD 714.[17] Beyond their exalted genealogical origins of descent from the sun god, the Sisodias of Mewar declared their pre-eminence for maintaining Rajput honour in two key areas.

---

[13] James Tod, *Annals and Antiquities of Rajast'han or, the Central and Western Rajpoot States of India*, 2 vols (New Delhi, 1971, reprint of 1914 edition), vol. 1, p. 107.

[14] Alfred C. Lyall, 'The Rajput States of India', in *Asiatic Studies, Religious and Social* (London, 1882) is representative of British officials and Robert W. Stern, *The Cat and the Lion: Jaipur State in the British Raj* (Leiden, 1988), pp. 23–62 is a perceptive overview of the scholarly debate on Rajput feudalism.

[15] Ronald Inden, *Imagining India* (Oxford, 1990).

[16] Peabody, 'Tod's Rajast'han', p. 217. Peabody argues that Tod claimed that their feudal institutions made the Rajput similar to the English, distinct from other Indian groups such as the Mughals and Marathas, and served as a basis for Rajput nationality: pp. 185–220.

[17] Tod, *Annals*, vol. 1, p. 188.

First, they had refused to give daughters in marriage to Muslim rulers. Frances Taft has argued that the Mewar dynasty broadcast their resistance to Mughal overtures and to Rajput peers who entered marriage alliances with Mughals to enhance their position in Rajput clan and state rivalries.[18]

Second, the Mewar rulers committed *jauhar* in 1303, 1534 and 1567 when resisting superior Muslim forces. Jauhar is probably a Rajput custom from Central Asia that was practised when confronted with certain defeat. To preserve their honour, Rajput women and children were consigned to death by fire, and then Rajput men purified themselves, donned saffron-coloured robes symbolising martyrdom, and fought until death. The bravery of the Rajputs was affirmed, but the material costs were high. The Sisodias saw their territory shrink and entered the eighteenth century ensconced in their capital of Udaipur with much reduced resources compared to their two major rivals, Marwar and Amber, which were more willing to share power and daughters with the Mughals.

During the tenth and eleventh centuries, the Kachhawaha clan migrated into an area known as Dhoondar, south of Delhi and north of Mewar.[19] Dulha Rai, a Kachhawaha leader, supposedly granted estates to indigenous Minas in return for their allegiance, and their symbiotic relationship was acknowledged in two practices: first, a Mina placed the *tilak*, an auspicious mark, on an incoming Jaipur ruler during the installation durbar or ceremony, and second, the Minas were the hereditary guards of the Jaipur treasury.[20] This is another instance of the process described by Wink among the Marathas whereby neighbouring tribal groups are employed as watchmen and plunder specialists and thus 'the complementarity of order and disorder . . . made possible the establishment of sovereignty'.[21]

Amber was a relatively minor chieftainship until the Mughals incorporated it and other Rajput rulers, through marriage ties as well as rank, within the elite administrative hierarchy.[22] Bihar Mal of Amber was the first Rajput ruler to pay tribute to the Mughals, to give his eldest daughter in marriage to Akbar in 1562, and to have his grandson Man Singh I become a prominent administrator

[18] Frances H. Taft, 'Honor and Alliance: Reconsidering Mughal–Rajput Marriages', in Schomer, *Idea*, vol. 2, pp. 217–41, esp. pp. 230–3.

[19] Jadunath Sarkar, *A History of Jaipur c. 1503–1938*, revised and edited by Raghubir Sinh (Delhi, 1984), pp. 20–7. Highly critical of the negative views of Tod about Jaipur, Sarkar completed his manuscript in 1940, but according to the dust jacket, 'Rajput sensitivity towards incidents depicting Mughal–Rajput relations, and other obstacles, prevented publication'.

[20] Ibid., pp. 22–4.   [21] Wink, *Land*, p. 194.

[22] Norman P. Ziegler, 'Some Notes on Rajput Loyalties during the Mughal Period', in Richards, *Kingship*, pp. 229–31; Norman P. Ziegler, Action, Power and Service in Rajasthani Culture: A Social History of the Rajputs of Middle Period Rajasthan, PhD thesis, University of Chicago (1973).

or *mansabdar* under Akbar. As a Mughal general, Man Singh led the campaign that defeated Maharana Pratap Singh of Mewar-Udaipur at Haldighat on 18 June 1576 and ended the effective Rajput resistance to the extension of Mughal control into Rajasthan. These two Rajput rulers illustrated the consequences of two Rajput responses to an expanding imperial system. Amber's acceptance of a client relationship with a Mughal patron yielded an increase in territory, *jagirdari* rights to collect land revenue around his capital, and bardic condemnation, while Mewar's refusal brought loss of territory but poetic glory.[23]

Amber reached a peak in the early eighteenth century under Jai Singh II (1700–43), who used military force to capture it from a rival protégé of the Mughals. The victorious ruler proceeded to enlarge his territorial base by securing *ijara* or tax-farming rights to *pargana*s or districts surrounding his jagir from the impotent Mughal emperor.[24] In 1727 the foundation of a new capital city named Jaipur on the plain below Amber provided 'a center uniting local [Rajput] and Mughal organisational and ceremonial features'.[25]

Jai Singh reaffirmed his dual heritage as a Hindu-Rajput ruler and a member of the Mughal imperial mansabdari hierarchy. First, he achieved Mughal recognition of Jaipur as his capital in 1733, and then he consecrated it through the ancient Hindu ritual of the horse sacrifice, which asserted his sovereignty. He endowed Jaipur with Mughal-style gardens and palaces for the performance of Mughal-style celebrations, but also Hindu temples and lively bazaars that attracted Hindu and Jain merchants as well as jewellers, craftsmen and musicians from Delhi. Jai Singh made annual processions and occasional tours through the broad streets of Jaipur that provided, 'in an era before mass media and instant communications, a ceremonial relationship to his people parallel to that created in the *darbar* and halls for public audience'.[26]

Jaipur was not unique among Rajput states in its acceptance of Mughal suzerainty in return for confirmation of their local control. Three other key states in western Rajasthan, Marwar-Jodhpur, Bikaner and Jaisalmer, paid their homage to Akbar in 1570. In the sandy hills of the western Thar Desert known as Marwar, meaning region of death, a lineage of the Rathor clan founded a

[23] Susannne Hoeber Rudolph and Lloyd I. Rudolph, 'The Political Modernization of an Indian Feudal Order: An Analysis of Rajput Adaption in Rajasthan', in *Essays on Rajputana: Reflections on History, Culture and Administration* (New Delhi, 1984), pp. 41–5.

[24] Satya Prakash Gupta, *The Agrarian System of Eastern Rajasthan (c. 1650–c. 1750)* (Delhi, 1986), pp. 12–27.

[25] Joan L. Erdman, *Patrons and Performers in Rajasthan: The Subtle Tradition* (Delhi, 1985), p. 29; Sten Åke Nilsson, 'Jaipur: In the Sign of Leo', *Magasin Tessin* 1 (1987), pp. 49–51.

[26] Erdman, *Patrons*, p. 42.

Amber Palace with view towards Jaigarh Fort.

View of planned city of Jaipur.

state during the thirteenth century. In 1459 Rao Jodh established a new capital called Jodhpur, the city of Jodh, and its name became an alternative to Marwar. Until the Mughal period, Marwar was second in importance to Mewar in Rajasthan and frequently in conflict with Amber-Jaipur, with whom it shared a shifting border. Norman Ziegler has linked the transformation of Marwar into a centralised state with a shift from patrimonial domain, where control over land is inherited through membership in a kinship group, to prebendal domain, where control is granted in return for service to the state and is not inheritable. This process began around the mid-sixteenth century and was linked to the increased use of horses for warfare, which required greater resources but also enabled rulers to extend their territorial control because of the mobility that improved breeds of horses provided.[27] Eventually Jodhpur grew to be the largest state in Rajasthan. Although much of its territory was economically unproductive and its population remained limited, Marwar-Jodhpur was a valued ally of the Mughals. However, it became less prominent during the British period as the fortunes of a neighbouring state rose.

Bikaner was an offshoot of Marwar-Jodhpur. Its creation occurred during the first stage of the cycle outlined by Fox, when the absence of a strong imperial state allowed ambitious sons or brothers to take over new territories and thereby remove one potential threat to a newly established lineage. Rao Bika, the second and eldest surviving son of Rao Jodh, proclaimed himself king in 1472 in the inhospitable desert area northwest of Marwar. Karni Singh, the last maharaja of Bikaner and a historian, has argued that Bikaner's relations with the Mughals 'were forged by the needs of the rulers of Bikaner for protection against the invasion of the sister-State of Jodhpur and brigandage of the indigenous elements and the realisation of the Central Powers [Mughals] of the potential help that Bikaner could afford in consolidating their territories'.[28] Rao Kalyanmal of Bikaner and his son, Rai Singh, entered relations with Akbar in 1570 and received a mansab rank of 2000. Bikaner fared well until the eighteenth century when the absence of a strong central power intensified strife among the Rajput states themselves.[29] Brigands from the west ravaged Bikaner and Marwar, and Amber challenged it for dominance. Bikaner's location in the barren Thar Desert, however, saved its rulers from having to pay tribute to the more formidable Marathas.

[27] Norman P. Ziegler, 'Evolution of the Rathor State of Marvar: Horses, Structural Change and Warfare', in Schomer, *Idea*, vol. 2, pp. 193–201.

[28] Karni Singh, *The Relations of the House of Bikaner with the Central Powers 1465–1949* (New Delhi, 1974), pp. 41–2.

[29] Ibid., pp. 99–120; Fox, *Kin*, p. 124.

23

The last major Rajput state to enter the Mughal system was Jaisalmer, whose ruling clan claimed descent from Krishna. They are Yadu or Jadon Bhatti Rajputs and their bardic genealogy makes allusions to a possible retreat into Central Asia and then re-entrance to India accompanying Scythian invaders. In 1156 Jaisal, the putative founder, erected a fort on a commanding ridge situated near a water supply and caravan routes between Afghanistan and the western coast of India. In frequent conflict with Marwar-Jodhpur, Jaisalmer entered the Mughal mansabdari system to prevent the encroachment of other Rajput clients of the Mughals. Ultimately such loyalty to the Mughal Empire would serve as a prototype for their subsequent alliances with the British.

Successor states

Although Awadh, Bengal and Hyderabad, as former Mughal provinces, are considered the classic successor states, some antique states, most particularly Amber-Jaipur, which had been an active participant in the Mughal mansab-dari/jagirdari administrative system for over a century, had similar characteristics. S. P. Gupta has described how closely the Jaipuri revenue administration conformed to the Mughal model.[30] In many ways the Jaipur state followed the prototypical successor state in both its structure and the process of its expansion and illustrates the arbitrary nature of any typology of princely states. Because of its pre-Mughal origins, however, I have not treated it as a successor state.

In his pioneering analysis of Awadh, Richard Barnett outlined seven criteria of autonomy that marked the metamorphosis from province to successor state:

1. The provincial governor or the imperial military officer in a little kingdom nominates or appoints his own revenue officers.
2. Regional governors appoint their own successors.
3. Revenues are used within the region and only ceremonial remittances are made to the centre.
4. Governors engage in independent diplomatic and military activity.
5. Ruling families establish their principal residences at their provincial capitals rather than at the Mughal court.
6. A coinage is minted at least in silver to replace the imperial silver rupees.
7. Delivery of the *khutbah*, the Friday congregational sermon in the principal mosque, is in the name of the governor rather than the emperor.[31]

---

[30] Gupta, *Agrarian System*, pp. 1–26, 163–86.
[31] Richard B. Barnett, *North India Between Empires: Awadh, the Mughals, and the British 1720–1801* (Berkeley CA, 1980), pp. 21–2.

Most successor states appropriated the first five functions in a sequential order, but only a few minted coins and practically none took the seventh step.

The classic model for the development of a successor state is Awadh. In 1720 Saadat Khan, a relatively late Shi'a immigrant from Nishapur in Iran seeking his fortune at the Mughal court, was appointed *subahdar* of Agra but was later demoted to the less remunerative Awadh. Despite this reduction in income, he took the first four steps that Barnett outlined. Marriage alliances created a network of support.[32] Then Saadat Khan became the first governor of Awadh to appoint his revenue officers; to nominate his successor, his son-in-law and nephew, Safdar Jang; to reduce the portion of revenue remitted to Delhi; and to engage in direct military and diplomatic negotiations with a foreign invader, Nadir Shah. Safdar Jang and Shujaud-Daula, his son and heir, continued this transformation of a state.

In 1764 at Buxar, the upstart English East India Company defeated an alliance of Shujaud-Daula, the Mughal emperor, and Mir Kasim, the deposed nawab of Bengal. Shujaud-Daula yielded territory, paid an indemnity, and concluded a treaty with the British but also laid out an impressive capital at Faizabad complete with palaces, zoo, aviary and marketplaces to demonstrate his status as the ruler of a regional state.[33] Awadh would enjoy a reprieve until 1856. Bengal, the successor state that Alivardi Khan so brilliantly crafted, was much more short-lived.[34] After their victory in 1764, the British received the *diwani* or revenue-collecting rights in Bengal. Thus the East India Company emerged as a regional Indian state and the Nawab of Bengal became their pensioner. One successor state, however, would survive until 1948.

The third and most long-lived successor state was among the last territories to be incorporated into the Mughal Empire. Mir Kamar-ud-din, who is better known by his titles of Nizam-ul-Mulk and Asaf Jah I, was appointed subahdar of the Deccan Plateau province in 1713. After settling at the Mughal capital of Aurangabad, Asfar Jah campaigned against the Marathas and briefly served as *wazir*, the chief Mughal revenue minister. Disgusted with the political infighting in Delhi, Asfa Jah I returned to the Deccan where he eventually exercised the first four of Barnett's criteria for autonomy. After his death, rival claimants allied themselves with the French and English companies during their struggle over succession. Salabat Jang, with French support, emerged triumphant in

[32] Michael H. Fisher, 'Political Marriage Alliances at the Shi'i Court of Awadh', *CSSH* 24 (1983), pp. 598–601.

[33] Barnett, *North India*, pp. 67–95.

[34] P. J. Marshall, *Bengal: The British Bridgehead Eastern India 1740–1828*, The New Cambridge History of India, II, 2 (Cambridge, 1987).

1751 and remained in power for a decade. In 1761 he was deposed by Nizam Ali Khan, a younger brother, whose reign extended from 1762 to 1803. He evolved a distinctive political system, reduced hostilities with the Marathas, defined firmer boundaries, and established a new capital at Hyderabad city, near the former seat of the Qutb Shahi dynasty of Golconda.

The political system in Hyderabad was relatively complex. While high-lighting the Mughal pattern of its administrative institutions, Karen Leonard argues that these Mughal-named institutions operated differently in the Dec-can.[35] More recently, Sunil Chander has asserted that Hyderabad cannot be considered a successor state since a 'criss-cross pattern of alliances between small kings at the local level, "intermediaries" at the supra-local level, and foreign powers at the inter-regional level' moulded the central government of Hyderabad.[36] But he contends that Hyderabad became more like a successor state in the nineteenth century, so I have chosen to treat it as such. The *nizam*, as the head of state, controlled the largest territorial base and used revenues from it to support his personal household, his administration, and his mili-tary establishment. But the nizam and his nobles were revenue receivers and expenders since they farmed out revenue collection to intermediaries. Military campaigns, administrative commitments, the patronage of cultural clients such as poets, religious men and artisans, and their precarious fiscal base led this ruling elite to resort to loans from private bankers, frequently outsiders from northern and western India.[37]

Intermittent warfare with the Marathas (to be discussed later) dominated diplomatic and military affairs in Hyderabad. The nizams held these Deccani rivals at bay by allowing them to levy taxes in certain districts and by entering alliances with the English Company. In 1766 Nizam Ali Khan concluded an initial treaty with the British, on the basis of equality, which promised tribute from Hyderabad in return for support from Company troops when that was requested. Although Edward Thompson's claim that 'Hyderabad was saved only by the coming of the British'[38] overstated British power, Hyderabad benefited territorially from a subsidiary alliance in 1798. This treaty marked the beginning of unequal status. Hyderabad had to agree to disband its foreign troops and to support a regular, subsidiary force to be used only at the direction

---

[35] Karen Leonard, 'The Hyderabad Political System and Its Participants', *JAS* 30 (1971), pp. 569–82.
[36] Sunil Chander, From a Pre-Colonial Order to a Princely State: Hyderabad in Transition, *c.* 1748–1865, PhD Thesis, University of Cambridge (1987), p. 5.
[37] Leonard, 'Hyderabad System', pp. 569–82.
[38] Edward Thompson, *The Making of the Indian Princes* (London, 1978, first published in 1943), p. 14.

of the Company.[39] Hyderabad purchased a century and a half of continued existence by accepting a new patron. As Peter Wood succinctly stated, the price of survival was submission.[40]

Warrior or conquest states

Although the use of military force to establish political dominance was a key factor in the formation of most princely states, here conquest states will be construed as a third category. It designates states established by warrior groups who contested with an overarching authority to establish new political entities by offering military protection to local populations. Burton Stein asserts that Vijayanagara was a warrior state of the old regime that served as a structural precursor of the Maratha states.[41] The founders of conquest states were usually clan leaders who performed extraordinary services for a dominant ruler. These military entrepreneurs gained compensation ranging from rights to the produce of land, to clothing worn by the ruler, to honours such as titles, banners and other emblems of sovereignty. In south India Nicholas Dirks has described how the next step to assert one's legitimacy to rule was for such warrior chiefs to give gifts, especially of land, to Hindu temples and brahmans.[42] In north India, Hindu temples were less central to the political cosmology, but Hindu and Sikh as well as Muslim rulers also patronised a variety of religious, social and artistic institutions. At times, rising rulers agreed to nominal incorporation into the Mughal structure as mansabdars, but generally they did not participate in the governance of the empire on either provincial or imperial level, as had the successor states of the subahdars of Awadh, Bengal or Hyderabad. To validate their conquest or rebellion against their sometime acknowledged overlord, these emergent kings avowed divine sanction from myths as well as secular confirmation from a Mughal authority who did not have the power to refuse.

Conquest states are the most diverse of the three categories of princely states. Although the victories of the Persians under Nadir Shah and the Afghans under Ahmad Shah Abdali of the Durrani clan were external signals of the decline of the Mughal power, these foreign protagonists did not themselves establish

---

[39] Sarojini Regani, *Nizam–British Relations 1724–1857* (Hyderabad, 1963), pp. 187–213.

[40] Peter Wood, Vassal State in the Shadow of Empire: Palmer's Hyderabad, 1799–1867, PhD thesis, University of Wisconsin-Madison (1981), p. 39.

[41] Burton Stein, *Vijayanagara*, The New Cambridge History of India, I, 2 (Cambridge, 1989), p. 146.

[42] Nicholas B. Dirks, *The Hollow Crown: Ethnohistory of a Little Kingdom in South India* (Cambridge, 1987), pp. 128–38, 285–90.

states in India. Rather they served as new arbitrators of regional conflicts and new sources of legitimation to aspiring rulers who could also be supportive clients. A few Afghans nevertheless founded states that would remain internally autonomous until 1948. One was Rampur in western Uttar Pradesh, the sole remnant of Rohilla Afghan power after the revolt of 1857.[43] A larger one was Bhopal in central India.

Dost Muhammad Khan, the Afghan founder of Bhopal state, whose capital is approximately 200 miles south of Delhi, entered Mughal service in 1703. Four years later he began his career as an independent military entrepreneur with an ever expanding band of mercenary troops, many of whom were his relatives. During the 1720s he broadcast his political aspirations by taking the title of *nawab*, but Nizam-ul-Mulk, still ostensibly in Mughal service, defeated him. However, the future founder of Hyderabad state granted a *sanad* (letter, decree, contract) to Dost Muhammad Khan that recognised his right to collect revenues in return for a fort, the payment of Rs 50 000, and the pledge of 2000 troops. Upon the death of Dost Muhammad in 1728, the nizam again intervened by designating Yar Muhammad Khan, an elder but illegitimate son, as heir. Stewart Gordon has labelled this action as the '"weak candidate strategy" in Indian politics'.[44] Someone ambitious for suzerainty supported a vulnerable nominee who would then be willing to pay tribute because he could stay on the throne only with external support. A war of succession erupted after the death of Yar Muhammad Khan and eventually his widow, Mamola Begum, secured a compromise that gave actual power to a *wazir*. By 1763 Mamola Begum emerged as the de facto ruler of this state and remained so until the 1780s. She was the first of five formidable women who would be both rewarded with British honours such as the Star of India and lampooned on cigarette cards as savage rulers along with native American leaders.[45]

The Hindu ruling dynasty of Mysore traditionally dates its origin to 1399 and so it might possibly be considered an antique state.[46] However, because its greatest territorial and governmental expansion occurred from the late seventeenth century onward, Mysore seems more similar to warrior/conquest states such as Bhopal. Located in peninsular India, the rulers of Mysore were

---

[43] E. I. Brodkin, 'Rampur, Rohilkhand, and Revolt: The Pathan Role in 1857', *IBR* 15 (1988), pp. 15–30.
[44] Stewart Gordon, 'Legitimacy and Loyalty in Some Successor States of the Eighteenth Century', in Richards, *Kingship*, p. 291.
[45] Shaharyar M. Khan, *The Begums of Bhopal: A Dynasty of Women Rulers in Raj India* (London, 2000).
[46] C. Hayavadana Rao, *Mysore Gazetteer Compiled for Government*, new edn, 5 vols (Bangalore, 1930), vol. 1.

Begum Shah Jahan of Bhopal, ruled 1868–1901.

Her Highness the Begum Secunder, India and Princess Shah Jehan, India, cigarette cards of Savage and Semi-Barbarous Chiefs and Rulers of W. S. Kimball & Co.

petty chieftains in the Vijayanagara state where the ruler held ritual sovereignty over little kings (known to the British as *poligar*s) who collected the revenue and maintained law and order.[47] By 1610 the last agent of the Vijayanagara king sold the Srirangapatanam fortress to Raja Wadiyar (1578–1617), who began the transition from petty chief to little king.[48]

By the mid-eighteenth century, disputes over succession to the Mysore *gaddi* (literally a cushion and by extension a throne) had led one claimant, Krishnaraja II (1734–65), to seek the assistance of Haidar Ali (*c.* 1722–82), a Muslim general who had fought effectively in wars between rivals for the nawabship of the Carnatic, the area south of the Gundlekamma and Krishna Rivers that extended almost to Madras. After a successful coup in 1761, Haidar Ali became the effective ruler of Mysore, though the Wadiyar king remained his nominal suzerain. Once again an aspirant to autonomy retained a militarily impotent source of legitimacy, much as the governors of successor states used the Mughal emperor. Haidar Ali sought to create a centrally controlled military force that would enable him to subdue the petty chieftains within his state and to oppose external threats. Although he had to depend on tribute payments and

[47] Burton Stein, *Peasant State and Society in Medieval South India* (New Delhi, 1980) and 'State Formation and Economy Reconsidered: Part One', *MAS* 19 (1985), pp. 387–413.

[48] Ibid., pp. 400–1.

prebendial obligations, Haider Ali strengthened his military prowess by dominating the market for horses, cannon and foreign military officers – especially the French, who trained his troops in western techniques.[49]

When Tipu Sultan (1753–99) succeeded his father in 1782, he bolstered revenues to support a centralised military machine and intensified state control downward into local political units. Burton Stein has applied the concept of military fiscalism to his program while arguing that the same process had already begun from the local political base of petty chiefs and enterprising temples.[50] The state's share of the land revenue was maximised with the appointment of central officials as collectors in place of petty chiefs who had siphoned off much of the land revenue. To gain new sources of wealth, commercial crops such as sugar cane were encouraged and state-supported trade centres were developed that enabled the regional state to penetrate more deeply into the local economy and to undermine the position of intermediary chiefs and revenue farmers. Finally, *imam*s (gifts or assignments of revenues from parcels of land to support notable people or institutions) were carefully regulated. Tipu Sultan set in motion trends towards military centralisation and administrative modernisation, which the British and a restored Wadiyar dynasty would continue.[51]

As a Muslim ruler in a predominantly Hindu kingdom and a staunch opponent of the East India Company, Tipu Sultan has multiple personae in the historical record. Some British depicted him as a cruel, fanatical Muslim usurper; Pakistani historians claimed him as a defender of Islam; Indian historians have represented him as a prototypical nationalist; and in the 1980s some right-wing Hindu populist leaders have castigated him as a temple-destroying Muslim zealot. Kate Brittlebank has explored his diverse strategies to establish the legitimacy of his kingship, which was grounded on the material resources of a strong military force, an expanded tax base, and extended penetration of local politics. First, Tipu acted as a king, claiming universal kingship authorised by a *farman* (decree) from the Ottoman Caliph and minting coins in his own name. Second, he incorporated former enemies, neighbours and officials into

[49] Ibid. and Devadas Moodley, 'War and the Mysore State: Men and Materials 1760–1800'. Paper presented at the Ninth European Conference on Modern South Asian Studies, Heidelberg University, 9–12 July 1987 and provided by the author.

[50] Martin Wolf first developed the concept of military fiscalism in the context of fifteenth-century Renaissance France, and Stein is careful to underline the differences between Renaissance France and eighteenth-century India: Stein, 'State Formation', pp. 387–413.

[51] Ibid. and Mary Doreen Wainwright, 'Continuity in Mysore', in C. H. Philips and Mary Doreen Wainwright (eds), *Indian Society and the Beginnings of Modernisation c. 1830–1850* (London, 1976), pp. 165–85.

a hierarchy of subordination through gifts offered as a superior to subordinates and exchanges of women as marriage partners, concubines and possibly slaves. Third, although he destroyed some Hindu temples connected to his enemies, he extended protection and patronage to Hindu as well as Muslim sacred sites. Tipu Sultan also appealed to both Hindus and Muslims by his use of the tiger and the sun as royal emblems.[52] A potent symbol of secular and sacred power, the tiger appeared in various forms, as a tiger head, as stripes, or in calligraphy, on buildings, weapons, clothing and thrones.

It took four wars before, in 1799, the British defeated Tipu at Srirangapatanam, where he was killed. Subsequently the British appropriated many of Tipu's icons and possessions as war trophies to be displayed first in private collections and then in museums as testaments to imperial glory. The best-known image of Mysore's formidable challenge, now housed in the Victoria and Albert Museum, is the mechanical tiger with a British soldier in its mouth which is equipped with an organ that growled as the tiger opened its mouth.[53] Pursuing a policy inaugurated in Awadh in 1764, the British concluded a treaty, to be discussed in Chapter 4, that did not annex Mysore but restored the displaced Wadiyar dynasty to the gaddi.

Another remnant of the Vijayanagara state was the small principality of Pudukkottai (meaning new fort) created by the Tondaiman *kallars*.[54] By the mid-seventeenth century a Tondaiman chief had developed a military relationship with the Tamil Maravar Sethupati rulers of Ramnad. He then engaged in marriage politics by marrying a sister to his Sethupati ally and thereby elevating his status above that of rival kallar clans. In an innovative and elaborate analysis that combines archival research and ethnological fieldwork, Nicholas Dirks has traced the rise of the Tondaimans from petty chiefs with a reputation for banditry to little kings. Because of timely military service, in 1801 the British acknowledged them as an internally autonomous princely state.[55] Eventually Pudukkottai became a theatre state as hegemonic British colonial officials directed rituals and bestowed honours in a play devoid of actual participation by the subordinate Pudukkottai prince.

---

[52] Kate Brittlebank, *Tipu Sultan's Search for Legitimacy: Islam and Kingship in a Hindu Domain* (Delhi, 1997).

[53] Two major British collections of artefacts associated with Tipu Sultan are at Powis Castle in Wales and the Victoria and Albert Museum in London. Mildred Archer, Christopher Rowell and Robert Skelton, *Treasures from India: The Clive Collection at Powis Castle* (London, 1987); C. A. Bayly, *The Raj: India and the British 1600–1947* (London, 1990), pp. 152–60.

[54] Dirks, *Hollow Crown.*   [55] Ibid., parts 4 and 5.

In the mid-eighteenth century Martanda Varma created Travancore,[56] and an elaborate foundation myth is held to account for several distinctive cultural features in this state. The god Parasurama was exiled from India, and Varuna, god of the sea, allowed the homeless god to throw his axe and reclaim the land from the sea that his axe covered. It went from Cape Comorin at the tip of the Indian subcontinent to Cochin and covered a narrow strip of land 70 to 80 miles wide that arose between the Arabian Sea and the western Ghats. Parasurama created the *nambudiri*s, brahmans who were given ownership of the land and distinctive customs so that they would not migrate back to India over the Ghats. Then the god provided *nayar*s, who were *sudra*s who functioned as their servants and bodyguards. The nayars had a matrilineal system of family organisation and inheritance but no formal marriage, and their women were to satisfy the sexual desires of nambudiri brahmans. The historical ancestor of Travancore was the Chera Empire, but after its dissolution around 1100, petty chiefs ruling over little kingdoms dominated the area.

Martanda Varma (r. 1729–58) became the raja of Venad in 1729. Prepared to ignore traditional modes of warfare and governance, he sought to create a new type of centralised state. Martanda executed nayar chiefs, sold their wives and children into slavery, and conquered and absorbed the territories of neighbouring chiefs. He then imported 'foreign' Tamil and Maratha brahmans to administer these newly conquered territories and displaced the local chiefs. He employed a Belgian soldier, Eustace de Lannoy, to reorganise his military into a salaried, drilled and dependent army composed of diverse groups including Deccani and Pathan Muslims, Tamil Hindu warriors and local Syrian Christians.

Susan Bayly has pointed out the importance of the Kerala states in linking traditional warrior lineages and *kalari* martial training groups to the European-style military system. The central civil and military administration was largely paid with revenues from state monopolies in export crops such as pepper, cardamom and wood products, which made Travancore one of the most commercialised states during the eighteenth century.[57] This new structure represented a diminution of the powers of the local nayars and their dependants, but as Robin Jeffrey has analysed it, they were not excluded from power as long as

---

[56] A. Sreedhara Menon, *A Survey of Kerala History* (Kottayam, 1967); K. M. Panikkar, *A History of Kerala 1498–1801* (Annamalainagar, 1960).

[57] Susan Bayly, 'Hindu Kingship and the Origin of Community: Religion, State and Society in Kerala, 1750–1850', *MAS* 18 (1984), pp. 186–202.

they were willing to participate in the government on the terms that Martanda Varma dictated.[58]

Besides the need to maintain armies trained and equipped by Europeans, religious patronage and leadership in the establishment of states were of the utmost importance throughout south India in the eighteenth century.[59] To gain legitimacy and to conciliate the strongest opposition group, Martanda Varma dedicated the state to the tutelary deity Sri Padmanabha, an incarnation of Vishnu, in an act that incorporated all classes in his gift. But as his European-style military was ecumenical in membership, the aggressive ruler adjudicated leadership succession disputes among the Syrian Christians within his state and patronised brahmans.[60]

By 1758 Travancore included around 7000 square miles of territory. Under Maharaja Rama Varma (r. 1758–98) it became the focus of unwanted attention from Mysore. In 1795 the Travancore ruler expediently concluded a treaty of subsidiary alliance with the Company to secure additional protection from Tipu Sultan's aggrandising embrace. By 1800 Travancore had to accept its first British resident and reconfirmed its commitment to the British with another treaty in 1805.[61]

Cochin, a much smaller state of about 1500 square miles, shared with Travancore a legendary descent from the Chera Empire and the matrilineal system of family organisation and inheritance. It was, however, less successful than its southern neighbour in resisting external and internal challengers. The Portuguese arrived in the sixteenth century and the Dutch in the next century. When the latter left in the middle of the eighteenth century, the *zamorin* of Calicut invaded the state and was only repulsed with the aid of troops from Travancore. In 1775 Haidar Ali compelled the raja of Cochin to pay an annual tribute. Then in 1791 the raja shifted his allegiance and his tribute to the British.

André Wink has maintained that following the process begun by Rajputs in the fourteenth century, the Marathas, along with the Jats, Bundelas and Sikhs, represented the gentrification of India. As the Mughal Empire advanced southward, Maratha military entrepreneurs were able to expand their political control through the skilful negotiation of alliances with the contending Muslim

---

[58] Robin Jeffrey, *The Decline of Nayar Dominance: Society and Politics in Travancore, 1847–1908* (London, 1976), pp. 2–5.
[59] Susan Bayly, *Saints, Goddesses and Kings: Muslims and Christians in South Indian Society 1700–1900* (Cambridge, 1989).
[60] Susan Bayly, 'Hindu Kingship.'
[61] Susan Bayly's revisionist arguments in 'Hindu Kingship' and *Saints* are the basis for my interpretation, along with Jeffrey, *Decline*.

powers during the middle decades of the seventeenth century. Shivaji (1630–80), the founder of the Maratha state, came from a *deshmukh* family. Stewart Gordon has delineated the obligations and rights of deshmukhs, who as village headmen gradually achieved financial, military, judicial and ritual rights and obligations through the process of colonisation in abandoned or waste lands. As the 'hinge' between a king and cultivators, a successful deshmukh needed administrative and military skills.[62] By his death in 1680, Shivaji, a man of great personal courage, had built up a powerful base through adroit military campaigning, administrative reforms and ritual innovation. His main sources of revenue were *chauth*, a tax of one-fourth of the land revenue, which might be deemed tribute or fees for military protection, and *sardeshmukhi*, an assessment of about 10 per cent of the produce. Payment of the sardeshmukhi implied recognition of Shivaji as head of the deshmukhs, the dominant families in the districts.

By the early 1700s, Shivaji's political association had evolved into what Indian nationalists have labelled the Maratha Empire and British historians the Maratha Confederacy. Neither term is fully accurate since one implies a substantial degree of centralisation and the other signifies some surrender of power to a central government and a longstanding core of political administrators.[63] Maratha power was fragmented among several discrete elements. They included the raja of Satara, the nominal head and source of legitimacy; the peshwa, a brahman bureaucrat who became the de facto leader; and five major military leaders of whom three would survive until 1948. Shinde, who is frequently referred to as Scindia in British sources, was based at the ancient Hindu sacred site at Ujjain and later at the Rajput-constructed fort of Gwalior, south of Agra and the Chambal River. Holkar, a leader from a pastoralist background in the Vindhya Mountains and technically not a member of the Maratha caste group, eventually established his capital at Indore in central India. The *gaekwad* in Baroda remained on the periphery of Maratha politics because of his distant base in Gujarat. Bhonsle overcame the Gonds of central India and settled at Nagpur.

Just as the Rajput states had their British chronicler in Tod, the states of Central India had Sir John Malcolm (1769–1833). His account about the origin of the Scindia and Holkar families illustrates features common to other Maratha ruling families. Ranuji, the founder of the political good fortune of the Scindias, came from cultivators who were sudras and held the hereditary

---

[62] Stewart Gordon, *The Marathas 1600–1818*, The New Cambridge History of India, II, 4 (Cambridge, 1993), pp. 22–34.
[63] Ibid., pp. 178–9.

office of *patel* or headman of a village. Ranuji had supposedly entered the service of Baji Rao I, peshwa from 1720 to 1740, as slipper-bearer. One night Baji Rao came out from a long audience and discovered Ranuji asleep with the peshwa's slippers clasped tightly to his chest. The peshwa was impressed with his servant's faithfulness in small matters and promoted him to his bodyguard.[64] A similar story is related about the Holkar family. These foundational myths have common features: their natal or adoptive families had some sign of superior authority such as a village headman or the maintenance of armed supporters; despite low-status occupations, the founders performed some extraordinary act which attracted the attention of a superior political authority anxious to recruit talented, loyal supporters; and during the decline of a central power shrewd individuals at the right place at the right time could create their own political base with great speed.

During the eighteenth century the core of the Maratha political entity was the peshwas of Poona (now Pune) and the Scindias of Gwalior, the latter being intermittently challenged by the Holkars of Indore.[65] As the Mughal imperial structure lost the support of local elites, the Marathas spread out from their Deccan stronghold into a broad arc from the fringes of the Portuguese settlement at Goa across central India to the outskirts of the British enclave at Calcutta. They did not always seek direct control of land but were often content with indemnities and the right to collect chauth and sardeshmukhi.[66] However, Gordon has emphasised that in much of Malwa and the Khandesh, the Maratha state at the village and pargana level collected its revenue on the basis of extensive contracts specifying the amount of revenue in return for political stability.[67]

As the Marathas moved north they encountered the Rajputs, some of whom initially asked for their assistance as allies in succession struggles, first in Bundi in 1734 and later in Mewar, Marwar, Amber and Alwar. Wink has described these forays as 'conquests on invitation'.[68] The Rajput rulers soon discovered that Maratha demands for tribute to pay their expensive but potent military units could never be fully satisfied. Yet these princes could not form a successful

[64] Sir John Malcolm, *A Memoir of Central India including Malwa and Adjoining Provinces*, 2 vols (New Delhi, 2001, first published in 1823), vol. 1, pp. 116–17.
[65] Gordon, *Marathas*, pp. 132–77.
[66] Stewart N. Gordon, 'Scarf and Sword: Thugs, Marauders, and State-formation in 18th Century Malwa', *IESHR* 6 (1969), pp. 403–30.
[67] Stewart Gordon, Everyday Resistance and Negotiation in the Eighteenth Century Maratha Kingdom. Unpublished paper presented at the American Historical Association, Washington, D.C., December 1987.
[68] Wink, *Land*, p. 75.

alliance against the Marathas, even after the Afghans had defeated them in 1761.[69] The Rajputs might gain interludes of indifference when the forces of the Scindias and Holkars fought each other. But they were plundered for resources when a dynamic, able ruler like Mahadji Scindia concentrated on collecting tribute from the Rajputs not only on his own behalf but also that due to his nominal overlord, the Mughal emperor. Here is another instance of a rebel prince invoking the authority of the Mughal emperor ostensibly to protect the emperor but in reality to enable the nominal subordinate to strengthen his own military establishment. Mahadji was using the emperor, as had Saadat Khan and Safdar Jang of Awadh. Mahadji's death in 1794 provided a respite for the Rajputs, but in ten years they would be subjected to attacks by the *pindaris*, who were attempting to form their own resource base from the disarray of the Maratha possessions.[70]

By the 1790s the Maratha polity was debilitated by ineffective leadership and had lost what little internal cohesion it had earlier possessed. Like his nominal overlord in Satara, the peshwa had been reduced to a political cipher by his chief minister, Nana Fadrnavis. In Indore, Ahilyabai, the daughter-in-law of Malhar Rao Holkar, who had thoroughly trained her in administration and military strategy, assumed the throne in 1765 when her husband became mentally unbalanced, and kept Indore politically stable. Her executive skills, her recruitment of a supportive elite, and her kingly dharmic gift-giving to brahmans and pilgrimage sites from Kedarnath in the Himalayas to Rame-saram in the south reflected a possible pattern by which a few princely wives, widows or mothers were politically active in the public sphere.[71] Her death in 1795, however, left Indore in a politically weakened condition similar to that of Nagpur and Baroda. By 1805 the latter was a British-protected state and disengaged from its Maratha peers by treaty and by geography.

C. A. Bayly has characterised the Sikhs as a social movement like the Marathas, which derived strength from their ability 'to incorporate pioneer peasant castes, miscellaneous military adventurers and groups on the fringes of settled agriculture'.[72] Guru Nanak (1469–1539), the founder of Sikhism as a religious movement, proclaimed that his followers should approach the One, Formless God directly and live in the world on the product of their own labours. Guru Gobind Singh (1666–1708; the tenth guru 1675–1708) instituted the

[69] S. C. Misra, *Sindhia-Holkar Rivalry in Rajasthan* (Delhi, 1981).

[70] R. K. Saxena, *Maratha Relations with the Major States of Rajputana (1761–1818 A.D.)* (New Delhi, 1973), pp. 260–72.

[71] Gordon, 'Legitimacy', pp. 293–6, and Malcolm, *Memoir*, vol. 2, pp. 175–95.

[72] C. A. Bayly, *Rulers*, p. 20.

khalsa as the community of those who were baptised and accepted social practices such as not cutting their hair. W. H. McLeod has argued that these customs came from the Jats,[73] pastoralists who had moved into settled agriculture and were attracted to Hinduism and Islam as well as Sikhism. The Sikh community also acquired a commitment to political domination embodied in the slogan *raj karega khalsa* (the khalsa will rule).[74]

During the eighteenth century, Sikh *jathas*, military bands based on varying degrees of personal, kinship and regional bonds, coalesced into larger units called *misls* that extended protection over tracts in central Punjab in return for a share in the produce from the land. By 1799 Ranjit Singh had incorporated most of the misls into a kingdom of Punjab based at Lahore, which resisted British annexation until 1848. A few Sikh *misldars* or rulers, mainly those south of the Sutlej, survived as allies of the British for another century. The principal ones controlled the three Phulkian states of Patiala, Nabha and Jind. The Phulkian clan traced their ancestry remotely to Jaisal, the Jadon Bhatti Rajput founder of Jaisalmer state, and would maintain their right to Rajput status even in the twentieth century.

In return for supporting the Mughal emperor Babur during the battle of Panipat in 1526, Bariam, a Phulkian Jat, acquired *chaudhriyat*, or the right to collect revenue from a wasteland southwest of Delhi. When a descendant, Phul (d. 1652), was introduced to Har Govind, the sixth Sikh guru, the religious leader is reputed to have prophesied that Phul, whose name means 'flower' in Hindi, would bear many blossoms and satisfy the hunger of many. Phul had seven sons by two wives; the two by his first wife were Tilokha, the ancestor of the rajas of Nabha and Jind, and Rama, who was the ancestor of the Patiala ruling house. Ala Singh (1691–1765), the third son of Rama, was the first to take the name of Singh and is considered to be the founder of Patiala state. By 1765 the Afghan king-maker Ahmad Shah Durrani granted Ala Singh the title of raja, a robe of honour, and the right to coin money in return for an annual tribute. Indu Banga has emphasised that political expediency was Ala Singh's guiding principle in external relations,[75] and it is apparent that Sikh *sardars* or local leaders generally were profiting from judicious negotiations of alliances in an area where more powerful opponents were contesting for dominance. Amar Singh (b. 1748, r. 1765–82), the grandson of Ala Singh, accepted Sikh baptism

---

[73] W. H. McLeod, *The Evolution of the Sikh Community: Five Essays* (Delhi, 1975), pp. 51–2.
[74] J. S. Grewal, *The Sikhs of the Punjab*, New Cambridge History of India, II, 3 (Cambridge, 1990), ch. 5.
[75] Indu Banga, 'Ala Singh: The Founder of Patiala State', in Harbans Singh and N. Gerald Barrier (eds), *Punjab Past and Present: Essays in Honor of Dr. Ganda Singh* (Patiala, 1976), p. 155.

and continued the expansion of Patiala state through strategic alliances and successful military actions. A series of succession disputes after his death left Patiala vulnerable to better organised rival Sikh misldars and northward-bound Marathas.

In the 1790s female relatives of Patiala rajas, most notably Rani Rajindar (d. 1791), a cousin of Amar Singh, and Rani Sahib Kaur (d. 1799), the sister of Raja Sahib Singh (1773–1813), actively rallied the troops of Patiala against Maratha incursions. Lepel Griffin, a late-nineteenth-century British official in Punjab and hardly a feminist, remarked that 'it would almost appear that the Phulkian Chiefs excluded, by direct enactment, all women from any share of power, from the suspicion that they were able to use it far more wisely than themselves'.[76] The Phulkian states were soon to acknowledge the suzerainty of Ranjit Singh, but in 1809 Patiala, Nabha and Jind entered treaty relations with the English Company to secure protection from annexation by their formidable Sikh overlord. Yet again, Patiala would gain from its geographical position between two expanding states, the British and the kingdom of Punjab.

After Ranjit Singh's death in 1839, a series of rapid successions weakened the resistance of the kingdom of Punjab to British encroachment and the loyalty of petty chieftains of 'little kingdoms'. During the Anglo-Sikh war of 1845–46, the responses of the Sikh states varied. Patiala, Jind and Faridkot committed their resources to the British, willing to come to terms with whoever controlled Delhi. Nabha and Kapurthala hesitated or joined the Punjab kingdom and suffered losses but not extinction. The Anglo-Sikh war of 1848 meant the annexation of Punjab and confirmed the anomalous creation of the kingdom of Jammu and Kashmir. Since the British felt unable to defend an extended and remote frontier area in 1846, they transferred Kashmir, which Ranjit Singh had annexed to Punjab, to Maharaja Gulab Singh of Jammu, a Dogra who claimed Rajput status, in return for a payment of Rs 75 lakhs.[77] Thus a Hindu military ally of Ranjit Singh was made the ruler of the Muslim majority area of Kashmir for imperial strategic reasons.

Like their Phulkian counterparts, the Hindu Jat rulers of Bharatpur and Dholpur claimed Rajput origins. The ruling family of Bharatpur, located south-east of Delhi, reputedly forfeited its Rajput status when an ancestor Bal Chand, having no children by a Rajput wife, produced sons with a Jat woman. One

[76] Lepel H. Griffin, *The Rajas of the Punjab: Being the History of the Principal States in the Punjab and Their Political Relations with the British Government*, 2nd edn, 2 vols (Patiala, 1970, first published in 1870), vol. 1, p. 67.

[77] Bawa Satinder Singh, *The Jammu Fox: A Biography of Maharaja Gulab Singh of Kashmir 1792–1857* (Carbondale IL, 1974). A lakh = 100 000.

of their scions banded together with other Jats and offered protection to local populations as Mughals and Marathas fought around Delhi. By 1752 the Mughal emperor was compelled to recognise Badan Singh as a hereditary raja controlling a little kingdom near Delhi. As he rose from petty chieftain to raja, the Bharatpur ruler sought legitimation through his patronage of Vaishnavite ascetics and acknowledged their power to confer benediction.[78] On the material level Badan Singh constructed palaces, other kingly amenities in his newly founded capital of Bharatpur, and a fort. After shifting alliances with the British and the Marathas, in 1805 his descendant, Raja Ranjit Singh (d. 1805), calculated that his interests would be best served by a treaty with the British, who were more threatening than the Marathas. Dholpur, the other Hindu Jat-ruled state, captured the great Rajput fort at Gwalior after the defeat of the Marathas in 1761. After several exchanges of Gwalior fort among the British, Scindia and Dholpur, in 1805 the Dholpur ruling family were confirmed in their possession of the districts of Dholpur, Bari and Rajakhera.

No typology will ever include all examples, and Bahawalpur state followed perhaps a singular pattern of state formation.[79] Situated in barren desert territory along the left banks of the Indus and its tributaries between Jaisalmer in Rajasthan and Multan in Punjab, it was populated largely by Muslim Jats and had a pastoral-nomadic economy until the eighteenth century. Then warrior chieftains known as Daudputra (sons of Daud) and claiming descent from Abbas, the uncle of the Prophet Muhammad, as well as the Abbasid caliphs of Baghdad, expanded during the 1730s from a territorial base at the confluence of the Chenab and Indus Rivers. Soon the Daudputras devoted themselves to the promotion of agriculture, first by sustaining the construction of a simple but effective earthen canal network and then by supportive tax policies. Flourishing food and cash crops stimulated pan-Indian trade and the development of urban centres. Successfully resisting envious Rajput neighbours at Jaisalmer and Sikh states advancing from the north, Bahawalpur demonstrated the viability of indigenous forms of irrigation based on appropriate levels of technology. At the same time the rulers of Bahawalpur did not incorporate any imperial Mughal ideologies, administrative patterns, or cultural habits but rather 'were simply conducting business as usual, carving niches for themselves' and thereby reflecting the multiplicity of models for state formation.[80]

[78] C. A. Bayly, *Rulers*, p. 185.
[79] Richard B. Barnett, 'The Greening of Bahawalpur: Ecological Pragmatism and State Formation in Pre-British Western India, 1730–1870', *IBR*, 15 (1988), pp. 5–14.
[80] Ibid., p. 12.

PATTERNS OF STATE FORMATION

An analysis of the preceding early histories of groups of states reveals some broad patterns in the processes of state formation in India during the late eighteenth and early nineteenth centuries. Aspiring rulers of Indian states had to undertake three major tasks if they were to achieve political autonomy. First, they assembled supporters who would assist them in the initial conquest and the subsequent administration of their newly acquired territory. This elite generally comprised three elements: kinsmen and others who had participated in the military triumphs, indigenous elites, and administrators who possessed the literacy and management skills needed to implement the policies that ensured the penetration of the state.

Kinsmen of the ruler provided varying levels of support. Rajput rajas generally conquered their states with the assistance of warbands and kinsmen, who were rewarded with jagirs or ijaras in the classic Mughal pattern. Among Rajputs, a ruler was frequently considered the first among equals and faced continuing competition from his kinsmen. Thus many Rajput rulers sought emblems of sovereignty from some external source such as the Mughal Empire and later the English Company to differentiate themselves from their kinsmen. When a ruler showed signs of weakness, ambitious kinsmen, especially siblings, either seized power or left to create new states. During the fifteenth century, when the Lodis of Delhi exerted little control beyond Punjab, Bikaner split from Jodhpur. Later, during the Mughal decline in the eighteenth century, Alwar broke off from Jaipur and the states of Patiala, Nabha, Jind and Faridkot evolved from the Sikh Phulkian misl.

Many rulers of eighteenth-century states had moved into territories where they shared few cultural bonds such as language, religion, history or extended residence with those they governed. Consequently, to reduce active opposition to their new regime, they incorporated local elites who retained symbols of authority or the loyalty of subordinate social and economic orders. Most states eventually came to follow the Mughal model of granting or reaffirming jagirs or the right to collect revenue or receive a certain portion of the revenue from a specific tract of land to local elites. Some indigenous elites continued to perform bureaucratic or military services for the new ruler. Others received pensions that acknowledged past services and tried to ensure present loyalty. Although these older elites survived physically, their political power was usually diluted in an expanded pool of elites that included the kinsmen of the ruler, non-indigenous bureaucrats, and pan-Indian and local merchant groups.

Newly emergent rulers also recruited external groups with literacy and administrative abilities. These outsiders were sought for two reasons. First, the ruling elite and local land-controllers often did not possess the requisite skills. Second, newcomers would be more dependent on the ruler for their power and authority than kinsmen or locally based elites. Thus the Marathas employed Chitpavan brahmans; Travancore imported brahmans from Tamilnadu and north India; the nizams of Hyderabad recruited *kayasth*s (a kshatriya caste group with a tradition of administrative work in an imperial language such as Persian) from north India. These non-indigenous administrative elites were one of many strands that tied princely states to other parts of India. Although they were limited in number, some of these administrators came to form an informal, pan-Indian cadre comparable to the Indian Civil Service (ICS) of British India since they might spend much of their career in one state or region but could also move to posts throughout India.

Second, whether conquest states that relied heavily on military power to establish themselves, successor states that avowed imperial appointment as their basis, or states evolving from social movements, eighteenth-century states had to devote significant resources to the maintenance of an effective military force. Here was a significant change from earlier patterns of state formation. Rulers now needed more disciplined armies that were uniformed, drilled, equipped and paid according to European and Ottoman models. From the Seven Years War in the mid-eighteenth century onward, the French and English trading companies demonstrated the value of using Indian troops organised according to more efficient models. The importance of artillery and European techniques of sapping in waging successful seige warfare also became apparent. Initially the European mercantile companies themselves offered such military expertise to a few aspiring states, and then European mercenary officers provided it as individual consultants.

These new armies required cash for payrolls and the purchase of new weapons, equipment and uniforms. Rulers needed more revenue. First, they restricted the percentage that intermediaries claimed as their share of the revenue collected from agricultural production. Second, they penetrated local agricultural society more deeply by pensioning off some layers of intermediaries and establishing their own collection structures, which procured a larger percentage of the revenue for the state. Third, they extended their territory to gain new sources of revenue. Fourth, they provided protection to new client groups who would supply extraordinary sources of tributes. Fifth, they fostered expanded economic activities that generated new sources of revenues, such as the development of cash crops, the production of specialised goods, and the establishment of markets to facilitate the exchange of such goods and surplus agricultural produce.

Most states tried these strategies in varying combinations. In Mysore a Muslim usurper secured more revenue, and in Travancore rulers encouraged new crops and markets, as did some in north India including Bahawalpur. Marathas augmented their territories and exacted tribute from client groups such as the *pindaris*, mobile bands who accumulated resources through irregular expeditions among unprotected peasants. During the early eighteenth century Jaipur city attracted wealthy bankers and merchants, and artisans from Delhi in Jaipuri workshops fashioned luxury products that found a ready market beyond state territory.

Those who lacked a strong material resource base such as the western Rajputs or were unable to unite in order to use their limited resources more effectively could not create a military force comparable to their more favourably situated neighbours. Succession disputes and clan feuds fragmented the Rajputs, and the lack of modernised military forces weakened the Rajput defence against the Marathas. Consequently the western Rajputs were generally eager to secure alliances with external powers such as the British.

After aspiring rulers had created a diverse group of collaborators that included kinsmen, local elites and competent administrators, and enhanced their finances to support a modernised military force, they sought ideological legitimation of their power and increasing autonomy. Antique states, basically those ruled by Rajputs, had long supported bards who elaborated genealogies that traced descent from pan-Indian epic heroes; they had recorded compromises with indigenous inhabitants and had reconciled claims to high ritual caste status with their present positions through stories of marriages, usually undertaken to secure heirs, that inadvertently lowered ritual or caste status. Moreover, these antique states as well as successor and conquest states buttressed their right to rule with grants of legitimation from external sources and by personal dharmic actions, with patronage and gifts being a crucial link between the two spheres.

Perhaps the most potent external source of legitimation was a supernatural injunction to rule. Thus several Hindu rulers declared that they were deputies of a divinity. As mentioned earlier, Martanda Varma of Travancore gave his state to its tutelary deity Sri Padmanabha, whose temple was a centrepiece of the fort in the capital of Trivandrum (now Thiruvananthapuram). In the distant Himalayan foothills, the Rajput ruler of Mandi declared that he ruled as the diwan of Vishnu and that Tehri Garhwal was the speaking personification of the deity of the Hindu temple at Badrinath. Among the Sikh misls, the

Phulkian rulers affirmed the blessing of the tenth Guru on their founder. Muslim rulers might view themselves as shadows of Allah's authority on earth.

More earthly sources of external legitimation were recognition by the Mughal emperor, aspirants to imperial power such as Ahmad Shah Abdali, or the English Company. Most states became adept at using ties to the Mughal emperor to enhance their legitimacy and their claims to greater autonomy, even though such demands diminished the authority of the Emperor himself. Thus the nawabs of Awadh, as wazirs of the emperor, obtained grants of territory and possessions that reduced the resource base of the Mughal Empire while enhancing that of Awadh. Other rulers, such as Ala Singh of Patiala, did not see any incongruity in paying a ransom to Ahmad Shah Abdali and then accepting symbols of sovereignty from him. Rebel states such as the Marathas, which arose in opposition to the Mughal Empire, also saw no contradiction in seeking Mughal titles and eventually becoming protectors of the Mughal emperor when he had only authority and not power.

Rulers could also achieve legitimacy by acting according to established norms of kingly conduct. Following models recorded as early as the *Arthashastra*, they mediated disputes among castes and other social and religious groups. Here the work of Nicholas Dirks on Pudukkottai highlights the role of the rulers in settling caste disputes and thus the priority of political power in determining caste boundaries. Later the British census would reinforce a hierarchy among castes and indirectly resolve the claims of caste groups to particular statuses. Such activity was not limited to Hindu groups. In a discussion of Muslim communities in south India, Susan Bayly has remarked that 'eighteenth-century rulers had to use every possible strategy to reconcile disparate interest groups and associate valuable allies and client communities with their regimes'.[81] Even Martanda Varma of Travancore, a most Hindu ruler, arbitrated disputes over the leadership of the Syrian Christian community in Travancore.[82]

Another aspect of kingly dharma was to give gifts to and generally patronise religious institutions, whether Hindu temples, Muslim mosques and *dargah*s (tombs of Sufi saints), or Sikh *gurudwara*s (repositories of the Sikh sacred scripture). Religious scholars and people with the aura of sanctity were also prime recipients of kingly largesse. As might be expected, rulers nourished religious institutions and persons within their states and at varying points in state formation. For example, the Marathas did not begin such patronage until late in the eighteenth century, while south Indian rulers tended to give major gifts much earlier.

[81] Susan Bayly, *Saints*, p. 173.   [82] Ibid., pp. 269–70.

Temple of Sri Padmanabha in Trivandrum during Attukal Pongal Festival.

What is more striking is how several rulers extended their patronage across political and sectarian boundaries. During the early nineteenth century Maharaja Ranjit Singh of Punjab was especially catholic in his endowments to Hindu and Muslim institutions as well as to Sikh ones; his aid ranged from gilding the central Sikh gurudwara at Amritsar with gold leaf to generous grants to Sikh scholars. Moreover, there were other notable patrons on a pan-Indian scale. Jai Singh II of Jaipur constructed his great astronomical observatories on the basis of knowledge accumulated from Hindu, Muslim and European sources (the last generally transmitted by Jesuits) at major Hindu pilgrimage sites such as Banaras, Ujjain and Mathura and political centres such as Delhi. Martanda Varma of Travancore made gifts to north Indian Hindu pilgrimage centres as well as temples in Tamilnadu. The Maratha rulers of Tanjore supported a Muslim dargah at Nagore. Much research remains to be done on the extent and impact of such pan-Indian patronage, which continued into the twentieth century, but it clearly constituted another strand in the web of relationships among individual regional states and cultural institutions throughout India.

A third type of personal action affirming legitimacy was for the ruler to live like a ruler. Thus during the eighteenth century many regional rulers, whether of antique states such as Jaipur or successor states such as Awadh, constructed new capital cities or embellished older ones with elaborate palaces, gardens and walls and erected profit-making markets. These urban sites provided a stage for enhanced court rituals and the display of consumption that proclaimed one's status as ruler. Maratha and Sikh rulers as leaders of peasant bands were slower to erect complex capitals and to develop enhanced court rituals, but by the early 1800s Ranjit Singh would impress both his Indian rivals and the English Company with lavish public rituals such as the use of a gold chair as a gaddi. C. A. Bayly has pointed out that what western observers viewed as 'a frivolous misappropriation of the peasant surplus . . . was the outward mark by which rulers were recognised – the circulating life-blood of the traditional kingdom which nourished the princely, commercial and agrarian economies'.[83] From the 1760s to the 1810s, many servants of another regional state, the English East India Company, imitated this lifestyle of the so-called nawabi culture. Possibly the most extraordinary was David Ochterlony, the British resident at Delhi (1803–25), who also oversaw Rajputana. Bishop Heber has described Ochterlony as a 'tall and pleasing-looking old man, but was so wrapped up in shawls, kincob, fur, and a Mogul furred cap, that his face was all that was

---

[83] C. A. Bayly, *Rulers*, p. 57.

visible', while others remarked on his reputation for having thirteen elephants and thirteen wives.[84]

Thus the eighteenth century, which witnessed the declining power of the Mughal Empire and some Mughal elites, was also an era of creative state formation that extended into the early nineteenth century. Successor states, those formed by appointees of the Mughal Empire, and warrior states such as the Marathas, Mysore and the Sikhs, formed powerful entities. Their bases were a synthesis of a collaborative elite that included kinsmen, outside administrators, and the remnants of indigenous elites; important merchant groups; a modernised army; and the economic capacity to raise necessary revenue by penetrating the local society. Political power had been decentralised during the eighteenth century, but individual states intervened more directly in local communities than had any Mughal emperor or governor. Gradually the British Indian regional state, first established in Bengal, evolved a new political structure to incorporate their other Indian rivals.

---

[84] Reginald Heber, *Narrative of a Journey through the Upper Provinces of India, from Calcutta to Bombay, 1824–25*, 2 vols (London, 1829), vol. 2, pp. 392–3; Thompson, *Making*, pp. 182–5.

CHAPTER 3

THE BRITISH CONSTRUCTION OF INDIRECT RULE

Many empires, from the Roman to the Soviet Union, have employed indirect rule in an effort to extend their influence over disparate peoples and regions with a minimum of expenditure in material and human resources. This chapter delineates how the British devised and then sustained a system of indirect rule that reputedly provided a model that was adapted to many other imperial situations. In his comprehensive study of the British residency system, Michael Fisher has defined indirect rule in India as 'the exercise of determinative and exclusive political control by one corporate body over a nominally sovereign state, a control recognised by both sides'.[1] The four key elements are that:

1. both sides must recognise the control as effective;
2. only one entity can exercise control;
3. all other rivals must be excluded; and
4. the dominant power must recognise some degree of sovereignty in the local state.

Debate continues over the degree of the sovereignty or autonomy of the Indian princes before and after they concluded treaties with the British. Since its publication in 1943, Edward Thompson's classic work, *The Making of the Indian Princes*, about British relations with Mysore and the Marathas from the 1790s to the 1820s has been the bedrock of arguments that without the British the princely states would not exist. But this thesis has outlived its usefulness.

In most cases the British did not create the Indian princes as political leaders. Although many were coerced into subordination, princes usually sought political and material benefits from their agreements with the British. As discussed in the preceding chapter, most Indian kings or rulers who would come to be labelled princes during the nineteenth century had existed before the advent of the British or had evolved along with the British as regional powers. Their treaties with the British, however, would acutely affect their political futures. These agreements defined territorial boundaries, rendering them compact or diffuse but generally more restricted; they regulated relationships with

---

[1] Fisher, *Indirect Rule*, p. 6.

both stronger or weaker neighbours, and to varying degrees modified relationships within a state between a ruler and his or her kinspeople, administrators, merchant groups and peasants. Most importantly, the treaties appropriated resources of Indian states, including revenues in the form of subsidies or tribute, subjects as soldiers, and commercial goods, for the benefit of the English East India Company. So while British treaties did not beget Indian princes or princely states, they did shape their future form and activities by establishing parameters that increasingly restricted princely options.

Second, the British experimented with various political arrangements. Anxious to maximise their commercial profits, to limit their political liabilities, and to reduce their operational expenses, they first tried to collect revenues through the administration of the nawab of Bengal. The Company soon discovered that this system enriched its servants but did not produce the income needed to meet its expenditures in India or in England. Consequently Warren Hastings, governor of Bengal (1772–73), and the first governor-general of India (1773–85), introduced a more direct system of revenue collection through British officers, which culminated in the Permanent Settlement of 1793. Now the British acted as did other eighteenth-century Indian rulers such as Tipu Sultan of Mysore and enlarged their share of revenue from peasants in order to maintain an efficient army. This military strength would undergird a growing centralisation of political functions and a corresponding penetration by the state into local society. With the recognition of zamindars as tax-paying landlords in Bengal in 1793, the British sought to create a loyal, dependent intermediary group that would supply an assured revenue. But the British soon found that they had to protect their expanded territorial base from other assertive regional powers. Their mercantile corporation was being drawn into wider relationships by their operational objectives, and they soon sought new means of extending their political control.

Third, indigenous states had multiple reasons for allying with external invaders as well as other Indian states. They sought to achieve dominance in succession disputes, to establish a superior position vis-à-vis their kinspeople, and to gain needed support in military confrontations with other regional states. Succession disputes occurred before, during and after the entrance of the British into India. Multiple wives and concubines and the lack of any firm commitment to primogeniture among both Hindu and Muslim rulers could precipitate a contest among sons, each allied with mothers, male relatives, and ambitious job-seekers. Despite or perhaps because of assorted sexual relationships, some rulers and dynasties repeatedly lacked direct male heirs. In those cases the struggle would be among illegitimate or adopted heirs and cadet branches of the ruling family. For example, during the 1740s the Marathas were active in Rajput states as allies of one side or the other in succession disputes.

Fourth, rulers including both Rajputs and Marathas would appeal for signs of their pre-eminence over their kinspeople from powerful external rulers. The East India Company would gradually assume this function from the increasingly bereft Mughal emperor.

Finally, military attacks, such as those by the Marathas on Hyderabad, led the latter to forge alliances with the British, who would provide badly needed military assistance. Consequently treaties with the English Company fit into a pattern of political behaviour that initially did not appear to be particularly innovative or dangerous for beleaguered regional states and little kings. But the situation would soon change dramatically. By 1820 the British had created a monopolistic military despotism funded by resources acquired from peasants in the most productive areas of India and from Indian commercial groups.[2]

BUILDING BLOCKS OF INDIRECT RULE

Five elements were fundamental in the creation and maintenance of the British system of indirect rule from 1764 to 1857: a growing monopoly of expanded military forces; legal documents ranging from treaties to sanads to proclamations and letters of understanding; maps and surveys; political officers, called residents, and political agents who translated policies and documents into practice; and concepts of legitimation that included suzerainty, paramountcy, and a chain of succession from the Mughal emperor.

Military resources

The War of Austrian Succession (1740–48) and the Seven Years War (1756–63) transplanted European rivalries to India. The British military presence in India expanded to counter a European antagonist, namely the French, and then Indian rivals, most notably Mysore and the Marathas. The English Company initially maintained its own meagre military units to protect its coastal settlements, but by the 1740s it had limited use of British royal troops. From the 1760s, the Company increasingly came to rely on sepoys or Indian troops trained and officered by Europeans and equipped with European-style weapons. Each presidency maintained its own army centred on infantry units

---

[2] C. A. Bayly, *Indian Society and the Making of the British Empire*, New Cambridge History of India, II, 1 (Cambridge, 1988), pp. 103, 110.

but also including cavalry, artillery and sappers, the last of which were particularly effective in siege warfare.

Following the example of Joseph Dupleix, the governor of the French East India Company in Pondicherry, Robert Clive began to extract support from Indian rulers for military contingents. Theoretically these units were to protect the rulers from internal and external threats as well as to safeguard the interests of the English Company. After the object lesson of the British military victory at Baksar in 1764 against the forces of Awadh, Indian rulers would pay a subsidy or tribute to support what became known as subsidiary contingents. During the late 1700s some rulers mobilised these contingents against external enemies; for example, Awadh did so against the Rohilla Afghans. Sometimes troops were used internally to extract revenue payments. By the early 1800s the British increasingly reserved these contingents for the pursuit of their own strategic goals in India. Meanwhile the British would curb the power of Indian rulers to maintain independent military forces through treaty provisions, and their continuing and inflexible demands for subsidies would restrict the economic ability of Indian rulers to sustain more than a palace guard. Thus by the 1820s the British controlled one of the largest standing armies in the world through the three armies of its presidencies and the subsidiary contingents financed by Indian rulers. This formidable force defeated major indigenous rivals and then guaranteed general, though not uniform, compliance with treaty provisions among most Indian rulers.

Treaties, sanads and letters

Initially Mughal emperors, who did not consider foreign merchants to be their equals, declined to conclude treaties guaranteeing trading privileges to the English East India Company. Rather, in 1613 Jahangir granted a farman or imperial edict that extended permission to trade at Surat to the Company and thereby incorporated the British within the authority of the Mughal emperor. Since the farman was unilaterally issued and not a contract in the English legal sense, in theory it could be unilaterally withdrawn. By the 1730s lesser Indian rulers began to conclude treaties with the English Company, and from the 1760s the Mughal emperor and his nominally subordinate subadars or governors entered treaties on a basis of equality with the Company.

Although British indirect rule is sometimes called the treaty system, no more than forty Indian states actually signed a treaty with the Company or its successor, the British Crown.[3] A few states account for a disproportionate

---

[3] I am grateful to John McLeod for sharing his computations on the states with treaties.

number of treaties. Rulers of major states such as Awadh and Hyderabad were compelled to sign new treaties upon their accessions to the gaddi. Each subsequent treaty conceded more territory or subsidy to the Company. Most treaties focused on specific concerns related to a particular point in time, but many issues were not addressed. The interpretation of these treaties became arenas of manoeuvre and negotiation among British political officers, Indian rulers and their ministers, and British and Indian lawyers until the demise of the states in 1948. The attempt to codify treaty provisions and practices intensified in the late nineteenth century and will be discussed in Chapter 4.

The British actually issued greater numbers of *sanads* and letters to Indian states than treaties. Sanads were certificates or testimonials of protection or recognition that the British unilaterally extended, much as Mughal emperors had earlier dispensed farmans. The British also bestowed letters of understanding that formulated, again unilaterally, the conditions of relations between themselves and an Indian state.

Maps and surveys

Simultaneously with their use of military force and legal instruments to extend their control over Indian states, the British undertook mapping and survey expeditions based on post-Enlightenment techniques of measurement and visual representation to create a scientific, rational and uniform geographic archive.[4] Although the Great Trigonometrical Survey focused on directly controlled areas, British maps came to define visually their indirect rule over Indian states for British and Indian audiences. Ironically, the alleged rationalisation of such mapping fostered the seemingly irrational intertwining of princely state boundaries. As Matthew Edney has argued, 'boundaries were no longer vague axes of dispute (frontiers) between core areas of Indian polities but were configured as the means whereby those core areas were now defined. Political territories were no longer delineated with respect of the physical features that characterised or bounded them; nor were they defined by the complex feudal interrelationships of their rulers'.[5] Plotting boundaries on paper erased intricate affiliations and connections.

By 1833 Captain James Sutherland, a retired deputy surveyor-general, striving for precision, estimated that 'the area of native states who had signed a treaty of alliance with the Company amounted to 449 845 square miles, and territory under direct British rule, including small quasi-autonomous states, made

---

[4] Matthew H. Edney, *Mapping an Empire: The Geographical Construction of British India, 1765–1843* (Chicago, 1997).
[5] Ibid., p. 333.

up 626 746 square miles'.[6] According to this calculation, the princely states constituted slightly more than 41 per cent or two-fifths of the territory of the British Empire in India, although the boundaries of many frontier states, ranging from western Rajputana to Himalayan hill-states, would not be physically established until well after 1833. Moreover, Sutherland attempted to divide princely states into six classes on the basis of their relationship to the British and then to categorise them by religion and region.[7] This British intellectual exercise served to reify the princely states as political, religious and ethnic entities, with serious implications for popular political activity in the twentieth century.

Residents

The Mughal emperor, his governors, and autonomous, indigenous rulers such as those of the Rajput states had conducted relations through *vakils*. These agents transmitted communications between rulers and reported to their rulers daily events at the courts to which they were attached based on official court *akhbars* (newspapers), public knowledge, and covert intelligence. The number of vakils resident at a court was a visible mark of its importance. Initially the Company sent its officers to conclude treaties with Indian rulers, frequently after military encounters. Consequently many early British diplomatic agents were military officers rather than commercial or civil employees. These men came to be known as political officers and had the title of residents when posted to major states and political agents when assigned to less important ones. More intrusive than vakils, since they did not confine themselves to handling interstate relations or intelligence-gathering, political officers became involved in the internal administration of states and extended British control in myriad ways. While serving with the resident to Scindia in 1806, James Tod began a geographical and mapping survey of western Rajputana, which was completed in 1815.[8] Maps, revenue settlement reports, ethnographic reviews and genealogical accounts contributed to the colonial intellectual construction of Indian society in areas of indirect as well as direct rule. Besides being used by the British to conquer and control Indians and to legitimate their own policies and actions, these texts influenced Indian intellectuals, administrators and rulers of Indian states in their constitution of political reality.

---

[6] 'Computation of the Area of the Kingdoms and Principalities of India', *JASB* 20 (August 1833), pp. 488–91, cited in Sudipta Sen, *Distant Sovereignty: National Imperialism and the Origins of British India* (New York, 2002), p. 81.

[7] Ibid., p. 82.

[8] Anil Chandra Banerjee, *The Rajput States and British Paramountcy* (New Delhi, 1980), pp. 5–7.

Only within recent decades have historians focused on the impact of the residents themselves. The pioneers include K. N. Panikkar, who analysed the role of the Delhi Residency from 1803 to 1857 when it handled British relations with both the Mughal emperor and neighbouring clients such as Rajputana and cis-Sutlej states.[9] Robin Jeffrey has defined a typology of the modes of interaction among maharajas, diwans, and residents based on his research in Travancore:

(i) the 'dominant Resident', in which the Resident controlled the Minister and reduced the Ruler to a cipher; (ii) the 'balanced' system, in which British governments, impressed by anglicised Rulers and Ministers, instructed Residents to achieve an equitable division of functions and responsibilities among the three principals; (iii) 'laissez faire', in which Rulers and Ministers were left largely alone, providing that the state remained free of blatant disturbances or misrule; (iv) the 'imposed Minister', in which an anglicised, trustworthy 'native' from outside the state – or sometimes a European – was established as Minister.[10]

In this last scheme a resident participated indirectly through control of a chief minister or the appointment of an imposed minister. There were, moreover, cases elsewhere in which a political officer might share directly in the administration of an Indian state as a minister or as a member of a council of regency for a ruler during his or her minority.

In his study of the residency system in India from 1764 to 1857, Michael Fisher explores its institutional origins, its British personnel and their varying goals, and, most innovatively, the Indian employees of the residents who were the principal means of contact with their counterparts within the princely administration and other elements of local society.[11] When Warren Hastings appointed the first residents in the 1770s, he sought direct control of residents and faced challenges from his own Council and the governors of Bombay and Madras. Although governors-general were ultimately successful in achieving jurisdiction over the major residents, the Indian political service continued to be fragmented between the central and the provincial levels until the eve of independence. Besides these organisational divisions, Fisher's analysis emphasises how the variations between policy and practice illustrate the differing attitudes and objectives of the men who created and operated the British Empire in India.[12]

---

[9] K. N. Panikkar, *British Diplomacy in North India: A Study of the Delhi Residency 1803–1857* (New Delhi, 1968).

[10] Robin Jeffrey, 'The Politics of "Indirect Rule": Types of Relationship among Rulers, Ministers and Residents in a "Native State"', *JCCP* 13 (1975), p. 262.

[11] Fisher, *Indirect Rule*.

[12] Michael H. Fisher, 'Indirect Rule in the British Empire: The Foundations of the Residency System in India (1764–1858)', *MAS* 18 (1984), pp. 393–428.

Concepts of legitimation

In a system of indirect rule, the superior power must concede some degree of sovereignty to the dependent ally. To provide a theoretical justification for this anomalous legal and constitutional situation, the British evolved two key concepts of suzerainty and paramountcy. A suzerain power had superior sovereignty or control over states that possessed limited sovereign rights. In the context of indirect rule in India, the sovereign rights that each Indian ruler possessed were partially defined by treaty but were more generally in a state of flux.

As the first British governor-general who sought to implement an overt imperial policy in India, Lord Wellesley and his extraordinary subordinates acted as if they were the acknowledged dominant power of India.[13] During the 1810s his successor, Lord Hastings, and some of the British officials who had served under Wellesley began to use the word 'paramount' to describe their perceived position in India. Hastings also encouraged several Indian regional states including Hyderabad and Baroda to declare themselves independent of the Mughal Empire so that they then might enter a new and more direct 'feudal' relationship with the British. Nawab-Wazir Ghazi al-Din Haydar of Awadh was the only Indian ruler to respond by having himself crowned padshah or emperor on 9 October 1819, but his action did not significantly improve his position with the British.[14] Edward Thompson has claimed that the first formal articulation of paramountcy as a doctrine occurred in a letter from David Ochterlony, the nawabi-style resident at Delhi, to Charles Metcalfe in 1820 and that the latter was the first to use it to justify intervention during a succession dispute at Bharatpur in 1825.[15] Metcalfe claimed:

> We have by degrees become the paramount State of India. Although we exercised the powers of this supremacy in many instances before 1817, we have used and asserted them more generally since the extension of our influence by the events of that and the following years . . . [O]ur duty requires that we should support the legitimate succession of the Prince, while policy seems to dictate that we should as much as possible abstain from any further interference in their affairs.[16]

Metcalfe's caution about intervention in the internal affairs of so-called protected states would be increasingly abandoned as British officials invoked

---

[13] Thompson, *Making*, pp. 27–30; C. A. Bayly, *Indian Society*, ch. 3.
[14] Michael H. Fisher, *A Clash of Cultures: Awadh, the British and the Mughals* (Riverdale MD, 1987), pp. 120–41.
[15] Thompson, *Making*, pp. 283–4.
[16] Minute by Sir Charles Metcalfe, 1825, Document 28 in Adrian Sever (ed.), *Documents and Speeches on the Indian Princely States*, 2 vols. (Delhi, 1985), vol. 1, pp. 145–6.

paramountcy to justify whatever course of action they judged expedient for British interests. The definition of paramountcy and what it entitled the British to do remained contentious until 1947.

THE CREATION OF INDIRECT RULE

The tyranny of periodisation

British apologists and historians from many nations have long sought to discern distinct phases in the evolution of the relationships between the British and Indian rulers. I argue that the British policies of indirect rule and annexation existed in a dynamic tension with one or the other strategy in greater ascendancy but that neither was ever fully dominant. C. A. Bayly has pointed out how the inflexible demands of the British subsidiary alliance system frequently created conditions that then led to British annexations of indirectly ruled Indian territory as a solution to a problem initially created by the British.[17] Most annexations incorporated specific strategic or economic objectives, but at no point did the British have the resources to administer all of India directly. Even in Saran district of Bihar, part of the Bengal province under direct British rule since 1765, Anand Yang has revealed the limited nature of the British raj, which collaborated with the maharaja of Hathwa, a zamindar. In this case the British were willing to enhance the resources of this landholder, who maintained local control over the peasantry that produced the revenue on which both the zamindar and the British existed.[18] At the same time the British felt they had the right to intervene in the administration of both zamindari estates and princely states when it suited their interests.

My second premise is that intervention and non-intervention as British policies also persisted in close association. British officials interfered or did not interfere because of particular political imperatives, intellectual constructs, economic needs and Indian responses. Thus while a scheme of periodisation is useful for the purpose of justifying an imperial policy or organising a historical narrative, it should not obscure the persistent, underlying juxtaposition of indirect rule and annexation and British non-intervention and intervention in the internal structure and policies of Indian states.

Once Queen Victoria renounced annexation as a policy in 1858, some British officials sought to legitimate the system of indirect rule and to codify British practices towards the princely states. They forged an intellectual

---

[17] C. A. Bayly, *Indian Society*, pp. 104–5.

[18] Anand A. Yang, *The Limited Raj: Agrarian Relations in Colonial India, Saran District, 1793–1920* (Berkeley CA, 1989), pp. 67–97.

framework that many historians of the Indian princes used. Before presenting an alternative periodisation, I will examine the formulations of William Lee-Warner (1846–1914), one of the most influential systematisers of the history of princely states. A member of the Indian Civil Service from 1869 to 1895, Lee-Warner served mainly in the Bombay secretariat with brief assignments in Kolhapur and Mysore. This consummate bureaucrat concluded his career in London at the India Office and then with membership on the Council of India from 1902 to 1912. He wrote the widely cited constitutional history first entitled *Protected Princes of India* when published in 1893 and then retitled, more 'neutrally', *The Native States of India* in a second edition of 1910. He differentiated '[t]hree distinct periods in filling in the Treaty map' created by the British in India. The first one began when Warren Hastings inaugurated the 'ring fence' policy of non-intervention by the British in the internal affairs of Indian states, which supposedly prevailed until the exit of Lord Minto as governor-general in 1813. During this phase allied states were few and supposedly '[w]ithin the Company's ring-fence or on its borders'. The key phrases in treaties were 'mutual alliance' and 'reciprocal agreement'.

The second stage commenced in 1813 when these expressions of interdependence were exchanged for those of dependence, for example 'subordinate alliance or co-operation' and 'protection'.[19] Lee-Warner labelled the governor-generalship of Lord Hastings from 1813 to 1823 as one of 'subordinate isolation' when '[t]he large, indefinite blocks of Foreign Territory left by Lord Minto, with no external frontiers delimited and no internal divisons fixed, were now brought under elaborate settlement; and the multitude of principalities, which still claim separate and direct relations with the British Government, were classified and protected'.[20] Subsequently the British allegedly pursued a policy of non-intervention in the affairs of its dependent allies, which allowed the princes to exploit their subjects. According to this interpretation, because of British reluctance to intervene at earlier stages of misgovernment, Lord Dalhousie, governor-general from 1848 to 1856, was forced to annex delinquent states. The third era was one of union and stability after 1858.

Other British officials and assorted scholars have proposed more finely detailed chronologies that continue to associate vacillation between indirect rule and annexation with specific governors-general. Thus we have the 'ring fence' policy associated with Warren Hastings from 1772 to 1785; the subsidiary alliance with Lord Wellesley from 1798 to 1805; the achievement of

[19] Sir William Lee-Warner, *The Native States of India* (New Delhi, 1979, first published as a second edition in 1910), pp. 43–5.
[20] Ibid., p. 96.

paramountcy with Lord Hastings and his immediate successors from 1813 to 1828; and the triumph of annexation with Lord Dalhousie from 1848 to 1856. Aggressive use of both indirect and direct rule was punctuated with eras of retreat, consolidation or non-involvement, with Lord Cornwallis (1786–93), Sir John Shore (1793–98) and Lord Minto (1807–13) being the leading non-interventionist governors-general.

These periodisations are important since they have influenced British officials in their relations with Indian princes as well as the historiography on the princely states. But they obscure the overall continuities in British policies, which balanced direct and indirect rule to serve an expanding empire. From the Company's acquisition of the rights to collect revenue in Bengal until 1858 when the Crown assumed formal control in India, British governors-general used the strategies of indirect rule and of direct rule through annexation with varying frequency and effectiveness. For example, the non-interventionist Minto offered protection to the cis-Sutlej Sikh states. Labels can obscure the longue durée as well as highlight briefer trends.

British officials divided states into various categories based on their treaty-cum-legal relationships with the Company. Lord Hastings had separated them into feudatories and allied states.[21] Sir Richard Jenkins, who had extensive experience with Maratha rulers, first as acting resident with Scindia and then as resident at Nagpur from 1807 to 1827, drew the line between the subsidiary states who entered treaty relations as equals and the subordinates who accepted British protection through a sanad or unilateral proclamation. By the late 1840s Lord Dalhousie designated as independent states those that existed before the coming of the British, as tributary or dependent those that survived through British protection, and as subordinate those that the Company supposedly created or revived by sanads. But later Lee-Warner argued that the '[d]ifferentiation of states as allied, tributary, created, or protected is illusory. All are alike respected and protected'.[22] Contemporary scholars such as Urmila Walia have also pointed out that many states do not fit into these categories with any consistency.[23] Consequently I will not use these terms in my narrative to signify categories.

A provisional scheme

Starting with my premise that indirect rule through Indian princes and direct rule by Company officers consequent upon annexation coexisted in dynamic

[21] M. S. Mehta, *Lord Hastings and the Indian States* (Bombay, 1930).
[22] Lee-Warner, *Native States*, p. 51.
[23] Urmila Walia, *Changing British Attitudes Towards the Indian States, 1823–1835* (New Delhi, 1985).

tension from 1765 until 1858, I propose a scheme of three major periods when client states were incorporated into the British system of indirect rule: 1765–85, years dominated by Robert Clive and Warren Hastings; 1798–1805, the era of Lord Wellesley as governor-general; and 1813–23, when Lord Hastings prevailed. But annexations occurred simultaneously with the expansion of indirect rule and extended into a fourth period under Lord Dalhousie. From 1848 to 1856 no new states were brought into the system of indirect rule, and non-intervention continued to be practised along with the extensive annexations of Dalhousie.

Before embarking on a survey of the transformation of Indian kings into Indian princes and clients in a system of indirect rule, readers must be fore-warned that the existing scholarly charts for the journey supply many details and few sweeping vistas. Charles Lewis Tupper, one of most cited British officers writing on the evolution of British indirect rule in India, remarked that 'the tediousness of Indian history is proverbial'.[24] The dullness is not in the history but in the telling of it. To try to reduce the tedium, I will not trace the evolution of relationships between the British and individual states but will rather use specific examples to illustrate general patterns.

EUROPEAN AND INDIAN ORIGINS OF THE SUBSIDIARY ALLIANCE SYSTEM

From the 1740s, the French and then the English East India Companies began to ally themselves with Indian regional states when the latter sought their assistance during succession disputes, internal confrontations between rulers and elites, and external attacks. The French and British were different, however, from possible indigenous allies in that they operated from very limited territorial and revenue bases in India but had potential access to much larger resources beyond India. In addition, events in Europe and throughout the world impacted on the policies of the French and the British more forcefully than on those of Indian regional powers. For example, the advent of Napoleon stimulated French interest in India and his defeat increased the number of unemployed French mercenaries seeking employment in India.

Following the French example of Joseph Dupleix, the English Company offered military support to Indian contenders in succession disputes and to

---

[24] Charles Lewis Tupper, *Our Indian Protectorate: An Introduction to the Study of the Relations between the British Government and Its Indian Feudatories* (London, 1893), p. 25.

other allies threatened by rival regional powers. Treaties, usually but not always, stipulated the extent of and conditions under which such aid was extended. In a manner that reflects the imbricated relationship between power and knowledge, which Edward Said and Michel Foucault have so forcefully explicated, British treaty relations with Indian states have been extensively described. British political officials such as Charles Aitchison, William Lee-Warner and Charles Tupper during the nineteenth century, British historians, most notably Edward Thompson during the 1940s, and Indian historians such as A. C. Banerjee, Sukumar Bhattacharyya, M. S. Mehta and Urmila Walia all participated in this project.[25] While officials codified British practices, historians evinced disciplinary biases for the analysis of wars and treaties and for working with accessible primary sources.

Initially the British sought to restrict relations, first between Indian rulers and the French and then among Indian rulers. Gradually their influence permeated the internal administrations of the princely states. To illustrate how the treaty system evolved, I will trace the British relationship with Hyderabad over five crucial decades.

The British treaty system with one successor state: Hyderabad

During the War of Austrian Succession, first the French and then the English Companies allied themselves with rival candidates in a dispute over the succession to the nawabship of the Carnatic, a little kingdom north of their respective enclaves at Pondicherry and Madras. The Treaty of Aix-la-Chapelle (1748) brought a brief hiatus in overt European hostilities in India, but eventually the British-backed candidate, Muhammad Ali, was victorious in 1751 over the French-supported Nawab Chanda Sahib. The British had acquired their first political ally in India. Meanwhile, in 1748 the death of Nizam ul-Mulk Asaf Jah I, the nawab of the Carnatic's nominal overlord, launched a succession dispute with higher stakes, which tempted the Marathas as well as the French and the British to intervene.[26]

Renewed military engagements during the Seven Years War culminated in the British defeat of the French and the first treaty between the British and Salabat Jang, the nizam of Hyderabad, who had been an ally of the French. Concluded on 14 May 1759, this treaty was one between equals. Although

[25] Thompson, *Making*; Banerjee, *Rajput States*; Sukumar Bhattacharyya, *The Rajput States and the East India Company from the Close of the 18th Century to 1820* (New Delhi, 1972); Mehta, *Lord Hastings*; Walia, *Changing British Attitudes*.

[26] Much of the following account is based on Regani, *Nizam-British Relations* and Zubaida Yazdani, *Hyderabad during the Residency of Henry Russell, 1811–1820* (Oxford, 1976).

the nizam was a major regional power and the British were petty chieftains, the latter had the more formidable military force. Thus the nizam had little choice but to cede certain districts to the British, to employ no French, and to prohibit them from settling in the districts transferred to the British. The British in turn pledged not to assist or protect any of his enemies. The European orientation of the British is apparent. The Indian perspective of the nizam led to the isolation of his principal Indian rival, the Marathas.

Nizam Ali Khan, the diwan of Hyderabad who deposed his brother Salabat Jang to become nizam from 1762 to 1803, sought British aid against the Marathas. Despite having been bested by the Afghan forces in 1761, the Marathas could still inflict two major defeats on Hyderabad forces in 1760 and 1763, winning the right to collect chauth and sardeshmukhi from Hyderabad. Nizam Ali Khan thus agreed to a new treaty with the British in 1766 that confirmed the Company in possession of the Northern Circars (*Sarkar*s), a string of districts on the eastern coast of India, which provided a key link between the British base in Bengal and their outpost at Madras. In return, the Company consented to assist the nizam with troops in ventures that were not in conflict with their pre-existing commitments in the Carnatic and to an annual rent of Rs 9 lakhs, which could be used to pay for troops supplied to the nizam. The Company further pledged to place troops at his disposal. When the nizam attacked the Marathas at Kharda in 1795, the British governor-general refused any support since the peshwa was an ally of the British. After having to surrender territories and pay tribute to the victorious peshwa, the nizam decided to solicit the assistance of French officers in forming European-style contingents.

Arriving in 1798, Lord Wellesley (1760–1842) was the first governor-general to aspire to imperial power in India. To augment his limited resources for military expeditions, Wellesley concluded another treaty with Hyderabad in 1798 that became a template for subsequent subsidiary alliances. The treaty required that the nizam dismiss all French officers and pay Rs 24 lakhs for a subsidiary force or contingent of six battalions that would be integrated with the British military. The British were to arbitrate between the nizam and the Marathas at Poona. The British ability to exact cash from Hyderabad and other Indian states for military forces has led Sunil Chander to argue that military fiscalism was the main impetus to foreign intervention in India during the eighteenth century.[27] Moreover, Fisher's criterion of exclusive control by one corporate body over another was met.

---

[27] Chander, 'Pre-Colonial Order to State'.

After the British defeated Tipu Sultan in 1799, they concluded another treaty with Hyderabad in 1800 that more clearly registered the latter's subordinate status. The nizam's subsidiary force was increased by two battalions of infantry and one regiment of cavalry, and the British agreed to protect the nizam from enemies such as the Marathas, their erstwhile allies. The nizam also had to cede more territory, to abstain from open warfare, and to submit any disputes with other princes to British arbitration. He thus could not exercise one of the prime functions of external sovereignty, the conduct of foreign affairs. Moreover, he had accepted a major constraint on his internal sovereignty since the subsidiary force was to be a constant, inflexible drain on his revenues. The objectives of the Company and their attitudes towards their princely ally are reflected in Wellesley's despatch dated 4 February 1804 to his Resident at Hyderabad:

> The fundamental principle of His Excellency the Governor-General's policy in establishing subsidiary alliances with the principal states of India is to place those states in such a degree of dependence on the British power as may deprive them of the means of prosecuting any measures or of forming any confederacy hazardous to the security of the British empire, and may enable us to preserve the tranquillity of India by exercising a general control over those states, calculated to prevent the operation of that restless spirit of ambition and violence which is the characteristic of every Asiatic government, and which from the earliest period of Eastern history has rendered the peninsula of India the scene of perpetual warfare, turbulence and disorder. The irremediable principles of Asiatic policy, and the varieties and oppositions of character, habits and religions which distinguish the inhabitants of this quarter of the globe, are adverse to the establishment of such a balance of power among the several states of India as would effectually restrain the views of aggrandisement and ambition and promote general tranquillity. This object can alone be accomplished by the operation of a general control over the principal states of India established in the hands of a superior power, and exercised with equity and moderation through the medium of alliances contracted with those states on the basis of the security and protection of their respective rights.[28]

The restless ambition and violence that had characterised British policy since the mid-1750s were ascribed solely to Asian governments. Furthermore, unspecified characters, habits and religions foreclosed the possibility of the balance of power that supposedly regulated interstate relations in Europe. Based on this racist construction of Indian politics, Wellesley claimed moral justification for the British assumption of superior controlling authority in India.

Once the British assumed control of Hyderabadi foreign relations, they began to penetrate the internal administration of Hyderabad in 1803 through the

---

[28] Despatch of 4 February 1804 quoted in Tupper, *Indian Protectorate*, pp. 40–1.

appointment of a sympathetic diwan. After the British rewarded Hyderabad with the fertile Berar province they had appropriated from Nagpur and other Maratha districts, Nizam Sikander Jah had to accept the British-suggested appointment of Mir Alam as diwan. As their external and internal sovereignty was being curtailed, Sikander Jah and his successors retreated to their inner palace or *zenana*, where they exerted influence through the manipulation of factions at their courts.[29] The British came to view the nizams as indifferent to affairs of state that diwans controlled through alliances with domineering residents such as Henry Russell (1811–20), Charles Theophilus Metcalfe (1820–25) and James Stewart Fraser (1838–53). Here is an early instance of a continuing phenomenon where an Indian ruler withdraws from active involvement in administrative affairs when a British-sponsored diwan, or later a coterie of skilled bureaucrats, monopolises power within a state administration. A later example of an eclipsed ruler in Hyderabad occurred when Salar Jung served from 1853 to 1883 as chief minister of Hyderabad. He enjoyed such firm British support that they permitted his son, even though he was a minor, to succeed him as diwan.[30] Similar arrangements materialised in other states and will be discussed in subsequent chapters.

Further treaties refined the relationship between Hyderabad and the Company. In 1822 a treaty ended the obligation to pay to the British the chauth that Hyderabad theoretically owed to the Marathas, and it established well-defined boundaries for Hyderabad through an exchange of territories. One in 1829 guaranteed British non-intervention, but another in 1853 leased the revenue of Berar to the British as payment for the Hyderabad Contingent and gained them access to the raw cotton of Berar sought by both Chinese markets and Manchester textiles mills.[31]

From 1759 to 1853 the British concluded numerous treaties with Hyderabad that extended British control and reduced the nizam's autonomy. The four criteria of indirect rule were clearly met. Both sides acknowledged British control as effective; the British were undoubtedly the dominant power; all rivals, both foreign (French) and domestic (Mysore and Marathas), were excluded; but the Hyderabad administration still exercised significant sovereign rights such as the collection of revenues and legal jurisdiction over its subjects within its territories. Although Hyderabad had to concede substantial resources in

---

[29] Peter Wood, 'Vassal State', pp. 40, 64.

[30] Vasant K. Bawa, 'The Interregnum in Hyderabad after the Death of Salar Jung I: 1883–1884,' *IBR* 15 (1988), pp. 79–89.

[31] Tara Sethia, 'Berar and the Nizam's State Railway: Politics of British Interests in Hyderabad State, 1853–1883,' *IBR* 15 (1988), pp. 59–61.

British Residency at Hyderabad by Captain Grindlay, from *Views in India, China and on the shores of the Red Sea.*

men, revenue and commercial products to its British suzerain, the state and particular subjects gained some benefits.

Several of the early treaties increased and then consolidated the territory of Hyderabad. Even the controversial lease of 1853 might have reduced the likelihood of full annexation by Dalhousie. Many Hyderabadi military officers, revenue farmers and peasants suffered, but other groups profited from the British-induced reforms. Sunil Chander has described how the British promotion of military fiscalism in Hyderabad extended centralised state control over many intermediaries and benefited those willing to serve as collectors and officials for British-inspired land settlements that raised funds to pay for British-imposed military forces.[32] The system of indirect rule extended and reinforced British power, but Hyderabad continued to exist as a state.

From treaties to subsidiary alliances to indirect rule
Ring fence or first phase of treaties among equals, 1759–85

The earliest treaties that the Company negotiated with Indian states during the 1730s – two with the small coastal states of Sawantwadi and Janjira and one with the peshwa – regulated maritime and commercial affairs, especially the suppression of piracy. However, the first major phase of the treaty system is more appropriately dated to the turbulent years 1759–65. Then treaties did not include any formal mechanisms of intervention in internal affairs or restrictions on the external sovereignty of the Indian states. The earliest treaty of friendship and alliance, with vague promises of military assistance, was the one concluded with Hyderabad in 1759, described above.

In 1765 Robert Clive allied with Shuja ud-Daula of Awadh to maintain a buffer state between the Company's new base in Bengal and the Marathas. He laid the foundation for what Lee-Warner labelled the ring fence policy of using a barrier of Indian allies to insulate the trading and territorial frontiers of the Company from potentially hostile groups. Warren Hastings elaborated this policy in 1773 when he rented a subsidiary force to Shujaud-Daula of Awadh. Subsequently the nawab attacked the Afghan Rohillas, who had not paid their tribute to him, since as Richard Barnett has pointed out, 'The Rohillas thus became to Awadh what Awadh was to the Company, and when they failed to pay their installments on time, they provided a ready-made justification for annexation'.[33] Hastings' acquiescence would be one issue leading to his impeachment. Responding to contemporary critics who claimed that he loaned

---

[32] Chander, 'Pre-colonial Order to State,' pp. 89–140.   [33] Barnett, *North India*, p. 93.

troops to Awadh solely to obtain the rental payment, the governor-general asserted that he

engaged to assist the Vizier [Shuja-ud-Daula] in reducing the Rohilla country under his dominion, that the boundary of his possessions might be completed by the Ganges forming a barrier to cover them from the attacks and insults to which they are exposed by his enemies either possessing or having access to the Rohilla country. Thus our alliance with him, and the necessity for maintaining this alliance, so long as he or his successor shall deserve our protection, was rendered advantageous to the Company's interest, because the security of his possessions from invasion in that quarter is in fact the security of ours.[34]

In other words, Hastings assisted the nawab of Awadh in order to allow this faithful ally to expand at the expense of a mutual enemy. Strategic interests, clearly not moral superiority, informed British policy.

After his governor in Bombay undertook inconclusive military action against the Marathas, Hastings concluded treaties of friendship and military alliance with two Maratha rivals, Bhonsle and Scindia, in 1781. Madhaji Scindia agreed to intercede in negotiating peace with Haider Ali of Mysore and the peshwa at Poona, and the British pledged to remain neutral in the face of Scindia's expansion north and westward that would gain Gwalior as his capital.[35] The next year Scindia served as a guarantor for the Treaty of Salbai between the British and the peshwa, which established a status quo between those two powers. At the same time the British repudiated earlier treaties with the gaekwad of Baroda (1780) and with the Jat ruler of Dholpur which offered 'perpetual' friendship (1779). These reversals clearly revealed that the Company would sacrifice lesser allies to achieve accommodation with more powerful rivals. While the treaties with Bhonsle, Scindia, and the peshwa were made between equals for ostensibly strategic objectives, the British were influencing internal Maratha politics. For example, their treaties of 1781 and 1782 provided legitimation for Scindia as an autonomous power.

Lord Cornwallis, an aristocratic general whose political and military reputation survived the surrender of the British force at Yorktown in 1783 to the victorious American colonists, succeeded Hastings as governor-general in 1786. He had specific instructions to avoid costly military expeditions and annexations and to pursue a policy of non-intervention. Most sources view him as following instructions explicitly. Cornwallis nevertheless concluded a

---

[34] G. W. Forrest (ed.), *Selections from the State Papers of the Governors-General of India*, 4 vols (Oxford, 1910), vol. 1, p. 50.

[35] *A Collection of Treaties, Engagements and Sanads relating to India and Neighbouring Countries*, compiled by C. U. Aitchison, vol. 5; *The Treaties, &c., Relating to Central India (Part II – Bundelkhand and Baghelkhand) and Gwalior*, rev. edn of 1929 (Delhi, 1933), p. 379.

Triple Alliance with the peshwa and the nizam against Tipu Sultan in July 1790 and embarked on the Third Anglo-Mysore War from 1790 to 1792, personally taking command on the battlefield. He also concluded treaties of friendship and alliance with Coorg in 1790, which was annexed in 1834, and with Cochin in 1791 to secure his flanks against Mysore. Thus a desire to isolate Mysore, arguably the strongest antagonist of the British, spawned new treaties, commitments, and even military confrontations.

The record of Sir John Shore, the Company servant who succeeded Cornwallis as governor-general (1793–98), reveals that strategic opportunities could tempt another non-interventionist to expand the Company's political commitments. B. B. Srivastava admits that Shore 'did not possess the boldness of Lord Cornwallis or the initiative and aggressiveness of Lord Wellesley' but that his 'cautious non-intervention' did not preclude assertive actions.[36] In one instance, territorial considerations, namely the need to protect the districts on the Malabar coast recently acquired from Mysore, and the desire to counter the French, led Shore to accept the proposal of the raja of Travancore for a permanent treaty of friendship and defensive alliance in 1795.

In another case Shore deposed Wazir Ali, the adopted son and proclaimed heir of Nawab Asaf ud-Daula of Awadh, only four months after he had succeeded his putative father in 1798. The British masked their suspicions that Wazir Ali was engaged in anti-British activities by allegations regarding his legitimacy. Shore himself went to Lucknow and placed Sa'adat Ali Khan, the brother of Asaf, who had been living in Banaras under Company protection, on the gaddi. The grateful victor in this succession dispute entered a treaty with the Company in 1798 that accelerated Company penetration into Awadh affairs, granted the key fort at Allahabad to the British, and enhanced the annual subsidy of Awadh to Rs 76 lakhs.[37] These two incidents indicate that even under a reticent governor-general, the policies of intervention and non-intervention in the internal affairs of Indian states were not mutually exclusive. Rather, they were deployed with differing emphases or frequencies in response to political circumstances in Europe, to political visions of governors-general, and to strategic and financial imperatives of British power in India.

Lord Wellesley and subsidiary alliances, 1798–1805

The arrival of Lord Wellesley in 1798 inaugurated the second major phase of the evolution of the treaty system. The significance that he ascribed to this

---

[36] B. B. Srivastava, *Sir John Shore's Policy Towards the Indian States* (Allahabad, 1981), pp. 244, 234, 239; Barnett, *North India*, pp. 230–2.
[37] Fisher, *Clash*, pp. 90–3.

policy is represented in a print of 1807 where Wellesley stands before copies of subsidiary treaties with Hyderabad and Mysore on a nearby table.[38]

The subsidiary alliance system entrenched the superior position of the Company and the subordinate one of the princes by restricting their exercise of key sovereign powers, especially the waging of war and direct communication with other rulers. Wellesley had imperial ambitions for the Company and followed different policies towards the Marathas and Mysore, whom he deemed his two principal protagonists.

To defeat Mysore militarily and to contain the Marathas by treaties, Wellesley sought to isolate both from possible allies and then to acquire the military assistance needed to achieve his objectives.[39] Since the Court of Directors in London wanted to minimise expenses and maximise profits, this ambitious governor-general sought aid from the two Mughal successor states, with differing consequences for Hyderabad and Awadh. The treaty of 1798 with Hyderabad described earlier produced military support through a subsidiary force. Because the nizam became in arrears of payment for the so-called Hyderabad Contingent, the state contracted extensive debts to the Palmer & Sons Bank. Michael Fisher has emphasised that these obligations to the British bank and to British officials operating in their private capacity ultimately reduced the possibility of an annexation of Hyderabad.[40] Such action would kill a goose that laid golden eggs. As a result, Hyderabad would survive as a princely state but Awadh would not. Although the 1798 treaty, as discussed earlier, had obtained an increased subsidy from Awadh, Wellesley made new demands. After threatening to annex the entire Awadh state, in 1801 he concluded a treaty with Sa'adat Ali Khan that effectively ended the independent Awadhi army, imposed an enlarged subsidiary force, and annexed the districts of Rohilkhand, Gorakhpur and the Doab (the territory between the Ganges and the Jumna) as payment for the subsidiary force even though the nawab had been current in his tribute payments.[41] Although Sa'adat Ali Khan was able to consolidate his control over his one remaining province of Awadh and to develop a new capital at Lucknow, the British annexed Awadh in 1856.

After the defeat of Mysore in 1799, the British treaty added some Mysorean districts to their expanding Madras Presidency and rewarded their ally Hyderabad with other districts. As noted earlier, the British then returned a

---

[38] Robert Home (1752–1834) painted several portraits of Wellesley during his tenure in India, most of which included copies of the treaties with Hyderabad and Mysore: Mildred Archer, *India and British Portraiture 1770–1825* (London, 1979), pp. 314–17.

[39] This section relies heavily on Thompson, *Making*.

[40] Fisher, *Indirect Rule*, pp. 388–90; Peter Wood, 'Vassal State'.

[41] Barnett, *North India*, pp. 235–7; Fisher, *Clash*, pp. 90–107.

Lord Wellesley by James Heath after portrait by Robert Home,
London 1807.

truncated but geographically compact Mysore to the Wadiyars, the Hindu dynasty that had been usurped in 1761 by its Muslim military ally, Haider Ali. They emphatically proclaimed the subordinate position of the restored infant ruler, Krishnaraja Wadiyar, by mandating the exclusion of all French influence and the stipulation that Mysore could not communicate with any foreign power without the prior knowledge and *sanction* of the British. A more onerous sign of Mysore's subordination was the imposition of an annual subsidy of Rs 24.5 lakhs, which represented 57 per cent of the presumed state revenue. This sum came to constitute 50 per cent of the British tribute collected from 198 princely states. Burton Stein has argued that the need to secure revenues to pay this subsidy was one of the factors that led the durbar to reform its tax-farming system. Subsequently this extension of central control into previously semi-autonomous local areas in Mysore provoked the Nagar insurrection in 1830–31.[42] The British then used their suppression of this disorder to legitimate their direct management of Mysore state for the next fifty years.

With Mysore subdued with golden cords, Wellesley confronted the Marathas. Although entitled as a member of the Triple Alliance to a share of the territory taken from Mysore by the British in 1799, the peshwa refused in order to avoid the imposition of a subsidiary alliance. Wellesley then proceeded to deal separately with the individual members of the Maratha confederacy. His action reflected an imperial strategy of divide and rule. It was, however, facilitated by the longstanding rivalries among the Maratha states, the lack of astute Maratha leaders after the deaths of Mahadji Scindia and Ahilyabai of Indore, their geographical dispersion, and the diminished authority of the peshwa.

In Gujarat, where the gaekwad was geographically isolated from the Maratha home base in Poona, a succession dispute after 1800 gave Wellesley an easy entry into Baroda state. The governor of Bombay sent a force of 2000 troops under Major Alexander Walker (1764–1831) to arbitrate between two contenders for the Baroda gaddi, and this veteran of the Mysore campaigns decided in favour of Anandrao and his diwan, Raoji Appaji. After crushing the other rivals and replacing Arab mercenaries as guarantors of government measures and loans, Walker and his superior concluded a subsidiary alliance in 1802 with the newly enthroned gaekwad that imposed a subsidiary force in return for a cession of territories. Additional fertile districts were ceded in 1803 and 1805. A novel

[42] Burton Stein, 'Notes on "Peasant Insurgency" in Colonial Mysore; Event and Process', *SAR* 5 (1985), p. 22 and note 8 on page 25 based on work of Sebastian Joseph, 'Mysore's Tribute to the Imperial Treasury: A Classic Example of Economic Exploitation', Q *JMS* 70 (1979), pp. 154–63.

feature at this stage was a British guarantee to Raoji Appaji that his heirs would be diwans of Baroda. They would later regret this promise, but it gave the British useful leverage in the internal administration of Baroda. Walker, the first British resident in Baroda, reorganised its revenue collection and military organisation, disbanding the disruptive Arab mercenaries and re-forming the subsidiary force into an efficient unit.[43]

Meanwhile the peshwa himself became more amenable to a subsidiary alliance after Holkar had defeated the combined forces of his nominal overlord and Scindia. The Treaty of Bassein in 1802 imposed a subsidiary force of six battalions, the obligation to submit disputes with the nizam and the gaekwad to the British, and the need to consult with the British before negotiating with any other powers. A few months later, the British confronted Scindia and the bhonsle of Nagpur in the Second Maratha War. The British victory at Assaye, where Arthur Wellesley, brother of the governor-general and the future Duke of Wellington, was in command, led to the treaties of 1803 with both Scindia and Holkar. The former was removed from his position in the Ganges-Jumna doab in the north and from the Deccan to the south and accepted a subsidiary force that was stationed in British territory near his frontier. Here again, these treaties confirmed the independent status of Scindia and Bhonsle from their Maratha overlord while not yet making them tributary to the British since cession of territory paid for the subsidiary force. As a consequence of the campaign against Holkar, who had expanded northward beyond Delhi, Wellesley as a matter of expediency offered an offensive and defensive alliance to the relatively new Rajput state of Alwar, recently separated from Jaipur, and of perpetual friendship to the vacillating Jat ruler of Bharatpur in 1803. The other major Jat-ruled state of Dholpur entered the treaty map in 1806. These three allies would provide a friendly frontier on the western side of Awadh.[44]

Far to the south, 1803 witnessed an example of how timely assistance to the British created anomalies in the treaty map. When the British assumed the administrative powers of its longstanding ally, the nawab of Carnatic at Arcot in 1801, it claimed the overlordship of his petty tributaries, the poligars or *palaiyakkarar*s. The Permanent Settlement of 1803 in the Madras Presidency transformed these poligars into zamindars with extensive rights over the produce of the land but also regular revenue obligations to the British. The one Tamil poligar to escape this process was in Pudukkottai. He had rendered both

---

[43] John Edmond McLeod, The Western India States Agency 1916–1947, PhD thesis, University of Toronto (1993), pp. 16–24.
[44] Thompson, *Making*, pp. 43–124.

military assistance and badly needed supplies to the British from 1751 to their last campaigns against Mysore.[45] The lack of any treaty or sanad defining the status of Pudukkottai illustrates the haphazard process of incorporation of Indian political entities into the British treaty map. When Pudukkottai asked for certain honours that the nawab had granted, the British allowed him to have a white umbrella and gold *chubdar* sticks, Hindu symbols of sovereignty, carried before him as well as a fort and a district that the raja of Tanjore had seized some years before. The British demanded one elephant a year '"as a mark of homage for the tenure"', but the Tondaiman ruler avoided paying this tribute until it was excused in 1839.[46] Thus the British revealed a willingness to deal in the indigenous coin of honours as well as their imported specie of treaties, especially when stakes were deemed negligible.

Continuing British extension during an era of non-intervention, 1805–13

Lord Minto, the governor-general from 1807 to 1813, is usually characterised as a pacific interlude between two expansionists. Thompson has described Minto as 'quiet and friendly' and a writer of letters that were 'witty and observant, strangely modern in tone'.[47] While Minto remained steadfast in not extending Company protection to the Rajput states, he transplanted several clumps of smaller chiefs into the soil of British indirect rule. Perhaps other historians have played down this intervention since few treaties were concluded. Bonds, proclamations and sanads were the usual instruments. In the interregnum between Wellesley and Minto, the Company had first extended its protection and then recognition of their internal autonomy to little kings in Bundelkhand such as Baoni, Chhatarpur, Maihar in 1806, and Ajaigarh, Datia, Panna, Sarila in 1807. These client states barred any advances by Holkar against recently acquired British territory on the Jumna.

Another example of British aggrandisement during a supposedly non-interventionist era occurred in Gujarat, particularly in Saurashtra, the peninsula known as Kathiawar (from its Kathi rulers) during the British period.[48] Analysing the Bombay Presidency, Ian Copland has applied Cohn's structural model.[49] Until 1756 the imperial authority was the Mughal emperor, whom the peshwa then replaced. At the secondary level the provincial governors

---

[45] Dirks, *Hollow Crown*, pp. 192–9, 385–9.
[46] Ibid., p. 387.   [47] Thompson, *Making*, p. 150.
[48] Saurashtra was the ancient name and after 1947 was again used for this peninsula. Major sources are Copland, *British Raj*; John E. McLeod, *Sovereignty, Power, Control: Rulers, Politicians, and Paramount Power in the States of Western India, 1916–1947* (Leiden, 1999); Harald Tambs-Lyche, *Power, Profit and Poetry: Traditional Society in Kathiawar, Western India* (New Delhi, 1997).
[49] Copland, *British Raj*, pp. 19–25.

deriving their authority from the imperial level were the gaekwads of Baroda in the north and the rajas of Satara and Kolhapur in the south. The regional level in Gujarat consisted mainly of Rajput-ruled states such as the Jhala in Dhrangadhara, Limbdi, Wankaner and Wadhwan; the Jadeja ones of Kutch, Nawanagar, Rajkot, Dhrol, Gondal and Morvi; the Jethwa at Porbandar; and the Gohels of Bhavnagar and Palitana. Some Kathi-ruled states, such as Jasdan as well as Jungadh, a successor state founded by a Mughal official, also belong in this category. *Bhayad* (the brotherhood) and *girassia* (petty chiefs) constituted the fourth level of petty chiefs and landholders and were overlapping categories. Girassia were those to whom a ruler granted land, in return for which the recipients had obligations of military or religious service. Bhayad were younger sons to whom Rajput, and sometimes Kathi, rulers granted the right to collect revenue from a group of villages and to dispense criminal justice. Thus bhayad were a subset of girassia and distinguished by their hereditary ties to rulers. As provincial and regional rulers confronted aggressive challenges in the late 1700s, some bhayad and girassia developed little kingdoms.

After their 1802 treaty with Baroda, the British sought to stabilise conditions in western Gujarat. Recognising the inefficiency and destructiveness of the *mulkgiri* or yearly military expedition that the gaekwad used to extract tribute from subordinate rulers, Walker, the British resident, attempted to rationalise the system with two kinds of bonds. One pledged the regional or petty chief to promote peace, to protect the possessions of the British, the peshwa and the gaekwad, including their merchants, and not to give sanctuary to thieves. The other required fixed annual tributes in return for abolition of the mulkgiri. Bards were to be the guarantors of the payment since they could enforce payment by threatening to kill themselves, and Rajputs considered causing the death of a bard a grievous sin.[50] Most of the regional states signed such bonds in 1807. Further agreements pledged the Rajput chiefs to prohibit female infanticide within their realms and piracy on their coasts.

Although the Walker Settlement re-established order, it also provided the basis for extensive fragmentation of political authority in western India. Walker initially invited twenty-nine regional rulers to sign the bonds. But to secure all previous sources of revenue, he then concluded bonds with whoever was paying tribute, whether they paid directly to a regional ruler or to the higher levels of gaekwad or peshwa. John McLeod has argued that Walker and the bhayads had thought that the bonds maintained the status quo of the latter as petty landlords. However, later British officials, unaware of the diffused nature of

---

[50] McLeod, *Sovereignty*, pp. 17–18.

power in Rajput states, either consciously or unconsciously, misinterpreted the bonds and created 153 supposedly sovereign rulers from subordinate bhayad and girassia.[51] Despite the absorption of eighty of these little kingdoms into other estates, according to various authorities their number expanded during the nineteenth century from around 350 to 418. Rajput ruling families followed primogeniture, with younger sons receiving a small number of villages in giras, but Kathi ruling families divided states equally among all sons. In 1903 and 1904 the British attempted to impose the practice of primogeniture on Kathi-ruled states, but because of Indian resistance, they compromised in 1908 and agreed to consider each instance of succession on its merits.[52] Western India had the largest numerical concentration of princely states, but only a small percentage exercised internal sovereignty. The significance of this blurring of the broad category of princely states will figure in subsequent chapters.

To maintain law and order and to ensure a fixed amount of revenue that would allow for both a reduced military force and a more rationalised administration since the Baroda durbar would now be able to plan expenditures – one should not use the word budget – with greater regularity, Alexander Walker presaged the later British emphasis on the establishment of efficient administration within the princely states. At the same time he undercut the authority of the gaekwad by introducing the British as an alternative source of authority for the regional powers who paid tribute to the gaekwad.

As the British now allowed the gaekwad to collect his tribute independently of the peshwa, so now regional rulers could appeal to the British, thereby affirming their autonomy from their tributary lord, Baroda. Mani Kamerkar highlights the example of Morvi, a Jadeja Rajput-ruled state, which appealed to the British for remission of tribute in 1817 because of alleged natural disasters and lack of law and order. After extended deliberations, Captain Barnwell, the British resident, urged that Morvi make full payment to Baroda. His superior, the Government of Bombay, however, granted Morvi the concession of paying only a third of the arrears and decreed that in the future Baroda would continue to receive only one-third while the other two-thirds should go to the Company to whom the peshwa had yielded his claim.[53] Yet again, Indian rulers learned to appeal to differing levels of the British hierarchy to achieve a favourable decision

[51] McLeod, 'Western India', ch. 2.
[52] C. U. Aitchison (comp.), *A Collection of Treaties, Engagements and Sanads relating to India and Neighbouring Countries* (Calcutta, 1932), vol. 6, pp. 1–30.
[53] Mani Kamerkar, *British Paramountcy: British–Baroda Relations 1818–1848* (Bombay, 1980), pp. 35–6.

on a request. Simultaneously, British residents undercut the authority of their subsidiary allies by supporting claims of subordinates against the prerogatives of their allies.

Ultimately the British affirmed their political sovereignty in Gujarat by an agreement in 1820 with Baroda. Although it made no treaties with other states in Saurashtra, the Company further extended its political authority with the establishment of a Criminal Court of Justice at Rajkot in 1831. The political agent presided and three or four chiefs served as assessors to try capital cases and crimes by one chief against another.

Further to the north, Charles Theophilus Metcalfe (1785–1846), a serious, circumspect young man of 23, was sent by Minto in June 1808 to the Lahore court of Maharaja Ranjit Singh, the 28-year-old ruler of Punjab.[54] Metcalfe's instructions were to negotiate a treaty of offensive and defensive alliance to create a barrier against a British-imagined French advance towards India through Persia and Afghanistan. When the wily Ranjit Singh scoffed at a French threat and marched to Faridkot to demonstrate his dominance with an uncomfortable Metcalfe in tow, Minto and his envoy decided to stand forth as the protector of the cis-Sutlej, Sikh-ruled states which had earlier received a noncommittal reply to their plea for protection from their ambitious Sikh neighbour. Thus on 25 April 1809, Metcalfe and Ranjit Singh signed a treaty affirming a British attitude of laissez-faire towards any expansion by Ranjit north of the Sutlej. The Sikh ruler was therefore free to advance northward to Himalayan hill-states such as Kashmir and westward to Multan and Peshawar near the Khyber Pass. In return he agreed not to encroach southward. Eight days later the British proclaimed to the chiefs south of the Sutlej:

It is clearer than the sun, and better proved than the existence of yesterday, that the detachment of British Troops to this side of the Sutlege was entirely in acquiescence to the application and earnest entreaty of the Chiefs, and originated solely through friendly considerations in the British to preserve the Chiefs in their possessions and independence.[55]

Besides obtaining British protection, the cis-Sutlej rulers were exempted from the payment of tribute but obliged to provide military assistance to the British when requested. Lee-Warner contended that '[t]his treaty, which was practically forced upon Lord Minto, as much by the old scare of French aggression as by the bold policy of the ruler of the Punjab, fitly closed the

[54] Edward Thompson, *Life of Lord Metcalfe* (London, 1937) in Metcalfe and Grewal, *Sikhs of Punjab*, ch. 6.

[55] C. U. Aitchson (comp.), *A Collection of Treaties, Engagements and Sanads Relating to India and Neighbouring Countries*, vol. 1 (Nendlem, Lichtenstein, 1973, reprint of edition published in 1931), p. 156.

first period of the policy of non-intervention'.[56] Although Edward Thompson also emphasised the motivating factor of the French threat,[57] the cis-Sutlej states gained British protection because of political expediency. They were a functional buffer between British-controlled territory near Delhi and Agra and an astute, energetic Indian ruler who had demonstrated the power of troops officered, trained and equipped by Europeans and supported by solid revenues from agriculture and commerce.

In the same year Minto signed a vague treaty of eternal friendship with the Amirs along the Indus River, who pledged not to 'allow the Establishment of the tribe of the French in Sind'.[58] In 1812 the governor-general concluded treaties of alliance with Nawanagar in Kathiawar and the Rajput-ruled states of Orchha and Rewa in Bundelkhand. Minto probably acquired his reputation for non-intervention because his treaties did not follow military expeditions except for an invasion of Nawanagar. His actions, nonetheless, demonstrate that any British governor-general was prepared to risk criticism from the authorities in England to buttress the expanding Company state against Indian rivals.

The triumph of paramountcy, 1813–23

The arrival of Lord Moira, later to become Lord Hastings, as governor-general in 1813 accelerated the incorporation of the Indian states onto the treaty map of India and inaugurated the era of subordinate isolation for Indian princes. Lee-Warner portrayed Hastings as lacking Cornwallis' faith that stronger Indian states would encompass weaker ones and become good neighbours, on the model of Ranjit Singh, but also not believing as Lord Dalhousie would 'that the good of the people required annexations'.[59] Although most commentators mention that Hastings concluded more treaties than any other governor-general, they are less apt to point out that despite his alleged lack of interest in annexation, he was a major participant in rounding out the Company's directly controlled territories.

Hastings first had to confront the expansionist Gurkha rulers of Nepal. After the short but costly Anglo-Nepalese War of 1814–16, both sides accepted the need to compromise.[60] A treaty in 1816 allowed the British to recruit Gurkha soldiers for its military, but Nepal remained an internally autonomous state able to pursue independent relations with bordering states.[61] Neighbouring Bhutan and Sikkim were more clearly subordinated to Company

---

[56] Lee-Warner, *Native States*, p. 88.　　[57] Thompson, *Making*, pp. 157–66.

[58] Ibid., p. 156.　　[59] Lee-Warner, *Native States*, pp. 102–3.

[60] J. Premble, *The Invasion of Nepal: John Company at War* (Oxford, 1971); C. A. Bayly, *Empire and Information: Intelligence Gathering and Social Communication in India, 1780–1870* (Cambridge, 1996), pp. 97–113.

[61] Thompson, *Making*, pp. 188–200.

control. Further west in the Himalayan foothills, the British made several small political units south of the Sutlej independent of their larger neighbours, creating several minuscule states. Finally the British fed tidbits of the Himalayan foothills to newly acquired allies including the raja of Patiala.

After this curtain-raiser on the Company's northern frontier, Hastings performed his main act in the Maratha-dominated heartland of central India. His immediate antagonists were the pindari bands who accumulated the produce of the cultivating peasants through irregular marauding rather than bureaucratic land revenue settlements. Characterising state formation in Malwa, Stewart Gordon stresses that '"states" and "marauders" were not different in kind, but only in relative degrees of success in conquest, revenue collection, and infrastructure-building. All were involved in the same process, with the same ends, using the same sources of legitimatization'.[62] The British would even be willing to assist at least two pindari leaders, Tonk and Jaora, in the process of state formation.

Pindari raids into the British presidency of Madras in 1816 and 1817 hardened British resolve to terminate this recurring threat. The British invited its Maratha allies, who functioned as protectors to various pindari leaders, to join their efforts, which involved an army of over 100 000 including 13 000 Europeans.[63] This British force was divided into two units, a northern one under the personal command of Hastings and a southern one under the commander-in-chief of Madras, who was accompanied by John Malcolm as a military and political officer. Malcolm, whom Thompson judged the most popular man in India,[64] had an unusually wide range of experiences, from military service in Mysore to a diplomatic mission to Persia. He had eagerly sought this joint appointment, which reflected a continuing link between military and political service by Company officers who dealt with Indian states.

As Hastings advanced against the pindaris, he was able to invest much of Scindia's territory and so the most powerful Maratha leader agreed to a subsidiary alliance. This treaty of 5 November 1817 allowed Scindia to retain the tribute from his subordinate states after giving it up for three years to the British; it required him to fight in a coordinated manner with the British against the pindaris, not to shelter any of the pindaris, and to give two forts as security for lines of communications. The British obtained the right to make treaties with the Rajput states who had been tributary to Scindia. Afterwards the peshwa sarcastically advised Scindia that 'it is befitting you to put bangles

---

[62] Stewart Gordon, 'Scarf and Sword: Things, Maranders, and State-formation in 18th Century Malwa', *IESHR* 6 (1969), p. 425.
[63] Thompson, *Making*, pp. 208–23; S. Sen, *Distant Sovereignty*, pp. 52–4.   [64] Ibid., p. 167.

on your arms, and sit down like a woman'.[65] The bhonsle raja at Nagpur and belatedly Holkar at Indore tried to strengthen their position by ill-timed attacks on British stations; they paid for their ineffective resistance.

Four days later, the British formally invested Amir Khan, a prominent pindari leader, as the nawab of Tonk and confirmed his possession of the districts he had detached from Indore state. In their generosity to Tonk with Indore's territory, the British added the fort and district of Rampura. On 6 January 1818 two key political officers concluded treaties with the two remaining principal Maratha military rulers. Richard Jenkins negotiated with the bhonsle raja of Nagpur. Territory yielding Rs 24 lakhs was divided with the nizam, but Bhonsle Appa Sahib remained on his gaddi. Hastings had intended to dethrone Appa Sahib, but the political officer in the field exercised formidable authority. The governor-general soon had his way as Appa Sahib continued to intrigue against the British, and by March 1818 he was deposed and replaced by Raghuji I, a maternal grandson of his predecessor and brother. Malcolm dealt with the boy ruler of Indore. He had to accept the creation of Tonk, to cede further territories to the British, to discharge his army, to agree not to employ any Europeans or Americans, and to transfer his tributary Rajput states to the Company.

Malcolm then negotiated with Peshwa Baji Rao II, who was the last to surrender. The peshwa lost his title and his right to live in the Deccan, being asked to move to a sacred Hindu site on the Ganges. He eventually selected Bithur near Kanpur. A sympathetic Malcolm granted him a pension of Rs 8 lakhs, earning the censure of Hastings for this generosity. After the death of Baji Rao in 1851 his adopted son, Dhondo Pant, better known as Nana Sahib, was denied this pension and became one of the leaders of the revolt of 1857. Hastings in turn confirmed the descendants of the elder son of Shivaji as the rulers of Satara and is usually lauded as a king-maker for this action.

With Maratha power circumscribed by their treaty system and superior military force, the British extended their protection to many states tributary to the Marathas. Charles Metcalfe invited the Rajput chiefs, who had long sought protection, to become British feudatories and thereby transfer payment of any tribute owed to the Marathas to the Company. Karauli, Kotah, Marwar-Jodhpur, Mewar-Udaipur and Bundi joined in January 1818; Jaipur agreed in April 1818; Partabgarh, Dungarpur and Jaisalmer closed the circle by the end of 1818.

In central India the British concluded a treaty with Nawab Nazar Muhammad of Bhopal, who had been an informal ally of the British against the

[65] Surendra Nath Roy, *A History of the Native States of India* (Calcutta, 1888), vol. 1, p. 325.

pindaris. He agreed to furnish a military contingent and received five districts in Malwa. Bhopal now became the third most populous Muslim-ruled state in India. Finally Malcolm recognised 143 chieftainships by sanads, and thus the second major concentration (after that in western India) of little kings became allies of the Company. Malcolm's assessment of the British work in central India was optimistic.

With the means we had at our command, the work of force was comparatively easy: the liberality of our Government gave grace to conquest, and men were for the moment satisfied to be at the feet of generous and humane conquerors. Wearied with a state of continued warfare and anarchy, they hardly regretted even the loss of power: halcyon days were anticipated, and men prostrated themselves in hopes of elevation. All these impressions, made by the combined effects of power, humanity, and fortune, were improved to the utmost by the character of our first measures.[66]

What Malcolm viewed as anarchy were conditions that the British partially spawned when they reduced indigenous military forces and left many armed men underemployed. Furthermore, the inflexible British demands for tributes and subsidies to fund their military machine led many Indian rulers to increase their demands on hard-pressed peasants, whose resistance contributed to disorder in the countryside.

When Lord Hastings left India in 1823, the broad outline of what came to be known as princely or Indian India, in contrast to British India, had been defined on British maps. There were three great blocks of what were called native state territories. The largest one was the massive conglomeration of Rajput- and Maratha-ruled states, which spread from Gujarat in the west through Rajasthan to Malwa and Rewa in central India. This broad band included the states and estates of Saurashtra; the deserts of Rajasthan with Rajput rulers and large populations of aboriginal tribal groups; northern central India with the small states of Bundelkhand and Baghelkhand; and the Maratha holdings of the northern Deccan. In the east there was Maratha-ruled Nagpur and the Orissan states, constituting the Tributary Mahals of Chota Nagpur. With significant tribal populations, petty chieftains ruled in the latter states and came under British jurisdiction from 1817 to 1825. In the south, Hyderabad and Mysore dominated the interior, with Travancore and Cochin on the southwestern coast. There was also the outlying group of smaller states north of Delhi: the cis-Sutlej states of Punjab and some Rajput-ruled states in the Himalayan foothills. Historical contingencies were partly responsible for which areas were annexed and which remained under princes. The British were nevertheless

---

[66] Malcolm, *Memoir*, vol. 2, pp. 264–5.

anxious to control most coastal tracts, the hinterland of their major entrepôts, and economically productive areas such as the Gangetic Plain.

Not only had Hastings concluded more treaties than any other governor-general, but the relationships inscribed in the treaties had changed. The British now aggressively declared themselves the superior power. Lee-Warner highlighted this transition with a comparison between the 1803 treaty with the relatively new Rajput state of Alwar and the 1818 treaty with Mewar-Udaipur, which enjoyed ritual superiority among many Rajput groups and some British officers. The British specifically engaged to protect Udaipur but plainly enunciated its subordination in article 3, which demanded that the Udaipur ruler 'will always act in subordinate co-operation with the British Government and acknowledge its supremacy, and will not have any connexion with other Chiefs or States'.[67] The next article imposed isolation and prohibited any negotiation with other states without British sanction. Hastings, however, legally guaranteed British non-intervention in the internal affairs of the state, but opportunities for British interference abounded. The imposition of a subsidiary force and the transfer of tribute owed by the Marathas to the British made the irregular payment of such dues a pretext for intervention. The posting of British residents and political agents provided a channel for observation, and both overt and covert intervention. This topic will be explored in the next chapter.

An era ended in 1823. Afterwards governors-general would not take command on the battlefield, as Cornwallis and Hastings had done, and then sign treaties the day after they were concluded. Since the major Indian states, with the exception of Punjab, were now in treaty relations with the British, political officers would no longer participate in battles or negotiate treaties. The extraordinary galaxy of distinctive stars in the political firmament such as Malcolm, Jenkins and Metcalfe would not recur. Circumspect bureaucrats superseded the flamboyant David Ochterlony and the adventurous and empathic Malcolm.

Consolidation and rounding out borders, 1823–56

Although administrative rationalisation and social reforms were dominant British concerns after 1823, annexations continued, especially on the borders of the Company domains, with provinces of lower Burma in 1826 and Sind on the lower Indus in 1843 being the major acquisitions. Moving into the heartland of Punjab, in 1846 the British fought a short but successful war with the heirs of Ranjit Singh. As a result they acquired the districts between the Beas and the Indus including Kashmir, the hill areas east of the Beas, and

[67] Lee-Warner, *Native States*, p. 125.

control over traffic on the Beas and the Sutlej to the Indus and then the Indus to Baluchistan.[68]

The arrival of Lord Dalhousie (1812–60), at 36 the youngest man to be appointed governor-general (1848–56), did not reintroduce a policy of annexation but rather intensified it.[69] Lee-Warner argued that by 1848 annexation was the only possible response to 'a scrupulous avoidance of interference in the internal affairs of a multitude of isolated principalities'.[70] In other words, British restraint had allowed such princely misrule that annexation was the only means of improvement. However, the British protection of their allies from internal challengers was surely a form of intervention in the internal politics of states, where tensions between rulers and their relatives or nobility were a critical aspect of a dynamic political process. Dalhousie's policy of annexation was informed by strategic concerns and 'revenue maximisation'.[71]

Pragmatic, autocratic, hard-working, Dalhousie used military victories, the denial of the right to adopt heirs to rulers whose states he classified as British creations, and allegations of misgovernment as the bases for annexation.[72] Economic and strategic concerns are reflected in his support for a second war against the now dependent kingdom of Punjab in 1848, even supervising the military operations to the dismay of his commander-in-chief in the field, and his decision to annex the remainder of Punjab in 1849. In contrast to his predecessors, Dalhousie tended to consume all the territory of a defeated state rather than nibbling morsels. In 1852 he returned to the piecemeal approach after the defeat of the Burmese in 1852 with the informal acquisition of Pegu province. Upper Burma would be annexed in 1885.

Dalhousie's other acquisitions of Indian territory were more controversial because of their justifications and because they were later deemed to be immediate causes of the revolt of 1857. They began three months after he arrived in India. The first state was small but symbolically significant. The Maratha ruling house of Satara, which descended from the elder son of Shivaji, had adopted several times to maintain the dynastic line, as did many Hindu families. When Raja Appa Sahib of Satara adopted a son a few hours before he died on 5 April 1848, Dalhousie recommended against recognition of the adopted heir and for annexation. His argument was that the British had essentially created the Satara state in 1818 when they reconstituted it with territory captured from the

---

[68] Aitchison, *Collection of Treaties*, vol. 1, pp. 50–4.
[69] William Lee-Warner, *The Life of the Marquis of Dalhousie K. T.*, 2 vols (Shannon, Ireland, 1972, first published 1904).
[70] Lee-Warner, *Native States*, p. 129.   [71] C. A. Bayly, *Indian Society*, p. 134.
[72] S. N. Prasad, *Paramountcy under Dalhousie* (Delhi, 1963); Muhammad Abdur Rahim, *Lord Dalhousie's Administration of the Conquered and Annexed States* (Delhi, 1963).

peshwa. However, arrogant imperialism is clearly reflected in the often quoted minute of 30 August 1848:

I cannot conceive it possible for anyone to dispute the policy of taking advantage of every just opportunity which presents itself for consolidationg the territories that already belong to us, by taking possession of states which may lapse in the midst of them; for thus getting rid of these petty intervening principalities, which may be made a means of annoyance, but which can never, I venture to think, be a source of strength, for adding to the resources of the public treasury, and for extending the uniform application of our system of government to those whose best interests, we sincerely believe, will be promoted thereby.

Strategic and revenue gains are more sharply articulated in the less well known article 32, which noted that the territories of Satara

are interposed between the two principal military stations in the presidency of Bombay; and are at least calculated, in the hands of an independent sovereign, to form an obstacle to safe communication and combined military movement. The district is fertile, and the revenue productive; the population, accustomed for some time to regular and peaceful government, are tranquil themselves, and prepared for the regular government our possession of the territory would involve.[73]

In defending the lapse or annexation of three other states when they sought British recognition of an adopted heir, Dalhousie cited both pragmatic and political reasons. Sambalpur, now a district on the western border of Orissa state and then a little chieftainship astride the Mahanadi River on the road between Bombay and Calcutta, was swallowed up in 1849. With a brahman ruling family from Maharashtra, Jhansi had been carved from Orchha, southwest of the British Northwestern Provinces. A buffer between the territories of Scindia of Gwalior and the Rajput-ruled states of Bundelkhand, Jhansi had first entered treaty relations with the British in 1804, and had assisted them against the Marathas and Burmese. Such support did not prevent extinction to secure the border of a British province.[74]

The 1854 annexation of Nagpur was the most substantial and most contentious one justified by the doctrine of lapse. Since it encompassed 80 000 square miles with an annual revenue exceeding Rs 40 lakhs and a population of more than 4 million, Nagpur could not be classified as a 'petty intervening principality'. Dalhousie, perhaps feeling the need for legitimation, cited three additional reasons. First and foremost, he argued that 'the prosperity and happiness of its [Nagpur] inhabitants would be promoted by their being placed

---

[73] As cited in Sever, *Documents*, vol. 1, p. 200 from Minute by Lord Dalhousie dated 30 August 1848 in *House of Commons (Sessional Papers), 1849*, vol. 39, pp. 224–8. 'Papers Relative to the Raja of Sattara'.

[74] Rahim, *Dalhousie's Administration*, ch. 7, especially pp. 206–14.

permanently under British rule'. Second, the essential interests of England would be served by ready access to 'the best and cheapest cotton grown in India . . . in the valley of Berar'. Third, the general interests of India – by which he obviously meant the British establishment in India – would benefit territorially by making British possessions contiguous by providing a direct line of communication between Calcutta and Bombay and by surrounding the nizam's state with British territory; economically by adding a large and wealthy province; and militarily since 'the present army of Nagpore was organised by ourselves, and still retains much of the form and of the feelings it received under British command'.[75] Despite all these supposedly positive outcomes, Dalhousie faced opposition from British as well as Indian sources. Colonel Sir John Low, a distinguished political officer who after extensive service in Rajputana and as a resident in Hyderabad had risen to membership on the Council of the Governor-General (1853–58), thought that additional annexations were inappropriate. He stressed that British rule would not be safe and prosperous 'till there shall be among its native subjects a much more general attachment to the ruling powers than there is at present among the inhabitants of British India' and that the British should seek 'to remove from the minds of those princes their present feelings of uncertainty and distrust', which had arisen because of the conquest of Sind, an attack on Gwalior, and the annexation of Satara.[76]

Dalhousie, possibly in response to such critics, elaborated on the principles guiding his exercise of the doctrine of lapse. He categorised the Hindu-ruled states into independent, dependent and subordinate. Independent states had never been subordinate to a paramount power and were not tributary. Here he placed the Rajput states and ignored their incorporation into the Mughal structure, their payments of tribute to the Marathas, and sometimes to the British. Dependent states were subordinate to the British as the paramount power in its role as successor to the Mughal emperor or the peshwa. The payment of tribute or a subsidy was a sign of their dependency. Subordinate states were those which the British created or revived through its treaties or sanads. Over the first category the British had no right to refuse adoptions; over the second they had a right to refuse but usually agreed; and over the third they should never allow succession by adoption.[77] He classified Nagpur as both dependent and subordinate and so any adoption required British ratification. Dalhousie

[75] As cited in Sever, *Documents*, vol. 1, p. 213 from *House of Commons (Sessional Papers), 1854*, vol. 48, pp. 337–52. 'Papers relating to the Rajah of Berar'.
[76] As cited in ibid., Minute dated 10 February 1854, pp. 216–18 and HC Rajah of Berar, pp. 355–9.
[77] Lee-Warner, *Life*, vol. 2, pp. 115, 155–6; Rahim, *Dalhousie's Administration*, pp. 372–3.

therefore decided not to sanction the adoption and to annex the state.[78] It became the basis for the sprawling Central Provinces, now conveniently linked to the Northwestern Provinces through the corridor of the recently annexed Jhansi.

Maladministration had been cited in the decision on Jhansi along with lapse, but it was the only rationale for the annexation of Awadh in 1856. The British had long pursued contradictory policies towards one of their oldest allies. On the one hand the British had encouraged the nawab to establish his independence of his suzerain, the Mughal emperor. Thus they abetted Nawab Ghazi al-Din Haydar's efforts to declare his independence, first by minting coins in his own name in 1818 and then by crowning himself king of Awadh in 1819.[79] On the other hand the British resident extended his protection over groups at court and society at large. These British clients included Europeans employed by the nawab; 'natives' of Awadh who were employed by the Company, especially the soldiers or sepoys in its armies; and Awadh officials whose pensions were to be paid from the interest the British owed on loans extorted from nawabs. Michael Fisher has pointed out that the Company had already gained crucial political adherents in Awadh before the actual annexation occurred in 1856.[80] Earlier historians writing on the events of 1857 would castigate Dalhousie for pursuing a reckless policy of annexation, while subsequent apologists such as Lee-Warner viewed him as a great humanitarian for extending the benefits of British rule to India – including the misgoverned masses of Awadh.[81]

A searing shock to the British in both India and at home, the events of 1857 provoked an extensive and ongoing literature. The precipitating action of sepoys at Meerut meant that for many British historians, 1857 was a mutiny. Other historians have focused on civilian involvement, especially of peasants,[82] landlords[83] and a few Indian princes, and their work labelled 1857 as the first war of Indian independence, a rebellion, or a revolt. Nana Sahib of Satara and Rani Lakshmi Bai of Jhansi were highly visible leaders whom both British and

---

[78] Ibid., pp. 229–34; Lee-Warner, *Life*, vol. 2, pp. 176–81.
[79] Michael H. Fisher, 'The Imperial Coronation of 1819: Awadh, the British and the Mughals', *MAS* 19 (1985), pp. 254–5, 258–75.
[80] Michael H. Fisher, 'British Expansion in North India: The Role of the Resident in Awadh,' *IESHR* 18 (1981), pp. 69–82, esp. pp. 81–2.
[81] Lee-Warner, *Life*, vol. 2, pp. 363–73, 381.
[82] Eric Stokes, *The Peasant and the Raj: Studies in Agrarian Society and Peasant Rebellion in Colonial India* (Cambridge, 1978); Gautam Bhadra, 'Four Rebels of Eighteen-Fifty-Seven', in Ranajit Guha (ed.), *Subaltern Studies IV* (Delhi, 1985), pp. 229–75.
[83] Metcalf, *Land*.

Indian historians have constructed as heroes of Indian resistance to colonial rule.[84]

Although some troops from princely states, notably Gwalior and Indore, joined rebel contingents, the loyalty of Hyderabad, most Maratha and Rajput rulers, and especially the cis-Sutlej princes, confined military resistance to the Gangetic Plain. Some princes aided the British more directly. Besides providing supplies and protecting Europeans, the rulers of Patiala, Nabha, Jind, Kapurthala and Faridkot personally led their troops to maintain civil order in Punjab or in military engagements further afield.[85] Moreover, a newswriter for Jind at the Delhi court became a key source for British intelligence.[86] Once the military revolt was suppressed in 1858, British officials and apologists reaffirmed the strategic value of indirect rule. Indian princes were deemed natural leaders of their Indian subjects and valuable British allies. A grateful imperial government fed them morsels of territory, new honours, and occasionally monetary rewards.[87]

CONCLUSION

The British did not create the Indian princes. Before and during the European penetration of India, indigenous rulers achieved dominance through the military protection they provided to dependants and their skill in acquiring revenues to maintain their military and administrative organisations. Major Indian rulers exercised varying degrees and types of sovereign powers before they entered treaty relations with the British. What changed during the late eighteenth and early nineteenth centuries is that the British increasingly restricted the sovereignty of Indian rulers. The Company set boundaries; it extracted resources in the forms of military personnel, subsidies or tribute payments, and the purchase of commercial goods at favourable prices, and limited opportunities for other alliances. From the 1810s onward as the British expanded and consolidated their power, their centralised military despotism dramatically reduced the political options of Indian rulers. The latter could not easily manipulate the corporate British Government of India, which did not experience the succession struggles or division of resources among heirs that had plagued

---

[84] Joyce Lebra-Chapman, *The Rani of Jhansi: A Study in Female Heroism in India* (Honolulu, 1986).

[85] Lepel H. Griffin, *The Rajas of the Punjab* (Patiala, 1970, reprint of 1873 2nd edn), pp. 213–18 on Patiala, pp. 355–8 on Jind, pp. 422–4 on Nabha, pp. 526–8 on Kapurthala, and p. 526 on Faridkot.

[86] C. A. Bayly, *Empire*, pp. 327–8.

[87] Thomas R. Metcalf, *The Aftermath of Revolt: India, 1857–1879* (Berkeley CA, 1964); Bhupen Qanungo, 'A Study of British Relations with the Native States of India, 1858–62,' *JAS* 26 (1967), pp. 251–65.

earlier overlords such as the Mughals and the Marathas and which offered attractive possibilities for 'conquest by invitation'. Indian rulers had to learn how to exploit the interstices of the increasingly bureaucratic British structure in order to gain political, ritual and economic advantages. Thus they might appeal to a sympathetic resident for concessions that a more distant governor-general in Calcutta or Company directors in London might not grant, or vice versa to the remote official over the objections of a hostile man on the spot.

British policies towards Indian rulers are an excellent prism for viewing the complex interaction of varying views, priorities and resources of the multiple levels of the British hierarchy in India, which portrayed itself as a monolith to outsiders. In reality the British never were able to enforce a tight chain of command from the metropolitan authority in London to local officials in India. Further, the scholarly debate over British annexation is an example of the British efforts to categorise Indian political phenomena in order to conquer, to control, and to justify. Wellesley and Hastings uninhibitedly used imperialist and strategic explanations. Dalhousie's particular contribution was to combine economic, political, moral and legal arguments in an age when reform was a prominent motif in British domestic political discourse. In the face of increasing Indian challenges to the British right to rule in India, later nineteenth-century commentators such as Tupper and Lee-Warner shifted the emphasis from material causes such as desirable access to superior cotton to moral and legal rationales. Twentieth-century scholars underscore economic and political arguments and do not allow moral and legal principles to have any role in the decision-making of nineteenth-century British administrators. This purely materialist approach simplifies the decision-making process of these men in an ahistoric manner.

A recent trend to an institutional approach promises a more balanced explanation. Thus a good start would be more exploration of the growing centralisation of decision-making within the Government of India, which allowed a confident, strong-willed governor-general such as Dalhousie to ignore the advice of experienced men on the spot such as Low. While the British GOI was becoming more centralised, its growing bureaucratisation rewarded those who implemented policy and frequently penalised those who challenged it. Dalhousie was possibly no more of an imperialist than Wellesley or Hastings. But he was not balanced as they were by brilliant, independent-minded political officers such as Mountstuart Elphinstone, John Malcolm and Charles Metcalfe, who were sympathetic to Indian rulers, willing and able to suggest alternative policies, and even to make commitments to Indian rulers that would be honoured even though a governor-general might disagree with them.

The British treaty system created a structure in which the British directly ruled a combination of those parts of India held by any major aspirant to a centralised imperial status, from the Mauryan Empire to the Congress Party, with those parts of India prized by seaborne traders, whether foreigners such as Arabs or indigenous south Indian kings. Thus British India was an innovator in its administrative integration of the Indo-Gangetic Plain with the ports and coastal plains of the triangular subcontinent, from the mouth of the Indus to the mouth of the Ganges. But no state at Delhi ever sought to govern directly the Thar desert area of Rajasthan, the remote salt flats of Cutch, or the jungly tracts of central India and Orissa. The British system of indirect rule over Indian states and a limited raj even in directly ruled areas such as Bihar and the United Provinces provided a model for the efficient use of scarce monetary and personnel resources that could be adopted to imperial acquisitions in Malaya and Africa. Thus there were multiple reasons why the British continued a system of indirect rule after they were clearly the dominant power in India. Moreover, the dialectic between British intervention and non-intervention in princely states continued to exist until 1947.

CHAPTER 4

THE THEORY AND EXPERIENCE OF INDIRECT RULE IN COLONIAL INDIA

COLONIAL SOCIOLOGY, CLASSIFICATION AND HIERARCHY

Throughout their imperial tenure in India, British administrators described and categorised Indian legal practices, religious beliefs and rituals, social structures and customs, and languages and literatures. British officials in India and in the metropole used these data to construct a static, underdeveloped India that legitimated British political dominance. This knowledge was not disinterested or objective but imbricated with political power. Analysed by Edward Said as Orientalism, this information has also been termed colonial sociology or, more broadly, colonial knowledge.[1] More recently, C. A. Bayly has argued that Indians participated significantly in the creation of the British information order, which remained contested and incomplete.[2] Although these intellectual constructions and scholarship have focused on the directly ruled territory and peoples of British India, several subsumed the indirectly ruled domains and peoples of princely states. They included gazetteers that were compendia of geographical, historical and statistical data; the Great Trigonometrical Survey that supposedly provided a scientific skeleton for surveys, mapping and a spatial conception of India; and decennial censuses issued from 1871.[3] After 1858 colonial knowledge specifically targeted the princes and their states.

Initially British officials discovered that there were relatively few documentary bricks with which to erect the intellectual framework of indirect rule. Treaties had been concluded depending on the exigencies of war, financial need, personal inclinations of men on the spot, internal politics of the Company, and a state's relationship to the Mughal Empire or other indigenous political entities. There were few documents of explication and no comprehensive collection of treaties or other legal documents such as sanads and letters of understanding. There was no accepted definition of an Indian prince and no authoritative list of those recognised as princes. Using data from archives, surveys, maps and

---

[1] Two influential sources are Bernard S. Cohn, *Colonialism and Its Forms of Knowledge: The British in India* (Princeton NJ, 1996) and Inden, *Imagining India*.

[2] C. A. Bayly, *Empire*, ch. 2 and conclusion.

[3] Edney, *Mapping*, pp. 318–40; Bernard S. Cohn, 'The Census, Social Structure and Objectification in South Asia', *Folk* 26 (1986), pp. 30–8.

censuses, British officials defined and enumerated Indian princes; naturalised princely associations with their British sovereign in London and her representatives in India; and demarcated appropriate relationships between princes and their subjects.

During the second half of the nineteenth century the number of Indian princes multiplied, and it remains difficult to trace the chronology of this inflation and the reasons for it. As mentioned in Chapter 3, the British had concluded treaties with about forty princes. When Lord Canning, governor-general and the first viceroy from 1856 to 1862, extended sanads guaranteeing the right of princes to adopt heirs subject to British confirmation, the need to limit them to ruling princes was widely discussed. Approximately 140 such sanads were granted on 11 March 1862.[4] Later another twenty were tendered, mainly in Kathiawar. However, by the last decades of the nineteenth century, references to 500–600 Indian princes began to appear in both official and popular publications. The largest concentrations were in western and central India where the British policy to treat petty chieftains as rulers created many princes lacking much internal autonomy. Like the diverse and supposedly divisive caste and religious groups of India, this large number of disparate, dependent rulers was one more justification for a strong, impartial overlord, namely the British GOI, to maintain order.

The British also tallied the population of the princely states. By 1881 the largest had their own census commissioners, initially someone loaned from the Indian Civil Service and increasingly an Indian officer; census officials from neighbouring British Indian provinces counted the smaller ones. The princes now had extensive data on their subjects. But there is little research on how the princes used this newly acquired information to enhance their control within their states or their relationship to their British overlord. There is one exception to this: Robin Jeffrey, who has illuminated how the subjects of one prince employed such data. In Travancore the first 'scientific' census of 1875 disclosed that nayars constituted about 20 per cent of the population instead of the 30 per cent that earlier censuses had estimated. Subsequently Syrian Christians and lower-caste groups used census data to claim their civil rights and a greater share of government positions.[5]

Besides formulating a hierarchy of numbers, the British regularised a salute table that ranked both Britons and Indians, including princes, by gun salutes in relation to their common suzerain, the British Crown. At the pinnacle, Queen Victoria had a salute that rose to 101 guns when she acquired the title

---

[4] Quanungo, 'Study,' pp. 264.   [5] Jeffrey, *Decline*, passim but esp. p. 14.

of Empress of India in 1877. The governor-general, who assumed the title of viceroy in 1858 as the representative of the monarch within the GOI, came next, along with other members of the British royal family, with a more modest salute of thirty-one guns. The rank of twenty-one guns eventually included five princes: the rulers of Hyderabad, the most populous state; Kashmir, the largest in territory; Mysore, third in size and population; and Baroda and Gwalior, the principal remnants of the Maratha polity. Nine was the lowest level. Each succeeding category included more princes, so the salute table resembled a pyramid with 9-gun princes at the base. (Interestingly, the governors of the three British presidencies were assigned seventeen guns, lieutenant-governors of the other British provinces fifteen until the 1920s when they were granted the title of governor and elevated to seventeen, and residents had thirteen guns.) Rulers and states were assigned salutes according to diverse criteria: historical importance such as relationship to the Mughal Empire; regional status; extent of territory; size of population; conspicuous service to the British; and later modernising reforms. There were anomalies at all levels that neither the British nor the princes, despite their shared aptitude for classification, could ever resolve. Gradually the British resorted to a system of local salutes enjoyed within a state and personal salutes that were granted to a ruler for his or her life as a reward or possibly a sop to silence a clamorous petitioner. Salutes became particularly contentious as princes and the British met more often in formal settings where salutes would be fired.

CEREMONY AS MANIFESTATION OF THEORY AND HIERARCHY

Durbars, the formal occasions when the princes met with British representatives – either local political agents, the viceroy, or more rarely members of the royal family – encoded British ideas about their relationships with Indian princes. As durbars became more frequent with easier transportation by railway, their protocol became more precise. Regulations evolved about where a prince greeted the British official upon arrival, how many officials accompanied the British official and the prince, seating arrangements, and appropriate dress. These rituals were most elaborate for the highly coveted status symbol of a visit by a viceroy or a member of the British royal family to an individual princely state. Earlier governors-general such as Lord Amherst (1823–28) had made extended tours, but Lord Canning (1856–62) was the first to visit systematically the princely states after 1858 in order to distribute rewards for faithful service during the revolt. In 1869 the Duke of Edinburgh was the first member of the royal family to tour India, and in 1875–76 the Prince of Wales undertook a highly publicised tour that stopped in several princely states.[6] States developed distinctive attractions to entertain visitors, such as the *keddah* or elephant round-ups in Mysore and sand grouse shoots in Bikaner. Although these staged events were financially burdensome for their subjects, princes esteemed them as signs of imperial favour. The British in turn used such excursions as rewards and withheld them in retaliation for alleged misbehaviour. Moreover, these meetings could serve British political purposes, as in 1920–21 when the Prince of Wales gained a respite from nationalist protests in British India in the princely states, where he could also display his masculinity in pig-sticking, polo and tiger-shooting.[7] But the most significant ritual arenas for the articulation of British ideas about their relationship to the princes were the Imperial Assemblage of 1877 and the Imperial Durbars of 1903 and 1911 at Delhi.

Bernard Cohn has argued that after 1858 the British enunciated

> two divergent or even contradictory theories of rule: one which sought to maintain India as a feudal order, and the other looking towards changes which would inevitably lead to the destruction of this feudal order . . . If India were to be ruled in a feudal mode, then an Indian aristocracy had to be recognized and/or created, which could play the part of 'loyal feudatories' to their British queen.[8]

For Cohn, the Imperial Assemblage at Delhi on 1 January 1877, when Queen Victoria was declared Kaiser-i-Hind or Empress of India in a carefully orchestrated gathering of British and Indians that prominently displayed sixty-three ruling princes, was the cynosure of this feudal mode. Disraeli as prime minister, Lord Salisbury as secretary of state for India, and Lord Lytton, the recently arrived viceroy, were the principal architects of this spectacle. Specialists designed the site, its structure, uniforms for the participants, and even created banners with coats of arms for the princes. These banners, with both British and Indian iconography, replaced the earlier Mughal exchange of *nazar* (gold coins) and *peshkash* (valued objects) with clients for *khilats* (robes of honour that had been touched to the superior's body). The Mughal practice had symbolised the incorporation of the recipient into the person of the ruler, but the British

---

[6] Two eyewitness accounts are J. Drew Gay, *The Prince of Wales in India: From Pall Mall to the Punjaub* (New York, 1877) and Val. C. Prinsep, *Imperial India: An Artist's Journal* (London [1877?]). Gay was a correspondent for the London *Daily Telegraph*, and Prinsep, from an old Anglo-Indian family, was commissioned to paint a portrait of the Imperial Assemblage for Queen Victoria.

[7] L. F. Rushbrook Williams, *The History of the Indian Tour of H. R. H. the Prince of Wales 1921–22* (Calcutta, 1922); Bernard C. Ellison, H. R. H. *The Prince of Wales's Sport in India* (London, 1925).

[8] Bernard S. Cohn, 'Representing Authority in Victorian India', in Eric Hobsbawm and Terence Ranger (eds), *The Invention of Tradition* (Cambridge, 1983), p. 166.

one indicated a linear hierarchic order in which princes now owed fealty and obedience to their liege lord, the empress, from whose representative they had received their banners.[9]

A third arena that reinforced the notion of a feudal hierarchy was the new orders of royal knighthoods that the British had instituted in the aftermath of 1857 to reward loyal Indian allies as well as status-conscious British officials. The Order of the Star of India, which included both princes and British military and civilian officers, was established in 1861 with twenty-five members. The maharajas of Gwalior and Patiala, who remained loyal in 1857, were its first princely initiates. The insignia included a necklace with alternating Tudor roses and Indian lotuses with the image of the Queen on a pendant.

Some rulers, such as the nizam of Hyderabad, refused to wear the insignia because of Muslim injunctions against any representation of the human form.[10] But many other princes as well as British officials sought inclusion in the Order, and after 1865 the Star of India Order was expanded to three levels to accommodate hundreds of knighthoods. Subsequently more orders were instituted to recognise other categories of aspiring Britons and Indians.

Salute tables, imperial orders, and imperial rituals such as the Imperial Assemblage of 1877 and visits of British officials to the states are key evidence for David Cannadine's argument that bonds of class and status linked the empire to the metropole. However, his description of *imperialism as ornamentalism*, which he defines as 'hierarchy made visible, immanent and actual',[11] ironed flat the wrinkled texture of the cloth of British perceptions and policies towards the princes of India and how these changed over time and place. Imperial officials attempted to constitute the princes into a feudal hierarchy and promoted them as natural leaders; they also constrained, pressured, restricted and deposed them when it was expedient to strengthen or maintain their political power and to gain economic benefits.

CONSTRUCTING A THEORY FOR A PATRON—CLIENT SYSTEM

Bureaucratic codifications

Although the salute table, durbar rituals and honours provoked reams of correspondence requesting higher positions from disgruntled princes and British

---

[9] Ibid., pp. 185–96.
[10] Bernard S. Cohn, 'Cloth, Clothes and Colonialism: India in the Nineteenth Century,' in *Colonialism*, pp. 119–20.
[11] David Cannadine, *Ornamentalism: How the British Saw Their Empire* (New York, 2001), p. 122.

Maharaja Jaswant Singh of Marwar/Jodhpur with Star of India.

officials, they were a concrete, multifaceted ranking system, as Cannadine has asserted, that both British and princely participants understood. It was far more difficult to achieve agreement on the codification of the theory and the precedents that reputedly guided British policies. When some foreign department officials confronted this task after 1858, they found little besides a survey of the

Company's relations with selected states that John Sutherland, who had served in the major posts of Hyderabad, Delhi, Gwalior and Rajasthan, had compiled in 1833; a few departmental memoranda; letters from governors-general and British political agents to individual princes which enunciated principles that became precedents for other cases; speeches by governors-general; and scattered treaties. To provide a basic reference, Sir Charles U. Aitchison (1832–96), the foreign secretary from 1870 to 1877 and lieutenant-governor of Punjab from 1882 to 1888, edited a *Collection of Treaties, Engagements and Sanads Relating to India*.

It first appeared in 1862, was continually updated, and eventually reached fourteen volumes by the fifth edition published from 1929 to 1933. Each volume focused on particular states or regions including frontier and border areas extending from Siam in the east to Aden in the west. Besides including legal documents, each section began with a narrative of British relations with that particular state which appeared as potted histories in other reference works such as the *Memorandum on Indian States* issued periodically as a handbook for political officers. As a complement to Aitchison, Sir H. Mortimer Durand (1850–1924), another foreign secretary (1885–93) best known for his service in Afghanistan and Persia and as a boundary-maker, compiled *Leading Cases*, a selection of past decisions in disputes between the British and individual states. His collection yielded precedents that the British had introduced as concepts into Indian law in areas where treaties were silent.

Other British officials developed theoretical justifications for both past and future British policies. In an 1864 minute on the Kathiawar states, Sir Henry Maine (1822–88), the noted legal scholar and law member of the governor-general's Executive Council (1862–69), argued that sovereignty was divisible.

Sovereignty is a term which, in international law, indicates a well-ascertained assemblage of separate powers or privileges. The rights which form part of the aggregate are specifically named by the publicists, who distinguish them as the right to make war and peace, the right to administer civil and criminal justice, the right to legislate, and so forth. A sovereign who possesses the whole of this aggregate of rights is called an *independent* sovereign, but there is not, nor has there ever been, anything in international law to prevent some of those rights being lodged with one possessor and some with another. Sovereignty has always been regarded as divisible.[12]

This interpretation of sovereignty meant that the British, as the only 'independent' sovereign, suzerain or paramount power, had exclusive control over such

[12] Minute by Sir Henry Maine dated 22 March 1864 in Sever, *Documents*, vol. 1, p. 251. Emphasis in the original.

Sir Charles U. Aitchison

sovereign rights as war and foreign relations, while Indian princes could collect revenues and administer justice within their states. If sovereignty were indivisible, then the British would not have any legal ground to maintain alliances with the princely states.[13]

The convenient concept of usage was elaborated in 1877. T. H. Thornton, briefly the acting foreign secretary but without any service in a princely state, declared:

For a proper understanding of the relationship between the British Government and the Natives States regard must be had to the incidents of the de facto supremacy as well as to the treaties and charters in which the reciprocal rights and obligations have been recorded . . . A uniform and and long-continued course of practice acquiesced in by the party against whom it tells . . . must be held to exhibit the relations which in fact subsist between them.[14]

Princely toleration of practices implied consent, and thus the precedent of usage was created. According to Lee-Warner, usage 'amends and adapts to circumstances duties that are embodied in treaties of ancient date, and it supplies numerous omissions from the category of duties so recorded'.[15] Besides providing flexibility in a haphazard collection of treaties that had been concluded in particular times and circumstances, usage enabled the British to reinterpret inconvenient clauses and promises to serve current strategic needs. In short, usage could rationalise breaking promises made in treaties and sanads.

Discussed in Chapter 3 with regard to their periodisation of the relations between the British and the princely states, William Lee-Warner and Charles Lewis Tupper worked 'to bring system and uniformity into the disordered world of Indian feudatory policy'.[16] Competitors for official favour, both men had limited service in the princely states and worked mainly at provincial capitals – Tupper in Punjab and Lee-Warner in Bombay. So their theories tended to be based on documentary evidence and not direct field experience. Asserting that the ties between the British and the princes were constitutional, Lee-Warner based much of his argument on Durand and sought the assignment to revise Durand's compilation.

In *Our Indian Protectorate*, published in 1893, Tupper contended that the relationship between the states and the British Raj was essentially a feudal one since 'the Indian Protectorate rests on ideas which are fundamentally indigenous . . . There were many tendencies making for feudalism in the India of our predecessors; and . . . our protection has been sought in India as vassals

---

[13] I am grateful to an anonymous reviewer who pointed out the significance of this distinction.
[14] Quoted in Copland, *British Raj*, pp. 214–15.
[15] Lee-Warner, *Native States*, p. 204.   [16] Copland, *British Raj*, p. 217.

sought the protection of their lords'. Tupper cited Charles Metcalfe, who wrote of the requests of Rajput princes for treaties in 1816 that Rajputs 'say that there has always existed some power in India to which peaceable states submitted, and in return, obtained its protection'.[17] Since the vision of princes as feudal vassals was congenial to many officials, Tupper was chosen to update Durand. He eventually produced the three volumes, plus an index, of *Indian Political Practice*, printed privately in 1895 for the use of British political officers.[18]

Tupper's work was to remain the classic reference, but later documents and manuals reflected evolving British theories and practices. Sir Harcourt Butler, the foreign secretary from 1907 to 1910, who had never been in the political service before being appointed its head, issued an influential handing-over note for his successor that strongly advocated less interference in princely affairs. In 1917 a new edition of the *Manual of Instructions for Political Officers* attempted to regularise procedures. These documents were particularly important in the absence of any formal training for political officers.

Definitions of paramountcy and usage

During the late nineteenth century, British officials invoked paramountcy and usage to justify diverse policies. In 1877 Lytton advised Lord Salisbury, his superior in London, that '[t]he paramount supremacy of the British Government is a thing of gradual growth; it has been established partly by conquest; partly by treaty; partly by usage'.[19] Thus paramountcy would buttress the British right to confirm all successions to the gaddi in princely states; the extension of British jurisdiction over railway lines that crossed the borders of states; intervention in struggles between princes and their nobles; and the extension of advice to princes about the need to improve or reform their administrations.

Although many Indian princes had complained individually throughout the nineteenth century against British encroachment in their internal affairs, by the beginning of the twentieth century some began to protest collectively in new sites of constitutional debate and legal inquiry. The Chamber of Princes (to be discussed below) was the primary locus of this challenge. Another was the Indian States Committee that Lord Irwin, viceroy from 1926 to 1931, appointed in 1928 to investigate princely grievances. Chaired by Harcourt Butler, an advocate of minimal interference in princely state affairs, with W. H. Holdsworth, a distinguished jurist, and Sidney Peel, a financier with

---

[17] Tupper, *Indian Protectorate*, p. 240.
[18] C. L. Tupper (comp.), *Indian Political Practice: A Collection of the Decisions of the Government of India in Political Cases*, 4 vols. (Delhi, 1974 reprint of 1895 edn.)
[19] Despatch dated 11 June 1877, in Tupper, *Practice*, vol. 1, p. 7.

experience in the City and in Parliament, as the other members, this Committee refused to define paramountcy. It concluded that '[p]aramountcy must remain paramount; it must fulfil its obligations, defining or adapting itself according to the shifting necessities of time and the progressive development of the States'.[20] It rejected the contractual basis for the British relationship with the princes that Lee-Warner had advanced and that the princes and Leslie Scott, their expensive King's Counsel, had revived. The British made their last effort to resolve the constitutional relationship between themselves and the princes and the princely states and British Indian provinces in a federal structure enshrined in the *Government of India Act* of 1935 that promised responsible government with fully elected ministries in British Indian provinces. This aborted solution will be discussed in Chapter 8.

British officials were not the only group constructing images and theories of the native states. Indians produced histories and reference works on the Indian princes and their states. Surendra Nath Roy, a vakil at the high court in Calcutta, published one volume on Gwalior of an incomplete multi-volume project entitled *History of the Native States of India*. Roy sought 'to let war-like nations know that among our "imbecile" princes and chiefs could yet be found brave and patriotic men who would prove matches for any warriors of ancient and modern times who could be named'.[21] In some cases the authors or editors appear to be oriented to profit rather than policy. A. Vadivelu produced *The Ruling Chiefs, Nobles and Zamindars of India*, a compendium whose uneven quality might be related to subventions from individuals listed or to possibly unacknowledged collaborators. His inclusion of large landlords and zamindars blurred the category of what constituted an Indian prince. His volume, however, provided a counterpoint to such British references as G. R. Aberigh-Mackay's *The Native Chiefs and Their States in 1877*.[22]

THE INDIAN POLITICAL SERVICE

Structure

Although Company servants called political officers negotiated with Indian rulers from the 1760s onward, they were only organised into a formal Indian

---

[20] *Report of the Indian States Committee*, p. 31.
[21] Surendra Nath Roy, *A History of the Native States of India*, vol. 1, Gwalior (Calcutta, 1888), p. ii.
[22] A. Vadivelu, *The Ruling Chiefs, Nobles & Zamindars of India*, vol. 1 (Madras, 1915); G. R. Aberigh–Mackay (comp.), *The Native Chiefs and Their States in 1877: A Manual of Reference*, 2nd edn with index (Bombay, 1878).

Political Service in 1937 on the eve of their demise.[23] Cornwallis initiated bureaucratic specialisation to eliminate corruption and to increase efficiency. Company officers had to choose between the commercial and the administrative branches, the latter including revenue collection, judicial work, and relations with Indian states. Those who negotiated with Indian states were called foreign or political officers and the three presidencies appointed them as needed. Michael Fisher has outlined three broad phases in the development of the political service under Company rule. From 1764 to 1797 residents and political agents were diplomatic agents negotiating between equals. By 1840 there were 116 political officers who exercised increasing hegemony vis-à-vis the princes. From 1841 to 1856 their number contracted to fifty-one as fewer political officers were posted to Indian states.[24] In 1843 the GOI organised a foreign department that oversaw relations with frontier areas and external states such as those in the Persian Gulf as well as the princes. In 1914 this entity was renamed the foreign and political department.

Despite the efforts of governors-general to consolidate political officers under central control, the Bombay Political Service was only the most prominent of the continuing provincial cadres of political officers.[25] A major confrontation between the GOI at Calcutta and the Bombay Government during the 1870s over affairs in Baroda epitomised the ongoing tensions within the imperial structure over policy and its implementation.[26] When the Bombay Government appointed Colonel Robert Phayre as resident in Baroda in 1873, he embodied the Bombay orientation to a *mission civilisatrice* and tactlessly intervened in internal affairs of the Baroda durbar, even seeking the dismissal of the eminent Indian nationalist Dadabhai Naoroji from the post of diwan. Gaekwad Malhar Rao vigorously opposed the resident's activities, and the GOI's commitment to non-intervention led them to demand that Bombay dismiss Phayre. After an alleged attempt by the Baroda durbar to poison the resident with diamond dust, the GOI secured Phayre's removal, took over control of Baroda from Bombay, and eventually deposed Malhar Rao. This episode highlights the inconsistencies between theory and practice as well as

---

[23] Terence Creagh Coen, *The Indian Political Service: A Study in Indirect Rule* (London, 1971), a general overview by a former political officer; W. Murray Hogben, The Foreign and Political Department of India, 1876–1919: A Study in Imperial Careers and Attitudes, PhD thesis, University of Toronto (1973).

[24] Fisher, *Indirect Rule*, pp. 54–9, 72–7.

[25] Ian Copland, The Bombay Political Service, 1863–1924, PhD thesis, Oxford University (1969); Copland, *British Raj*, chs 2, 4.

[26] I. F. S. Copland, 'The Baroda Crisis of 1873–77: A Study in Governmental Rivalry', *MAS* 2 (1968), pp. 97–123.

the existence of continuing bureaucratic rivalries within the British imperial structure.

The final act in this bureaucratic drama occurred four decades later. In 1919 when the *Indian Councils Act* introduced some elected Indian ministers into provincial governments, Edwin S. Montagu, the secretary of state for India (1917–22), and Lord Chelmsford, the governor-general (1916–21), recommended that states in direct relationship with provincial governors be transferred to the central government. Ostensibly this change would consolidate lines of communication, but there was growing concern within the GOI about the impact of elected, responsible Indian ministers in the provincial governments on relations with the Indian princes. Two governors argued strongly against the transfer: Sir George Lloyd of Bombay (1918–23), who conducted relations with numerous states, estates and shareholders of western India and the Deccan, and Sir Michael O'Dwyer of Punjab (1913–19), who had served in several states before his greater notoriety as the civilian authority condoning the firing at Amritsar in 1919. They countered that the GOI would be too distant from the smaller states, whose territories were often dispersed within their respective provinces, and that governers feared the loss of status for their governorships if the princes were transferred, of control over these safe havens from nationalist agitators, and of patronage over the political appointments in these states. After some vacillation, the princes generally endorsed direct relations. Upon the departure of O'Dwyer and Lloyd from India, the bureaucratic continuity of the GOI effected the transfer of the Punjab states in 1921 and the western Indian states in 1924.[27]

Because of the special relationship between the British Crown and the princes, the governor-general headed the foreign department, with a secretary supervising its daily operation. Usually the foreign or, after 1914, the political secretary had had a career in the provincial and central secretariats of British India, such as Lee-Warner, rather than service in princely states. Personal contact paved the way to such promotions, and extensive field experience might make it difficult to formulate a supposedly rational code for universal application. The influence of political secretaries varied. Under an authoritarian viceroy such as Lord Curzon, they were faceless bureaucrats. But Harcourt Butler, who had no experience in the princely states, was a forceful foreign secretary from 1907 to 1910 since Lord Minto (1905–10) was more willing than Curzon to delegate authority and responsibility. Finally, the post

---

[27] Barbara N. Ramusack, *The Princes in the Twilight of Empire: Dissolution of a Patron–Client System, 1914–1939* (Columbus OH, 1978), pp. 85–8; Copland, *British Raj*, pp. 250–62.

could also serve as a dumping ground for controversial officials such as J. P. Thompson (1873–1935), the chief secretary of the Punjab Government during the Jallianwala Bagh massacre in 1919, who was political secretary from 1922 to 1927.

The hierarchy within the political service mirrored the British ranking of their princely allies. At the apex, four to eight first-class residencies were responsible for major states (those with a 21-gun salute) or large clusters of states such as those in Rajputana or Central India. The titles of these officers changed over time; those who were responsible for one large state were termed residents and those overseeing several states were known as agents to the governor-general (AGGs). In 1937 the title of AGG was abolished and usually replaced by resident. With overall responsibility for as many as thirty states, AGGs were assisted by political agents in charge of smaller groups of states. On the next level were second-class residents, and on the third was the pool that supplied political agents and assistants to the residents. Recruits to the political service came from both the military and the ICS cadres. They had no formal training in either administration or the conduct of relations with the princes beyond a rudimentary examination on some departmental references such as Butler's *Manual of Instructions*[28] and historical works, chiefly the ubiquitous Tod and Malcolm. The political service trusted to on-the-job training.

Recruitment and personnel

From the late eighteenth century there was an ongoing debate over the appropriate ratio of military and civilian officers in the political service.[29] The Company's Court of Directors in London and many governors-general preferred civilians to be dominant, as they were during the first phase of the Company's expansion. However, as the newly annexed provinces under direct rule absorbed civilian officers, the military element in the political service climbed to 80 per cent during the 1830s before levelling off to 55 per cent during the 1850s. Both ICS and military officers frequently owed their appointments more to patronage, either from a relative who had been a political officer or a mentoring senior officer at the provincial or central secretariat, than to any personal combination of talents.

For military personnel accustomed to regimental duties, a transfer to the political service was a more crucial career change than for their civilian

---

[28] *Manual of Instructions to Officers of Political Department*, 2nd edn (Simla, 1924).
[29] Ian Copland, 'The Other Guardians: Ideology and Performance in the Indian Political Service', in Jeffrey, *People*, pp. 275–305.

counterparts, for whom the administrative work in a British Indian district had many similarities to political service, particularly if one were acting as regent for a minor ruler. Thus military men tended to stay in the political service while civilians moved more easily back into administration in British India. Although they were frequently denigrated by their civilian counterparts and their military brethren as either narrow or soft respectively, military men could be effective. Those with strong personalities and initiative could shape institutional relationships both within and between states and the British Raj. Others such as James Tod, who entered the Company's army as a cadet in 1798 before he chronicled the Rajputs, produced regional histories and ethnographies that influenced generations of officials and historians.

After the reorganisation of the GOI in 1858, military men remained dominant within the political service despite renewed pleas for more civilians. Lepel Griffin, author of *The Rajahs of the Punjab* (1873), argued for dividing the appointments equally after all had served a probation of two years in a British district. He emphasised the importance of selecting 'patient, intelligent, self-reliant and discreet' officers since they had a special influence in forming Indian opinions of the virtues of the British Government in princely states, 'where the political agent is often the only Englishman with whom chief and people come in contact'.[30] Based on his experience as AGG for the central Indian states (1881–88), Griffin also declared that the people there looked 'to the English officer as their last and surest refuge against oppression, with the result that the people in India most attached to the Government, and most ready to obey its slightest wish, are often to be found among the population of native States'.[31]

Such appeals were futile, and the basic ratio within the political service stabilised at 70 per cent officers from the Indian Army and 30 per cent civilian officers from the ICS.[32] Copland has argued persuasively that the Bombay Government preferred military men because they were cheaper. Moreover, British officials alleged that men with military bearing, good character and athletic ability were needed to impress and influence the princes under their control.[33] Expense, however, remained a significant factor. First, military officers were carried on the army budget and not that of the GOI. Second, ICS officers received a higher pay equal to their level in the ICS, until 1925 when both military and civilian officers received equal pay for equal work but not

[30] Lepel Griffin, 'Native India,' *AR* 1 (April 1886), pp. 454–5. [31] Ibid., p. 452.
[32] W. Murray Hogben, 'An Imperial Dilemma: The Reluctant Indianization of the Indian Political Service,' *MAS* 15 (1981), p. 752.
[33] Copland, *British Raj*, pp. 70–5.

equal pensions because of the differing formulae of the ICS and the Indian Army.

An even more vexatious question was the recruitment of Indians for the Indian political service. With limited personnel and little knowledge of the Persianised court ritual that governed relations with the Mughal Empire and the major princely states, the early British residents relied heavily on Indian employees for their language and literary skills and knowledge of court rituals. During the 1770s and 1780s Indians were occasionally allowed to function independently as vakils or agents for the British in negotiations with individual princes, but by the 1790s the British generally excluded Indians from the political service.[34]

Although Indians in the ICS only gradually increased from two in 1869 to 367 (with 894 Europeans) in 1929, they were practically invisible in the political service. Despite the prodding of Indian members of the Central Legislative Assembly and supportive British members of the British Parliament, in 1921 it was noted in the Legislative Assembly that Indians held less than 1 per cent of the posts above the Rs 1000 salary level in the foreign and political service. These few appointments were exclusively in the Northwest Frontier Province. Privately, British officials argued that the Indian princes objected to their relations being handled by Indians rather than British officials.[35] In postings abroad, the British Foreign Office were concerned about the trustworthiness of Indian officers with access to cipher files and codes. Many British officials also held racial assumptions that Indian candidates lacked the decisiveness needed for success. The Lee Commission recommended that Indians should gradually constitute 25 per cent of the political service. By July 1947 there were 124 political officers out of a cadre with an authorised strength of 180, and Indians held only seventeen posts, all on the northwest frontier or in the newly created external affairs ministry. W. Murray Hogben has analysed this phenomenon and concluded that the British political officers allowed their sense of racial-cum-moral superiority and their conservative departmental ethos to influence their policy decisions.[36]

This analysis overlooks two additional issues. First, during the twentieth century British ICS officers who disliked the growing democratisation in Britain and in India were attracted to the political service, where such democratisation was less evident.[37] For example, Edward Wakefield (1903–69) transferred from Punjab to the princely states because political service 'opened up

---

[34] Fisher, *Indirect Rule*, chs 7, 8.   [35] Hogben, 'Imperial Dilemma', pp. 757–8.
[36] Ibid., pp. 755–6, 766–8.   [37] Ramusack, *Princes*, pp. 238–40.

a pleasing vista of possibilities and uncertainties' and in the princely states he 'would be out of range of irresponsible criticism from a hostile Legislative Assembly'.[38] *The Jewel in the Crown*, Paul Scott's epic portrayal of the last years of the British rule in India, maintains a post-colonial fascination with the princely states as a refuge for many Britons and some Indians. Through the patronage of a well-connected aunt in Britain, Nigel Rowan gained an appointment to the political service and worked to secure the accession of the Nawab of Mirat to independent India. Ronald Merrick, the anti-hero, sought refuge in the police service of the states where, as an authoritative father, he could treat Indians as children. Guy Perron, the sceptical observer, later wrote a dissertation on the princely states from 1830 to 1857; he was enchanted with hawking, a princely pastime, as was Sarah Layton. As independence approached, Layton retreated to life in the princely state of Mirat and a relationship with one of its officials, Ahmad Kasim. Although his father was a prominent Congress Muslim politician and his brother joined the Indian National Army organised by Subhas Chandra Bose, Ahmad Kasim had remained in the political backwater of Mirat rather than becoming involved in British Indian politics.

Second, superior British officials who professed support of the demands for Indianisation acquiesced in the foot-dragging of conservative political officers and the sensitivities of the princes. Secretaries of state and viceroys were possibly ready to accede to such requests when they deemed such concessions would not have major repercussions in British India. Thus Indianisation of the political service was a symbolic issue on which the British were willing to concede to their princely clients since they could respond to critics by saying that there was increasing Indianisation in the cadre serving in British Indian provinces.

The viceroy, advised by his political secretary, had primary responsibility for assignments in the political service. After 1858 many British officials felt that political service was not the avenue to achieving administrative plums, although O'Dwyer and Bertrand J. Glancy (1941–47), who were governors in Punjab, and Francis Wylie, who served as governor in the Central Provinces (1938–40) and the United Provinces (1945–47), indicated that such mobility was possible. Within the political service, it was patronage, mentors and seniority rather than initiative that facilitated promotions. Princes also influenced the placement and sometimes the appointment of political officers.

---

[38] Edward Wakefield, *Past Imperative: My Life in India, 1927–1947* (London, 1966), p. 81.

Functions

Political officers were, first and foremost, representatives of the Company and later the British Crown. Yet they were janus-faced functionaries. On the one hand they implemented policies decided in London, Calcutta and, after 1911 Delhi, and practices codified in Calcutta and Delhi designed to enhance and protect British prerogatives. On the other hand they represented the princes within their jurisdicions to the GOI. During the Mughal period, nobles and allied princes maintained vakils as intermediaries and intelligence-gatherers at the imperial and provincial courts. Initially the British had allowed Indian rulers, especially pre-eminent ones such as Hyderabad, Mysore and Gwalior, to maintain vakils in Calcutta. During the 1790s restrictions were placed on this practice, until by the 1820s British political officers were to handle all relations between a ruler and the Company.

These dual functions spawned continual disagreements within the British hierarchy. Political officers might judge policy formulated in distant capitals to be unworkable or destructive of British hegemony in the field. Extended service in a particular state might create sympathy for a ruler, his subjects and his culture that made it difficult to implement harsh policies. During the early nineteenth century some political officers such as John Malcolm were noted for their clement attitude towards their charges; James Tod retired from his post in Rajputana in 1822 because of growing criticism of his pro-Rajput orientation.[39] Others such as Colonel Phayre in Baroda supervised state affairs more rigorously than the GOI thought expedient. During the twentieth century some political officers would prejudice princes against proposed constitutional reforms, especially federation during the 1930s. But such dissidents became less influential as the avenue to promotion lay through the secretariat and conformity to policy from above.

TENSIONS BETWEEN INTERVENTION AND LAISSEZ-FAIRE

Queen Victoria's proclamation in November 1858 that there would be no further annexations and that indirect and direct rule would coexist has been considered a major shift in British policy towards the princes. In practice, however, elements of continuity persisted since transfers of territory did occur. First, Lord Canning rewarded some princes who had actively assisted the British during 1857 with grants of territory. Jind, Patiala, Rampur, Gwalior,

---

[39] Banerjee, *Rajput States*, pp. 226–37.

Hyderabad and Bhopal received districts adjacent or near their states and Kapurthala gained two confiscated estates in Awadh.[40] New princely entities emerged with the formal recognition of Cooch Behar as a state in 1873, the designation of the maharaja of Banaras as an internally autonomous prince in 1911, and the creation of Swat from tribal territory on the Afghan frontier between 1916 and 1926. The Wadiyar ruling family was reinstalled in Mysore in 1881. There were realignments of Kathi states in Saurashtra and lapses of estates such as Peint in Maharashtra to direct British rule.[41]

Although no major shifts in territory occurred, the territorial basis for statehood was reaffirmed as boundaries were frozen and made more precise. Anomalous situations were created where districts of princely states swam in the sea of British India, chiefly in western and central India and in eastern Punjab. The often heard remark is that some princely states were so intertwined that they shared two sides of a street. But while the British would no longer use annexations or fear of annexations to intimidate princes, they had no intention of relinquishing their right to intervene in princely states to secure their imperial interests.

British policies about when and how to intervene in the princely states had long vacillated. In the early 1800s the Court of Directors in London, desiring cheap administration, enjoined its servants 'not to interfere in the internal affairs of other states'. Its officers in India often thought otherwise. In 1825 Charles Metcalfe, then resident at Delhi and proposing intervention in a disputed succession at Bharatpur, claimed 'we are continually compelled to deviate from this rule, which is found untenable in practice'.[42] During the 1830s and 1840s the British remained ambivalent. In Rajputana the British, alarmed by the influence of militant Nath ascetics over Maharaja Man Singh II of Jodhpur, actively pursued the expulsion of the Naths.[43] However, they refused to mediate in the more isolated states of Jaisalmer and Bikaner. This oscillation between intervention and laissez-faire continued after 1857. While they assumed a less overt profile in princely states affairs, the British argued that they retained the right and responsibility to mediate to ensure good government. The occasions for such interference form three clusters: succession, especially when adoption or minor rulers were involved; disputes

---

[40] Quanungo, 'Study', p. 262; Metcalf, *Aftermath*, pp. 222–3.
[41] I am grateful to John McLeod for pointing out several of these transfers to me.
[42] Minute by Sir Charles Metcalfe, 1825, in Sever, *Documents*, vol. 1, p. 145.
[43] Daniel Gold, 'The Instability of the King: Magical Insanity and the Yogis' Power in the Politics of Jodhpur, 1803–1843', in David N. Lorenzen (ed.) *Bhakti Religion in North India: Community Identity and Political Action* (Albany NY, 1995) pp. 120–32.

between princes and their nobility; and rationalisation of a state's administration. The British methods of intervention included 'advice' to a ruler, participation in a minority administration, the education of young princes, and 'suggestions' about the appointment of ministers. In practice there was considerable overlap among causes for interventions as well as the means of doing so.

The politics of succession, adoption, and minority administrations

The princes eagerly received the sanads of 1862, which permitted the adoption of children in accord with Hindu and Muslim customs and laws. But adoption sanads were a double-edged boon. While they assured the preservation of princely dynasties, they also proclaimed that '[t]he British Government will recognise and confirm any adoption of a successor made by yourself or by any future Chief of your state'.[44] Invoking the authority of paramountcy and usage, the British gradually claimed that no succession, whether or not adoption was involved, would be valid without their assent. A state might not lapse, but the British could exert significant influence at the crucial transfer of power from one generation to another. Critical issues were the timing of adoptions, the appropriate role of widows, nobility (jagirdars and thakurs), and state officials in selecting heirs when there was no natural or adopted heir, and the principles on which the British approved adoptions and posthumous selections.[45]

One of the most famous adoption cases occurred in Baroda. While a commission of inquiry was investigating charges of misgovernment and attempted assassination against Gaekwad Malhar Rao, Maharani Jamnabai, the widow of Malhar Rao's predecessor, was 'allowed to adopt... [anyone] whom the Government of India "*may select*" as the most suitable person'.[46] The British, desiring to rationalise the administration, and the maharani, wanting to delay any challenge to her authority, both preferred to have a minor adopted. They agreed on a young village boy from the Kavlana branch of the Gaekwads who was renamed Sayaji Rao (b. 1863, r. 1881–1939) upon his adoption in 1875. Other adoptions that would set precedents included those at Kolhapur in 1871; Udaipur in 1874 where the maharani and the state council selected the heir (Sajjan Singh), the Maharana Sambhu Singh having died without adopting an heir; Alwar in 1874–75 where an election was held among female relatives

---

[44] Canning to Hindu Rulers, Sever, *Documents*, vol. 1, p. 245.
[45] Tupper, *Practice*, vol. 2, pp. 81–116.
[46] Fatesinghrao P. Gaekwad, *Sayajirao of Baroda: The Prince and the Man* (Bombay, 1989), p. 41. Emphasis in the original.

and jagirdars of the late ruler;[47] Dhar in 1890; and Jhabua in 1893. At the other end of the political spectrum, in Mysore the British reluctantly agreed to recognise the adoption of an heir (Chamarajendra Wadiyar [d. 1894]) in 1865 even though the maharaja had not received a sanad granting the right to adopt in 1862 since he was not then a ruling prince. Eventually the British returned control of Mysore state in 1881 to the adopted heir after an extended period of minority administration.[48]

K. M. Panikkar credits Lord Mayo, governor-general from 1869 to 1872, with establishing the practice of forceful intervention during minority administrations.[49] British officials frequently denigrated local appointees to councils of regencies as motivated by self-interest.[50] Their most caustic criticism was directed at the minor ruler's female relatives. Since the British did not have direct access to the zenana or women's quarters, they were particularly anxious to reduce the influence of Indian women, whom they stereotyped as superstitious and of doubtful morality. Here the British conflated their Orientalist concepts of the exoticism of Asian women, especially an uncontrolled sexuality and lack of intelligence, with British disdain for alternative sources of identity for young princes.

Ostensibly to counter the zenana's impact in the public sphere and to preserve the patrimony of young princes, British policy was to appoint a local political agent to the council of regency or to approve its membership. Such councils frequently rationalised princely administrations according to British models that furthered British economic and political interests. Their measures included reorganised administrative structures and judiciaries, state-managed forests and, most importantly, land revenue settlements. These settlements measured land, defined who was responsible for land taxes, the major source of state income, and set rates. They were crucial in shaping economic and social hierarchies in the princely states where agriculture was even more dominant than in British India, as well as in enhancing state revenues at the expense of both nobles and peasants.

In western India during the peak year of 1876–77, almost half of the total princely area, twenty-eight states with a combined area of 24 000 square

---

[47] Edward S. Haynes, 'The British Alteration of the Political System of Alwar State: Lineage Patrimonialism, Indirect Rule, and the Rajput Jagir System in an Indian "Princely" State, 1775–1920', *SH* 5, n.s. (1989), pp. 27–71.

[48] C. Hayavadana Rao (ed.), *Mysore Gazetteer*, 5 vols., new edn (Bangalore, 1930), vol. 2, part 4, pp. 2923–60.

[49] K. M. Panikkar, *Indian States and the Government of India* (London, 1930), p. 56.

[50] Ajit K. Neogy, *The Paramount Power and the Princely States of India, 1858–1881* (Calcutta, 1979), pp. 76–7.

miles, was under minority administration.[51] During the Baroda minority from 1875 to 1881, the late Maharaja Fateh Singh Rao lamented that the British-sponsored diwan, T. Madhava Rao, was unnecessarily responsive to British requests for concessions in such areas as the manufacture of arms, opium, salt, and even alcohol.[52] For example, in 1880 the British secured Baroda's agreement to implement a tax on toddy trees. Raising the price of toddy in Baroda was designed to discourage smuggling from Baroda districts into south Gujarat, where the British were attempting to limit the consumption of alcohol through economic disincentives.[53]

In Hyderabad, Mir Mahbub Ali Khan succeeded to the gaddi in 1869 at the age of 2 and was only invested with full powers in 1884. Although Salar Jung, the diwan, and Nawab Shams-ul-Umra Amir-i-Kabir, a prominent noble, were to be co-administrators, the diwan recognised the British right 'to associate themselves with the education of the Nizam and the mode of administration of the state during his minority'.[54] Indeed the British secured substantial economic concessions during this period. One of the most consequential was to have Hyderabad underwrite at ruinous financial terms the construction of a broad-gauge railway connecting it with the Great Indian Peninsula Railway along a route that served British military strategy and not the economic growth of the state.[55] Hyderabad also consented to prohibit the export of salt to British India, tightening the British monopoly on salt and increasing British revenues from this regressive tax.

Frequent minority administrations in Rajputana and in the Punjab states and extensive British involvement raised other issues. During the minority of Mangal Singh in Alwar from 1874 to 1877, Alfred Lyall, the AGG for Rajputana, cautioned his superiors in Calcutta:

The natural tendency of a system which makes the Political Agent necessarily responsible for good government during a minority is, I think, to draw the whole conduct of affairs more and more within his personal control . . . This tendency should, if possible, be to a certain degree guarded against, in order that the transfer of power at the end of the minority, should not involve a radical change of system.[56]

---

[51] Copland, *British Raj*, pp. 138, 300, 316.   [52] Gaekwad, *Sayajirao*, pp. 67–73.

[53] David Hardiman, 'From Custom to Crime: Politics of Drinking in Colonial South Gujarat', in Guha, *Subaltern Studies IV*, p. 126.

[54] Vasant Kumar Bawa, *The Nizam between Mughals and British: Hyderabad under Salar Jang I* (New Delhi, 1986), p. 52.

[55] Bharati Ray, 'The Genesis of Railway Development in Hyderabad State: A Case Study in Nineteenth Century British Imperialism', *IESHR* 21 (1984), pp. 45–59; Sethia, 'Berar', pp. 59–78.

[56] AGGR to FSGOI, Camp Ajmer, 24 December 1874, Pol. A Progs, February 1875, 133, quoted in Haynes, 'British Alteration', p. 66.

To prevent a sharp break, Colonel P. W. Powlett, the political agent on the spot, interpreted this warning as a good reason for developing a state bureaucracy that would continue the British-influenced system inaugurated during a minority. Thus he accelerated the trend towards the employment of western-educated Indian administrators from outside the state who grew in power at the expense of local jagirdars. This course was accelerated during the minority of Maharaja Jai Singh from 1892 to 1903 and widened the gulf between nobles and prince.

Patiala state had minority administrations for thirty of the fifty years from 1860 to 1910. Ajit Neogy discusses how the British felt that Indian members of the Regency Council during the minority of Mohinder Singh during the 1860s had ruined the character of the ruler and the quality of the administration.[57] The British kept a tighter control over subsequent councils of regency, and under Curzon, loaned British officers effected changes that enhanced state control in Patiala. During the minority of Maharaja Bhupinder Singh (b. 1891, s. 1895, r. 1910–38), Major F. Popham Young revised the land settlement in 1901 and J. O. Warburton reorganised the police department. Although the British were not directly responsible for princes being unable to produce male heirs or being short-lived, they readily seized the opportunities offered.

While ministers constructed centralised administrative and economic institutions during minority regimes, British officials debated how best to prepare young princes to rule. Education that synthesised a British-style curriculum with indigenous elements so as not to estrange princes from their cultural heritage and subjects became a panacea. It would reduce the zenana influence, broaden the horizons of the princes, and most importantly motivate rulers to continue the reforms and practices once the regency ended. The British tried two methods. One was the approval of British tutors for the princes if education within the state was deemed most appropriate. There was particular concern regarding the heirs of major states such as Nizam Mahbub Ali of Hyderabad, whose education was a contentious issue between Salar Jung, residents, and viceroys. The British desired a rigorous, western education while Salar Jung wanted instruction in Arabic as well as Urdu and English, in Muslim religious subjects, and control over the appointment of the British tutor.[58] An alternative occurred in Baroda when F. A. H. Elliot, an ICS officer, set up a small school in which the newly adopted, non-literate Sayaji Rao would be educated with eight to ten carefully selected pupils.[59]

---

[57] Neogy, *Paramount Power*, p. 76.   [58] Bawa, *Nizam*, pp. 107–11.
[59] Stanley Rice, *Life of Sayaji Rao III Maharaja of Baroda*, 2 vol. (London, 1931), vol. 1, pp. 33–5.

By the 1870s the British decided that princes might be better educated as 'traditional' rulers and partners in the imperial enterprise in the Indian equivalent of a British public school. The activist Mayo inaugurated the policy with the founding of Rajkumar College at Rajkot in 1870 for the education of princely sons from Kathiawar. The princes and gentry of Rajputana established Mayo College at Ajmer two years later. Its Indo-Saracenic campus was a synthesis of architectural elements from Dig, the eighteenth-century Jat capital near Agra that combined indigenous Hindu, Bengali and Mughal elements with British ones. The distinctive modern element was a prominent clock tower whose height symbolised British dominance, as the Qutb Minar in Delhi did the Muslim conquest. The clock's hourly tolling would supposedly promote punctuality, discipline and order and a desirable modernity.[60] Subsequently Aitchison College (1886) was erected at Lahore for princes from Punjab, Daly College (1898) at Indore for those from central India, and Rajkumar College at Raipur. Both British and Indians were critical of their graduates. Many felt that the young princes acquired the veneer of a public school education with its addiction to sports, some unfortunate vices, and little of the substance of a classical education or commitment to duty. In 1913 Lord Hardinge, viceroy from 1911 to 1916, called the first of two conferences of princes to discuss the establishment of a Higher Chiefs' College in the new imperial capital of Delhi. Although this institution, intended to provide an all-India perspective for princes, never came into being, these conferences served as a stepping stone towards the Chamber of Princes.

Balancing princes and nobles

During the eighteenth century the relationship between a prince and his aristocracy was dynamic. A prince required military and civil support, but a follower skilful in forming alliances, military leadership and the acquisition of material resources could become a ruler himself. Expanding British power reduced opportunities to create new states and restricted the latitude for nobles to augment their political and material resources at the expense of their rulers. Many British officials who saw their relationship with the princes as a feudal one between lord and vassal inherited from the Mughal Empire were reluctant to interfere on behalf of vassals of their vassals. Others, using the analogy of the feudal barons and the Magna Carta, characterised the nobility

---

[60] Thomas R. Metcalf, *An Imperial Vision: Indian Architecture and Britain's Raj* (Berkeley CA, 1989), pp. 66–80.

within a state as rightful co-sharers of power and a check on the autocracy of the princes. Once committed to the maintenence of the princes as allies after 1858, the British did not want civil war or brigandage threatening the survival of client princes. The imperial suzerain tried to mediate internal power struggles while it simultaneously pursued policies that exacerbated such relationships.

Appealing to their role in the establishment of the state, nobles resented their loss of political clout, economic privileges and ritual status. As princes sought to rationalise their administrations, to extend control over their subjects and to enhance revenues, nobles became increasingly restive. They attempted to protect their interests by participating in the adoption of heirs, the education of minor heirs and the appointment of officials. Sometimes they resorted to poison for the quiet despatch of a ruler or to armed insurrections that could degenerate into outlawry, especially in more remote areas such as Saurasthra, the deserts of Rajputana and the rugged ravines of central India. The British derisively labelled these processes court intrigues, perhaps because they reminded them of their own domestic politics in earlier eras or seemingly substantiated their Orientalist construction of Indian politics as the incoherent Other demonstrating the superiority of British institutions.

But the British efforts to rationalise administrations heightened friction between rulers and nobles. Centralised administrations employed an educated elite and required a secure financial base to pay for railways, telegraph systems, roads, irrigation projects and disciplinary institutions such as schools, hospitals and prisons. The older aristocracy was affected in two ways. First, they frequently lacked the educational qualifications required for bureaucratic positions. By the 1870s Travancore and Hyderabad began to replace ministers drawn from a local nobility, who had an independent power base in their landholdings and networks of relatives, with western-educated Indians.[61] In other states British as well as Indian officers were used. Second, the incomes of nobles were largely derived from lands that the ruler had alienated to them. As princes bolstered their income by restricting and if possible resuming jagirdari or zamindari rights and increasing rates of land revenue, the incomes of nobles as well as peasants were reduced. Scholarship has so far uncovered more opposition from nobles than from peasants – until the rise of popular agitations during the 1930s and 1940s.

---

[61] Jeffrey, *Decline*; Karen Leonard, 'Hyderabad: The Mulki-Non-Mulki Conflict', in Jeffrey, *People*, pp. 65–106.

Different levels of the British hierarchy had conflicting ideas about how to handle disputes between rulers and their nobles. In Alwar bureaucrats from British India exacerbated the relationship between the ruler and his jagirdars.[62] In 1858 there was a jagirdari uprising against the so-called 'Delhi diwans' (two Muslim brothers), who were assuming significant control as officials within the state and allegedly attempting to convert to Islam Sheodan Singh, a minor who had succeeded as raja in 1857. After stifling the dispute, the British appointed a ruling council of jagirdars, but these lacked education, experience, and the required commitment to a modern-style administration. By 1870 brigandage and the possibility of open warfare intensified as some senior jagirdars protested their deteriorating status as marked in durbar ceremonies, the recruitment of non-Rajputs for a state military force in place of their jagirdari levies, and an alleged anti-Hindu stance of the prince as well as the growing authority of bureaucrats. Posted as political agent to Alwar to prevent civil war, Thomas Cadell advocated the removal of Sheodan Singh, who was imputed to have serious personal flaws:

His removal would, I think, be a step toward the solution of the great 'Chief *versus* Thakoor' question. It would show that we are ready and able to punish a Chief, who, after repeated warnings, drives his nobles into rebellion . . . and it would be a lesson which, I am sure, is needed in many parts of Central India and Rajpootan.[63]

The more distant Lord Mayo, while admitting that the raja's acts were 'contemptible, spiteful and discreditable', declared that Cadell 'must make up his mind to put up with his [Sheodan Singh's] petty annoyances, for I am determined to carry forbearance to its utmost limit'.[64] Even an aborted assassination attempt on Cadell did not evict Sheodan Singh from remaining on the Alwar gaddi until his death in 1874. In contrast, Malhar Rao of Baroda was deposed the following year, partly because of a similar assault on a political officer. Not only did assorted levels of the British hierarchy have differing attitudes towards intervention, but the incidence of deposition varied.

Meanwhile the jagirdars of Alwar would suffer further diminution of their prerogatives as 'foreign' administrators extended state authority through reformed land revenue settlements that ended jagirdari exemption from such

---

[62] Edward S. Haynes, 'Alwar: Bureaucracy versus Traditional Rulership: Raja, Jagirdars and New Administrators, 1892–1910', in ibid., pp. 32–64.

[63] Demi-official (confidential letter), PAA (Cadell) to AGGR (Keatinge), 1 September 1870, Pol. A Progs., October 1870, 167, quoted in Haynes, 'British Alteration', p. 55.

[64] Note which was a 'Keep-with' (KW) by Viceroy, 18 May 1871, Pol. A Progs., June 1871, quoted in ibid., p. 56.

taxes and forest policies brought grazing and common lands under state jurisdiction. The British argument that these measures were a boon rather than a deliberate extension of state control is reflected in the memoirs of Sir Michael O'Dwyer, who revised the land settlements in Alwar and Bharatpur from 1897 to 1901. Claiming that he 'had experienced some difficulty in getting the State authorities to agree to my limiting the State share to two-thirds or three-fourths of the estimated rental', O'Dwyer related that he 'imposed an assessment about double of what I should have imposed on them if they had been British districts'. He asserted that 'my assessments were welcomed by the people, and were regarded as decidedly moderate in comparison with other Native States'.[65] In contrast, Shail Mayaram criticises the British for their land and forest settlements, which created oppressive conditions for jagirdars and peasants alike and eventually precipitated Meo peasant revolts and British charges of financial mismanagement against Maharaja Jai Singh in Alwar.[66]

Support for social reform and rational administration

Britain's ambivalence about intervention or laissez-faire pervaded its promotion of social reform and efficient administration in the princely states. Although British officials claimed that after 1858 Indians themselves would have to inaugurate social reforms, the imperialists continued to exhort princes to take action on certain issues. In 1861 the GOI warned its AGG in Rajputana that the durbars under its jurisdiction should more vigorously prohibit sati, still practised in Rajputana. If a prince neglected his duty, the GOI threatened to 'consider the propriety of reducing the number of guns with which the Chief of the State is saluted', to demonstrate the displeasure of the Queen's Government.[67] These instructions indicate the continuing British obsession with sati, which afflicted far fewer women than the less public practice of female infanticide. The proposed punishment also indicates how the threat of a demotion subtly inculcated among the princes the value the British overlord placed on salutes and titles as a system of rank. Rudyard Kipling satirised the fetishisation of honours and disparaged Indian indifference or opposition to modernising, disciplinary institutions in 'A Legend of the Foreign Office':

[65] Sir Michael O'Dwyer, *India as I Knew It 1885–1925*, 3rd edn (London, 1926), p. 97.
[66] Shail Mayaram, *Resisting Regimes: Myth, Memory and the Shaping of a Muslim Identity* (Delhi, 1997), pp. 75–82.
[67] GOI to AGG in Rajputana, 20 December 1861 as quoted in Tupper, Practice, vol. 1, p. 78. These directives were also sent to the AGG in Central India.

Rustum Beg of Kolazai
slightly backward Native State
Lusted for a C.S.I.
so he began to sanitate.
Built a Gaol and Hospital
nearly built a City drain
Till his faithful subjects all
thought their ruler was insane.[68]

Although Canning had hesitated to preach the doctrine of 'good government' to the princes, some of his successors did not. Both John Lawrence, governor-general from 1864 to 1869, who energetically proclaimed the gospel of public works, and Lord Mayo, his successor, fostered greater state control through modernising institutions. The desired reforms included metalled roads and railways; public health measures, especially piped water, vaccination campaigns and medical dispensaries; and elementary schools. Although some subsequent viceroys were more low-key, Lord Curzon, viceroy from 1899 to 1905, epitomised British intrusion in princely administrative affairs and personal lives.

Curzon's ambivalent attitudes towards them indicate some of the problems created by the contradictory aims of British policy for the Indian princes.[69] On the one hand this ambitious viceroy glorified the feudal image of the princes during the great imperial durbar held in 1903 to commemorate the coronation of Edward VII and considered the conservative Madho Singh II of Jaipur to be the ideal prince. On the other hand he wanted princes to be hardworking administrators but not too efficient. His personal favourite among the princes was Maharaja Madho Rao Scindia of Gwalior (b. 1876, s. 1886, r. 1894–1925) since, as he commented to the secretary of state in London, 'In his (Scindia's) remorseless propensity for looking into everything and probing it to the bottom, he rather reminds me of your humble servant'.[70] David Cannadine uses an iconic photograph of Curzon and Madho Rao Scindia as a frontispiece in *Ornamentalism* to represent the ways in which Britons accepted the princes as their social equals and both sought to broadcast their hierarchical superiority through spectacular public rituals and buildings.[71]

[68] I am indebted to Edward Haynes for this reference, Rudyard Kipling, 'A Legend of the Foreign Office', in *Rudyard Kipling's Verse: Definitive Edition* (Garden City NJ [1940]), p. 8. Originally published in *Departmental Ditties*, 1885.

[69] S. R. Ashton, *British Policy towards the Indian States 1905–1939* (London, 1982), pp. 23–5, 45–7.

[70] Curzon to Lord George Hamilton, 26 November 1899, OIOC, MSS Eur F111/159 as quoted in ibid., p. 16.

[71] Cannadine, *Ornamentalism*, pp. 45–57. Despite the visual prominence given to Madho Rao of Gwalior, Cannadine later confuses him with Sayaji Rao of Baroda on p. 147.

Maharaja Madho Rao Scindia II of Gwalior and Lord Curzon in 1899 after shikar.

Although Sayaji Rao of Baroda was hailed for his progressive administration and social services, which included universal compulsory primary education, by Curzon's standards the latter prince indulged in too frequent, extended stays in Europe at spas and first-class hotels. Some princes apparently retreated to Europe to avoid having to respond to British demands, much as Nawab Sa'adat Ali Khan of Awadh went on hunting trips in the 1810s to avoid such confrontations. Curzon responded as had the British resident in Awadh by requiring his personal permission before princes journeyed to Europe.[72] Curzon and many British officials were racist in their desire to have the princes conform to British constructions of paternalistic and hard-working rulers and in their disdain for princes who challenged the self-image of the British as the only progressive administrators in India.[73]

Under Curzon's successor, there was a perceived shift to a policy of laissez-faire regarding governmental reforms. In an often quoted speech at a durbar in Udaipur on 3 November 1909, Lord Minto (1905–10) announced that he was 'opposed to anything like pressure on Durbars with a view to introducing British methods of administration' and 'preferred that reforms should emanate from Durbars themselves and grow up in harmony with the traditions of the State'. Curzon and generations of political officers must have turned red with rage when Minto asserted that '[i]t is easy to overestimate the value of administrative efficiency' and then added that 'administrative efficiency, if carried out on lines unsuited to local conditions, would lessen or impair the personal loyalty of the people to his rulers'. The viceroy tried to assuage wounded egos by claiming that he spoke 'in no spirit of criticism' but wanted to remind political officers 'that they are not only the mouthpiece of Government and the custodians of Imperial policy' but they are 'to interpret the sentiments and aspirations of the Durbars'.[74] This speech reflected Minto's aristocratic sentiments and those of his foreign secretary, Harcourt Butler, who had strongly supported the taluqdars of Awadh when governor of the United Provinces.[75]

Many princes considered Minto's speech to be their Magna Carta setting limits on their British suzerain. Most political officers committed to the promotion

---

[72] Fisher, *Clash*, p. 105.

[73] Manu Bhagavan, 'Demystifying the "Ideal Progressive": Resistance through Mimicked Modernity in Princely Baroda 1900–13', *MAS* 35 (2001), pp. 385–409; Ian Copland, 'Sayaji Rao Gaekwar and "Sedition": The Dilemmas of an Indian Prince', in Peter Robb and David Taylor (eds), *Rule, Protest, Identity: Aspects of Modern South Asia* (London, 1978), pp. 28–48.

[74] Quoted from Speeches by the Earl of Minto (Calcutta, 1911), pp. 321–6 in Sever, *Documents*, vol. 1, pp. 376–7.

[75] Ashton, *British Policy*, pp. 42–5; Copland, 'Sayaji Rao Gaekwar', pp. 30–1.

of reforms within the states saw it as an unwise constraint. S. R. Ashton agrees, arguing that non-interference permitted 'a rapid deterioration of administrative standards in the states' and made them 'wholly unreliable allies' since they no longer had the support of their subjects.[76] But he ignores the fact that popular expectations of governments changed dramatically from 1910 to the 1940s and that in 1947 many state subjects still respected and supported their rulers. Morever, Minto was responding to the immediate, strategic need to renew bonds between the British and the princes in the face of nationalist challenges that erupted dramatically in the agitation over the partition of Bengal in 1905 and would escalate with Gandhian civil disobedience and peasant protests over economic hardship. By the late 1920s, Lord Irwin, the Conservative viceroy (1926–31) who was sympathetic to the princes, acknowledged the disadvantages of the 'sledge-hammer' policy of intervention and tried to persuade the princes to undertake significant internal reforms, particularly the establishment of an independent judiciary and a designated portion of state revenues as a privy purse, to head off political protests. Irwin met with the princes in Simla in 1927, circulated a note on the basics of good government, and tried to achieve through persuasion what Curzon sought through harangue.[77] Laissez-faire remained a dominant motif in British policy but more subtle forms of intervention stayed in the British arsenal.

Alternatives to annexation for trangressive princes

Despite their overwhelming military power and the pervasiveness of their informal instruments of intimidation, the British still had to confront princely refusals to perform their expected roles on the imperial stage. There were two major issues. One was to delimit the boundaries between appropriate, inappropriate and unacceptable princely behaviour. While arguing that 'to draw a hard-and-fast line between cases for punishment and cases to be ignored would be impolitic in a high degree', in 1895 Tupper declared:

first, that the British Government holds Ruling Chiefs responsible for the prevention and punishment of such barbarous practices as mutilation, torture, sati, samadh, impalement and the like; *and secondly*, that the British Government will not recognise the right of a Ruling Chief to order or secretly compass without trial the death of any person in his territories who has committed no offence, but has simply become obnoxious to him.[78]

---

[76] Ashton, *British Policy*, pp. 197–8.
[77] Minutes of Conference at Simla on 6 May 1927, NAI, GOI, F&P, 1928, Pol, File No. 201–R and Note by Lord Irwin dated 14 June 1927, NAI, GOI, F&P, 1927, Pol, File No. 727.
[78] Tupper, *Practice*, vol. 1, p. 74. Emphasis in the original.

As with paramountcy, it was inexpedient to define and thereby limit what might be considered princely misconduct. At times political officers and some viceroys were prepared to tolerate behaviour unacceptable by British standards but bearable in Indian clients who, according to racist ideas, could not be expected to measure up to such lofty models. During the twentieth century the British would expand misconduct to include financial malfeasance and oppressive treatment of state subjects, particularly when it triggered popular protests that threatened neighbouring British Indian provinces. Even so, such misconduct might be overlooked if the prince had political value for the British or had forged a supportive network among political officers and viceroys in India or members of Parliament in London.

The second concern was to develop effective deterrents once annexation was no longer a viable threat. Low-level sanctions ranged from the posting of a political agent to the denial of a viceregal visit, the demotion of a prince in the salute table, or the refusal of permission for a prince to travel outside his state. The next level was to require the appointment of an external official, either an Indian trained in British India or a British ICS officer, to a major post such as diwan or finance minister in the state administration. Some prominent examples were the British support initially for Salar Jung (diwan from 1853 to 1883) and for his son in Hyderabad and for T. Madhava Rao (1828–91), an astute, western-educated Maratha from Thanjaur (Tanjore), in Baroda in 1875. During the late nineteenth and early twentieth century, the British frequently used Indian surrogates in princely administrations with only an occasional British political officer. By the 1930s and 1940s, the number of British officers serving as prime minister in princely states had increased. They included M. Frederick Gauntlett as financial minister in Patiala during the 1930s, Francis Wylie as prime minister in Alwar in 1933, and Edward Wakefield as minister in charge in Rewa in 1943. Once again, Paul Scott reflects that reality in the person of Tusker Smalley, an unambitious, efficient army officer, who was deputed to Mudpore state, which his wife proclaimed as 'the *real* India'.[79]

The appointment of a British prime minister could presage the more drastic measure of a commission of inquiry to investigate grievances against a ruler. The threat of such a commission sometimes impelled a ruler to relinquish his powers temporarily or to abdicate permanently. Ashton has documented fifteen princes who so reacted during the viceroyalty of Lord Curzon.[80] Accusations of either public or private misbehaviour continued to trigger such

---

[79] Paul Scott, *Staying On* (London, 1978), p. 86. Emphasis in the original.
[80] Ashton, *British Policy*, p. 24.

responses until 1947. Maharaja Ripudaman Singh of Nabha (b. 1883, r. 1911–23), who was charged with abduction and illegal detention of prisoners from Patiala and British India, first moved outside his state and then abdicated in 1928.[81] Maharaja Tukoji Rao III of Indore (b. 1890, r. 1911–1926, d. 1978) abdicated in 1926 rather than face a commission investigating his alleged involvement in the murder of the husband of a woman rumoured to be his mistress.[82]

Several princes were scrutinised by such commissions, and the varied consequences indicate how theory and practice diverged. A few survived after agreeing to internal changes in government or spending patterns. Two prominent examples are Bhupinder Singh of Patiala and Hari Singh (b. 1895, r. 1925–48, d. 1961) of Jammu and Kashmir, who benefited from British and Indian advocates. After they advised Bhupinder Singh to curb his financial commitments and to appoint a finance minister who would oversee the payment of state debts, the British launched an official inquiry in 1930 in response to a highly critical report from the All-India States' People's Conference (AISPC) entitled *Indictment of Patiala*.[83] They selected J. A. O. Fitzpatrick, the AGG for Punjab, who was certainly familiar with the state but someone the maharaja had suggested. Although his report exonerated the ruler, Fitzpatrick urged reforms in the judiciary and police. Despite vociferous campaigns by the AISPC and the Punjab Riyasti Praja Mandal (the local states' people's group), Bhupinder Singh retained his gaddi because of sympathetic British supporters, his prominence in constitutional negotiations regarding the princes, and his shrewd participation in Sikh politics, where he divided his attackers.[84] As Harold Wilberforce-Bell, then officiating deputy-secretary in the political department, noted, 'We cannot afford to see a state of importance & position of Patiala crack'.[85]

In July 1931 Maharaja Hari Singh of Jammu and Kashmir confronted demonstrations protesting at discriminatory measures towards the Muslim majority. The opposition escalated as the Ahmadiyyas, a heterodox Muslim

[81] Barbara N. Ramusack, 'Incident at Nabha: Interaction between Indian States and British Indian Politics,' *JAS* 28 (1969), pp. 563–77.
[82] Lord Reading, the governor-general, proposed an inquiry to Lord Birkenhead, secretary of state for India, 4 December 1925, OIOC, MSS Eur E 238/14.
[83] *Indictment of Patiala: Being a Report of the Patiala Enquiry Committee Appointed by the Indian States' People's Conference* (Bombay, 1930).
[84] Barbara N. Ramusack, 'Punjab States: Maharajas and Gurdwaras: Patiala and the Sikh Community', in Jeffrey, *People*, pp. 188–90; Ian Copland, *The Princes of India in the Endgame of Empire 1917–1947* (Cambridge, 1997), pp. 81–2.
[85] Note by Wilberforce-Bell, 31 December 1929, OIOC, CR, R/1/19/509.

sect based in Punjab, and the Ahrars, an urban political party in Lahore, sent jathas to join Muslim comrades in Kashmir.[86] B. J. Glancy, a senior political officer, chaired a commission of inquiry that included two Muslim and two Hindu members.[87] Their report satisfied neither the Hindus nor the Muslims. Initially the GOI appeared ready to appoint a British administrator for the state, but lobbying by Nawab Hamidullah of Bhopal and two Kashmiri brahmans, Tej Bahadur Sapru, a leading Liberal lawyer based in Allahabad, and K. N. Haksar, his relative through marriage, persuaded Hari Singh to dismiss key officials and Lord Willingdon, the viceroy (1931–37), to agree to the milder but still significant alternative of the appointment of E. J. Colvin as prime minister of Kashmir.[88] Hari Singh faced an even more tumultuous future and would eventually be forced to live outside Kashmir in 1949 and to accept his son, Karan Singh (b. 1931), acting as his regent and then as head of state from 1952.[89] A third ruler, Maharaja Jai Singh (b. 1882, r. 1903–33, d. 1937) of Alwar, confronted popular resistance by the sizeable Meo Muslim minority beginning in 1932 over the state imposition of Hindi, the lack of educational facilities for Muslims, and most importantly, oppressive taxation. After he refused to implement recommendations from a British commission and A. C. Lothian, the local political officer, the maharaja was deposed and exiled in 1933 and died in Paris in 1937.[90] Having developed a reputation for cruelty to animals and people as well as irrational demands for deference, Jai Singh could expect little indulgence.

The ultimate British sanction of recalcitrant princes was deposition. The most prominent deposition was that of Gaekwad Malhar Rao of Baroda. As discussed earlier, this ruler had been caught in bureaucratic crossfire between differing British policies towards the princely states. Lord Salisbury, the secretary of state in London, even proposed to make an example of Malhar Rao's misgovernment by transferring some of Baroda's territory to a prince 'who had behaved well'.[91] Despite opposition from Bombay and London, Lord Northbrook, a liberal viceroy (1872–76), appointed a commission of three British officials and three Indians, the rulers of Jaipur and Gwalior and Sir Dinkar Rao,

[86] Ramusack, *Princes*, pp. 171–4; Ian Copland, 'Islam and Political Mobilization in Kashmir, 1931–34', *PA* 54 (1981), pp. 228–59.
[87] Prem Nath Bazaz, *The History of Struggle for Freedom in Kashmir* (New Delhi, 1954), pp. 151–71.
[88] K. N. Haksar to T. B. Sapru, 7 February 1932, NLI, Sapru MSS, I, H 51.
[89] Karan Singh, *Heir Apparent: An Autobiography* (Delhi, 1982), pp. 77–102.
[90] Arthur Lothian, *Kingdoms of Yesterday* (London, 1951), pp. 124–6; Mayaram, *Resisting Regimes*, ch. 4; Ramusack, *Princes*, pp. 179–80.
[91] Salisbury to Northbrook, 22 January 1875, as quoted in Copland, *British Raj*, p. 148.

the former prime minister of Gwalior, to investigate the charges of misgovernment. After the commission split on racial lines, with the Indian members declaring the gaekwad not guilty, the GOI deposed Malhar Rao on grounds of 'gross misrule' in 1875.[92] This action probably prompted other princes to take evasive action rather than risk an inquiry and to decline to serve on such commissions.

Although not frequent, depositions occurred until the British departure. In 1867 Nawab Muhammad Ali Khan (d. 1895) of Tonk was deposed for his collusion in an attack on the uncle of a tributary. In 1891 the ruling family of Manipur was debarred from the gaddi after an attack in which five British officers were killed, and the state was regranted to a collateral branch. The last major deposition reflects that the fluctuations in British attitudes between laissez-faire and intervention continued into the 1940s. In the difficult atmosphere of early 1942, the British appointed a commission of inquiry to investigate charges including fraud, bribery, the obstruction of justice and being an accessory to murder against Maharaja Gulab Singh of Rewa (b. 1903, s. 1918, r. 1922–45, d. 1950). Their verdict was not guilty and the prince remained in power while the British dealt with the Quit India movement and peasant demonstrations as well as the war effort. But in 1945 Francis Wylie (1891–1970), a more determined and aggressive political officer, deposed Gulab Singh as an example to other princes of the need for reform.[93] Long before 1945, however, the British were devising new roles for ambitious princes on the broader stages of all-Indian and imperial politics.

NEW FUNCTIONS FOR PRINCELY CLIENTS

Manly military allies

Initially the princes had concluded treaties as military allies and supplied troops and funds during the Company's expansionist wars. After 1857 British military power precluded further internal military challenges, so the British fashioned new duties for these military allies. Since the British viewed India as the centre, the reputed jewel in the crown, of their far-flung empire, they commandeered Indian resources to defend this empire. When a Russian contingent defeated an Afghan army near Panjdeh in 1885 and reignited smouldering British concern about the security of its frontiers, the GOI launched the Imperial Service Troops scheme to upgrade the military capability of the princes' troops. Selected princely states would be given the 'honour' of maintaining a contingent of state

---

[92] Ibid., pp. 141–53; Copland, 'Baroda Crisis'.   [93] Copland, *Princes*, pp. 187–8, 198.

subjects trained and inspected by British officers and supplied with British equipment. Paid from state revenues, these units could be used only for the defence of British imperial interests. The objective was to have units that could efficiently coordinate with British Indian units in battle. First employed along Indian borders in military expeditions to sites such as Chitral and Tirah, the Imperial Service Troops would fight in the Boer War, the Boxer Rebellion and the two world wars. Some princes such as Madho Singh of Jaipur would parlay his support for Imperial Service Troops into British backing in his struggles with his thakurs.[94]

Extending the commitment of their ancestors, some princes crossed the *kala pani* or black waters to safeguard the empire. The 19-year-old Maharaja Ganga Singh (b. 1880, r. 1898–1943) of Bikaner went to China during the Boxer Rebellion, along with Maharaja Madho Rao Scindia of Gwalior and Maharaja Pratap Singh (1845–1922), first a minister in Jodhpur, then ruler of Idar from 1902 to 1911, and twice regent of Jodhpur. Numerous princes including Ganga Singh, Pratap Singh and Maharaja Ranjitsinhji (b. 1872, r. 1907–33) of Nawanagar, who was most renowned for his exploits on the cricket field, enthusiastically volunteered during the First World War. However, these princes served for only brief periods as they lacked modern military training and were fairly ineffective in the field.

Consequently the British sought to transmute personal services from the princes into financial contributions and recruiting activities. Nizam Osman Ali Khan (b. 1886, r. 1911–48, d. 1967) of Hyderabad donated over Rs 35 lakhs to the war effort. Others funded aeroplanes and hospital ships, and some provided buildings for convalescing soldiers.[95] Equally important were recruiting efforts. Maharaja Bhupinder Singh, whose state contained so many of the Punjabi Sikhs and Muslims characterised by the British as martial races, was a zealous recruiter. In one speech he proclaimed that it was far better to die a manly death on the field of battle than to remain at home and meet the angel of death through the unmanly diseases of cholera and plague.[96] Some princes also served during the brief third Afghan war in 1919. But by the Second World War few princes were on active duty, although some such as Maharaja Yadavindra Singh (b. 1913, r. 1938–48, d. 1974) of Patiala made inspection tours of units from Patiala that were serving in North Africa.[97]

---

[94] Stern, *Cat*, pp. 198–203.   [95] Ramusack, *Princes*, pp. 38–40.
[96] *Khalsa Advocate*, 28 October 1916, p. 4.
[97] John McLeod has pointed out that Maharao Raja Bahadur Singh of Bundi (b. 1920, r. 1945–48, d. 1977) fought and was wounded in the Burma campaign a few months before his ascension to the gaddi.

Faithful feudatories

After 1857 British officials extolled the princes as 'natural leaders' and as faithful feudatories. The Imperial Assemblage at Delhi in 1877 inaugurated a series of ritual representations in which the British proclaimed the breadth of their imperial enterprise and sought to reaffirm ties with loyal clients through the dispensation of honours. Subsequently, princes provided opulence characterised as native at the even more elaborate Imperial Durbars held in India in 1903 and 1911 to mark the coronations of British sovereigns. King George V and Queen Mary were the first British monarchs to visit India for the 1911 Durbar, where most but not all princes competed in the lavishness of their dress, jewels and accommodations. It was here that Maharaja Sayaji Rao of Baroda achieved notoriety by allegedly challenging the British ritual order. His sartorial sins were to wear a simple white Maratha dress without the jewellery the British deemed appropriate for a prince, not to don his sash of the Order of the Star of India, and to carry a walking stick rather than a sword. Even more egregious was his perceived insult when he turned his back on his suzerain in less than the designated distance after performing a bow.[98] Charles Nuckolls says that this incident, which was initially labelled seditious, was transformed into 'bad manners' as then it could remain in the feudal context which the British felt able to control.[99] However, in an analysis of the newsreels of the Durbar, Stephen Bottomore shows that several rulers, including Begam Sultan Jahan of Bhopal, turned their back after bowing to their suzerain.[100]

Many scholars assert that the British fabricated their Indian feudal order by appropriating elements of both European and Indian traditions in order to appeal to the Indian mind – a mind that the British themselves had constructed.[101] The British also incorporated the princes (as well as Canadian and Antipodean politicians and African chiefs) into ceremonies held in Britain that were designed to affirm British superiority when Germany and the United States began to challenge it. Some princes travelled to the metropole to attend the Jubilee Celebrations of Queen Victoria in 1887 and 1897, where they would meet their suzerain in person and could appeal to her over the heads of her officials in India. These visits also helped the princes to predicate a

---

[98] Charles W. Nuckolls, 'The Durbar Incident,' *MAS* 24 (1990), pp. 529–59. In an authorised biography, the maharaja's action is described as an accident: Rice, *Sayaji Rao III*, vol. 2, pp. 16–18.

[99] Nuckolls, 'Durbar Incident', p. 559.

[100] Stephen Bottomore, ' "Have You Seen the Gaekwar Bob?": Filming the 1911 Delhi Durbar', *HJFRT* 17 (1997), pp. 330–5. On 24 November 1998 Queen Elizabeth II agreed that the Lord Chancellor, after handing her the government's speech at the opening of Parliament, could turn his back when walking away instead of walking backward: *CE*, 25 November 1998, p. A4.

[101] Cohn, 'Representing Authority', pp. 165–209: Nuckolls, 'Durbar Incident'.

Maharaja Sayaji Rao of Baroda in 1899.

special relationship with the British Crown. Several were present at the coronations in 1902, 1911 and 1937. They ranged from the youthful Ganga Singh of Bikaner, educated at Mayo College, who aspired to a broader role in the imperial political arena and attended both the 1902 and 1911 ceremonies, to Madho Singh of Jaipur who took two huge brass containers of Ganges water to

London for purification rituals in 1902. In Westminister Abbey and Bucking-
ham Palace, Indian and African clients were prized tokens of the submission
of exotic peoples to British rule.

Constitutional counterweights

After 1857 the British attempted to include the princes as least peripherally in
the constitutional structure they evolved for British India.[102] In 1861 Maharaja
Narinder Singh (r. 1845–62) of Patiala had been appointed to the Imperial
Legislative Council, and from 1906 to 1908 Ripudaman Singh, then heir of
Nabha state, also served on the Council. Neither prince distinguished himself
in this forum. In 1876 Lord Lytton had proposed a privy council of princes, but
the India Office in London feared that it would not be possible to secure parliamentary approval for the enabling legislation. In 1905 Lord Curzon revived
the proposal, linking it to princely contributions as military allies since the
twenty-five members were to be princes who had maintained Imperial Service
Troops. Lord Minto suggested a council of nobles as a possible counterweight
to Congress activities during the agitation over the Partition of Bengal in 1905.
Although some princes, most notably Madho Rao Scindia of Gwalior, lobbied
for such a council, the resistance of leading rulers such as those of Hyderabad
and Mysore, as well as political turmoil in British India, led Minto to drop this
scheme.

As mentioned earlier, Lord Hardinge had twice assembled some princes to
discuss a Higher Chiefs College. Lord Chelmsford, his successor from 1916 to
1921, continued to hold conferences of princes but broadened the topics of
discussions. Princes began to meet informally with British Indian politicians
and some British officials argued that these gatherings constituted a major and
ill-fated shift in the policy of 'subordinate isolation'. Michael O'Dwyer even
characterised them as 'encouraging them [the princes] to form themselves into
a sort of trade union' and asserted that 'it is bound to lead to intrigue between
the Chiefs and the political leaders of British India'.[103] In fact the isolation
of the princes had long been breached informally both by British-sponsored
rituals such as the imperial assemblage and coronation durbars and by private
princely ceremonies such as marriage celebrations and religious pilgrimages.

---

[102] This section is based largely on Ashton, *British Policy*, chs 1–2; Copland, *Princes*, ch. 1; Gerard
Douds, Government of Princely India, 1918–39, PhD thesis, University of Edinburgh (1979),
chs 1–2; Ramusack, *Princes*, chs 1–3.

[103] J. P. Thompson, Chief Secretary, Punjab Govt, to J. B. Wood, Political Secretary, GOI, 28 December
1917, Pro. No. 28, NAI, GOI, F&P, S-I, February 1918, Pro. Nos 28–34.

In a fascinating study of marriage patterns in Rajasthan, Frances Taft Plunkett has called attention to the importance of marriage alliances among the polygynous Rajput princes in maintaining ties with other states, not only in Rajasthan but elsewhere in Gujarat.[104] More recently, Indira Peterson has analysed how Serfoji II (r. 1798–1832) of Thanjaur used the private act of pilgrimage to Banaras from 1820 to 1822 to reaffirm his status within the framework of British colonial authority and among other princes as well as to collect religious and scientific manuscripts.[105]

There was renewed princely lobbying for a forum to discuss common problems during the negotiations preceding the Montagu-Chelmsford reforms of 1919. In response, the British inaugurated the Chamber of Princes, a consultative, advisory body, in 1921. Composed of 108 princes with salute of eleven guns or more and twelve princes who were selected to represent 127 other states, the Chamber did not fulfil most British or princely expectations. There were structural weaknesses. The viceroy was the presiding officer and set the agenda, so the princes rarely discussed what they considered difficult and sensitive issues such as minority administrations. Their resolutions were only advisory to the GOI and were subject to endless circulation within its bureaucracy.

Among the princes there were debilitating differences. Once again prominent princes, especially those from southern regions such as Hyderabad, Mysore and Travancore, disdained to participate in a group venture that they viewed as an encroachment on their sovereignty. Subsequently a coalition of western-educated princes from medium-sized states in Rajputana, western India and Punjab, most notably Ganga Singh of Bikaner, Bhupinder Singh of Patiala, Jai Singh of Alwar, Ranjitsinhji of Nawanagar, and later Nawab Hamidullah (b. 1894, r. 1926–49, d. 1960) of Bhopal, dominated the deliberations of the Chamber and its standing committee. British officials and others soon questioned the representativeness of the Chamber, some claiming it was a preserve of Rajput princes. Princely factions and personal jealousies, particularly between Ganga Singh and Bhupinder Singh, the first two chancellors of the Chamber, meant that the princes rarely spoke with a unified voice on controversial issues such as the need for a codification of British political practices to preclude what the princes perceived as excessive British intervention.

---

[104] Frances Taft Plunkett, 'Royal Marriages in Rajasthan', *CIS*, n.s. 6 (1972), pp. 64–80.

[105] Indira Viswanathan Peterson, 'Subversive Journeys? Travel as Empowerment in King Serfoji II of Tanjore's 1820–22 Pilgrimage to Benares', New England Conference of the Association for Asian Studies, Brown University, 30 September 2000.

Throughout the 1920s some assertive princes laboured to achieve a definition of paramountcy and greater security in an era of political challenges. In 1926 Lord Reading alarmed the princes with his reply to the nizam's request for the reincorporation of Berar into Hyderabad when he claimed that 'where Imperial interests are concerned or the general welfare of the people of a State is seriously and grievously affected by the action of its Government, it is with the Paramount Power that the ultimate responsibility of taking remedial action must lie'.[106] Princes feared that the welfare of state subjects opened endless opportunities for intervention. Simultaneously, some Chamber stalwarts raised economic issues. One was the impact of increased customs duties because of the institution of a protective tariff in 1922 on goods imported through British Indian ports but destined for princely states. Another was a more equitable distribution of the salt revenues collected by the GOI.

The report of the Indian States Committee appointed in 1928 by Irwin to assuage princely grievances shocked both princes and Indian nationalists, though for different reasons. Disappointed by the committee's refusal to define paramountcy, the princes were even more startled by the claim that intervention might be justified if there was a widespread popular demand within the states for changes. Although the Butler Report, so named after its chair, reaffirmed the treaty relationship of the states with the British Crown and therefore recommended that the states should not be transferred without their agreement to a responsible GOI (thereby frustrating Indian nationalists), the princes were dejected at what they saw as increased opportunities for British encroachment on their rights and prerogatives.[107] The princes had contradictory aims: wanting the benefits of closer economic ties with British India but safeguards from British interference in their internal affairs. For varying reasons the princes and the British soon viewed federation as a viable arrangement for resolving these longstanding constitutional debates.

Political partners

As Indian nationalists intensified their challenge to the British, the imperialists exploited the princes as political collaborators in all-India politics. Some princes had aroused British apprehensions because of their support for Indian nationalist leaders. The most notable example was Sayaji Rao of Baroda, who employed

---

[106] Reading to Nizam, 27 March 1926, NAI, GOI, F&P, No. 13-Political (Secret), 1924–26, Nos 1–49.

[107] Copland, *Princes*, pp. 65–71; Ramusack, *Princes*, pp. 143–52.

Indian nationalists ranging from Romesh Chandra Dutt, the moderate Bengali economist, to Aurobindo Ghose, the Bengali political philosopher who was vice-principal at Baroda College, and lesser-known Maratha activists.[108] In 1909 Minto asked residents to consult the princes on cooperative measures to contain seditious activities within their states. Several princes replied that they had strengthened their police and intelligence services and tightened control over the circulation of literature deemed seditious. They also requested the exchange of intelligence information, protection from negative press attacks on themselves and their administrations, and restrictions on religious aspects of political activities.[109]

During the 1910s the princes emerged overtly as political allies of the British, especially in the arena labelled communal politics.[110] As the British were not Hindu, Muslim or Sikh, they lacked the legitimacy that princes possessed as religious spokespersons. Thus the nizam of Hyderabad could issue a farman declaring that since the First World War was not a jihad, it was religiously permissible for Muslims to fight for the Allies against the Central Powers, who included the Ottoman Empire headed by the Muslim Caliph. When orthodox Hindus in 1917 protested against the construction of an irrigation channel at Hardwar where the sacred Ganges emerges from the Himalayas onto the north Indian plain, the British invited princes from Alwar, Banaras, Bikaner, Gwalior, Jaipur and Patiala to participate in the resolution of the dispute. All of them, except Alwar, who quoted Sanskrit legal texts that Banaras claimed were irrelevant, eventually supported a compromise that allowed a channel of free-flowing water past the bathing *ghats*, while a parallel channel serviced the irrigation system. During the early years of the war, the Punjab princes, especially Bhupinder Singh, implemented various measures to control disturbances related to the Ghadr movement, a Punjabi effort to secure German support for the overthrow of the British Government. After 1919 the Patiala ruler would increasingly collaborate with the British as Sikhs who followed the prescriptions of Guru Gobind Singh sought to wrest control over Sikh gurudwaras from Hindu *mahants*. Bhupinder Singh frequently functioned as an intermediary between the British and the leaders of the Shiromani Gurdwara Prabhandhak Committee, which achieved legal recognition and control in 1925 of Sikh gurudwaras in Punjab.[111] Not all princes participating in British Indian associations and politics served British strategies, but some continued as political collaborators until 1947.

---

[108] Copland, 'Sayaji Rao', pp. 33–40.   [109] NAI, GOI, F&P, S-I, March 1910, Pro. Nos 42–45.
[110] Ramusack, *Princes*, ch. 4.   [111] Ramusack, 'Punjab States', in Jeffrey, *People*, pp. 183–7.

CONCLUSION

From 1858 to the 1920s, the British developed a theory of indirect rule that helped to maintain hegemony in India without any further annexation and with the least possible expenditure of personnel and economic resources. Key elements included a hierarchy with the British at the apex and the princes as vassals, a system of honours, most notably the Order of the Star of India, and the salute table, which established one's rank in the hierarchy. Although the British frequently argued that such honours had particular appeal to Indians, they themselves devoted much attention to their own position in these ranking systems, which affirmed their superior status in India during a period of growing democratisation at home. Next, British officials constructed legal arguments to legitimate and to provide precedents for policy decisions regarding their princely clients. Major components were the semi-official histories by Tupper and Lee-Warner, the collections of treaties by Aitchison, the political manual by Butler, and finally the Indian States Committee Report of 1928–29. These documents would be adapted to changing imperial interests through concepts such as usage.

Although they eschewed annexation, the British continued to intervene in the internal politics of the princely states for political or economic advantage. Such intrusion ranged from advice about policies and appointments of state officials, to control over minority administrations, to the deposition of a ruler. The education of princely heirs according to British models was a more subtle means of influencing the future. Official support for intervention varied and reflected evolving British priorities and the complex interactions within the imperial chain of command.

The British corporate structure had eliminated succession struggles and enjoyed an unprecedented monopoly of military power, but that government was more factious than was generally admitted. The British theories about and policies towards the princes are an excellent prism for seeing how these differing levels of authorities actually operated. There were conflicts between Parliament and the India Office at the metropole and between the viceroy and his political secretary in the colony. Since viceroys had immediate responsibility for policies towards the princes, a succession in viceroys could mean varying magnitudes of change in policies. The most dramatic was the shift between the interventionist Curzon to the laissez-faire Minto. At the next level there were tensions between the viceroy at the centre and provincial governors, who were closer to the local situation and concerned about bureaucratic prerogatives, as in the long-term disputes between the GOI and the Bombay presidency. Finally, at the bottom there were political officers serving as political agents, AGGs, and residents who were expected to compartmentalise their professional selves into a British representative to the princes and an advocate of the princes to their overlord. They did so with differing degrees of success.

As the challenges to British power evolved, their princely clients accepted new tasks. First and foremost, the princes remained an inexpensive means of providing for the administration of large tracts of economically unproductive or geographically inaccessible areas. For an imperial power with limited monetary and personnel resources, the princes provided a key link to local levels of society. Second, the princes continued to be substantial contributors to the British imperial military establishment through the Imperial Service contingents, monetary contributions, and recruiting activities. Third, the symbolic role of the princes was enhanced. Besides their participation in ritual encounters ranging from lavish coronation durbars, the princes supplied a stage for viceregal visits and tours of the royal family that affirmed the British imperial order. Fourth, the princes could be useful allies in all-Indian and communal politics, to which their hereditary status and their financial patronage accorded access that the British lacked. So the princes continued as valued imperial clients until 1947.

CHAPTER 5

PRINCES AS MEN, WOMEN, RULERS, PATRONS, AND ORIENTAL STEREOTYPES

Indian princes played multiple roles on diverse stages. Thus their actions triggered complex and sometimes conflicting perceptions among various audiences. The last chapter documented shifting British official images of the princes from natural Indian leaders to loyal allies to naughty schoolboys. But just as British policies did not create the Indian princes as rulers, they influenced but did not circumscribe princely lives and political functions. This chapter explores what it meant to be a ruling prince in India, with particular emphasis on the period from 1870 to 1947. There are four main themes. First, the life cycle of a prince from birth through education to marriage to succession to rulership will exemplify their interlocking private and public lives. Second, an analysis of the sources of legitimacy for Indian rulers and the inconstancy of British policies will disclose opportunities for princes to manoeuvre in the interstices of indirect rule. Third, princely patronage of religious specialists and institutions, visual and performing arts, luxury crafts, secular scholarship, and sports will reveal how princes fostered cultural nationalism while fulfilling their princely dharma. Fourth, an examination of the construction of the princes as concerned, indulgent or decadent rulers, as benevolent fathers and as cunning, inept or naive politicians will detail the shifting perceptions of their disparate audiences as well as the unequal abilities, ambitions and achievements of Indian princes. These images reflect the ambiguous sources of political authority, the tangled ritual and social status of princes, and a mixture of fact and fantasy in public consciousness.

LIFE CYCLE OF A PRINCE

In princely as in most Indian families, the birth of a first son was exuberantly greeted.[1] A son was an heir to the family fortune, a supporter of his parents in old age, and in Hindu families, a crucial perfomer of rituals at the death ceremonies of parents. Since sons in princely families ensured succession that brought control of extraordinary resources, elaborate ceremonies heralded the

---

[1] Charles Allen and Sharada Dwivedi, *Lives of the Indian Princes* (London, 1984), chs 1–6 provides many examples of the patterns outlined.

birth of a first son. The beating of drums, an Indian insignia of sovereignty, and the firing of gun salutes, a British symbol of rank, accompanied public announcements to largely non-literate audiences. Other customs reflected the role of a ruler as a provider of material benefits and a fount of justice. Distributions of sweets indicated benevolence, and the release of prisoners from jails expressed justice tempered with mercy. As British power became dominant, news of a birth was communicated quickly to the colonial hierarchy. A letter or telegram of congratulations from the British sovereign and her or his representative in India authenticated legitimacy – a crucial factor since many princes had multiple wives and concubines. Subsequently there would be private ceremonies of purification and naming.

When a daughter was born, these elaborate festivities were conspicuous by their absence. Travancore and Cochin, where descent was matrilineal, were notable exceptions. There 18-gun salutes were fired for girls although boys received 21-gun salutes.[2] Another anomaly occurred in Bhopal. Upon the birth of her granddaughter, the formidable Begum Qudsia (r. 1819–37) was quick to petition British officials about the legitimacy of her succession to rule.[3] Otherwise daughters were more likely to be prized when sons had already appeared or there had been no daughters for an extended period. Female infanticide was a possibility in princely families as well as in non-ruling families, but hearsay is the most often cited evidence of this practice.

Young children in princely families resided with their mothers in the palace zenana. Many princes and princesses remember the women of the zenana and their servants as being indulgent and even fawning. When they were judged ready to become apprentices to power, sons, particularly heirs, were allocated semi-independent establishments replete with family servants. By the end of the nineteenth and especially in the twentieth century, many princely fathers followed the pattern of elite, westernised Indians and employed European, usually British, nannies, governesses and tutors. These foreigners were recruited primarily to teach English and to socialise their young charges into a western lifestyle and perhaps to offset more indulgent Indian caretakers.

Technical or applied training for ruling was unstructured. Indian tutors were mainly responsible for transmitting the history of the state and the princely dynasty and the sources of dynastic legitimacy. They were also to teach literacy and some mathematics. Then, much as a medical intern does in the early twenty-first century, heirs to princely gaddis who were titled *yuvrajs* or

---

[2] Ibid., p. 25.   [3] Khan, *Begums*, p. 83.

*tikka sahib*s might spend a few years in various state departments learning administrative routines. More important was touring within the state, sometimes done in conjunction with hunting excursions, a traditional means of developing appropriate masculine and royal skills in deploying weapons and conspicuously displaying physical courage.

After 1858 when the British began to endorse the princes as natural leaders of their peoples, they evinced more concern over their education. Other factors were also influential. One was the debate in Britain over the proper education for elite British men who were to rule at home and in an empire abroad. The other was the growing British disdain for the western-educated Bengalis, whom the British deemed effeminate and alienated from other Indians because of inappropriate education. Although British anxiety to mould princes as clients responsive to their political needs is evident, it is less apparent why Indian princes responded to British initiatives. Possibly these allies wanted to ensure that their heirs learned how to function effectively within the British system of indirect rule.

Many princes who played significant political roles in the twentieth century were educated at chiefs' colleges, such as Bhupinder Singh of Patiala at Aitchison College. But several princely families continued to educate their sons at home with Indian and western tutors, such as Ganga Singh of Bikaner who had a British tutor, Sir Brian Egerton, for three years after a five-year stint at Mayo College in Ajmer.[4] By the 1930s and 1940s, new patterns emerged. Some princes went to the Doon School, which had been established in 1935 as a boarding school for elite Indians from British Indian provinces. In 1942 Maharaja Karan Singh of Kashmir started a four-year stay at the Doon School that left him with vivid memories of inedible food, high academic standards and a rigorous regime of sports.[5] Some Indian princes went to England for their education with mixed results. Maharaja Mayurdhwajsinhji (later Meghrajji III) of Dhrangadhara enrolled in Haileybury 'on the theory that "since the Indian public schools were imitations of the schools in England, why go to an imitation and not to the original?" '[6]

Although princes received ruling powers at younger ages in the early nineteenth century, the British gradually established 18 to 21 as the age of investiture for princes who had succeeded as minors. They maintained that the higher age allowed for the training and personal maturity essential to fulfil the responsibilities of a ruler. But the appropriate age for investiture remained

---

[4] K. M. Panikkar, *His Highness The Maharaja of Bikaner: A Biography* (London, 1937), note by Egerton, pp. 46–9.

[5] Singh, *Heir Apparent*, pp. 24–7.   [6] Allen and Dwivedi, *Lives*, p. 121.

a hotly debated topic among the princes, their advisers, and British political officers.

First marriages for princes occurred from around 12 onward. As was common practice throughout Indian society, marriages were alliances of families and were carefully arranged to reinforce or enhance political, ritual, social and economic status. Some marriages maintained longstanding ties between families. Maharaja Man Singh II of Jaipur was married at 12 to an older princess from Jodhpur and then at 21 to her niece, continuing traditional matrimonial liaisons between Jaipur and Jodhpur.[7] Modern political objectives were also influential. Maharaja Yadavindra Singh of Patiala was married in 1931 at the age of 20 to a princess of Seraikella. Then in 1938, after succeeding his father, he married Mohinder Kaur, the daughter of a popular political leader.[8] Some princes, such as Nizam Osman Ali Khan of Hyderabad, went much further afield. In 1931, to enhance his credentials as a Muslim ruler, he married his first son to the daughter of the last Caliph of Islam and his second son to the great-great-granddaughter of Sultan Murad V of the Ottoman Empire.

Some princes and princesses chose not to enter arranged marriages, and these exceptions precipitated social or political crises. Princess Indira of Baroda, the daughter of the reputedly progressive Sayaji Rao, rejected the alliance proposed by her parents with Maharaja Madho Rao Scindia of Gwalior, who was many years her senior. Such a union of the two most powerful Maratha ruling families would have made the headstrong Indira a second wife expected to maintain purdah. She chose instead to marry the heir to the gaddi of Cooch Behar and become a highly publicised hostess in London and Calcutta. Ironically her daughter, Gayatri Devi, accepted the proposal of Man Singh of Jaipur to become his third wife and to observe purdah within Jaipur state.[9]

Even more problematic were those princes who chose to marry European, American or Australian women. Both Britons and Indians censured miscegenation. British society in India viewed white women who were sexually attracted to Indian men, and thus subverting the colonial hierarchy, as overtly betraying the imperial mission and covertly undermining claims of British masculinity and Indian male effeminacy. During the nineteenth century miscegenation was disparaged in official discourse and literature and during the twentieth century in novels translated into films and video series such as *The Rains Came*,

---

[7] Joshi, *Polygamy*, p. 46.

[8] Christiane Hurtig, *Les Maharajahs et la politique dans l'Inde contemporaine* (Paris, 1988), pp. 284–5.

[9] Gayati Devi of Jaipur and Santha Rama Rao, *A Princess Remembers: The Memoirs of the Maharani of Jaipur* (Philadelphia, 1976), chs 8–10.

Heat and Dust, and *The Jewel in the Crown*, where the fate of the transgressing woman was usually death.[10] For Indian princes, there was the question of the legality of marriages between Hindu men and non-Hindu women and the legitimacy of children born in such relationships. Both state officials and British political officers opposed these unions as straining bonds between a ruler and his subjects.

Despite and perhaps partly because of such objections, a few ruling princes married non-Indian women. The most prominent examples were the rulers of Kapurthala, Pudukkottai and Indore. In 1910 Maharaja Jagatjit Singh of Kapurthala married Anita Delgrada, a Spanish dancer, whom some of his relatives as well as the British never recognised as a legal wife or a maharani. Jagatjit Singh's heir and his European-educated Rajput daughter-in-law refused to meet or attend functions with Delgrada,[11] while in 1921, at an official reception, a British political officer took care to direct the Spanish woman to an alcove carefully screened with palms from the British gaze.[12] Beyond these social snubs, the maharaja of Kapurthala was not affected politically by this relationship, though Delgrada's sentiments are unknown. Two other Indian princes experienced political repercussions. Like Jagatjit Singh, Raja Martanda Bhairava Tondaiman (b. 1875, r. 1894–1928) travelled extensively in Europe and decided to marry an Australian woman, Molly Fink. Although British and local Indian opinion agreed that such a marriage would not be considered orthodox and children from it could not succeed to the throne, Martanda Tondaiman married Molly in 1915. After an alleged attempt to poison her in Pudukkottai and extended stays in Australia, Martanda asked to abdicate in return for a pension. Nicholas Dirks has highlighted the ultimate irony in this situation since the British had sought to remove the raja from the influence of the zenana by education in Europe, preparing the stage for the marriage that separated the ruler from his state.[13] Maharaja Yeshwant Rao Holkar (b. 1908, r. 1926–48) of Indore had two American wives sequentially. The second one, whom he had married in 1943, produced a son, Richard Shivaji Rao Holkar, whom the GOI recognised as legitimate in 1950.[14] But Richard did not succeed to the title of maharaja when his father died in 1961.

---

[10] Prem Chowdhry, *Colonial India and the Making of Empire Cinema: Image, Ideology and Identity* (Manchester, 2000), pp. 205–10.

[11] Brinda, Maharani of Kapurthala, *Maharani: The Story of an Indian Princess*, As Told to Elaine Williams (New York, 1953), pp. 112–13.

[12] Conrad Corfield, *The Princely India I Knew: From Reading to Mountbatten* (Madras, 1975), p. 17.

[13] Dirks, *Hollow Crown*, pp. 391–6.   [14] Copland, *Princes*, pp. 93–4, 267.

RULERSHIP

Two ceremonies that solemnised succession illuminate the multiple sources of princely authority and legitimacy. Upon the death of a ruler, his heir was installed on the gaddi. Subsequently there was a separate ceremony when the successor was invested with full ruling powers. Using over twenty-five oral interviews with former ruling Maratha princes in central India and Rajputs in Rajasthan and central India, Adrian Mayer has analysed installation protocols and princely perceptions of the nature of their authority. In their ceremonies and symbols of sovereignty, there were similiarites and differences between Maratha and Rajput princes.[15] Since there is no comparable analysis of the succession ceremonies of Sikh and Muslim rulers, the following discussion is mainly about Hindu princes.

Shortly after the death of a ruling Hindu prince and before his body was removed for the funeral procession, an accession ceremony confirmed the heir as successor. This rite involved the placing of a tilak, a vertical line sweeping up the centre of the forehead from the eyebrows to the hairline, made by a thumb usually with kumkum, a red powder. Generally the new ruler remained seated on the gaddi in the palace during the funeral procession.[16] Since the accession ceremony was held quickly and privately, there is little evidence that a British representative attended. Upon completion of a 12-day period of mourning, the new ruler would be publicly installed in a ceremony with an affusion (*abhisheka*) and enthronement. The affusion, a sprinkling of the new prince with consecrated substances ranging from clarified butter, milk, curds and honey to sanctified water, represents an element of continuity with a practice recorded in classic texts marking the installation of Hindu kings.[17] The affusion had an important place in Maratha installation ceremonies, possibly because of an association with Shivaji, but it was also performed in an abbreviated version for Rajput princes. This ritual is said to give the ruler some degree of sacredness but not to transform him into a deity.[18]

The enthronement had two crucial aspects. The first one was the application of a *rajatilaka*, which was possibly more significant for Rajput rulers than for Marathas. In several Rajput states, such as Jaipur and Dungarpur, an *adivasi*, or

---

[15] Adrian C. Mayer, 'Rulership and Divinity: The Case of the Modern Hindu Prince and Beyond', *MAS* 25 (1991), pp. 765–90.

[16] Adrian C. Mayer, 'The King's Two Thrones', *Man* (n.s.) 20 (1985), p. 215.

[17] J. Gonda, *Ancient Indian Kingship from the Religious Point of View* (Leiden, 1969); J. C. Heesterman, *The Inner Conflict of Tradition: Essays in Indian Ritual, Kingship, and Society* (Chicago, 1985); Ronald Inden, 'Ritual, Authority, and Cyclic Time in Hindu Kingship', in Richards, *Kingship*, pp. 47–52.

[18] Mayer, 'Rulership', pp. 767–73.

representative of another indigenous group antecedent to the formation of the state, inscribed the rajatilaka to symbolise their acceptance of the sovereignty of the prince. These men traditionally applied blood from a cut in their thumb, but kumkum was the more usual substance. In Gwalior, perhaps appropriately considering Maharaja Madho Rao Scindia's success in investing in Indian stocks, the rajatilaka was made with a gold coin, a symbol of Lakhsmi, the goddess of wealth.

The second element of an installation was the ascension of the gaddi. Although a gaddi can mean either a cotton stuffed cushion or a family home, it has been used in this book to indicate a *rajgaddi*, an ensemble of cushion with cotton or silk coverings that was the Hindu equivalent of a European throne. Usually a rajgaddi was on the floor, but sometimes it was placed on a chair of wood, silver or stone. Mayer has described how in most Hindu states the rajgaddi was viewed as a female deity who imbued the rajgaddi with her *sakti* or life force. When a prince was enthroned on the rajgaddi and his body was in direct contact with it, sanctified royal qualities were transmitted to him. The rajgaddi was the key symbol of the state, the ground of the guardian deities of the state. Mayer claimed that the rajgaddhi 'was believed to maintain and protect the kingdom and to carry the kingship over [an] interregnum, as well as to give the ruler his royal divinity'.[19] Being seated on it was therefore the defining moment in the installation ceremony for both Rajput and Maratha rulers.

As their system of indirect rule evolved, the British proclaimed their authority over succession in the installation and investiture ceremonies. The first step was to arrogate to themselves the right to determine who was the legitimate heir. Debates over succession were frequent when rulers had several wives and concubines or did not have a legitimate son. Dalhousie's doctrine of lapse tried to deny the right to adopt those princes whose states the British claimed to have created, but after the revolt of 1857 the British allowed adoptions if they had imperial sanction. At the same time they staked a claim to jurisdiction over all successions. In 1916 the GOI evoked a sharp retort from the princes when they reaffirmed that

> Every succession required the approval and sanction of government.
> It is essential that such approval and sanction should be announced in a formal installation durbar by a representative of the British Government.[20]

---

[19] Mayer, 'King's Two Thrones', p. 217.
[20] *Proceedings of the Conference of Ruling Princes and Chiefs: Held at Delhi on the 30th October 1916 and Following Days* (Delhi, 1916), p. 7.

In response to vociferous protests from the princes, the British conceded that installation and investiture durbars should be held in the name of the princes and that the British representative should be seated as the chief guest at the right hand of the presiding prince.[21] Although this dispute might appear as one over symbols, it revealed princely fears of imperial encroachment on their autonomy just when they confronted new challenges from political activists.

Princely families, as do most Hindu families, have tutelary deities whose blessings are sought daily and during crucial life cycle ceremonies.[22] But many Hindu princes had intense relationships with pan-Indian and regional deities and divine qualities that were important sources of legitimacy. Some Rajput princes claimed descent from the gods of sun (Surya) and moon (Chandra). Sages in a fire-sacrifice allegedly created the Agnikul Rajput clans. Many Hindu rulers were associated with Vishnu or Siva. Because of Martanda Varma's dedication of Travancore state to Lord Padmanabha, an incarnation of Vishnu, his successors conceived of themselves as the *dasa* or servants, constitutionally and symbolically, of Lord Padmanabha.[23] The maharaja of Bikaner declared himself to be the prime minister of Lord Lakshminarayan, an avatar of Krishna, while the Rajput ruler of Mandi in the Himalayas considered himself the diwan of Vishnu. The maharana of Udaipur was the servant of Siva in his manifestation as Eklinga, where Siva's linga has one face. The maharaja of Banaras, an eighteenth-century little king whom the British declared to be a ruling prince in 1911, is viewed as the representative of Siva, the lord of the ancient city of Kasi now known as Banaras or Varanasi. But these divine commitments were not restrictive. While they retained their commitment to Siva, the maharajas of Banaras became the dominant patron of the public recitation of the *Ramayana* and the dramatic performance of the Ramlila that honour Rama, an incarnation of Vishnu.[24]

Reflecting the complex network of divinity within the Hindu tradition, Hindu rulers might call upon more than one divine source for legitimacy and as a role model. Maharaja Vikramsinhrao of Dewas Senior (b. 1910, r. 1937–47, adopted as the maharaja of Kolhapur, 1947 and ruled as Chhatrapati Shahaji II

[21] Ramusack, *Princes*, pp. 69–77.
[22] Lindsey Harlan analysed the relationship between women and these tutelary deities in *Religion and Rajput Women: The Ethic of Protection in Contemporary Narratives* (Berkeley CA, 1992).
[23] Koji Kawashima, *Missionaries and a Hindu State, Travancore 1858–1936* (Delhi, 1998), pp. 18–23.
[24] Philip Lutgendorf, 'Ram's Story in Shiva's City: Public Arenas and Private Patronage', in Sandria B. Freitag (ed.), *Culture and Power in Banaras: Community, Performance, and Environment, 1899–1980* (Berkeley CA, 1989), pp. 34–61.

until 1949) reflected on his appropriation of Rama in an extended series of interviews with Adrian Mayer. Vikramsinhrao argued that Rama embodied a utopian world where a ruler could be passive and simply follow rules. This world did not exist during the dark age of the *kaliyuga*. Now Krishna, the shrewd manipulator for his allies in the *Mahabharata*, was a better model. Krishna and Indian princes had to use *danda*, literally a stick but metaphorically power, to achieve equity for their subjects. Thus Vikramsinhrao offered an explanation for the legitimacy of overriding laws and regulations, ostensibly to achieve the greater good of the people. The model of sensual Krishna also permitted rulers considerable latitude in their personal sexual lives as long as they fulfilled their duties as a righteous ruler.[25] However, as clients of the British imperial patron, the princes had to live with significant constraints on their use of danda and on some aspects of their personal lives. Late Victorian British officials were not sympathetic to Krishna as a sexual role model for Indian princes.

Because of their concepts of one, indivisible god, Sikh and Muslim princes differed from their Hindu counterparts in their claims to divinity. The Sikh rulers of the Phulkian states asserted the blessings of Guru Gobind Singh, the tenth and last guru of Sikhism. A few Muslim rulers such as the nizams of Hyderabad and the nawabs of Pataudi and Malerkotla traced their descent to Sufi *shaikhs* or mystical holy men. Muslim princes also evoked religious legitimacy through the protection and patronage of indigenous and pan-Indian Muslim religious institutions.

PRINCES AS PATRONS

A prime component of rajadharma was to bestow gifts. Even though the princes might be political clients in relationship to a British patron, they continued to act as patrons to multiple constituencies. These groups include religious specialists and institutions such as temples, mosques, schools and pilgrimage sites; visual artists, especially painters and architects; secular scholars in literature, language, history and archaeology; musicians and dancers; artisans who produced luxury crafts; and sportsmen. Through their patronage the princes were active, if unconscious, creators of cultural idioms that shaped regional and national identities and of public arenas for popular imagination of a national community.

---

[25] Adrian C. Mayer, 'Perceptions of Princely Rule: Perspectives from a Biography', in T. N. Madan (ed.), *Way of Life: King, Householder, Renouncer: Essays in Honour of Louis Dumont* (New Delhi, 1982), pp. 127–54; Mayer, 'Rulership', pp. 783–7.

Religious practices and institutions

Princes nourished religious activities within and beyond their states, further evidence that the British policy of isolating the princes was never as rigorous as represented. Pan-Indian endowments included those of Hindu rulers to sacred pilgrimage sites such as Banaras where they built bathing ghats on the banks of the Ganges for the use of pilgrims and those that the Sikh princes distributed to sites associated with the ten gurus such as the Golden Temple in Amritsar. Besides supporting Muslim mosques and their attached *madrasas*, Indian Muslim rulers, most notably those of Hyderabad and Bhopal, bestowed grants to holy places in Mecca and Medina.

In the late nineteenth century, princely patrons were quick to respond to fresh opportunities such as educational institutions established to reform and revitalise religious learning. The rulers of Hyderabad, Bhopal, Rampur and Patiala endowed the Muhammadan Anglo-Oriental College at Aligarh (founded 1875) to synthesise religious instruction with western secular education.[26] During the 1910s Bhupinder Singh of Patiala contributed Rs 5 lakhs to the new Banaras Hindu University, while the maharajas of Alwar, Jodhpur, Kashmir and Mysore each initially gave 1 lakh.[27] With their contributions to Sikh, Hindu and Muslim institutions, the princes of Patiala were notable examples of the cultural pluralism of royal patronage, but rulers tended to bolster their own religious and ethnic communities. Hyderabad, Bhopal and Rampur subsidised the Muslim seminary at Deoband in the United Provinces, which imparted rigorous instruction in Muslim religious texts and socialised its graduates to foster a reformed Indian Islam among all classes of Muslims.[28] Princes in western India, especially the brahman chiefs of Jamkhandi, Ichalkaranji and Miraj Senior, the Maratha rulers of Baroda, Kolhapur and Mudhol, and the Rajput prince of Gondal accounted for over half of the contributions to the Deccan Education Society between 1884 and 1910. Maharaja Shahu Chhatrapati I of Kolhapur fostered education among Maratha non-brahmans and provided job quotas for them in his bureaucracy.[29] Size of state was no indication of generosity since the chief of Ichalkaranji gave Rs 44 640, while the gaekwad of Baroda gave Rs 1000 to the Deccan Education Society.[30] All the

---

[26] David Lelyveld, *Aligarh's First Generation: Muslim Solidarity in British India* (Princeton NJ, 1978), pp. 139–41, 156, 184, 315.

[27] Ramusack, *Princes*, pp. 49–50.

[28] Barbara Daly Metcalf, *Islamic Revival in British India: Deoband, 1860–1900* (Princeton NJ, 1982), pp. 96, 116, 299.

[29] Richard I. Cashman, *The Myth of the Lokamanya: Tilak and Mass Politics in Maharashtra* (Berkeley CA, 1975), pp. 115–17.

[30] Ibid., pp. 100–2.

Sikh states, but especially Patiala and Nabha, donated to the Khalsa College in Amritsar, an institution designed to synthesise Sikh religious instruction and western learning. On the one hand these princely donations cultivated religious specialists and competent administrators. On the other hand princes strove to keep these institutions and their students away from anti-British demonstrations. Several princes tried to persuade the trustees of the Aligarh college to reject Gandhi's pleas to practise non-cooperation in 1920; the nizam tried to remove the director of the Deoband seminary, who was sympathetic to the civil disobedience movement in 1930; and Bhupinder Singh of Patiala urged students at Khalsa College to avoid political agitation.[31]

Printing presented a modern alternative to past patronage of copying and translations of sacred and literary works. With the possibility of mass production, princes now sponsored the publication of sacred works ranging from the Qur'an to the Guru Granth. Some rulers such as the nawabs of Tonk and Rampur amassed substantial collections of manuscripts, which are of great value to contemporary scholars.[32]

Princes were also attracted to communal associations. Some support was symbolic. Maharaja Sayaji Rao of Baroda chaired a session of the Arya Samaj, a Hindi revivalist reform organisation, at Ranoli on 26 February 1911 and declared that he welcomed 'the work of social enlightenment of the masses which the missionary zeal of the Arya Samaj has undertaken'.[33] The maharajas of Alwar, Bikaner, Kashmir and Patiala endorsed the Kshatriya Mahasabha, which fostered a militant image of Hinduism, as well as the interests of kshatriya caste groups, of which these princes consider themselves exemplary members. For example, in November 1924 Jai Singh chaired a session of the Kshatriya Mahasabha in Delhi and reminded his audience of their religious duties to protect the weak and to preserve the Hindu tradition. Later Jai Singh and Tej Singh of Alwar and Kishan Singh of Bharatpur actively cultivated the Hindu Mahasahba and the Sanatan Dharma Sabha outside and within their states. In January 1927 Jai Singh presided over the Fourth Provincial Sanatan Dharma Conference at Multan and buttressed his words with a donation of Rs 40 000.[34] Within Alwar he used these Hindu associations to legitimate a strong monarchy and to nurture a Hindu nationalism that represented Meos, a liminal group who drew from both Hindu and Muslim traditions, as Muslims and outsiders.[35] Eventually Tej Singh, his successor, appointed N. B. Khare, a former president

---

[31] Ramusack, *Princes*, pp. 107–8 on Aligarh, ibid., p. 163 on Hyderabad, and Ramusack, 'Punjab States', pp. 182–83 on Patiala.
[32] Metcalf, *Islamic Revival*, pp. 53–4.   [33] Quoted in Rice, *Sayaji Rao* III, vol. 2, p. 138.
[34] Ramusack, *Princes*, pp. 158–60.   [35] Mayaram, *Resisting Regimes*, passim.

of the Hindu Mahasahba, as prime minister. In 1947 there were rumours that Alwar provided facilities for the training of members of the militant Rashtriya Swayamsevak Sangh (RSS) and a refuge for the assassins of Gandhi. Although the maharaja and Khare were subsequently exonerated of this charge,[36] the rulers of Alwar and Bharatpur supported the Hindu Mahasahba and the RSS during the trauma of partition.[37]

My own research has explored the considerable role of Maharaja Bhupinder Singh in the formation and subsequent activities of the Shiromani Gurdwara Parbhandhak Committee (SGPC). Initiated in 1920 and legally recognised in 1925, the SGPC was a committee of 175 men who controlled the gurudwaras in Punjab. Although he was never dominant, Bhupinder Singh, his son (Yadavindra Singh) and a grandson (Amarindar Singh) would function as intermediaries between colonial and independent central governments in New Delhi and this powerful communication and patronage network.[38]

Princely support for Muslim *anjumans*, which could be cultural, educational or political associations, and the Muslim League is not well researched. Lucien Benichou has emphasised that the nizams of Hyderabad had promoted religious toleration and until the mid-1940s avoided cultivating distinctly communal Muslim organisations.[39]

Education and medical aid for women

Princes and their consorts aided institutions for women. Foremost among the beneficiaries was the National Association for Supplying Female Medical Aid to the Women of India or the Dufferin Fund, as it came to be called after the vicereine Lady Dufferin, its founder. Established in 1885, this institution provided medical training for women, medical assistance for women in institutional settings, and trained nurses and midwives. About Rs 70 000, almost half of its initial endowment of Rs 148 344, came from princes who contributed at least Rs 500 each to become life councillors. By 1886 Mysore had the first branch of the Dufferin Fund in a princely state,[40] and Dufferin hospitals were built in other princely states. Maharaja Madho Singh of Jaipur gave Rs 135 000 to the Dufferin Fund from 1885 to 1902, with the stipulation that it be used for women in purdah, and Rs 10 000 to Lady Minto's

---

[36] V. P. Menon, *The Story of the Integration of the Indian States* (London, 1956), pp. 253–4.
[37] Mayaram, *Resisting Regimes*, ch. 6. [38] Ramusack, 'Punjab States'.
[39] Lucien D. Benichou, *From Autocracy to Integration: Political Developments in Hyderabad State (1938–1948)* (Chennai, 2000).
[40] Maneesha Lal, 'The Politics of Gender and Medicine in Colonial India: The Countess of Dufferin Fund, 1885–1888', *BHM* 68 (1994), pp. 35–6.

Nursing Fund in 1918.[41] When vicereine Hardinge appealed to 'her friends amongst the Ruling Chiefs' for funds to establish a women's medical college in New Delhi to attract 'women of the right type', Jaipur granted Rs 3 lakhs, the largest donation. As the major princely donors, including Jaipur, Gwalior, Patiala, Hyderabad, Udaipur, Jodhpur and Kotah, did not have a reputation for being socially progressive, it seems the concept of an institution that could be feminist in its support for women's professional education appealed to princes whose female relatives lived in various forms of purdah. It also might be polit- ically inexpedient to deny a vicereine.[42] Evincing regional variations, the ruler of Travancore, where purdah was not observed, established a scholarship for women at the co-educational Madras Medical College.[43]

The patronage of women in princely families focused on medicine and edu- cation. Jadonji Maharani, a wife of Madho Singh of Jaipur, gave Rs 1 lakh to the Lady Minto's Nursing Fund in 1907.[44] It is noteworthy that her gift occurred shortly after the fund was started and over a decade before that of her husband. The begum of Bhopal and maharanis of Gwalior provided small contributions to the Lady Hardinge Medical College.[45] Schools for girls were early recipients of princely largess. Maharani Suniti Devi of Cooch Behar and her sister, both daughters of Keshub Chandra Sen, a leader of the Brahmo Samaj, financed the Maharani School, established in 1908 in Darjeeling. Begum Sultan Jahan of Bhopal was variously president of the All-India Muslim Ladies Conference and the All-India Women's Conference, which promoted education for women.[46] The first chancellor of the MAO College at Aligarh, in 1916 she chided her audience:

No less important than the education of the male members of your community is the education of the weaker sex . . . Female education has been a part of your programme from the very outset and there had been a deal of talk about it for more than a quarter of a century. But these efforts have been too spasmodic to produce any appreciable good.[47]

Princesses from Bharatpur, Dharampur, Indore, Limbdi, Nawanagar, Phaltan, Porbandar and Wadhwan each contributed Rs 1000 to the Shreemati Nathibai Damodar Thackersey Indian Women's University that D. K. Karve had

---

[41] Sarkar, *History*, p. 376. [42] 'Lady Harding Hospital', *JAMWI* 5 (February 1916), pp. 33–4.
[43] Countess of Dufferin Fund, Twenty-eighth Report of the Madras Branch (Madras, 1914), p. 53, OIOC, ST/84.
[44] Sarkar, *History*, p. 376. [45] 'Lady Hardinge', p. 34.
[46] Siobhan Lambert-Hurley, Contesting Seclusion: The Political Emergence of Muslim Women in Bhopal, 1901–1930, PhD thesis, University of London (1998); Khan, *Begums*, pp. 179–80.
[47] Speech delivered in March 1916 at Aligarh, *Speeches of Indian Princes* (Allahabad, n.d.), p. 45.

established in 1916, first in Poona and then in Bombay.[48] It is difficult to determine how autonomous princely women were as patrons or what were the sources of their funds. Their male relatives might have promoted such philanthropic activities to acquire prestige in the colonial hierarchy through honours and titles for themselves or their female relatives. But there was a longstanding pan-Indian custom that one aspect of queenly dharma was to patronise religious and social service institutions.[49]

Literature and history

In literary studies and historical research, the sacred and the secular are closely intertwined. In south India the maharajas of Mysore and Travancore accumulated substantial collections of Sanskrit manuscripts, while in north India the maharajas of Baroda, Bikaner, Kashmir, Jaisalmer and Jodhpur and their subjects (especially Jains and other mercantile communities) gathered significant libraries.[50] By 1874 the Bikaner Library held 1400 manuscripts that Dr G. Buhler, then an education inspector on special duty in Rajputana, characterised as 'a good deal of trash, a few nearly unique, and a dozen or two of rare works. Its strongest points are the Vedas, Dharmasastra or sacred law, Samgita, or the art of singing and dancing, and Mantra'.[51] During the 1910s Sayaji Rao of Baroda began to assemble Sanskrit manuscripts that became the core of the Oriental Institute of Baroda. To extend access, Benoytosh Bhattacharya began to edit, annotate and publish selected Sanskrit works in the Gaekwad's Oriental Series.[52]

A relatively unexplored area is the princely role in the construction of Indian history. The analysis of Indian historiography that sought to forge a nationalist identity has paid little attention to the princely states, or to whether a similar construction of Indian or nationalist identity was occurring where colonial power was one level removed.[53] Once again we have only stray bits of information. First, some princes such as those in Baroda and Patiala patronised

[48] SNDT Indian Women's University, *Silver Jubilee Souvenir* (1942), pp. 57–8.
[49] Joshi, *Polygamy*, pp. 131–2.
[50] Donald Clay Johnson, 'German Influences on the Development of Research Libraries in Nineteenth Century Bombay,' *SALNQ* 19–20 (Fall 1985/Spring 1986), pp. 25–6.
[51] Memorandum by Dr G. Buhler, NAI, GOI, Home-Public A, June 1876, nos. 143–4. Buhler would later produce an influential translation of the Laws of Manu.
[52] Rice, *Sayaji Rao* III, vol. 2, pp. 153–6; Gaekwad, *Sayajirao*, pp. 302–4.
[53] Two examples are Partha Chatterjee, *Nationalist Thought and the Colonial World: A Derivative Discourse?* (London, 1986) and Gyanendra Pandey, *The Construction of Communalism in Colonial North India* (Delhi, 1990).

scholars who wrote on the history of their regions, their dynasties and their religions. Second, a few princes joined nationalist efforts to shape icons for an Indian nation. Maharaja Sayaji Rao of Baroda and the chiefs of Ichalkaranji and Vishalgad, two feudatories of Kolhapur state, contributed to memorialise Shivaji, the Maratha hero, but many princes, such as Maharaja Shahu Chhatrapati of Kolhapur, refused support for the projection of a militant Shivaji.[54] More Maratha princes donated to commemorate M. G. Ranade, a mid-nineteenth-century moderate Maratha reformer and nationalist, rather than giving to the Shivaji Fund.[55] Their generosity might reflect that Ranade allegedly said that 'what is happening in the States is of even greater sociological interest than [what is] happening in British India. For the heart of India . . . beats in the Indian States'.[56]

Besides histories and heroes, museums and archaeological sites shaped Indian identity. Princes erected museums that housed disparate exhibits including indigenous flora and fauna, Indian painting and sculpture, European visual arts and industrial gadgets. In 1886 Maharaja Madho Singh opened the Jaipur Museum in Albert Hall, an Indo-Saracenic structure built specifically to be a museum. It contained Indian industrial exhibits as well as arts and antiquities.[57] In 1922 Maharaja Sayaji Rao of Baroda inaugurated a museum although his private collection of mainly modern Indian art had been available for public viewing since 1912.[58] Support for archaeology came in various forms. In September 1887 in his opening speech to the Mysore Representative Assembly, the diwan reported on the state-funded collection of inscriptions and proposed a 'complete' archaeological survey that would include illustrations but also conservation and restoration of buildings and monuments. He concluded that 'these undertakings cannot, it is hoped, fail to give life to the *national history* and lead to a great appreciation of *local interests*'.[59] A few princes subsidised the publication of opulent volumes on major archaeological and historical sites located within their states. The rulers of Bhopal supported volumes on Sanchi, a major Buddhist stupa and pilgrimage site within its territory, and the nizam of Hyderabad financially underwrote some volumes

---

[54] Cashman, *Myth*, pp. 106–15.   [55] Ibid., p. 112.

[56] Quoted by K. Natarajan, editor of *Indian Social Reformer*, when he presided over the Indian States' People's Conference at Delhi on 3 February 1934: N. Mitra, *IAR*, vol. I, January–June 1934 (Calcutta, 1934), p. 356.

[57] Metcalf *Imperial Vision*, pp. 133–5; Barbara N. Ramusack, 'Tourism and Icons: The Packaging of the Princely States of Rajasthan', in Catherine B. Asher and Thomas R. Metcalf (eds), *Perceptions of South Asia's Visual Past* (New Delhi, 1994), pp. 238–9.

[58] Gaekwad, *Sayajirao*, pp. 326–31.

[59] Printed Address, 30 September 1887, included in volume entitled *Proceedings of the Mysore Representative Assembly, 1881–1886*, KSA, B 20,451. Emphasis added.

on Ajanta and Ellora.[60] Since all three sites were either Buddhist, Hindu or Jain, the patronage of these Muslim rulers implied a pluralist, Indian cultural heritage. In the context of Southeast Asia, Benedict Anderson has argued that 'monumental archaeology, increasingly linked to tourism, allowed the state to appear as the guardian of a generalised, but also local, Tradition'. Then print capitalism disseminated archaeological reports and lavishly illustrated books that provided a 'pictorial census of the state's patrimony'.[61] Anderson claims that the colonial state used museums and archaeological sites to legitimate its exercise of power and that post-colonial states continued this practice. In India princes patronised museums and lavishly printed books on cultural sites as modern means of legitimating their authority and demonstrating princely dharma in a rapidly changing political context.

Visual and performing arts

For many centuries Indian rulers were generous patrons of architecture, sculpture and painting. Such support was a crucial aspect of kingly dharma and affirmed *izzat* (honour) and legitimacy.[62] Moreover, Hindu rulers, the Delhi Sultans and the Mughals, particularly Akbar, Jahangir and Shah Jahan, used architecture and painting to publicise their claims to absolute authority legitimated by semi-divine status. Mughal forts, palaces, gardens and tombs were physical representations of Mughal power strategically placed throughout conquered and incorporated territories.[63] In painting, portraits depicted Mughal emperors with halos indicating semi-divine status, as sources of light, and even standing on an hourglass and thus controlling time. Illustrations to imperial histories such as the *Akbarnama* showed emperors victorious in battle and supervising the construction of impressive forts and gardens. From the seventeenth century onward, Rajput rulers and successor princes blended Mughal and Hindu symbols of authority in architecture and painting.

Recent scholarship has reversed earlier judgements that Rajput patrons rather ineptly imitated imperial, whether Mughal or British, models in the

[60] John Marshall and Alfred Foucher, *The Monuments of Sanchi*, 3 vols (Calcutta, 1940–41); Vasudev Vishnu Mirashi (ed.), *Vakataka Inscription in Cave XVI at Ajanta*, Hyderabad Archaeological Series, no. 14 (Calcutta, 1941); Ghulam Yazdani, *Ajanta: The Colour and Monochrome Reproductions of the Ajanta Frescoes Based on Photography*, 4 vols (London, 1930–55).

[61] Benedict Anderson, *Imagined Communities: Reflections on the Origin and Spread of Nationalism*, rev. edn (London, 1991), pp. 181–2.

[62] Edward S. Haynes, 'Patronage for the Arts and the Rise of Alwar State', in Schomer, *Idea*, vol. 2, pp. 265–89.

[63] Catherine B. Asher, *The New Cambridge History of India, I: 4 Architecture of Mughal India* (Cambridge, 1992).

visual arts. In architecture Catherine Asher and G. H. R. Tillotson have emphasised that Mughal elements were incorporated within a Rajput frame of reference.[64] Thus the great Rajput forts at Amber, Jodhpur, Bundi and Gwalior are creative syntheses of imperial and local forms. During the late nineteenth century Rajput princes responded yet again to the architectural models of an imperial overlord. Although the British initially favoured classical styles recalling the imperial legacy of Rome, by the 1870s British engineers and architects had developed the Indo-Saracenic style as more suitable for public buildings serving Indians. Thomas Metcalf has documented this style, which combined Indic-Hindu elements such as lavish ornamentation and Muslim-Saracenic ones, especially arches and domes. He argues that the British believed that appropriate architecture influenced character and that the Indo-Saracenic style was particularly fitting for princely palaces and museums.[65] The former would be the setting for British imperial rituals, especially viceregal and imperial visits where banquets required new kinds of spaces, and the latter would display a reconstruction of the historical past of the state and the collecting habits of a ruler. On the one hand Sayaji Rao and Ganga Singh, princes eager to display their commitment to their imperial patron, used the Indo-Saracenic style when building Lakshmi Vilas Palace in Baroda and Lallgarh Palace at Bikaner. On the other hand Maharajas Ram Singh II and Madho Singh of Jaipur, generous patrons of Swinton Jacob, the high priest of Indo-Saracenic architecture, were careful to exclude this imposition of imperial cultural hegemony from their personal world of the City Palace. They confined the Indo-Saracenic style to public buildings such as Albert Hall for the Jaipur Museum and Rambagh Palace, their guest house for European visitors.

Other princes were more overt in their rejection of British prescriptions and built new palaces dominated by European references.[66] Maharaja Jayaji Rao Scindia of Gwalior used Doric and Corinthian columns and Palladian windows in Jai Vilas Palace and had a durbar hall with the most massive glass chandeliers in the world. This palace was finished in less than two years to provide a stage for the reception of the Prince of Wales in 1875. In the 1920s another Maratha prince, the holkar of Indore, built a Palladian-inspired palace whose location on the outskirts of the capital city seemed to indicate the ruler's retreat from active engagement in his state. British ideas about what was suitable for the princes also changed. In Marwar-Jodhpur, H. V. Lancaster, the architect of

---

[64] Ibid. and G. H. R. Tillotson, *The Rajput Palaces: The Development of an Architectural Style, 1450–1750* (New Haven CN, 1987).
[65] Metcalf, *Imperial Vision*, pp. 105–40.
[66] Maharaja of Baroda [Fateh Singh Rao Gaekwad], *Palaces of India* (New York, 1980).

Lakshmi Vilas Palace in Baroda.

Courtyard and City Palace in Jaipur.

Umaid Bhavan Palace, built between 1929 and 1944 partly to provide work during a famine, firmly rejected Indo-Saracenic features as inappropriate in Jodhpur since the area had been under only limited Muslim control.[67] Thus princely patronage of architecture reflected ambiguous political and aesthetic engagement with an imperial cultural hegmony. In independent India erstwhile rulers would recycle both Indo-Saracenic and European-inspired palaces as hotels to provide fantasy for international and domestic tourists.[68]

In painting, rulers of states such as Bikaner, Bundi and Marwar, who were early allies of the Mughals, were the first to borrow selectively from the Mughal style of imperial portraiture, but Mewar and others eventually followed. Vishakha Desai has analysed how Rajput princely portraits became more representative of physical characteristics of individual rulers and incorporated Mughal symbols such as the halo while they continued to emphasise indigenous conceptual aspects of idealised kingship. Thus painters at Rajput courts, whether Hindu or Muslims, were not trying to produce Mughal-style, psychologically sensitive images but rather were manipulating Mughal elements to enhance the visual representation of physical attributes of Rajput kingly ideals such as elephant-shaped legs and lotus-style ears. Moreover, by the eighteenth century Rajput princes in Rajasthan were more frequently painted in the context of their durbars, festivals, and kingly activities such as hunting than in the single, isolated portraits common in Mughal painting. Thus rulers acknowledged iconographically their position as first among equals and as protectors of their subjects, but in their bountiful patronage of painters they also advertised their legitimacy.[69]

Large-scale paintings from Mewar vividly indicate changing durbar scenes from the eighteenth to the mid-twentieth century. Now housed in the City Palace Museum in Udaipur, these paintings depict elephant fights, festival celebrations such as Holi and Dussehra, hunting scenes, and receptions of British agents. They provide visual evidence of changing power relations.[70] In 1818 James Tod, the first British agent to Udaipur, was received according to Indian protocols in the open air and seated on the ground. By 1930 L. W. Reynolds, the AGG for Rajputana and chief guest at the enthronement durbar of Maharana Bhupal Singh, participated in a British-approved

---

[67] Ibid., p. 48. [68] Ramusack, 'Tourism', pp. 242–5.

[69] B. N. Goswamy, 'Of Devotées and Elephants Fights: Some Notes on the Subject Matter of Mughal and Rajput Painting', in Vishakha N. Desai, *Life at Court: Art for India's Rulers, 16th–19th Centuries* (Boston, 1985), pp. xix–xxiii and passim; Vishakha N. Desai, 'Timeless Symbols: Royal Portraits from Rajasthan 17th–19th Centuries', in Schomer, *Idea*, vol. 1, pp. 313–42.

[70] Andrew Topsfield, *The City Palace Museum Udaipur: Paintings of Mewar Court Life* (Ahmedabad, 1990).

ceremony complete with armchairs. From the late nineteenth century onward, painters selectively borrowed European techniques such as a more naturalistic depiction of landscape and the use of photographs to paint more individualised faces for princely portraits. The impact of the camera is recorded in another way. A painting of Maharana Bhupal Singh celebrating the Gangaur festival, a women's celebration devoted to Gauri, the goddess of abundance, includes a British woman with a camera.[71] She was one in a long procession of camera-carrying foreign visitors to Rajput princely states, ranging from Lady Dufferin, who enthusiastically photographed Udaipur's Pichola Lake in 1885, to contemporary tourists in search of fantasy.[72] But court painters and tourists were not alone in bringing photography to the princely states.

By the 1860s photography was a popular means of representation in the princely states. Many princes relied on British firms such as Bourne & Shepherd or Johnston & Hoffman to take their portraits whenever they visited Calcutta,[73] but a few chose Indians as their official photographers. Around 1869 Maharaja Malhar Rao of Baroda selected Hurrychund Chintamon as his official photographer, while the holkar of Indore subsidised Lala Deen Dayal, who was employed first as an estimator and draftsman in the Indore Public Works Department.[74] In 1884 Nizam Mahbub Ali Khan of Hyderabad appointed Dayal as his official photographer and later conferred the title of raja on him. While in the nizam's service, Dayal oversaw commercial studios in Indore, Bombay and Secunderabad. The last one even had a zenana studio where a British woman photographed Indian women. Dayal also secured commissions from viceroys and other prominent Britons and was the official photographer for Lord Curzon on his visits to the princely states and for the Imperial Durbar of 1903. Selections of the photographs of Raja Lala Deen Dayal are widely published, but there has not been an in-depth analysis of how this ubiquitous photographer-entrepreneur influenced the representation of Indian princes by both British and other Indian photographers.

Princes made other uses of photography. They documented viceregal visits and princely reform projects with albums elaborately bound in leather or velvet, ornamented with semi-precious jewels and closed with brass or silver

---

[71] Ibid., p. 146.

[72] Marchioness of Dufferin and Ava, *Our Viceregal Life in India: Selections from my Journal 1884–1888*, vol. I (London, 1890), p. 228.

[73] *The Last Empire: Photography in British India, 1855–1911* with texts by Clark Worswick and Ainslie Embree (New York, 1976).

[74] Clark Worswick (ed.), *Princely India: Photographs by Raja Deen Dayal 1884–1911* (New York, 1980) and Judith Mara Gutman, *Through Indian Eyes* (New York, 1982), pp. 28, 108–9.

clasps.[75] These collections visually chronicled their relationship with British patrons and princely administrative innovations. Their pages held views of clean, airy, spacious hospitals, schools and jails. These images chart Michel Foucault's provocative analysis of how modern states used such institutions to extend their control over the lives of individuals.

Other aspects of modernisation featured in photographs included a water-pumping station in Mysore; a town hall, a school of industrial crafts and arts and a golf pavilion in Travancore; and a state library, a college, a museum and a clock tower in Baroda.[76] These views do not appear in the continuing stream of coffee table books of Indian photographs published for mass consumption. Their emphasis on princely portraits and palaces reflect a nostalgia for Oriental exoticism embodied in opulent dress and fantastic architecture and sites of colonial performances, especially viceregal visits, dinner parties and sporting events.

Princes also exploited photography to publicise their efforts as benevolent protectors of their subjects. Two notable examples are the series of Nizam Mahbub Ali Khan of Hyderabad's Good Works Project – Famine Relief in 1895–1902 and of Maharaja Ganga Singh of Bikaner's famine relief programs in 1899.[77] One prince mimicked the British effort to classify Indian society and thereby employ knowledge as a means of control. In 1891 the maharaja of Marwar commissioned a three-volume census of the people of Marwar. One volume had photographs of individuals posed against studio backdrops as well as in outdoor settings, accompanied by descriptive texts. Firmly in the tradition of ethnographic photography in British India that documented and classified the varied 'racial' types and occupations of Indians – especially those characterised as primitive, such as Nagas and the Andaman Islanders – this census reflects another selective borrowing by Indian princes of imperial cultural forms.[78]

Some princes became enthusiastic photographers. The most noted were the rulers of Jaipur, Travancore and Tripura, the last joined by his wife in this

---

[75] Lord Curzon, OIOC, Photo 430, collected at least thirty-one albums recording his visits. On a more modest level, British political officers made similar collections, several of which are held at the British Library.

[76] Mysore, Curzon, OIOC, Photo 430/41; Travancore, ibid., Photo 430/45; Baroda ibid., Photo 430/24.

[77] Examples from Hyderabad are in Gutman, *Indian Eyes*, and the Bikaner's series is in Curzon, OIOC, Photo 430/25 with selected views in Naveen Patnaik, *A Desert Kingdom: The Rajputs of Bikaner* (New York, 1990), p. 34.

[78] John Falconer, 'Photography in Nineteenth-Century India,' pp. 264–77, and 'Anthropology and the Colonial Image', in C. A. Bayly (ed.), *The Raj: India and the British 1600–1947* (London, 1990), pp. 278–304; Gutman, *Indian Eyes*, pp. 141–3.

Victoria Diamond Jubilee Hospital, opened on 8 December 1900 by Lord Curzon.

Central Jail at Junagarh, *c.* 1900.

avocation. Maharaja Ram Singh of Jaipur established a department of photography that documented nobles over whom he was tightening control.[79] The interest in photography was not confined to states in geographical areas readily accessible to the outside world. In northeastern India the maharaja and maharani of Tripura not only took pictures but developed their own prints. Their second son invented a chemical process for coating his own printing paper.[80] In 1864 the raja of Chamba showed Samuel Bourne, then touring the Himalayas, his collection of cameras, lenses and chemicals.[81] The princely interest in photography reveals that these Indian rulers were willing to experiment with new artistic forms to enhance the representation of their authority

[79] Ibid., pp. 91–2. B. N. Goswami also reports a cache of photographs of Ram Singh in erotic poses with his favourite mistress at the City Palace Museum in Jaipur: Goswami, 'Devotees', pp. xix and xxiii.
[80] Vidya Dehejia, 'Maharajas as Photographers', pp. 227–9, in Vidya Dehejia, *India Through the Lens: Photography 1840–1911* (Washington DC, 2000).
[81] Ray Desmond, *Victorian India In Focus: A Selection of Early Photographs from the Collection in the India Office Library and Records* (London, 1982), p. 5.

as well as to satisfy their intellectual curiosity. Bourne might marvel that the Chamba prince was interested in such a modern invention, but he shared his cultural condescension with scholars who deplore the erosion of princely patronage of painting under British cultural hegemony without acknowledging that new political, economic and cultural factors might direct princely benefaction to emerging art forms such as photography or to new arenas for older ones such as music.

Both Hindu and Muslim rulers throughout India nurtured musicians, singers, instrumentalists and dancers. Joan Erdman has analysed the changing patterns of patronage in Jaipur from the early eighteenth century to the 1980s. Since the founding of Jaipur city, the Jaipur state maintained a *gunijankhana*, a royal department of virtuosos who were state employees providing music for official occasions as well as leisure activities. Jaipur rulers patronised both folk or non-classical as well as classical musicians. Maharaja Ram Singh II, who died in 1880, was the last ruler to be both patron and musical performer. His successors continued to maintain the gunijankhana, but Madho Singh mainly provided for orthodox religious activities and Man Singh was famous for his promotion of sports. Moreover, the gunijankhana was increasingly bureaucratised, with non-musicians becoming the chief administrators as the rulers changed from being connoisseurs of the arts to employers of artists and European manners became the preferred sign of status rather than the quality of the artists.[82] Other states were substantial supporters of the performing arts: Mysore for classical *bharatnatayam* dance and the Maratha-ruled states of Gwalior, Baroda and Indore for musicians. Even smaller states with limited resources, most notably Rampur in the United Provinces, were significant benefactors. One musician said he left a theatre company when approached by Rampur 'because it was a court service, and a respectable one'.[83] At Rampur the musicians played for the prince and his friends after dinner, reflecting how princes had adopted western-style dinner parties and times for entertainment.

Princely patronage was also involved in changing institutional structures for the performance of music and dance. Several *gharanas* that provide 'a repertoire of stylistic elements' and 'rules of appropriateness for performance practices in Hindustani music' are associated with princely capitals. Evolving during the late nineteenth and early twentieth centuries, the gharanas

---

[82] Erdman, *Patrons*, ch. 3, and pp. 110–13.
[83] Daniel M. Neuman, *The Life of Music in North India: The Organization of an Artistic Tradition* (Detroit, 1980), p. 170.

encompass 'a lineage of musicians, the disciples, and the particular musical style they represent'.[84] The oldest of the gharanas is associated with Gwalior, and others with states such as Indore, Kolhapur, Rampur, Jaipur and Patiala. In his comprehensive analysis of the changing organisation of music performance in north India, Daniel Neuman mentions princely patronage but has not examined in depth the relationship of rulers to the families who constituted the gharanas.

In 1916 the first All-India Music Conference convened in Baroda to define a nationalist agenda and an educational program for Indian music. Fatesinghrao Gaekwad characterised this event as 'a fest for lovers of music' where the performances by musicians from rival schools 'were in the nature of a competition'.[85] Several other maharajas contributed funds for the second All-India Music Conference held two years later, which also solicited public subscriptions.[86] Subsequently Sayaji Rao held annual musical conferences in Baroda and attempted to change the nature of Holi celebrations so that 'the rowdiness, obscenity and vulgarity that were traditionally associated with Holi were replaced by a running feast of wholesome and skilled artistic performance'.[87] Although more research is needed on princely patronage of musicians, there is clear evidence that princes were key figures during the transition of patronage from the personal, intimate world of the royal court to the bureaucratic, populist organisations of post-colonial India such as All-India Radio and the Sangeet Akademi.

Sports

Some commentators condemn the princes for shifting their patronage from elite activities such as the fine arts of painting and music to more vulgar activities such as sports. But participation in certain sports had long been part of kingly dharma in both the indigenous Hindu and the incoming Turkic and Persian traditions. Hunting was a form of preparation for battle, a display of physical courage, and occasionally an effort to protect one's subjects from destructive animals, particularly tigers. Mughal emperors and Hindu kings, most notably the maharajas of Kotah, immortalised their involvement with hunting in vibrant paintings.[88] During the late nineteenth and into the twentieth

---

[84] Ibid., p. 146.   [85] Gaekwad, *Sayajirao*, p. 291.

[86] Daniel M. Neuman, 'Patronage and Performance of Indian Music', in Barbara Stoler Miller (ed.), *The Powers of Art: Patronage in Indian Culture* (Delhi, 1992), pp. 247–58.

[87] Gaekwad, *Sayajirao*, p. 292.

[88] William G. Archer, *Indian Painting in Bundi and Kotah* (London, 1959), pp. 47–52; Stuart Cary Welch (ed.), *Gods, Kings, and Tigers* (Munich, 1997).

centuries, hunting continued to be a prominent emblem of princely dharma. It also developed into a ubiquitous cultural activity for British colonists in Asia and Africa. Comparing lion-hunting in Africa with tiger-hunting in northern India, William Storey argues that colonial big-game hunting 'articulated a language of power over "restless natives"' and implies that it displayed the dominance of western culture over nature and of colonists over colonised.[89] John MacKenzie adds that 'hunting represented a historic cultural interaction which the British were able to use to build social bridges with Indians, particularly the Indian aristocracy'.[90] However, no scholars have analysed the British imperial cult of hunting that evolved in the late nineteenth century, which 'represented an increasing concern with the external appearance of authority' from the perspective of the Indian princes.[91]

First, princes as protectors of their people were supposed to be courageous. Charles Allen recounts that Rajput princes including Dungarpur and Kotah and Muslim ones such as Palanpur and Pataudi recalled shooting their first panther or tiger, generally around the age of 11 or 12, as a rite of passage to adulthood. Although hunting is usually deemed a masculine activity in both British and Indian cultures, women in princely families also participated both in the Mughal period and in the twentieth century. In 1925 Madho Rao Scindia of Gwalior dictated that '[c]hildren of both sexes should be taken out shooting once a week, and when they have advanced in years they should, as a rule be made to spend not less than a couple of weeks annually on tiger-shooting'.[92] Later Gayatri Devi, the maharani of Jaipur, remembered shooting her first panther at the age of 12 in Cooch Behar.[93]

Second, the organisation of hunting expeditions indicated control of substantial material, animal and human resources. Thus the elaborate *shikars* or hunting expeditions of princes were one possible arena for displaying their assets to their subjects and their imperial overlord. Some princes liked to portray how they were more accessible to their subjects when they were hunting, especially in remote areas, than they were in their capitals. But the limited evidence for such encounters is mainly hearsay. More lavishly documented are the opulent hunting expeditions that the princes arranged for their imperial

---

[89] William K. Storey, 'Big Cats and Imperialism: Lion and Tiger Hunting in Kenya and Northern India, 1898–1930', *JWH* 2, 2 (Fall 1991), p. 137.

[90] John M. MacKenzie, *The Empire of Nature: Hunting, Conservation and British Imperialism* (Manchester, 1988), p. 169.

[91] Ibid., p. 171.

[92] Quoted from Gwalior's *General Policy Durbar*, 1925 in Allen and Dwivedi, *Lives*, p. 127.

[93] Gayatri Devi, *Princess*, pp. 65–6.

Prince George Jivaji Rao and Princess Mary Kamlaraja of Gwalior at March Past
during visit of Prince of Wales, 8–12 February 1922.

suzerains. The most famous hunts were for tigers in Gwalior, Jaipur and Alwar,
for sand grouse on Gajner Lake in Bikaner, for various birds in Bharatpur, and
using cheetahs to hunt wild buck in Baroda.

British overlords ranging from princes of Wales to viceroys and political
officers expected to participate in extravagant shikars, to bag spectacular
trophies, and to be surrounded by luxury while they were living in the
'wild'. Three princes of Wales (Edward VII [1875–76], George V [1905] and
Edward VIII [1921–22]) hunted extensively in the princely states. In the
midst of Gandhi's first major non-cooperation movement in late 1921, the
prince of Wales found refuge from the massive public protests against his visit
in hunting in the princely states and Nepal.[94] At Gwalior he would be greeted
by the children of the anglophile Madho Rao, who were named George and
Mary.

[94] Bernard C. Ellison, *H. R. H. The Prince of Wales's Sport in India*, edited by H. Perry Robinson
(London, 1925).

Maharaja Madho Rao Scindia of Gwalior seated among tigers with Prince of Wales standing, 8–12 February 1922.

Viceroys participated and even Edwin S. Montagu, the Liberal secretary of state, sought relief from the political negotiations during his tour of 1917–18 in shikar.[95] In describing a hunt in Alwar, Montagu revealed his attraction to and ambivalence about hunting as well as his equivocal attitudes toward non-elites, such as villagers and beaters.

Nothing thrills me so much as these shoots. The excitement and the arrangements make the day pass like lightning, but what I hate about them, which destroys the happiness, is that I am expected to shoot the tiger . . . I agree that it is essential to shoot them, for the damage that they do to the villagers' cattle, and sometimes to the villagers themselves, is infinite, but I would prefer that somebody else took the responsibility of the climax of a shoot, upon which so much depends, and upon which so much trouble has been taken.[96]

During that beat he eventually shot a tigress who had wounded a beater and concluded 'we would have been very happy except for the mauling of a man, which I am assured is incidental to this ritual. I cannot ascertain news of his health'.[97]

Shikar within princely states served multiple functions. Princes could exhibit their wealth and their managerial ability in overseeing such large-scale undertakings. They provided opportunities to lobby informally British officials on sensitive issues. For both princes and British, shikar was a substitute for warfare and an activity deemed appropriately masculine when gender roles and behaviours were being intensely questioned.[98] Subsequently some princes changed their attitudes and became leaders in game preservation and conservation. The rulers of Kashmir, Mysore and Bharatpur developed game sanctuaries before 1947, and their refuges and those in other princely states would be transformed into national wildlife parks during the 1950s.[99]

Another sport closely associated with kingship in India was wrestling. The connection between kings and wrestlers has been traced to the epic *Ramayana* where Hanuman, the monkey god devoted to Rama, was portrayed wrestling. Joseph Alter asserts that '[k]ings have kept wrestlers because the physical strength of the wrestler symbolises the political might of the King'.[100] The

---

[95] Edwin S. Montagu, *An Indian Diary*, edited by Venetia Montagu (London, 1930) hunted in Bikaner, pp. 52–5; Patiala, pp. 203–6; Dholpur, pp. 238–42; Bharatpur, pp. 280–1; Alwar, pp. 290–3; Jaipur, pp. 314–18; and Bhopal, pp. 327–9.

[96] Ibid., p. 290.   [97] Ibid., p. 293.

[98] Satadru Sen, 'Chameleon Games: Ranjitsinhji's Politics of Race and Gender,' *JCCH* 2, 3 (2001), pp. 23–4.

[99] Mackenzie, *The Empire of Nature*, pp. 283–91. Major parks in formerly princely territory are Bandipur in Mysore, Siraska in Alwar, the Gir Forest in Saurashtra, Periyar in Travancore.

[100] Joseph S. Alter, *The Wrestler's Body: Identity and Ideology in North India* (Berkeley CA, 1992), p. 72.

dedication to his calling, the valour, the diet and the exercise regime of a wrestler reflected the political power and the moral virtue of his royal patron. In turn, the status of a prince enhanced the esteem of his wrestlers.

During the late nineteenth and early twentieth centuries, the rulers of Aundh, Baroda, Datia, Indore, Jodhpur, Kolhapur and Patiala were prominent patrons of wrestling. One wrestler exemplifies this relationship. First nurtured by the maharaja of Jodhpur, Gama successfully captured the John Bull World Championship Competition in 1910. Indian newspapers widely celebrated his defeat of the best British wrestlers in the metropole. Two years later the maharaja of Patiala became his patron. In 1928 the Sikh prince sponsored a major bout in Patiala that attracted 40 000 spectators. After Gama once again defeated the opponent he had bested in 1910, Bhupinder Singh placed his own pearl necklace on the champion, had him ride the prince's elephant, and awarded a village and an annual stipend to him. Gama's victory certainly entertained people, but Alter stresses that it had political implications since 'Gama and his patron the maharaja came to symbolise the possibility of self-determination and independence'.[101] But Indian wrestlers have not viewed the independent GOI kindly. They lament the passing of princely patrons who preserved wrestling as a way of life during the British period and transferred the wrestler from the private world of the *akhara* or training pit to the public sphere of popular acclaim. The contemporary employment of wrestlers in government services does not promote public esteem or private self-respect and provides no pearl necklaces or villages. Princely patronage of Indian wrestlers was yet another way of performing kingly dharma.

The princes sponsored and participated in other sports embodying military and masculine values. Pig-sticking and polo were indigenous sports that the British appropriated as displays of manly daring, courage and horsemanship. Some princely clients joined them in these ventures, most notably Man Singh of Jaipur, who died of a heart attack while playing polo in England in 1970. Other princes such as Rajendra Singh of Patiala (1872–1900), who had achieved fame in pig-sticking and polo,[102] became enthusiastic participants and patrons of an imported aristocratic sport, cricket.

Although Rajendra was a vigorous batsman, he was more significant for recruiting a cosmopolitan team to play for Patiala. His son, Bhupinder Singh, expanded state patronage of cricket to the national level, and his grandson

---

[101] Ibid., p. 77.
[102] Rajendra's reputation in polo was acknowledged by a caricature in *Vanity Fair* on 4 January 1900 in Roy T. Matthews and Peter Mellini, *In 'Vanity Fair'* (London, 1982), p. 182.

Wrestling match at Patiala, *c.* 1930.

played, supported local and national teams, and organised the National Institute of Sports in Patiala.[103] Other princes overshadowed Patiala's fame for
cricketers. In 1894 Ranjitsinhji of Nawanagar became the first Indian playing
for an English county team.[104] According to Arjun Appadurai, he acquired an
Orientalist glow in which 'wile became guile, trickery became magic, weakness
became suppleness, effeminacy was transformed into grace' and thus came to
represent the obverse of British stereotypes of Indian effeminacy.[105] Satadru
Sen has elaborated on how Ranjitsinhji used his persona as a cricketer acclaimed
in England to cultivate friendships with senior Rajput princes, especially Partap

[103] Richard Cashman, *Patrons, Players and the Crowd: The Phenomenon of Indian Cricket* (New Delhi,
1980), pp. 27–35.
[104] Ibid., pp. 35–9; Satadru Sen, 'Chameleon Games'; Ranjitsinhji's caricature appeared in *Vanity Fair*
on 26 August 1897; Matthews and Mellini, '*Vanity Fair*', p. 183; Ian Buruma, *Playing the Game*
(New York, 1991) is a novel that examines his life and the ambiguities of cultural identity.
[105] Arjun Appadurai, 'Playing with Modernity: The Decolonization of Indian Cricket', in Carol
A. Breckenridge (ed.), *Consuming Modernity: Public Culture in a South Asian World* (Minneapolis,
1995), p. 30.

Singh, who would support his claims to status as a Rajput and to the gaddi of Nawanagar.[106] Defining the 1920s and 1930s as the golden age of princely involvement, Richard Cashman speculates that through cricket the princes gained advantageous contacts with British officials and popularity among Indian audiences during a period of political change. Princely patronage of cricket ironically contributed to the eventual decolonisation of cricket and its present status as perhaps the most popular Indian spectator sport. After independence, the nawabs of Pataudi and Loharu continued the tradition of celebrity prince-players.

NATURAL LEADERS OR ORIENTAL AUTOCRATS

From 1858 to 1947 when the British Parliament exerted direct control in India, British officials projected multiple and contradictory images of the Indian princes on the screen of public discourse. After proclaiming that the British desired 'no extension of our present territorial possessions', Queen Victoria promised to 'respect the rights, dignity and honour of the native princes as our own'.[107] Indian princes were to be preserved, glorified and rewarded for services rendered in time of imperial need during the revolt of 1857. As outlined in Chapter 4, British officials in the colony and the metropole long debated over how to relate to Indian princes legally, ritually and personally. After almost twenty years of experimentation, Lord Lytton incorporated the Indian princes into an imperial ceremonial hierarchy with Victoria at the apex as Empress of India. Declaring that '[p]olitically speaking, the Indian peasantry is an inert mass. If it ever moves at all it will move in obedience, not to its British benefactors, but to its native chiefs and princes, however tyrannical they may be', Lytton characterised the princes as a ' "powerful aristocracy" whose complicity could be secured and efficiently utilized by the British in India'.[108] The Indian princes were to be subordinated to their imperial British suzerain while remaining influential, legitimate, even if despotic, rulers vis-à-vis their Indian subjects.

The public pronouncements and private views of British officials towards the Indian princes continued to show striking ambiguity. Lord Curzon, the epitome of British paternal imperialism, and Sir Walter Lawrence, his private

---

[106] Satadru Sen, 'Becoming Rajput: The Politics of Race in Ranjitsinhji's Empire', paper delivered at annual meeting of the American Historical Association, 4 January 2003. I am grateful to the author for permission to cite this paper.

[107] Proclamation by Queen Victoria, 1 November 1858, in Sever, *Documents*, vol. 1, p. 233.

[108] Lytton to Lord Salisbury, secretary of state for India, 11 May 1876, OIOC, E 218/518/1, pp. 147, 150 and quoted in Cohn, 'Representing Authority', pp. 191–2.

secretary, reflect these enigmatic images, which indicate conflicting and at times uncertain conceptions of British rule in India. An ICS officer who had served in both British India and the princely states, Lawrence celebrated the personal qualities and administrative effectiveness of the Indian princes. In his memoirs he wrote:

As a boy he [the prince] has listened to his father, and even to his grandfather, telling of the problems and incidents of past generations. The Raja is proud of his stored-up knowledge of customs, precedents, proverbs; he has a memory for faces and names, and knows the value of prompt and laconic decisions. Legends grow up of his wise and pithy judgements . . . Durbar justice is prompter and less ruinously expensive than it is in [British] India, and in the long run just as fair; for the Raja knows the facts, and understands the people. The Rajas – and I have known many of them – are men of great courtesy and dignity, and these qualities appeal to all Indian hearts.[109]

Lawrence cited personal experience including informal conversations and visits as well as official assignments as the basis of his assessment.

Lacking casual, personal rapport with Indian princes, Curzon thought in terms of imperial policy on a grand scale. Shortly after his arrival in India, he declared: 'The Native Chief has become, by our policy, an integral factor in the Imperial Organisation of India. He is concerned not less than the Viceroy or the Lieutenant-Governor in the administration of the country. I claim him as my colleague and partner.'[110] But like Lytton, Curzon did not view princes as equals of the British. Subsequently Curzon wrote privately to Lord George Hamilton, the secretary of state for India in London, that he accepted that the British acted as schoolmasters to the princes – 'For what are they, for the most part, but a set of unruly and ignorant and rather undisciplined school-boys?'[111]

A combination of concern for protocol and possibly racist and sexist attitudes colour Curzon's characterisations of social relations with Indian princes. He once complained of being nauseated by the sight of '"English ladies . . . of the highest rank" curtseying before the most insignificant princes . . . as if they were royalty'.[112] A stickler for observing tables of precedence, Curzon's nausea might have been occasioned by the women's ignorance of precedence. Even so, Curzon like other British men might also have been anxious over the perceived challenge presented to British masculinity when British women of any class

---

[109] Walter Roper Lawrence, *The India We Served* (London, 1928), pp. 180–1.
[110] Speech by Curzon at Gwalior, 20 November 1899, in Sever, *Documents*, vol. 1, p. 343.
[111] Curzon to Hamilton, 29 August 1900, in ibid., p. 346.
[112] Curzon's minute, 29 February 1904, PSCI, 1875–1911, vol. 163, No. 694/1904 quoted in Ashton, *British Policy*, p. 24.

publicly deferred to or were sexually attracted to Indian men. When asked for the participation of Indian orderlies in ceremonies related to the coronation of Edward VII, Curzon remarked: 'The "woman" aspect of the question is rather a difficulty, since, strange as it may seem, Englishwomen of the housemaid class, and even higher, do offer themselves to these Indian soldiers, attracted by their uniform, enamoured by their physique, and with a sort of idea that the warrior is also an Oriental prince.'[113]

Although the princes might be administrative partners, they were not to be treated as social or sexual equals. In the twentieth century, British officials continued to be ambivalent about the image of the Indian princes even as they instituted constitutional innovations such as the Chamber of Princes, which accorded the princes a defined but circumscribed political forum. But the ambiguity of imperial images was matched by an array of images of the princes that Indian nationalist leaders epoused. Romesh Chunder Dutt, best known for his theory that the British drained India of its economic resources but also a former ICS officer and minister in Baroda state, was an early nationalist apologist for the princes. When referring to Mysore and Baroda in the closing decades of the nineteenth century, he claimed that '[n]o part of India is better governed today than these States, ruled by their own Princes'.[114] Furthermore, he asserted that the princes as well as leaders of the Indian National Congress should represent and govern India. For many nationalists the princes, especially those acclaimed as progressive, were living examples of the Indian ability to govern themselves and to do so with wisdom and innovation. Like the British officials they sought to replace, some nationalists also lauded the personal relationship between a prince and his or her subjects, as opposed to the aloof one between British bureaucrats and Indian subjects.

During the twentieth century, Indian nationalists projected other images of Indian princes. Born in a princely state, Mahatma Gandhi regarded the princes as trustees for their people and consequently advocated that the Indian National Congress should not intervene in princely states. Other Congress leaders, especially those such as Jawaharlal Nehru who were affiliated with the left wing of the Congress, were critical of princely autocracy and promoted Congress support for popular political activists in the states. In his presidential address at the Lucknow Congress in 1936, Nehru claimed that 'Indian rulers

---

[113] Curzon to Lord Hamilton, 1 October 1900, MSS EUR F 111/159 as quoted in Rozina Visram, *Ayahs, Lascars and Princes: Indians in Britain 1700–1947* (London, 1986), p. 176.

[114] Romesh Dutt, *The Economic History of India in the Victorian Age: From the Accession of Queen Victoria in 1837 to the Commencement of the Twentieth Century*, 4th edn (London, 1916), p. 32.

and their ministers have spoken and acted increasingly in the approved fascist manner'.[115] Two years later Nehru characterised princes as puppets but then conceded that '[o]ur fight is not against any individual but against autocracy and oppression itself. Some rulers of the native states may be good people, but when they get power in their hands, they become inhuman'.[116] In other words Nehru opposed the sin of autocracy and the imperial patron–client system that protected the sinner but did not condemn the erring prince if he would repent. In 1935 when urging greater Congress intervention in princely state politics, Kamaladevi Chattopadhyay, like Nehru a socialist, had characterised the princes as slaves (in their relationship with the British) when she referred to the subjects of Indian states as slaves of slaves.[117] In contrast, Sarojini Naidu, Kamaladevi's sister-in-law by marriage and another Congress leader born in a princely state (Hyderabad), opposed intervention by the Congress and accused Nehru of 'picking' on the Muslim rulers of Bhopal and Hyderabad with 'unjustified' criticisms.[118] These conflicting attitudes among the Congress hierarchy towards the Indian princes reflected ambivalent relationships both before and after 1947.

CONCLUSION

Despite British dominance in India, the princes remained significant protagonists in multiple public and private spheres. Relatives, subjects and British officials participated in their personal life cycle ceremonies. Princely education, marriages and succession disputes involved factions contending for control over or access to the current or future occupant of a gaddi. Shrewd and ambitious princes manipulated these competing groups to achieve their goals. British officials, who might wish that the princes would behave in officially defined, appropriate ways, had to overlook personal and administrative transgressions if the political consequences of deposition or abdication were judged too costly.

---

[115] Presidential Address at Lucknow Congress, 12 April 1936, *Selected Works of Jawaharlal Nehru*, vol. 7 (New Delhi, 1975), p. 189.
[116] Article in *The Hindu*, 23 October 1938, and then speech at Bombay, 18 November 1938, in *Selected Works of Jawaharlal Nehru*, vol. 9 (New Delhi, 1976), pp. 405–7.
[117] Speech at meeting of the All India Congress Committee at Madras, 18 October 1935, in N. N. Mitra (ed.) *IAR*, vol. 2, July–December 1935 (Calcutta, 1936), p. 279.
[118] Sarojini Naidu to Padmaja Naidu, 16 January 1938, Padmaja Naidu Papers, NMML, quoted in Ian Copland, 'Congress Paternalism: The "High Command" and the Struggle for Freedom in Princely India, *c.* 1920–1940', *SA*, n.s. 8, 1 & 2 (1985), p. 81.

In the cultural arena, princes were not the only patrons of religious special-ists, activities, and association, of visual and performing arts and of sports, but their resources were widely sought in other arenas. Because of the tangled rela-tionships between religious associations, communalism and political violence (shown, for example, by the assassination of Mahatma Gandhi), the role of Indian rulers and their families in religious communalism and nationalism has not been fully researched. My own work on the maharajas of Patiala and the Sikh community outlines some continuity of participation from the colonial to the post-colonial era. The activities of Rajmata Vijayraje Scindia of Gwalior (1919–2001) in the Bharatiya Janata Party (BJP), an electoral party, and the Vishwa Hindu Parishad (VHP), a worldwide organisation promoting Hindu culture, during the 1980s and 1990s and of Dilip Singh Ju Deo, son of the last raja of Jashpur who is a major BJP leader in Chhattisgarh, indicate that the mutual attraction of erstwhile princely families and religiously oriented associations has not ended.[119] If the princes were without political or cultural resonance, their appearances at public meetings would not be featured in the news media. But it must be emphasised that only a limited number of erstwhile princes are prominent in such organisations.

Common wisdom is that princes helped to maintain cultural forms such as Indian dance and music during the colonial period. The evidence supports these assumptions. The independent GOI established a bureaucratic infras-tructure that assumed responsibility from the princes and distributed public resources to promote indigenous art forms. However, princely activity as cul-tural innovators in establishing museums, promoting photography, developing a national structure for music festivals, and providing the transitional stage in the evolution of some sports, especially cricket, as mass entertainment has often been ignored.

Finally, the diverse images that both British officials and Indian nationalists projected of the Indian princes manifest complex assessments of the Indian princes. Even if they were publicly and privately caricatured or disdained, the princes had to be accommodated. Most importantly, the princes remained in-ternally autonomous rulers within their own territorial units and were seen as embodying their states. One example is the manner in which many British and Indians referred to princes by the name of their state as if they were synony-mous with the states they ruled. Another is the many histories of states that chronicle succession struggles, the activities of rulers, and their relations with

[119] Vijayaraje Scindia with Manohar Malgonkar, *Princess: The Autobiography of the Dowager Maharani of Gwalior* (London, 1985) and Amrita Basu, 'Feminism Inverted: The Real Women and Gendered Imagery of Hindu Nationalism,' *BCAS* 25, 4 (1993), pp. 25–36.

the British. In them administrative elites, merchants and peasants constituted a dim background. Scholarship on the princely states as political entities with elites and subalterns, with varying levels of economic development, and with religious and cultural associations and activities has emerged only in the 1970s. Moreover, it generally focuses on the largest states, especially Hyderabad and Mysore, and certain clusters such as those in Rajasthan and western India.

CHAPTER 6

PRINCELY STATES: ADMINISTRATIVE AND ECONOMIC STRUCTURES

Among the slightly more than one hundred states that were ensconced in the British salute table, the antique, the successor and the rebel-warrior categories, as outlined in Chapter 2, all survived into the twentieth century. The internal evolution of these princely states as political and economic units has not been as extensively studied as their relationships with the British suzerain. The importance of the British renunciation of an aggressive policy of direct annexation can be overemphasised since some changes in territory continued. After 1858, however, the number of princely states and their boundaries remain relatively constant until 1947 and it is useful to observe their evolution over the *longue durée*, even though much of the scholarship on individual princely states is usually limited to a few decades or the reign of an individual prince. This chapter will focus on government structures within the princely states; their indigenous and 'foreign' administrators; the expanding bureaucratisation; and princely efforts to modernise their economies under the constraints of the ambivalent economic policies and restrictions of their imperial suzerain from the 1860s to the 1940s.

GOVERNMENT STRUCTURE

In most states rulers remained in power as long as they successfully manipulated alliances with external allies and internal supporters, mainly relatives, military entrepreneurs and land-controllers. Although relations with their external competitor, the East India Company and its successor the British Crown, involved continual negotiation, princes also confronted crucial challenges from internal co-partners. Coalitions of a clan, groups of clans, or military allies had created many states. Leaders of such ventures might initially differentiate themselves from their allies by seeking recognition from an outside power, as had the Tondaiman Kallars in Pudukkottai. If the newly ascendant ruler were to achieve internal stability, he or she also had to accommodate cohorts. The classic means was to provide internal allies with grants to collect land revenue from tracts within the conquered areas and thereby create a landed nobility or gentry. This practice alienated substantial sources of revenue from the central government, but without the collaboration of the nobility there would be no state.

The ruler, as the most powerful of the elite, generated the income to maintain an administration from land that was designated as khalsa or crown lands and from indirect levies such as customs, salt and stamp taxes. Occasionally there would be a separation between the private holdings of a ruler that supported his or her household and the khalsa tracts that funded the state administration. Usually this division was not explicit.

Indian rulers tended to replicate more powerful models, and so the Mughal administration served as an archetype for successor states, and to some extent for rebel and antique Rajput states. When government functions were limited, an Indian prince had a minimal administration led by a diwan or chief minister to supervise the collection of taxes. Other officers headed departments of finance, military affairs, the judiciary, and household affairs. From the mid-nineteenth century onward, a few states such as Travancore, Mysore and Baroda established departments of public works and education.

The revenue department had immediate jurisdiction over khalsa lands, which paid land revenues directly to the ruler, while jagirdars, mainly early military allies, relatives of the rulers, state officials, and religious establishments, collected the land revenue from tracts beyond the control of the state administration. States with sizeable numbers of jagirdars included Hyderabad, where only half the land was khalsa, and several in Rajasthan such as Alwar and Jaipur.[1] Views on the origins of the jagirs differed. Rulers asserted that they granted jagirs, retained control over succession to them, and had their superior position acknowledged by the payment of tribute from jagirdars. Jagirdars often challenged this interpretation. In the case of Sirohi state in Rajasthan, Denis Vidal has documented how nobles argued that their ancestors had obtained their lands when the kingdom was in the process of formation and thus had autonomous rights in the land.[2]

Larger states were divided into divisions and then districts, but as in British India, the state structure often did not penetrate into local society below the district level. Village headmen (*patels*), accountants (*patwaris*), and councils were responsible for the collection and payment of revenues to state-appointed district officers or revenue contractors. In Mysore, patwaris presented their records and collections to district officers at an annual collection day (*jamabandi*). Accompanied by festivities celebrating the end of the harvest, the proceedings confirmed the local autonomy, which the ruler tolerated as long as order

---

[1] Rudolph and Rudolph, *Essays* contains their influential essays on Jaipur.
[2] Denis Vidal, *Violence and Truth: A Rajasthani Kingdom Confronts Colonial Authority* (Delhi, 1997), pp. 56–7.

was maintained and revenue transmitted.[3] State revenue records often did not itemise the amount collected but only the amount forwarded. Larger jagirdars had their own revenue officers, but, like the British and the princes, they usually did not collect revenue directly from peasant cultivators or tenants but from local intermediaries.

A central treasury to hold state funds and a finance department to dispense them were rare during the nineteenth century. Karen Leonard has described how banking firms controlled by Gujaratis, Marwaris and local families functioned as state treasurers and accountants in Hyderabad by giving loans to the nizam's government and paying salaries of state officials against the collection of revenues. The state finance department negotiated these loans and paid them off when revenues were received. Diwans therefore needed the support of these creditors to survive politically. Although they solved a short-term problem, many of the bankers in Hyderabad became jagirdars and thus alienated more income from the state. Long-term solutions included the modernising reforms of Salar Jung, the cession of Berar to the British for payment of the salaries of the Hyderabad Contingent, and the establishment of a state bank in 1868.[4] G. S. L. Devra analysed the social mobility of Marwaris, especially in Bikaner. As privileged land-controllers in the eighteenth century, they moved into revenue farming, long-distance trade, and merchant banking for Rajput princes and the Muslim rulers of Hyderabad.[5] Although there are occasional references to princes such as those in Jaipur being heavily indebted to bankers for the payment of tribute to the British, the role of private bankers awaits further research, as does the establishment of state banks.

Many states, with a few exceptions such as Mysore, were dependent on military contingents that jagirdars supplied. Consequently, Indian rulers initially found the British-trained and equipped subsidiary forces attractive. They were more capable than local levies of repelling external enemies, suppressing internal challenges, and coercing recalcitrant taxpayers. However, princes were increasingly disappointed by their lack of control over forces for which they paid but could not command. By the mid-nineteenth century, reforming diwans sought to replace poorly disciplined jagirdari forces and British-dominated subsidiary contingents with centrally controlled military units. In 1854 Salar

---

[3] James Manor, *Political Change in an Indian State: Mysore 1917–1955* (New Delhi, 1977), pp. 16–17.
[4] Karen Leonard, 'Banking Firms in Nineteenth-Century Hyderabad Politics', *MAS* 15 (1981), pp. 177–201.
[5] G. S. L. Devra, 'A Rethinking on the Politics of Commercial Society in Pre-Colonial India: Transition from Mutsaddi to Marwari', Occasional Papers on History and Society, No. 38, NMML (New Delhi, 1987).

Jung I (1829–83) initiated such a reform in Hyderabad. By 1862 he had delegated the task to Raja Girdhari Pershad, a Saksena kayasth whose family came to Hyderabad as record-keepers but gradually moved into military service, which provided more remunerative opportunities.[6] Alwar also created reformed state forces that became the core of Imperial Service Troops. In the twentieth century some rulers such as the maharaja of Patiala reorganised their police departments as educated elites, jagirdars and peasants challenged princely autocracy. Compared to the extensive research on the police and definitions of crime in British Indian provinces, there is a paucity of such research on those topics in the princely states.[7]

The judicial system reflected both the autocratic nature of states and their narrow infiltration into local society. Caste panchayats, village headmen and religious leaders settled most civil and some criminal disputes at the local level. In larger states the lowest-level revenue collector, either a state-appointed officer, variously named a *tahsildar* or *amildar*, or a relatively autonomous jagirdar, decided revenue claims and other civil disputes. By the early twentieth century appeals went to district courts and then to a high court of the state located in the capital, or in smaller states to a consolidated regional court. High courts might have some original jurisdiction. In many states the ruler was the highest court of appeal in both civil and criminal cases and frequently approved death sentences. Thus intervention of the ruler at the highest level and revenue authorities at the lowest sharply reduced the independence of the judiciary.

Since household establishments were the crucible of succession to leadership and ritual ceremonies that symbolised the distinctive position of the ruler, most state administrations had a formal or informal department of household affairs. Its multiple responsibilities ranged from management and construction of forts, palaces and hunting lodges, to oversight of the zenana of the ruler's female relatives, the staging of private ceremonies such as the life cycle rituals at birth, marriage and death, and the negotiation and management of public ones, especially visits of imperial patrons. British officials usually regarded this department as a wellspring of intrigue and corruption. Considering how much attention and expense the British lavished on the Imperial Assemblage in 1876 and their expectations of princely largess during British official visits, it is ironic that the colonial government was so critical of princely expenditures on

---

[6] Karen Leonard, *Social History of an Indian Caste: The Kayasths of Hyderabad* (Berkeley CA, 1978), pp. 104–6.
[7] Two notable exceptions are Vidal, *Violence*, and Nandini Sundar, *Subalterns and Sovereigns: An Anthropological History of Bastar, 1854–1996* (Delhi, 1997).

public and private life cycle ceremonies. Since they reinforced and extended princely claims to authority within their states, among their clan members and their fellow princes, these rituals were vital in the maintenance of princely authority. Joanne Waghorne has carefully documented British ambivalence in the specific case of Raja Ramachandra of Pudukkottai, whose expenditures had to be sanctioned by the local British authorities. Among many examples, they denied a 'request for Rs 10 000 for his daughter's puberty rites' in 1867 but allowed Rs 20 000 in 1870 for the ruler to attend a reception for the Duke of Edinburgh.[8]

'Progressive' princely states

Mirroring the diversity among princely states, there were numerous variations on the model outlined. One category was that of 'progressive' states that included Baroda, Mysore, Travancore and Cochin. Here progress meant administrative modernisation with some introduction of representative institutions. But most princes remained autocrats and allowed little popular political participation until the 1940s. Other reforms included state support for social services, chiefly education and public health measures based on western medicine. Education supplied employees for an expanding bureaucracy and enhanced the productive capacity of the state, but there was little concern for the promotion of equality among state subjects. If medical programs improved the health of subjects, there were economic benefits for the state.

In Travancore the conjunction of a sympathetic young ruler (Ayilyam Tirunal), an able young diwan (T. Madhava Rao), and a new British resident (F. N. Maltby) led to major reforms during the 1860s and 1870s. Robin Jeffrey has outlined the modernisation that took place: in the collection of land revenue that enabled the state to pay off its debts; in the establishment of a public works department which built roads that promoted internal trade, provided alternative wage labour for lower castes, and broadened the social horizons of many groups; and in the bureaucratisation of the administration.[9] Most importantly, the diwan fostered the establishment of state-supported schools that linked government service to educational qualifications.[10] Until the 1890s this Hindu state helped Christian missionary schools with grants-in-aid since the foreigners mainly nurtured lower castes and girls, who were not the focus of state efforts.[11] As high-status Nayars and Syrian Christians

---

[8] Joanne Punzo Waghorne, *The Raja's Magic Clothes: Re-Visioning Kingship and Divinity in England's India* (University Park PA, 1994), p. 48.

[9] Jeffrey, *Decline*, ch. 3.   [10] Ibid., ch. 2.   [11] Kawashima, *Missionaries*, ch. 3.

and low-caste ezhavas became educated, their rising expectations of government employment and awareness of civil disability aroused social and political tensions and strained relations between the administration and the missionaries.[12] Although neighbouring Cochin, with a fifth of the area and a quarter of the population of Travancore, was slower to implement administrative reforms, it achieved rates of literacy comparable to those in Travancore by 1931.[13]

When explaining the 'advanced' government of Mysore, some historians attributed much of its administrative modernisation to the extended period of British management from 1831 to 1881 when colonial officers instituted an administrative structure similar to that in Madras. On the one hand, the research of Donald Gustafson emphasises that Indian ministers were active agents in implementing reforms.[14] On the other hand, James Manor argues that many reforms in Mysore were designed to cultivate a positive image with the British suzerain and Indian nationalists.[15] Expenditures were channelled to urban-based or state-level projects such as industrial enterprises and the provision of electric lighting in Bangalore, before it was available in British presidency capitals. Despite limited funds, these efforts gained favourable publicity and did not trespass on local power arenas. Manor asserts persuasively that the Mysore ruling family with a tiny social base tried to maintain internal order by allowing considerable local autonomy while retaining autocratic control at the state level.[16] Even so, the powers of local government boards were restricted, while their fiscal responsibilities for roads, compulsory education and health services were extensive.

The Mysore state also ventured into the contested terrain of social reform. Despite the opposition of a majority in the new Mysore Assembly, in 1894 Diwan Seshadri Iyer (1845–1901) pushed through a regulation that prohibited marriage for all Hindu girls below 8 and of girls below 16 to men over 50. The latter provision was designed to promote companionate marriages. The administration implemented this legislation through prosecutions, generally of lower-caste individuals, that disseminated its provisions at the very least by rumour.[17] Thus Mysore was in sharp contrast to the GOI, which did not vigorously enforce the controversial *Age of Consent Act* of 1891 that made illegal

[12] Ibid., chapter 6; Jeffrey, *Decline*, chs 3–5.   [13] Kawashima, *Missionaries*, ch. 6.
[14] Donald R. Gustafson, Mysore 1881–1902: The Making of a Model State, PhD thesis, University of Wisconsin at Madison (1968).
[15] Manor, *Political Change*, chs 1, 3.   [16] Ibid., pp. 11–13.
[17] Janaki Nair, 'Prohibited Marriage: State Protection and the Child Wife', in Patricia Uberoi (ed.), *Social Reform, Sexuality and the State* (New Delhi, 1996), pp. 157–86.

sexual relations with girls under the age of 12. Janaki Nair argues that Mysore was not primarily concerned with the condition of women but rather sought '[t]o encompass and absorb those aspects of civil and social life that had long lain outside its reach, thereby producing a civil society which recognised the overarching authority of the state'.[18] By the 1920s the administration decided that its objectives had been achieved. Thus it was not worth the cost to override local opposition to raising the age of marriage to match the provisions of the Sarda Act in British India that legislated 18 as the minimum age for men and 14 for women.[19]

For Baroda, David Hardiman has described how Sayaji Rao and his diwans, T. Madhava Rao (served 1875–81), Manubhai Mehta (served 1916–26) and V. T. Krishnamachariar (served 1926–44), achieved political stability and a 'progressive' reputation. Because Baroda's rich plains lacked natural defences, large landlords and jagirdars had not survived and thus did not constrain its ruler. Rather, landowning peasant cultivators, among whom *patidars* were dominant, were the most significant class. The diwans, allied with village shareholders, instituted a modern bureaucracy and promoted trade and industrialisation. The bureaucracy countered the power of local notables and was responsive to the interests of the village shareholders and open to their sons because of an extensive educational system. The state-sponsored construction of railways fostered trade and contributed to state income. Because of the growth of textile and chemical industries during the 1930s and 1940s respectively, the state was able to reduce the proportion of revenue that the rural sector paid and defuse peasant grievances. In 1938 the rate of land revenue was lowered by 20 per cent, while income and super tax rates that affected relatively few urban dwellers were raised.[20]

In general, the antique states of Rajputana did not have a reputation for being progressive, but some undertook administrative reforms that significantly influenced the lives of their peasant subjects.[21] During the late nineteenth century Maharaja Ram Singh of Jaipur implemented major public works programs and extended railways. Robert Stern has described how during the twentieth century British administrators in Jaipur followed a strategy similar to that in Baroda to achieve peasant support and political stability. When Man Singh was a minor during the 1920s and 1930s, a *ryotwari* settlement began to bring peasants into direct relations with the central administration. Simultaneously

---

[18] Ibid., pp. 168–9.   [19] Ibid., pp. 178–83.
[20] Hardiman, 'Baroda', in Jeffrey, *People*, pp. 122–3.
[21] Rudolph and Rudolph, 'Rajputana under British Paramountcy: The Failure of Indirect Rule', *Essays*, pp. 7–17.

there was an effort to complement income from land revenue with that from the state's investment portfolio, which was in GOI securities, interest-bearing loans to states such as Bikaner, and state railways.[22]

In an ecologically precarious position in the western Rajasthani desert, Ganga Singh in Bikaner developed an extensive famine relief program during the 1890s and then undertook more permanent solutions. The Gang Canal, opened in 1927, brought water from the Sutlej River to the northwestern area of this fertile but rain-deficient state. Subsequently the maharaja and his successor pushed through a land settlement on both khalsa and jagirdari lands that regularised the relations of peasants to the land they cultivated. Furthermore, from 1900 to 1931 the state expended 44 per cent of its revenue on social overhead capital, which represents 5.04 in constant rupees per capita. Thus Bikaner was second only to Cochin, which allocated 47 per cent of its revenues to social overhead, but ahead of Mysore and Baroda.[23] These expenditures on irrigation canals and social overhead retarded the evolution of popular political associations in Bikaner.[24]

Rulers could implement extensive programs of public works and administrative reforms but not achieve the reputation of being progressive. Thakore Saheb Lakhaji Raj (b. 1885, r. 1907–30) of Rajkot in western India established a representative assembly in 1923 that was unique in being fully elected. Although Rajkot joined a small group of states that took this ultimately abortive advance towards popular government, it has not gained the epithet of progressive or modern.

Mysore was the first princely state to inaugurate a representative assembly in 1881; it added a legislative council or upper house in 1907. Travancore launched an appointive legislative council in 1888 and created an elective consultative assembly in 1904. Other states with such bodies ranged from Baroda, Bhopal, Gwalior and Hyderabad, to much smaller units such as Bhor, Cochin, Datia and Pudukkottai. These assemblies began as appointed bodies with a majority of official members and were initially advisory in function. In the states with a reputation for being modern, the diwan was the chair. In others the ruler moderated, as occurred in 1929 in Datia or in Gwalior where

---

[22] Stern, *Cat*, pp. 250–1.

[23] John Hurd II, 'The Economic Consequences of Indirect Rule in India', *IESHR* 12 (1975), p. 175. Mysore spent 37 per cent and Baroda spent 25 per cent of their revenues and 1.80 rupees per capita and 2.16 rupees per capita respectively on social overhead: John Hurd II, Some Economic Characteristics of the Princely States of India, 1901–1931, PhD thesis, University of Pennsylvania (1969), p. 242.

[24] Richard Sisson, *The Congress Party in Rajasthan: Political Integration and Institution-building in an Indian State* (Berkeley CA, 1972), pp. 91–2.

View of famine relief work at Gajner, c. 1900.

the senior maharani, a regent for the minor heir, assumed control. Where the prince presided, the assembly was similar to a Mughal durbar in which elites presented their grievances but had no legal authority to influence policy. Some states introduced a restricted franchise. During the 1930s in Travancore and Cochin, about 5 per cent of the population could vote in regular elections. Most of these assemblies did not control the budgets or have the right to initiate legislation. When they did have such powers as in Mysore, the ruler could authorise expenditures or legislation in 'emergencies'. As the resources they managed were so restricted, these assemblies rarely became the focus for popular political activity.

Princely women as mothers, wives and power-brokers

Although neither British officials nor earlier historians considered the zenana as a component in the administrative structure of a princely state, the women who resided there had three significant political functions. First, they were responsible for producing sons. Varsha Joshi has stressed that Rajput rulers practised polygyny to obtain heirs as well as younger sons who could serve in their armies or extend Rajput control through the creation of new states.[25] When Mughal and British dominance eliminated the possibility of expansion, polygyny continued to strengthen clan and kinship networks and to maintain status. Such marriages simultaneously triggered succession disputes when princely wives supported candidates through strategies that ranged from alliances with nobles to murder and false pregnancies.[26] Despite polygyny, many princes lacked natural heirs. Surviving wives and mothers of a ruler often claimed a role in the adoption of heirs. In Alwar in 1874, the British political agent sought opinions about two contestants for the gaddi from the Rathor widow and the mother of the late Raja Sheodan Singh and also from jagirdars.[27] The mothers of natural or adoptive heirs frequently had an even more crucial role as regents when their sons had succeeded as minors. Rani Lakshmibai (*c.* 1835–58) of Jhansi is the most famous example of an activist regent who literally fought and died in 1858 to protect the interests of her adopted son. Numerous less well known queen mothers served as regents.

During the nineteenth century the British tended to reduce the influence of these women despite their professed intention to follow custom and avoid unwarranted intervention. Perturbed by the hostility of two queen mothers in Jaipur and the state's delinquency in forwarding its tribute payments during

---

[25] Joshi, *Polygamy*, ch. 2.   [26] Ibid., ch. 3.   [27] Haynes, 'British Modification', pp. 60–1.

extended regencies, the British assumed more direct control in 1839, with the justification that

[w]e had had sufficient experience of the bad effects of yielding to the caprices of females claiming a right to interfere in the government of Jaipur, and the present was the time to decide whether it was consonant with the prosperity of the country that a *zenana* influence shall for many years be exercised over all the affairs of the state, or whether it has not become the duty of the paramount power to free the ministry from all such thralldom.[28]

This misogyny was not limited to British officials since Jadunath Sarkar, when describing these regencies, claimed that '[t]o *the two evils of woman's rule on behalf of a child on the throne* and faction among the nobility, was now added financial collapse'.[29]

The second crucial responsibility of queen mothers was the education of heirs to the gaddi. Since most princely women had marginal exposure to western education in English, British officials viewed them as the repositories and promoters of all that was 'traditional' and increasingly 'decadent'. From the 1870s onward, therefore, the paramount power prodded their partners in empire to remove young princely heirs from the zenana. During the late nineteenth century Indian nationalists, particularly in Bengal, were exhorting women to raise heroic sons to combat the British and to remain as guardians of the spiritual essence of India in the home,[30] but they seem to ignore the mothers of princes as nurturers of potential leaders. Gradually princes began to appoint British nannies and tutors for their children and to send their sons to British-established schools for princes. This practice could produce a backlash. In 1934 the maharani of Faridkot, a small Sikh state in Punjab, was commended for 'sparing no pains in the upbringing of her worthy son and in making her sons perfect gentlemen and perfect Princes' and even moving to Lahore when her eldest son went to school there. She supposedly pitied 'those society woman [*sic*] who leave the care of her sons to nurses and governesses thereby surrendering to them the exercise and potent influence of a mother's love and counsel'.[31]

---

[28] GOI, F&P Procs, 26 June 1839, No. 30 quoted in Stern, *Cat*, pp. 82–3.

[29] Sarkar, *History*, p. 332. Italics added.

[30] Influential articles include Tanika Sarkar, 'Nationalist Iconography: Image of Women in Nineteenth Century Bengali Literature', *EPW* 22 (21 November 1987), pp. 2011–15; Partha Chatterjee, 'The Nationalist Resolution of the Women's Question', in Kumkum Sangari and Sudesh Vaid (eds), *Recasting Women: Essays in Colonial History* (New Delhi, 1989), pp. 233–53; Jasodhara Bagchi, 'Representing Nationalism: Ideology of Motherhood in Colonial Bengal', *EPW* 25 (20–27 October 1990), WS-65–WS-71; Samita Sen, 'Motherhood and Mothercraft: Gender and Nationalism in Bengal', *GH* 5 (1993), pp. 231–43.

[31] Makhan Singh, *Investiture Ceremony. Of His Highness Farzand-i-Saadat Nishan-i-Hazrat-i-Kaisar-i-Hind Brar Bans Raja Harindar Singh Sahib Bahadur Ruler of Faridkot State* (Lahore [1934?]), pp. 37–8.

In official documents and scholarly literature, women in princely families are usually characterised as manipulative when they functioned as power-brokers. The stronger the ruler, the more desirable was, and is, direct access to him. Wives, mothers and concubines enjoyed such access. In a system of personal government they might secure official appointments, the ouster of rivals, or lucrative boons.[32] The British and rival factions of Indian officials were critical of this channel of influence that was outside their control.

Women of the zenana irritated British sensibilities in the sphere of sexuality. As Victorian ideas linking uncontrolled sexuality and the 'other' became pervasive, the British constructed the Indian princes as addicted to the satisfaction of their sensual appetites, especially sexual ones. Consequently zenana women, because they could gratify such passions, became convenient scapegoats for the refusals of Indian males to conform to Victorian constructs of appropriate sexuality and rulership. Robert Stern has pointed out how the retreat of Maharaja Madho Singh of Jaipur to his zenana and his deference to Rup Rai, a concubine, and her male patron influenced the British to exert strong control over his adopted heir, Man Singh.[33]

Mothers were also castigated for wielding too much influence over princely sons. In 1938 the British resident described the junior maharani, Setu Parvathi Bai (1896–1983), of Travancore as 'arrogant, uncharitable, egotistical, bad-tempered, insular and vindictive'. He also claimed that the diwan, Sir C. P. Ramaswami Aiyar (1879–1966), was so loyal to her that the Briton was '[a]bsolutely certain that some of his [Ramaswami Aiyer's] most unpopular and . . . mistaken ideas have emanated from the Junior Maharani'.[34] Setu Parvathi Bai may have been a forceful influence on both her adult son and a Tamil brahman lawyer whose career included service on the Madras Executive Council, but the evidence so far comes mainly from British sources. Robin Jeffrey argues that the junior maharani's ascendancy persisted and was behind Ramaswami Aiyar's declaration that Travancore would assert its independence.[35] But V. P. Menon, the perceptive collaborator of Sardar Patel in achieving the integration of the princely states at independence, claimed that '[i]n view particularly of his [Aiyar's] position in the public life of the country, this statement [advocating the independence of Travancore] had deleterious

---

[32] Joshi, *Polygamy*, ch. 4.   [33] Stern, *Cat*, pp. 238–40.

[34] C. P. Skrine, resident for Madras States, to Bernard Glancy, secretary to viceroy as crown representative, Political Dept, 11 October 1938, OIOC, CR, R/1/29/1849, quoted in Robin Jeffrey, 'A Sanctified Label - "Congress" in Travancore Politics, 1938–48', in D. A. Low (ed.) *Congress and the Raj: Facets of the Indian Struggle 1917–47* (London, 1977), p. 444.

[35] Ibid., p. 461.

repercussions and encouraged the rulers who were not favourably disposed towards the Indian Dominion'.[36] Menon may be more discreet than was the British resident in not mentioning the maharani, but the evidence is still inadequate for a full assessment of the political clout of Setu Parvathi Bai and other princely women.

British frustration with any constraints on their exercise of power and their Orientalist stereotypes of Asian women as sexual objects fostered their condemnation of women in princely families. In some cases Indian rulers might have concurred with this negative stereotype of the zenana since it could be a convenient excuse for not responding positively to British advice or demands. A few more nuanced assessments are available. Besides the work of Varsha Joshi, which concentrates on Rajputana from the thirteenth to the early nineteenth century, Uma Chakravarti and Kumkum Roy have analysed the historical characterisations of such women during the pre-colonial era, and Gita Mehta has placed a sharp-witted woman from a princely family at the centre of her historical novel, *Raj*.[37] The agency of elite and non-elite women in princely states during the colonial era begs for further analysis.

INDIGENOUS AND 'FOREIGN' POLITICAL COLLABORATORS

The diwan or chief minister was potentially the dominant state official. Rulers such as those in Travancore had employed non-Malayali brahmans as diwans from the mid-eighteenth century to create an administration personally loyal to them. From the early nineteenth century the British adapted this practice to their own ends. They expanded the category of 'outside' or 'foreign' administrators to include both British political officers and Indians from a British Indian province who were educated in British political and bureaucratic techniques and rituals. Although the British preferred that British officers not be employed as the diwans, they occasionally sanctioned such a practice. Examples range from Colonel John Munro (*c.* 1770–1858), diwan in Travancore from 1811 to 1814, to Jaipur, where a series of British ministers from 1922 to 1939 used administrative reforms to contain peasant unrest.

The more common British policy was to support the appointment of Indian collaborators who had demonstrated support and loyalty to British interests.

---

[36] Ibid. and Menon, *Story*, p. 114.
[37] Joshi, *Polygamy*; Uma Chakravarti and Kumkum Roy, 'In Search of Our Past: A Review of the Limitations and Possibilities of the Historiography of Women in Early India,' *EPW* 23 (30 April 1988), WS-2–WS-10; Gita Mehta, *Raj* (New York, 1989).

In south India Maratha and Tamil brahmans who had served in the Madras presidency were employed as diwans in Travancore, Cochin and Mysore and often favoured the appointment of caste fellows or regional associates. With backing from the British resident in Travancore, T. Madhava Rao, whose father and uncle had both been diwans in this state, was appointed a district officer there in 1855 and confirmed as diwan in 1858. During his tenure, which ended in 1872, Madhava Rao acquired wide renown as the administrator who modernised Travancore and favoured non-Malayali brahmans. Later he migrated north as diwan first to Indore from 1873 to 1875 and then to Baroda from 1875 to 1882. Similarly, in Mysore Seshadri Iyer, a Tamil brahman who was diwan from 1883 to 1896, was reputedly responsible for inducting over a hundred men from Madras into the gazetted service of Mysore.[38]

Two groups in north India were conspicuous in princely state administrations. Western-educated Bengalis, generally *bhadralok* or respectable people and more particularly kayasths, had followed British armies and administrators into newly annexed areas of Punjab, Awadh and Rajput states. In Jaipur one British resident noted that 'the employment of Bengali ministers in the state has become almost traditional'.[39] Around 1873, Maharaja Ram Singh of Jaipur had recruited Babu Kanti Chander, an energetic, shrewd Bengali, who used his knowledge of the English language and culture to enhance Jaipuri relations with the paramount power and foster a more professional bureaucracy but also to check the powerful Champawat Rajput bureaucratic lineage within the Jaipur administration.[40]

Kashmiri brahman pandits who, like the Bengali kayasths, had a long tradition of administrative service based on fluency in a link language – initially Persian under the Mughals and then English under the British – had migrated to Delhi, Lucknow and Lahore from the late eighteenth century onward. By the 1820s they had entered princely states as educators and administrators. The Haksar family was prominent in Indore and Gwalior, the Kak family in Jodhpur, and others in Bharatpur. Henny Sender has pointed out how the British were ready to use this community as needed but that 'the indispensability of the Kashmiris had its limits' and they would be sacrificed to British interests.[41] But

---

[38] Vanaja Rangaswami, *The Story of Integration: A New Interpretation in the Context of the Democratic Movements in the Princely States of Mysore, Travancore and Cochin 1900–1947* (Delhi, 1981), p. 30.
[39] Quoted in Stern, *Cat*, p. 182.
[40] Susanne Hoeber Rudolph and Lloyd I. Rudolph with Mohan Singh, 'A Bureaucratic Lineage in Princely India: Elite Formation and Conflict in a Patrimonial System', in Rudolph and Rudolph, *Essays*, pp. 96–106.
[41] Henny Sender, *The Kashmiri Pandits: A Study of Cultural Choice in North India* (Delhi, 1988), p. 112.

Kashmiri pandits remained active in princely states until 1947. Daya Kishen Kaul served in Patiala during the 1910s despite British opposition, and Kailas N. Haksar was a prominent figure in Gwalior during an extended minority in the 1920s, then in the Chamber of Princes during the 1930s, and eventually as diwan from 1943 to 1944 in his ancestral state of Kashmir.

Indians and Britons were attracted to employment in princely states for differing and even conflicting reasons. In the late 1830s Raja Banni Singh of Alwar recruited the so-called Delhi diwans, Aminullah Khan and his two brothers, but the British, who then favoured the local nobility, forced out these Muslim administrators in 1858. Here a Hindu ruler preferred officials who did not share religious or ethnic ties with his local challengers, and the Delhi diwans remained influential in Alwar politics through the 1860s.[42] Other rulers used outsiders to reduce the power of their nobles. During the 1860s and 1870s Maharaja Ram Singh of Jaipur appointed non-official Europeans along with Bengalis since they combined professional competence with personal loyalty – they owed their positions entirely to him.

For a few decades some princes recruited Western-educated Indians with nationalist credentials. In response to British demands for administrative reforms, Maharaja Malhar Rao of Baroda appointed Dadabhai Naoroji, the eminent Parsi from Bombay and later the first Indian member of Parliament, to be diwan in 1874. Occasionally a ruler retained Indians of whom the British disapproved. Sayaji Rao of Baroda employed Bengali nationalists, most notably Romesh Chandra Dutt and Aurobindo Ghose. When opportunities for Indians were limited in the ICS, some Indian nationalists joined the administrations of princely states where they could demonstrate their administrative competence and exercise significant executive power. By the early twentieth century, however, relatively few nationalists sought such experience. The example of Mahatma Gandhi is idiosyncratic but illustrative. Although his grandfather and father had served in the administrations of Kathiawadi states, Gandhi felt compelled for personal and ideological reasons to seek a legal career in British India.

Employment in the princely states nevertheless continued to lure educated Indians who did not aspire to electoral or agitational political activity but preferred administrative authority. The most prominent among them formed an all-India cadre that circulated through several Indian states. One such person was Sir Mirza Ismail (1883–1959), who began his career as a 'native' diwan in

---

[42] Haynes, 'British Alteration', pp. 43–8.

Mysore, serving from 1928 to 1940, but went as a 'foreign' diwan to Jaipur in 1942 and then to Hyderabad in 1945.[43] Other examples exist. Patiala state retained both Hindustani Muslims such as the Sayyid brothers during the nineteenth century and Punjabi Muslims such as Liaqat Hayat Khan (1887–1952), the brother of Sikandar Hayat Khan (the Unionist Chief Minister of Punjab 1937–42), and Mir Maqbool Mahmud (d. 1948), a sometime elected member of the Punjab legislature, during the twentieth century. Unfortunately there is no study of this all-Indian bureaucracy and whether they functioned as a homogenising or reforming force within princely administrations. Furthermore, there is little analysis of their mediation between their princely employers and the British and between British Indian and princely state popular politics.

Although the British and the princes found 'foreign' diwans and middle-level administrators to be functionally useful, two groups within the states were vocal critics of them. Local aristocracies disliked the ready access of the diwans to the ruler and their influence in securing the appointment of other outsiders. By 1900 newly emerging, educated elites within the states resented the dominance of these outsiders and their recruits. Outsiders who peopled the second level of the administration in princely states were even more disliked than 'foreign' diwans. Their importation accelerated with growing bureaucratisation. Initially elites within the princely states who owed their position to land control, military skills or blood ties did not possess or seek the kind of education that would equip them for bureaucratic employment. Thus western-educated outsiders were the most readily available pool. Gradually, however, groups of individuals in some states secured such education either in British India or within the state. They resented what they perceived as monopolies by foreigners, whether Indian or British. Susanne and Lloyd Rudolph have incisively analysed the extended struggle of the Champawat thikanadars against Bengali and British administrators to regain control of both lands and bureaucratic appointments in Jaipur.[44]

In Travancore animosity was tempered with ambivalence against both 'foreign' diwans and middle-level administrators. T. Rama Rao (1830–95), a Maratha brahman who had been born in Trivandrum, was always considered a foreign diwan (1887–92) because of his ancestry, although S. Shungarasoobyer (1836–1904), a Tamil brahman who was also born in the capital, was considered a native when he succeeded Rama Rao as diwan (1892–98). Robin Jeffrey has traced how the hostility to middle-level foreigners in Travancore

[43] Mirza Mahomed Ismail, *My Public Life* (London, 1954).
[44] Rudolph and Rudolph with Singh, 'Bureaucratic Lineage'.

state service was a key factor in the efforts of first indigenous nayars, then Syrian Christians, and eventually low-caste ezhavas to organise to demand greater representation in government services.[45]

In Hyderabad and Kashmir, associational activity among their subjects to secure government jobs raised especially complex issues as the rulers were from a minority religious community. Salar Jung had created a modern diwani administration in Hyderabad that was staffed largely with Muslims from north India who were labelled non-*mulkis* (not of the soil). As education spread among indigenous Hyderabadis known as *mulkis*, they grew increasingly hostile towards the non-mulkis and demanded more government posts. Coupled with the usual problems of how a previously disadvantaged group catches up with one entrenched in a limited number of powerful positions was the issue of when an individual passed from non-mulki to mulki status. During the 1880s a legal definition evolved of a mulki 'as a person who had permanently resided in Hyderabad state for fifteen years or who had continuously served under the government for at least twelve years',[46] but the social usage of the term broadened as new categories appeared such as first-generation mulki or son of the soil.

In Kashmir, the largest princely state in territory, the Hereditary State Subjects movement around 1894 began calling for preferential employment of state subjects and culminated with the legal definition of Hereditary State Subjects in 1927. The situation was complicated as Kashmiri brahman pandits, who were a small minority, would be the immediate beneficiaries because of their acquisition of Persian and English language education rather than the majority Muslim community, who had been seeking proportional representation for Muslims in state service from 1907.[47]

ECONOMIC STRUCTURE AND DEVELOPMENT

As the English Company extended its political control throughout India, it annexed the most economically productive areas, both agriculturally and commercially. Thus it began in Bengal, long fabled as one of the richest Indian provinces; it quickly gobbled up most coastal areas to facilitate commercial enterprises and gradually engorged the fertile Gangetic plain to Punjab. When Queen Victoria renounced any further British annexation, the princely states were located mainly in less economically productive areas. Jammu and Kashmir

---

[45] Jeffrey, *Decline*, ch. 6.   [46] Leonard, 'Hyderabad', p. 76.
[47] U. K. Zutshi, *Emergence of Political Awakening in Kashmir* (New Delhi, 1986), pp. 206–14; Bazaz, *History*, pp. 135–63.

encompassed majestic but desolate mountains; Rajputana was a rain-deficit area; some Rajput-ruled states of Gujarat had unhealthy and unproductive tracts such as the salt marshes of the Rann of Kutch; the Orissan states stretched across the inaccessible jungly hills behind the Coromandel coast; and the large block of central Indian states was riven by the deep defiles of the Vindhya Range.

Notable exceptions with extensive natural resources included the coastal states of Travancore and Cochin with a small but lush agricultural base in both food and cash crops, the cis-Sutlej Punjab states possessing fertile soils and early access to canal irrigation, and Hyderabad and Mysore with diverse economies. However, even the latter were not immune to predatory British economic interests. Hyderabad was coerced into giving up control over Berar, its rich cotton-producing northern province, to the Company in 1853. In Mysore private British enterprise controlled the mines of Kolar, the main gold-producing area in India.

Unfortunately the economic landscape of the princely states remains clouded by a lack of scholarly research. Many works on the economic history of India ignore the princely states or make occasional remarks on their similarity or difference from British India. In over a thousand pages of text, the second volume of *The Cambridge Economic History of India, c. 1757–c. 1970* has less than twenty references to the princely states.[48] Many are a single sentence. Thus much of the following overview is impressionistic and calls attention to the need for intensive research on the economic structure and development of the princely states.

Agriculture

As in British Indian provinces, the economies of most princely states were mainly agricultural with widely differing patterns of land control, land revenue assessment and tax collection. Many rulers monopolised a significant portion of their states as khalsa or crown lands but frequently more would be under the jurisdiction of jagirdars, as in Rajputana states such as Alwar and Jaipur. In some, such as Baroda and Patiala, there were powerful cultivators-owners. Many observers claimed that princes extracted more from their peasants than did the British Indian Government, but that the peasants in princely states were 'happier' than those under colonial rule. However, little rigorous research on the agricultural economies in the princely states supports these opinions. The major exception is Amber/Jaipur in eastern Rajputana during the eighteenth

---

[48] Dharma Kumar (ed.), *The Cambridge Economic History of India*, vol. 2 (Cambridge, 1982).

century. Here Indian scholars have used an abundance of records to present a finely grained picture of state finances, grain production and marketing, increasing economic stratification in villages, and the growing importance of merchants or *mahajans* in providing credit to villages, facilitating the sale of the state's revenue grain, and entering tax-farming contracts with the state.

For Jaipur during the first half of the eighteenth century, S. P. Gupta has calculated that on khalsa lands the total taxation was around 44 per cent with about $33\frac{1}{3}$ per cent in direct taxation of produce and another 10 per cent in direct and indirect cesses. This burden was shared unequally in villages. The upper levels, such as the patels and patwaris who had high-caste status and a role in the land revenue administration, paid at concessional rates. The lower levels, of either middle and low-caste status, carried a disproportionate share of the tax burden.[49] When the state collected its taxes in kind, it evolved into the dominant force in local grain markets. Mahajans became increasingly important to the efficient functioning of the state. Madhavi Bajekal has analysed how the state maintained careful records that enabled it to control the price of grain. The state coerced merchants to purchase its grain stocks either directly through forced sales or indirectly by restricting commercial transactions and inter-regional grain movements.[50] It also allowed a margin of profit to traders through the mechanism of deferred payments, which enabled the merchants to pay off their contracts as prices rose during the months after the harvest sales when prices had been lower.

For the second half of the eighteenth century, Dilbagh Singh has argued that repeated Maratha incursions had disastrous effects on agricultural production and the internal grain trade in eastern Rajputana. There was a qualitative shift in agriculture from cash crops and inferior food crops to superior food crops that could be sold for better prices. A quantitative decline in total production also ensued as cultivators migrated to the more secure areas of Malwa and Harauti. Gradually the state administration alienated control of land to zamindars, merchants and bankers for long terms on ijara (tax-farming) contracts. Although this tactic provided some stable income over the short term for the Jaipur administration, it strengthened economic rivals to the state and intensified economic stratification in villages.[51] Thus a class of rich bankers in Jaipur was amassing capital resources similar to the revenue officials in

---

[49] S. P. Gupta, *Agrarian System*, pp. 144–55.

[50] Madhavi Bajekal, 'The State and the Rural Grain Market in Eighteenth Century Eastern Rajasthan', in Sanjay Subrahmanyam (ed.), *Merchants, Markets and the State In Early Modern India* (Delhi, 1990), pp. 98–104, 110–20.

[51] Dilbagh Singh, *The State, Landlords and Peasants: Rajasthan in the 18th Century* (Columbia MO, 1990), pp. 65–6, 199–207.

western Rajasthan described by Devra, who were moving increasingly from tax-farming into merchant ventures. These so-called Marwaris were benefiting from the difficulty Rajput princes had in maintaining effective revenue administrations when confronted by Maratha offensive raids.

Scholars have yet to analyse in similar detail what happened during the nineteenth and twentieth centuries to agriculture in the princely states. Official sources, mainly gazetteers and census reports compiled by British and British-trained Indian administrators, remain the starting place for scholars. The gazetteers include both volumes in the imperial series and those on individual states generated on the British Indian model.[52] Descriptive in nature, they detail the composition of soils, climate, availability of rainfall and irrigation, types of crops, patterns of cultivation, varieties of draft animals, horticulture, transportation networks, internal and external grain trade, and the incidence of famine. However, the data vary from the specific to the simplistic, and the interpretive remarks are often stereotypical. For example, the imperial gazetteer volume on Hyderabad declared that 'the ryots [peasant-cultivators] have taken no interest in improving the quality of their crops by selection of seed, or by the cultivation of new varieties, or by introducing improved agricultural implements'.[53] The volumes that the states themselves assembled report on individual districts and provide more information on variations in crops and production, reflecting ecological and social diversity. However, none of these gazetteers nor the administrative reports, which states striving for a reputation as progressive produced during the twentieth century, provide much data on long-term trends. For example, there is little information on the commercialisation of agriculture. In the key area of irrigation there are limited data on how much the princes and the land-controlling elites spent on the maintenance and extension of wells in north India and tanks in the south, the traditional sources of irrigation. There are slightly more data on canal irrigation, perhaps because it was regarded as modern and often undertaken in conjunction with British India.

Irrigation

In 1861 Maharaja Narinder Singh of Patiala offered to pay for the surveying, project preparation and construction within his state of the Sirhind Canal, which would carry water from the Sutlej River through the western part of his state. Because of his conspicuous loyalty during the revolt of 1857 and their

[52] A strikingly graphic presentation of the coverage of gazetteers is in Joseph E. Schwartzberg, *A Historical Atlas of South Asia* (Chicago, 1978), p. 141.

[53] *Imperial Gazetteer of India. Provincial Series. Hyderabad State* (Calcutta, 1909), p. 32.

interest in expanding canal irrigation in Punjab, the British responded affirmatively. After overcoming the technical obstacles in constructing a weir across the Sutlej at Rupar, the Sirhind Canal was opened in 1882. When Maharaja Ranbir Singh of Jammu and Kashmir requested a similar collaborative venture, the response was more lethargic, although eventually the Upper Chenab Canal, which watered parts of Jammu, was built. These two canals did not open up new lands for cultivation but rather enabled more intensive cultivation of existing crop lands.[54]

A bolder experiment that extended cultivation to fertile but hitherto waste lands was the Gang Canal in Bikaner state. Shocked by loss of human and animal life during the great famine of 1899–1900, which occurred just after he was invested with full ruling powers, Ganga Singh of Bikaner considered the development of railways and canal irrigation to be the long-term preventives of future famines. In 1905 he proposed to Viceroy Curzon the construction of a canal branching off the Sutlej at the northern border of Bikaner state. The Punjab Government and the neighbouring princely state of Bahawalpur objected. The Sutlej coursed through Bahawalpur but not Bikaner. The former state was unwilling to have a reduction in water available for irrigation. After many compromises over the location of the head-works that determined the area to be irrigated and negotiations to secure the requisite financing through private borrowing, the canal was finally opened in 1927. It brought around 1000 square miles under cultivation.[55] This irrigation project also stimulated an increase of 49 per cent in the non-agricultural workforce in Bikaner between 1901 and 1931. This rise was the fourth highest among the princely states.[56] Once the debts for the Gang Canal were retired, Ganga Singh was eager to participate in the Sutlej Valley Scheme, which involved the first storage dam in the Indus Valley at Bhakra.[57] Bahawalpur joined the Sutlej Scheme but its earlier concerns proved realistic in that it received less water for irrigation than expected. As less land could be irrigated, land prices and revenues fell during the 1930s and the Bahawalpur administration became in arrears in payments on its debts incurred for this scheme.[58] Irrigation clearly had both positive and

---

[54] Aloys Arthur Michel, *The Indus Rivers: A Study of the Effects of Partition* (New Haven CN, 1967), pp. 67–72.

[55] John Hurd states that from 1921 to 1933 in Bikaner 'the area under crops that was irrigated by government canals increased forty-one fold, and the percentage of total area under crops irrigated by such canals increased from 1 per cent to 19 per cent': Hurd, 'Economic Characteristics', p. 20.

[56] Ibid.

[57] Panikkar, *His Highness*, pp. 288–306, and Michel, *Indus*, pp. 120, 316–40.

[58] Ibid., pp. 85–98; Penderel Moon, *Divide and Quit: An Eyewitness Account of the Partition of India*, new edn (Delhi, 1998), pp. 99–101.

negative results for states and their subjects. In western Rajasthan irrigation projects extended state control over local populations as rulers attempted to transform pastoralists into sedentary agriculturists.[59]

Such princes as Ram Singh of Jaipur and Chamarajindra Wadiyar and Krishnaraja Wadiyer of Mysore reaped enhanced revenues and social benefits from irrigation projects. Ram Singh bargained with the British to eliminate a provision of their 1818 treaty that Jaipur state was to pay five-sixteenths of its annual revenue of over Rs 4 million to its British suzerain. Since Jaipur's revenue was never reported as being over the stipulated sum, in 1871 Viceroy Mayo rescinded this claim in return for a promise that the ruler would commit an increased share of his state revenues to public works. In 1867 Jaipur had hired Swinton Jacob, a military engineer, to lead the public works department, which managed irrigation, roads, palaces and other government buildings. By the time Jacob left Jaipur, the state had invested Rs 5 million in irrigation and subsequently received over Rs 9 million in increased land revenue. Ram Singh shrewdly confined most irrigation works to his crown lands where cash crops such as opium, which carried multiple taxes, were cultivated. Thus irrigation in Jaipur furthered the commercialisation of agriculture and made the khalsa lands more attractive to cultivators when the rains failed than those of neighbouring jagirdars.[60] In Mysore the rulers first subsidised renovation of irrigation tanks during the 1880s. Later, under the energetic leadership of M. Visvesvaraya (1861–1961), an engineer who also served as diwan from 1912 to 1918, the durbar constructed the Krishnaraja Sagar dam and reservoir on the Cauvery River, which were completed in 1931.[61] This elaborate project supplied water for the irrigation of paddy rice and sugar cane as well as hydro-electric power. Irrigation had multiple benefits for princely states, but scholars have yet to assess fully its impact on agricultural production, state revenues, or the lives of peasants.

Railways

Closely linked to irrigation was the construction of railways in the princely states since both were seen as key elements in the prevention of famine. Many advocates argued that railways would facilitate the commercialisation

---

[59] Carol Henderson, 'State Administration and the Concepts of Peasants and Sedentary Agricultural Production in the Thar Desert', paper presented at the Wisconsin Conference on South Asia, 6 November 1993.

[60] Stern, *Cat*, pp. 142–4.

[61] Bjørn Hettne, *The Political Economy of Indirect Rule: Mysore 1881–1947* (London, 1978), pp. 233–4, 269–71.

of agriculture and would help Indians to modernise because of the transfer of technology.[62] So far scholarship has concentrated on how railways expedited the movement inland of British manufactured goods, especially cotton textiles, the transport of raw materials, mainly cotton, opium and food grains, to ports, and the strategic deployment of imperial troops. Since railways were closely associated with communications and defence – two of the three areas that the princely states had ceded to the British as paramount power – there were numerous disputes over their construction within and across princely states. Key issues were finance because of British controls on the ability of states to raise money in public markets in Britain and in India, the routes to be followed, the type of gauges to be used, and political control over the right-of-ways. Railway development in Mysore and Hyderabad illustrates these themes.

A railway line connected Bangalore, the administrative capital of Mysore, to Madras in 1870. Twelve years later the first line within Mysore state was opened from Bangalore to Mysore city, the seat of the maharaja. Shortly after the British rendition of Mysore in 1881, the durbar sought to extend its rail infrastructure. But the British pressured the diwan to turn over railway development to a private British firm, the Southern Maharatta Company, in return for a delay of ten years until 1896 in raising Mysore's annual subsidy to the GOI from Rs 24.5 lakhs to Rs 35 lakhs.[63] Thus a foreign rather than an indigenous enterprise was to undertake railway expansion in a progressive princely state. Although this settlement was clearly not to Mysore's overall financial advantage, it would not be as disastrous for state finances as what would occur in its neighbour to the north.

Perhaps because of its status as the most populous state and its geographical location astride the Deccan Plateau in the centre of peninsular India, Hyderabad has attracted the most scholarly attention. Vasant Kumar Bawa and Bharati Ray have considered the development of railways in Hyderabad as a key issue in the increasingly troubled relationship between the princely state and the imperial suzerain during the diwanship of Salar Jung.[64] This chief minister was a fervent promoter of railways despite the reluctance of the nizam, who perceptively feared that the railways would intensify British influence without sufficient financial benefits.[65] Tara Sethia has linked railway development in

[62] Daniel R. Headrick, *The Tentacles of Progress: Technology Transfer in the Age of Imperialism, 1850–1940* (New York, 1988), pp. 49–96.
[63] Hettne, *Political Economy*, pp. 57, 235–7.
[64] Bawa, *Nizam*, pp. 92–7, 117–22; Bharati Ray, 'Genesis', pp. 45–69.
[65] Bharati Ray, *Hyderabad and British Paramountcy 1858–1883* (Delhi, 1988), pp. 137–8; Tara Sethia, British Imperial Interests and the Indian Princely States, PhD thesis, University of California at Los Angeles (1986), p. 48.

Hyderabad state during the 1870s and 1880s to the overwhelming desire of Salar Jung to recover control of Berar and to the grant of coalmining concessions.[66] Consequently Hyderabad experienced many of the problems that hampered the extension of railways within the princely states.

One controversy erupted over the linkages between all-Indian routes and the princely states. Bartle Frere, the governor of Bombay, and the India Office in London had proposed that the Great Indian Peninsular Railway (GIPR) between Madras and Bombay should meet at Hyderabad city. But because of political and military considerations, the governor of Madras and the GOI at Calcutta prevailed over their colleagues and ordered that the mainline should pass through Hyderabad territory at Raichur, 100 miles south from the alleged political dangers of the capital city.[67] The British still wished to have Hyderabad city connected to their railway network. So the multiple levels of the imperial hierarchy began tortuous negotiations with Salar Jung over the route, financing, and the gauge of a link between the GIPR and Hyderabad city. The princely state was eventually constrained to agree to conditions overwhelmingly favourable to the British. At first they had proposed to share the cost of construction, with the state's portion coming from the surplus revenue of the Berar province, which was allocated to Hyderabad. Because of his desire to regain Berar, Salar Jung vetoed this suggestion, offered to pay all costs, and formed the Nizam's State Railway (NSR) to build the link. The proposed route was conducive to British strategic objectives since it went through Secundarabad, its military cantonment near Hyderabad city, and the broad gauge that the British demanded was much more expensive to construct than the narrow gauge that Salar Jung had recommended.

Salar Jung sought to raise capital for the NSR from *sahukar*s (local bankers), but they were reluctant to make the extensive commitment. Salar Jung therefore employed British intermediaries to raise Rs 5.5 million on the London market to circumvent a 1797 parliamentary act requiring GOI approval of any loans between British subjects and the princely states. Following the pattern established in British India, the nizam's government guaranteed a 5 per cent return to local investors and a generous 6 per cent return to British investors. Since the NSR never earned more than 1.5 per cent, this settlement was a continual drain on the state's revenues.[68] In 1881 London investors, with the support of the India Office, began to explore the capitalisation of an extension of the NSR northward to Chanda in the Godavari coalfields and eventually to Nagpur in British India and southward to Bezwada. Gradually Salar Jung was

---

[66] Sethia, 'Berar', pp. 59–78.   [67] Ray, *Hyderabad*, pp. 133–6.   [68] Sethia, 'Berar', p. 72.

drawn into the scheme in the hope of increasing traffic and income. The NSR was to be dissolved and a new enterprise formed, the Nizam's Guaranteed State Railway (NGSR). Eventually this new company required an annual payment of over Rs 30 lakhs, which was more than any surplus revenue of the Hyderabad Government. The creation of the NGSR illustrates chicanery among private British investors in London eager to profit from stock manipulation, contradictory opinions within the British official hierarchy about what would be beneficial for Hyderabad, and ultimately the British goal of facilitating the extraction of Hyderabadi coal to fuel its railways in south India. The imperial patron was unconcerned by the damage to their princely client. These disadvantageous terms provoked unprecedented political demonstrations against the nizam's government. Dr Aghorenath Chattopadhyaya, the Bengali principal of Hyderabad College and the father of Sarojini Naidu, the first Indian woman president of the Indian National Congress, was a prime organiser of this response.[69] Popular opposition to foreign financing of railways that mortgaged tax revenues prefigured popular outbursts in twentieth-century China, first against the imperial government in 1911 and then against the warlord regime of Yuan Shih-kai and his successors.

Since the British were determined to expand railway lines throughout India, some princes shrewdly secured benefits from what they could not stop. Madhava Rao constructed light railways that were cheaper than metalled roads since Baroda, composed largely of alluvial plains, lacked useful road-building materials. By 1934/35 the state system of 707 miles of railway earned 9 per cent of the state revenues.[70] Other states such as Gwalior also constructed light railway systems that were reputed to be profitable investments for the durbars.[71] The rulers of Jaipur were to benefit even more handsomely from collaboration with the British and the construction of their own state system of railways.

Because of its geographical position across routes from the Gangetic Plain to Bombay, which became the major entrepôt for imports from Europe upon the completion of the Suez Canal in 1869, Jaipur was soon traversed by two major British lines. In return for his cooperation, Ram Singh won concessions on such issues as the siting of stations. As a result, the railway lines enabled the maharaja to undercut traffic through lands controlled by his jagirdars, thereby decreasing their customs income and increasing his. Coincidentally, easy access by rail put Jaipur city, proclaimed 'the finest of modern Hindu cities'[72] and

[69] Sethia, 'British Interests', esp. pp. 172–83.
[70] Hardiman, 'Baroda', in Jeffrey, *People*, p. 120.
[71] H. M. Bull and K. N. Haksar, *Madhav Rao Scindia of Gwalior 1876–1925* (Lashkar, 1926), p. 110.
[72] W. S. Caine, *Picturesque India: A Handbook for European Travellers* (London, 1891), p. 95.

favourably compared by Rudyard Kipling and others to Paris,[73] on the route of late-nineteenth-century tourists seeking the real India and handmade Jaipuri souvenirs.[74] Meanwhile Ram Singh was able to withhold from the British any useful information on the economic benefits for Jaipur from the railway.[75] Maharaja Madho Rao Scindia of Gwalior became an investor in British railways and a builder of the Jaipur State Railway. Although initially the British had refused the request of the Jaipur, Gwalior and Indore durbars to invest in sections of the Rajputana–Malwa line that passed through their territories, in 1905 the GOI reconsidered on the recommendation of its foreign and political department. It eventually decided there was 'political advantage of the chiefs of India having a large monetary interest in the Indian railways'.[76] On an investment of Rs 5 million secured in the London market, the Jaipur durbar would earn Rs 9.5 million in two decades. Around the beginning of the twentieth century, Madho Singh of Jaipur began the construction of the Jaipur State Railway, which would serve his political as well as economic interests. This line extended his physical control to Shekhawati, the remote base of several Marwari clans, directed the trade and social orientation of that area to Jaipur and away from Jodhpur and Bikaner, and earned a 10 per cent profit on the northern extension to Shekhawati and a 12 per cent one on the southern section.[77] As the Jaipur State Railway expanded, in 1936 the durbar took over its management from the British-owned Bombay, Baroda and Central Indian Railway Company. In 1940/41 the income to the Jaipur durbar from its own system and its investment in British Rajputana–Malwa line was Rs 1.6 million.[78]

Not all Rajput princes were such enthusiastic supporters of railways. The British Rajputana–Malwa line travelled through Udaipur state via Chittor, but Maharana Fateh Singh cancelled further railway expansion upon his accession in 1884. Later he reluctantly agreed to a rail extension from Chittor to his capital at Udaipur in return for permission to dismiss a reform-minded official, Mehta Panna Lal, whom he viewed as an agent of the British.[79]

Railways came to the princely states in varying degrees, but their long-term impact has not been adequately analysed, either for the microcosm of individual states or for the macrocosm of the princely states and British India. The

[73] Rudyard Kipling, *Letters of Marque* (New York, n.d.), pp. 13–14.
[74] Barbara N. Ramusack, 'The Indian Princes as Fantasy: Palace Hotels, Palace Museums and Palace on Wheels', in Breckenridge, *Consuming Modernity*, pp. 66–89.
[75] Stern, *Cat*, pp. 139–40.
[76] GOI, F&P, August 1911, Internal A., nos 27–31 quoted in Stern, *Cat*, p. 191.
[77] Stern, *Cat*, pp. 187–92.   [78] Ibid., p. 251.
[79] Rajat K. Ray, 'Mewar: The Breakdown of the Princely Order', in Jeffrey, *People*, pp. 223–4.

latter would be difficult to achieve without the former. Railway development has been viewed narrowly as a site of contestation between the durbars and the British, with a focus on the high construction cost of railways attributed to the guaranteed interest system that lessened the incentive for cost containment. More analysis is needed of the extent to which railways precluded the British policy of isolating the princes and their states from each other, fostered ties between social, religious and political associations in the princely states and British India, and affected the commercialisation of agriculture and the development of industries in the states.

Industrialisation

The terms of scholarly debate on industrialisation in the princely states set during the 1970s have yet to be revised. In his pioneering dissertation and two often cited articles, John Hurd tried to compare 'development' in the princely states with that in British India. Based on a sample of ninety-eight states containing 89 per cent of the total population of the princely states in 1931, with fifty-four British districts selected as comparable, Hurd focused on three variables: the structure of the male labour force, namely the percentage of males employed in non-agricultural work; migration, specifically the percentage of males born outside the state; and urbanisation. He concluded that although economic development declined in both British and princely India from 1901 to 1931, the princely states in general lagged behind the British districts. Two basic categories of factors were responsible. One was British policies that hindered growth, such as the refusal to extend any guarantee for developmental loans. The other was the historical evolution of the states. For example, the higher the percentage of jagirdars in a state, the lower was the level of development, and Hurd argued that jagirdars siphoned off revenue from the state treasury.[80]

In a subsequent analysis confined to twenty-eight states, each with over 500 000 people, which comprised 71 per cent of the populations of the princely states, Hurd added male literacy to his original three criteria of development. Political factors were mainly responsible for differences in economic development between princely and British India. By 'preserving the princely states as separate political units, the British contributed to the disparities in economic development in India'.[81] In another article on industrial development, Hurd postulated an argument similar to Sethia's. He claimed that the British acted ambivalently to safeguard their interests. They intervened in the princely states

---

[80] Hurd, 'Economic Characteristics', pp. 145–50.   [81] Ibid., pp. 175.

to secure the abolition of transit duties and the construction of transcontinental railways and roads to facilitate British trade. But they did not intercede for the princes in British capital markets since industrial development in the states was not a colonial priority.[82] In a comparison of industrial development in Alwar state and the adjoining Gurgaon district of Punjab, Edward Haynes supports Hurd's assessment that industrialisation in the princely states was delayed by contradictory British policies that coupled protection from unscrupulous 'foreign' investors with frequent opposition to projected indigenous industrial enterprises (such as a cotton mill in Alwar). Equally important for Alwar was its lack of integration into the all-India transportation network except for one railway line financed by state revenues and built during the 1870s when the British dominated the state administration.[83]

C. P. Simons and B. R. Satyanarayana challenged Hurd on his selection of samples and asserted that comparisons between the states and British India are invalid. The economy of imperial India was indivisible, comparisons conceal more than they reveal, and there are no scientific means to measure the factors that influenced economic development in such a heterogeneous area as India. In turn, using Hurd's four indices, they compared statistics on the princely states and British India as a whole. They concluded that differences in favour of British India were statistically insignificant and that economic development in British India and the princely states was commensurate.[84] Although railways and metalled roads provided a framework for an all-Indian economy, it remains important to analyse the development of discrete political units, whether they are British Indian provinces or districts or princely states. Furthermore, the numerous general overviews of Indian economic development under the British do not evaluate in any depth agricultural or industrial activity in the princely states, even as part of the indivisible imperial economy. So once again, case studies must suffice to illustrate industrial development within the princely states.

Here again Mysore and Hyderabad are significant examples. During the 1870s and 1880s, first under British and then indigenous control, Mysore had granted generous terms for prospecting to a British syndicate who discovered

---

[82] John Hurd II, 'The Influence of British Policy on Industrial Development in the Princely States, 1890–1933', *IESHR* 12 (1975), pp. 409–24, esp. pp. 423–4.

[83] Edward S. Haynes, 'Comparative Industrial Development in 19th and 20th-Century India: Alwar State and Gurgaon District', *SA*, n.s. 3, 2 (1980), pp. 25–42, esp. pp. 38–9.

[84] C. P. Simmons and B. R. Satyanarayana, 'The Economic Consequences of Indirect Rule in India: A Re-appraisal', *IESHR* 15 (1979), pp. 185–206. Simmons and Satyanarayana are responding primarily to Hurd's article 'Economic Consequences', since they do not cite his dissertation and find his subsequent article on industrial development in the princely states to be much more useful than his first one (note 13, p. 192).

gold in the Kolar area in 1884. Although the Mysore durbar gained royalties, the development of the Kolar fields had little ripple effect on the Mysore economy. The heavy equipment and supervisory personnel were imported from England, the labourers from Madras,[85] coal from Bengal, and wood from western India. Profits were remitted to British shareholders. Mysore provided some infrastructure in a railway line constructed in 1893, a hydro-electric plant at Sivasamudram in 1902, and eventually the Krishnasagar project. Hettne has argued that the durbar, driven by its need to pay a large subsidy, a stagnant land revenue income, and possibly the dominance of Madrassi administrators, was content with assured royalties of almost Rs 2 crores by 1911.[86]

In the sphere of mining concessions as in railway development, Hyderabad suffered more egregiously than did Mysore. The discovery in 1872 of significant coal deposits in the Singareni area near Warangal and the Godavari River interested the GOI since its railways in the south were dependent on expensive coal imported from eastern India or even Britain.[87] In the early 1880s some Hyderabadi and British officials sought to combine the railway and mining concessions since the prospect of profitable freight would be an incentive to British investors in an expanded NGSR. Under strong pressure from the GOI and despite warnings from London, the nizam's government granted mining concessions on extremely favourable terms to British investors. After convoluted negotiations Abdul Haq, a Hyderabadi minister, with British support purchased heavily watered shares of the company holding the concessions. He and private British investors profited while the Hyderabadi Government headed towards bankruptcy.

When some British newspapers and MPs began to question the British Government's role in this venture, British officials placed the primary responsibility on Haq, whom both the British and Hyderabad had earlier agreed lacked skill as a negotiator. Contrasting cultural constructions of manipulative and gullible Indians and well-connected, greedy British investors overlay a lack of official concern about the fiscal stability of a princely ally. The *Financial News* claimed that 'a small band of speculators' in collaboration with a 'machiavellian mahomedan', namely Abdul Haq, had victimised Hyderabad. Another paper referred to the scandal as 'milking the Rajahs', which occurred because the 'milker' on the London Stock Exchange had influence with the

[85] Janaki Nair, *Miners and Millhands: Work, Culture and Politics in Princely Mysore* (Walnut Creek CA, 1998), chs 2–3.
[86] Hettne, *Political Economy*, pp. 246–7. A crore is 100 lakhs.
[87] Sethia, 'British Interests', chs 5–7.

authorities.[88] Once again the GOI interfered in the economic affairs of states when it suited their interests, turned a blind eye when they would be unaffected, and was indifferent to its princely allies when unscrupulous investors concluded questionable deals.[89]

Ultimately the fraudulent practices of the London financiers led to a parliamentary inquiry and a restatement in 1891 of a potentially more restrictive or protective policy depending on one's viewpoint. Subsequently the GOI was to approve all loans and concessions for railways and mining between the princely states and British subjects. The imperial overlord wished to 'protect' the states from 'mischief' but also to prevent any infringement on the British position in India. This statement would be modified in 1930 to allow Indians, whether or not they were subjects, to make investments in princely states without British approval. In fact these policy directives were routinely but circumspectly evaded.[90] Mysore and Baroda illustrate the possibilities of and limitations on the expansion of manufacturing in the princely states. In Mysore the most vigorous promoter of capital-intensive projects was an engineer attracted to state service by the offer of authority not available to Indian professionals in British India; in Baroda it was a 'modernising' maharaja. In both cases cotton textile factories were the initial industries. The Mysore Spinning and Manufacturing Mills were established in 1884, three decades after the first cotton textile mill in Bombay, and the Bangalore Woollen, Cotton and Silk Mills two years later. Janaki Nair emphasises that Mysore faced significant obstacles to industrialisation such as the lack of an entrepreneurial class and indigenous sources of capital as well as restrictive imperial policies in areas such as tariffs.[91] It persisted in order to effect a social transformation that would strengthen its resource base. M. Visvesvaraya, a brahman from Mysore, trained as an engineer in Poona and was employed by the Bombay public works department until 1909 when he was appointed chief engineer in Mysore.[92] He favoured large-scale, state-sponsored schemes to build an infrastructure and was willing to use non-indigenous capital. Alfred Chatterton was recruited as the first director of the department of industries and commerce in Mysore in 1912. He proposed small-scale manufacturing projects based on agrarian

---

[88] Ibid., p. 267.   [89] Ibid., pp. 280–3.
[90] Hurd, 'Economic Characteristics', pp. 65–75.
[91] Janaki Nair, The Emergence of Labor Politics in South India: Bangalore, 1900–1947, PhD thesis, Syracuse University (1991), pp. 41–4.
[92] In *Tentacles*, pp. 359–60, Headrick implies that Visvesvaraya left the British service because of remote prospects of becoming the chief engineer.

products launched with local capital. Mysore state pursued both options with varying success.

Visvesvaraya had a longer tenure than Chatterton since he was diwan from 1912 to 1918 and later a consultant. He coined the motto 'industrialise or perish' and later became a leader in the campaign for *swadeshi* or 'Mysore for the Mysoreans', by which the administration meant to exclude Indians from outside Mysore, mainly Madrassi bureaucrats and Marwari traders, as well as British agency houses. First, Visvesvaraya fostered an institutional infrastructure supportive of industrial development. The Mysore Bank was established in 1913, the Mysore Chamber of Commerce in 1916, and Mysore University, the first university in a princely state, in 1916.[93] In collaboration with the GOI and in response to an initial offer from J. N. Tata, the Parsi industrialist, Mysore helped finance the first Indian Institute of Technology, which opened in Bangalore in 1911.[94] Second, Visvesvaraya ostensibly pursued heavy, light and rural industrialisation but personally favoured capital-intensive schemes such as the Cauvery Reservoir Project and the Mysore Iron and Steel Works. Both required heavy infusions of state aid and only the first was notably successful.

Alfred Chatterton advocated more small-scale, intermediate industrialisation. His endeavours included an Experimental Weaving Factory, a Sandalwood Oil Factory, and the Mysore Soap Factory based on agricultural products such as coconut and groundnut oils. After a slight hiatus during the 1920s, Visvesvaraya's technocratic emphasis on industrialisation and the push for economic autonomy continued under the diwanship of Sir Mirza Ismail. During the late 1930s it was proposed to establish an automobile factory financed by the shipping magnate Walchand Hirachand, which would assemble Chrysler cars in India, but British resistance rendered that undertaking stillborn.[95] Ismail claimed that this rejection prompted his resignation in 1941. Other significant industrial units in Mysore included a small ammonium sulphate plant outside Mysore City (1937), the first autonomous fertiliser plant in India, and Hindustan Aircraft, a direct result of the Second World War. Although Mysore did not attain the economic autonomy Visvesvaraya envisioned, its

---

[93] Hettne, *Political Economy*, pp. 264–7; Manu Belur Bhagavan, Higher Education and the 'Modern State': Negotiating Colonialism and Nationalism in Princely Mysore and Baroda, PhD thesis, University of Texas at Austin (1999), pp. 130–99.

[94] Headrick, *Tentacles*, pp. 335–6. The maharaja offered free land, Rs 500 000, and an annual pledge of Rs 50 000 a year and the GOI supplied Rs 250 000 and an annual pledge of Rs 90 000. Tata's initial offer was Rs 3 million for the buildings, equipment, and endowment fund.

[95] Hettne, *Political Economy*, pp. 295–6; Nair, 'Emergence', ch. 2.

industrial enterprises and higher education framework prefigured crucial industrial development in the decades ahead.

Baroda followed a different path. Influenced by the example of Europe, Sayajirao and his diwans used state resources to generate an industrial base. During the swadeshi era after 1905, the durbar abolished customs duties, established the Bank of Baroda, organised a department of commerce and industry, and extended loans.[96] By 1918 there were eleven textile manufacturers who formed the Baroda Millowners Association, the first noteworthy business organisation in the state. It developed into the Federation of Gujarat Mills and Industries in which Baroda textile, engineering and chemical/pharmaceutical interests dominated. Early engineering firms included a tractor repair and importing firm that became the nucleus of Hindustan Tractors and Bulldozers. Alembic Industries, which moved from Bombay to Baroda in 1907, was a major success story in the chemical field. By the early 1940s it had spawned two sizable subsidiaries, Alembic Glass and Jyoti Engineering. Attracted to Baroda by economic incentives and easy land acquisition, the Sarabhai family of Ahmedabad began small-scale chemical and pharmaceutical firms in the mid-1940s. After independence, chemical, pharmaceutical and engineering firms overshadowed textiles with the opening of a major public sector oil refinery that supports a large contemporary fertiliser complex.[97] Although several states experienced accelerated industrial growth when the Second World War cut off imported goods and stimulated domestic demand, Baroda sustained exceptional growth.[98] However, historians have yet to analyse the relationship between these early efforts at creating an industrial infrastructure in Baroda and Mysore and the subsequent emergence of Baroda as the core of a major petrochemical complex and of Bangalore as the Indian equivalent of Silicon Valley. Further study is needed before judgements about the lack of success of princely industrialisation schemes are canonised.

As most princes did not have a defined privy purse until the last decades of their rule, those in major states controlled significant sums of money. A few chose to invest in industrial enterprises in British India and British government securities, the latter with active British encouragement. Fifteen princes held 13 per cent of the shares of the Tata Iron and Steel Company (TISCO), with Madho Rao Scindia of Gwalior injecting £400 000.[99] Gwalior

---

[96] Hardiman, 'Baroda', in Jeffrey, *People*, p. 121.
[97] Howard L. Erdman, *Political Attitudes of Indian Industry: A Case Study of the Baroda Business Elite* (London, 1971), pp. 5–16.
[98] Copland, *Princes*, pp. 184–5.
[99] Kumar, *Cambridge Economic History*, vol. 2, p. 591; Headrick, *Tentacles*, p. 290.

was also a major investor in Bombay-based industries, but his activities have not been studied. Another Maratha prince, Sayaji Rao of Baroda, had invested in TISCO. Unfortunately he also put capital into the Villiers Companies, which failed to fulfil their promises to develop coal mines and a new steel mill in Bihar. The gaekwad eventually lost Rs 7 million of his private and state assets.[100]

During the minority of Man Singh of Jaipur, British administrators invested surplus Jaipur state revenues in GOI securities. By then the earlier British prohibition on princes lending to their peers had been lifted, possibly in an effort to promote princely solidarity and prevent financial crises from weakening conservative allies. The Jaipur durbar extended loans to Bikaner, Bharatpur, Alwar and Tonk, and so by 1940/41 it was earning Rs 2 million annually from these loans and its British securities.[101] There is fragmentary evidence that for some durbars such as Jaipur and Baroda, income from investments outside the states and in state railways reduced their critical dependence on land revenue. Consequently they would be able to make some concessions on land revenue rates in response to peasant protest movements.

Ports

Although most of the princely states were landlocked, fourteen of them, generally located in western India, had coastal ports. At first these ports received little freight destined for British India. However, the expansion of railways provided shorter transportation links between these princely ports and the major urban centres of northwestern India than the established ports of Bombay and Karachi in British India. In the twentieth century, princes attempted to attract trade by developing their port facilities to receive ocean-going ships and thereby benefit from increased customs duties. The most prominent developers were Baroda at Okhla, Nawanagar at Bedi, and to a lesser extent Kutch at Kandla. As trade increased at Bedi and Okhla and began to decrease slightly at British Indian ports, the British and the princes hotly debated the issue of customs duties. John McLeod has analysed the situation for seven coastal states of the Western India States Agency, namely Bhavnagar, Jafarabad, Junagadh, Kutch, Morvi, Nawanagar and Porbandar.[102]

Goods from ports in princely states coming into British India were supposed to pay British Indian tariffs as they were ostensibly entering from foreign territory. Since traffic was so light before 1900, little effort was made to collect

---

[100] Gaekwad, *Sayajirao*, pp. 337–40.   [101] Stern, *Cat*, p. 250.   [102] McLeod, *Sovereignty*, ch. 5.

customs duties. Once rail links were in place, some importers began to land goods at princely ports that had lower duties and then avoid paying British Indian tariffs at the borders. They also benefited from shorter distances. Moreover, smugglers tended to favour the more lightly patrolled ports in the princely states. Concerned about its customs revenues, in 1905 the GOI established the Viramgam Line as a customs cordon around Kathiawar and Kutch. At each border crossing the British collected customs duties according to their established rate, so goods entering through the princely ports had to pay twice. Even with lower transportation costs, this practice made the princely ports uneconomical and soon the coastal states experienced declining customs revenues. When the British needed wartime allies, they compromised with the protesting princes. In 1917 they removed the Viramgam Line in return for a promise from the princes to charge the British Indian rate of tariffs at their ports, with the proviso that the customs cordon could be reimposed if warranted by British fiscal interests.

After 1917 the princes sought to increase trade to their ports by lowering port fees that were not regulated and by enhancing their port facilities. Nawanagar was the first to open a modernised port at Bedi by 1927, and between 1925/26 and 1926/27 its customs duties increased from Rs 30 lakhs to Rs 78 lakhs. That sum represented 2 per cent of the total of British Indian customs duties. The GOI quickly decided its fiscal interests needed to be safeguarded and devised the so-called certificate system. The princes had to remit to the GOI the duty collected on all goods imported into British India. Thus they would retain only the custom duties on goods consumed within the princely states of Kathiawar. Although this system was slightly modified in 1929 to allow princely retention of all duties below Rs 2 lakhs and thus satisfy princes with smaller ports, the rulers with larger ports remained alienated. Ranjitsinhji of Nawanagar and Sayaji Rao of Baroda objected sharply to customs policies at the Round Table Conference of 1930 and during subsequent negotiations over federation. Neither was a firm ally during those critical years. After federation became a mute issue in 1939, the British made no further efforts to conciliate any of the western Indian states on the customs issue.[103]

McLeod points out that the British were motivated primarily by fiscal objectives, while the princes were concerned with any attenuation of their sovereignty. In general the GOI was willing to make concessions to the princes when their political support was needed, as in 1917 or in 1929, but heeded

---

[103] Ibid., pp. 103–8.

their financial department when they felt less threatened politically. Although McLeod focuses on the political aspects of the dispute over the ports, his work illustrates how British policies restricted economic developments in the princely states that might affect British fiscal or economic well-being.[104] At the same time the princes never ceased to resist incursions on their sovereignty. Moreover, some undertook significant economic investments within restricted circumstances that laid the groundwork for post-colonial economic developments.

CONCLUSION

The princely states of India were enmeshed within the overall political and economic framework of the British India empire. Their autonomy was restricted in numerous ways through treaty provisions but even more extensively through the never defined doctrines of usage and paramountcy. However, the significant variations among the princely states that existed until 1947 indicates the possibilities for autonomous activity in some spheres. Ecological and historical factors were influential, but personal initiatives were also vital. Thus rulers in three disparate geo-cultural spheres – the coastal Travancore and Cochin, the peninsular Mysore, and the plains of Baroda – could craft highly centralised, bureaucratised governmental structures that made significant improvements in the lives of their subjects through increased literacy, opportunities for government employment, and sometimes changes in land revenue rates. In even more difficult climatic environments such as Bikaner, a maharaja could decisively influence the economic development of his state and the position of his subjects through an irrigation project such as the Gang Canal.

Overall, the centralisation of power under the princely durbar that had begun in Mysore and Baroda as early as the late eighteenth century continued. The expanding bureaucratisation of princely state administrations countered the power of the nobility but also intensified the intervention of the princely states into the daily lives of their subjects. This process of intrusion was extremely uneven. It was strongest in the progressive states that expanded their functions to include support for primary schools, mobile libraries and public health facilities. For example, in 1930 Mysore had the first public hospital in India to dispense information on contraception. But even where the state's role remained more circumscribed, durbars encroached on the lives of subjects

---

[104] Ibid.

with British-style land revenue assessments that gave rights to some and curtailed them for others. Irrigation projects designed to increase productivity and revenues, as well as modern forms of transportation and communication, also caught state subjects in an expanding web. The impact of these policies would be one factor in stimulating the rise of new forms of popular political activity within these states.

CHAPTER 7

PRINCELY STATES: SOCIETY AND POLITICS

The paucity of research on social change and popular political activity in the princely states contributes to Orientalist representations of the princely states as the epitome of unchanging India. Fortunately the adventurous scholarship of a few social and cultural historians challenges such interpretations. Karen Leonard's path-breaking study of the kayasths of Hyderabad illuminates the adaptations of a literate, urban-based caste group to opportunities in a large princely state bureaucracy and then in a post-colonial successor state.[1] Robin Jeffrey has traced the gradual attenuation of nayar dominance in Travancore and the role of women in the evolution of the Kerala model of economic development in independent India.[2] Analyses of non-elite groups include David Hardiman's work on a low-caste reform movement within Baroda; Nandini Sundar on the tribal population in Bastar; Mridula Mukherjee and Mohinder Singh on peasant movements in the Punjab princely states before and after 1947 respectively; Shail Mayaram on the construction of Muslim identity among the marginalised Meos in Alwar; and Janaki Nair on labourers in Mysore.[3] Their work explores the internal dynamics of group formation and identity and political struggles for a greater portion of scarce political, economic, and ritual resources.

Other scholars have concentrated on the political associations and agitational activity of elite and non-elite groups. Actors range from newly educated young men ambitious for political power, to peasants who found their lives and resources increasingly circumscribed by jagirdars, who were being squeezed by centralising durbars and commercialised agriculture, to landlords challenging constraints on their authority and resources. The political activities of these groups provide a framework through which the complex interplay between agitational political activity in British India and in the princely states and

---

[1] Leonard, *Social History*.

[2] Jeffrey, *Decline*; Robin Jeffrey, *Politics, Women and Well-Being: How Kerala Became 'a Model'* (Houndmills, Hampshire, 1992).

[3] David Hardiman, *The Coming of the Devi: Adivasi Assertion in Western India* (Delhi, 1987); Sundar, *Subalterns*; Mridula Mukherjee, 'Peasant Movement in Patiala State', *SH* 1 (1979), pp. 215–83, and 'Communists and Peasants in Punjab: A Focus on the Muzara Movement in Patiala, 1937–53', *SH* 2 (1981); Mohinder Singh, *Peasant Movement in PEPSU Punjab* (New Delhi, 1991); Mayaram, *Resisting Regimes*; Nair, *Miners*.

the diversity of political actors and agendas within the states themselves may be deciphered. To provide a grid on which popular political activity may be plotted, I will first discuss the evolution and relationship of the territorial boundaries of the princely states to the linguistic and religious composition of their populations. During the twentieth century, both rulers and ambitious popular political leaders in the princely states increasingly appealed to language and religion as the basis for their legitimacy and for group identity.

TERRITORIAL BOUNDARIES AND THE POPULATIONS OF STATES

The frontiers of most princely states during the eighteenth century oscillated frequently depending on a ruler's and his clansmen's control of military resources and their skills in the negotiation of alliances. As the British consolidated their political dominance in India from 1765 onward, their surveyors produced maps cataloguing conquests and marking boundaries, at least on paper, between their possessions and those of their adversaries and allies.[4] It is important to note that the formal inauguration of a British political colony in India occurred in the same decade as John Harrison's invention in 1761 of the chronometer, on which the measurement of longitude, and thus modern mapping, is based. This scientific discovery aided in the imaginary and physical construction of the modern empires and nation-states.

In the revised edition of his highly influential work on the genesis of nationalism, Benedict Anderson has analysed the role of mapping in the creation of the modern Thai state. Thongchai Winichakul, Anderson's key source on this topic, has argued that in the Thai experience

[a] map anticipated spatial reality, not vice versa. [A] map was a model for, rather than a model of, what it purported to represent . . . It had become a real instrument to concretize projections on the earth's surface. A map was now necessary for the new administrative mechanisms and for the troops to back up their claims . . . The discourse of mapping was the paradigm which both administrative and military operations worked within and served.[5]

A similar process appears to have occurred in the British colonial empire in India. During the nineteenth century both the British and the princes extended their authority over the populations that were inscribed within the boundaries

[4] Sen, *Distant Sovereignty*, pp. 65–84.
[5] Thongchai Winichakul, *Siam Mapped: A History of the Geo-Body of Siam*, PhD thesis, University of Sydney, 1988, p. 310, quoted in Benedict Anderson, *Imagined Communities: Reflections on the Origin and Spread of Nationalism*, rev. edn (London, 1991), pp. 173–4.

of their respective political spheres. In Chapter 6 I have described how princely administrations augmented their power by reducing that of their nobles and strengthening that of their appointed bureaucrats. In the princely states, borders were only gradually defined by maps, and later and haphazardly by physical markers. Boundaries were firmer where princely states abutted British Indian provinces, as in Mysore and Hyderabad, or where strategic considerations were important, as in Punjab. In western Rajputana the demarcation of boundaries continued into the nineteenth century. In more forbidding locales such as the Rann of Kutch and northern Kashmir there was never a precise definition, so the post-colonial states of India and Pakistan still dispute their international boundaries in those regions. During the nineteenth century British India and some princely states such as Hyderabad occasionally exchanged territory to gain borders regarded as strategically or economically more rational. Sometimes, as after the revolt of 1857, the British also rewarded loyal princes with small grants of territory that were not always contiguous with their states. In general, the boundaries of the princely states became frozen at varying stages in state formation.

Hyderabad, Mysore, Travancore and Cochin were coherent territorial units. In Rajputana many states had compact boundaries on maps, but they would be unmarked and vague in physical reality because of the desolate, unproductive character of the desert terrain. In these states princes shared control over the land with numerous intermediary jagirdars and thikanadars. In western and central India, many states ended up having pieces of territory widely dispersed among British Indian provinces and other princely states. Baroda was a prime example – on a map its territory looked like a piece of Swiss cheese.[6] E. M. Forster claimed that in Dewas Senior and Dewas Junior in central India boundaries might be in the middle of streets in the capital city they shared.[7] In many states with borders that resembled the seams of a crazy quilt, rulers might not share the language and religion of their subjects. Before the 1870s such a situation was not considered unusual since a ruler claimed legitimacy largely by conquest and then subsequently by offering protection from other invaders. Moreover, new ideas of nationalism and political legitimacy infiltrated unevenly into British Indian provinces and the princely states.

As theorists of nationalism from Hans Kohn to Benedict Anderson have argued, the idea that a state should incorporate a ruler and a population who

---

[6] See Kenneth X. Robbins, 'Use of Numismatic and Philatelic Source Material in the Study of the Princely States of India', *IBR* 15 (1988), pp. 144–6.

[7] E. M. Forster, *The Hill of Devi* (Harmondsworth, Middlesex, 1965, first published in 1953), pp. 33–6.

spoke a common language, had a common history, and shared a common religion within a defined territorial unit fostered new bases of political legitimacy. This emphasis on language, history and religion, coupled with the movement towards representative and responsible government in which the people of the nation-state were to have a voice, preferably through the election of representatives, profoundly influenced the development of popular political activity in the princely states. Numbers now counted. The decennial censuses on which the Imperial Government counted in order to control its subject populations demanded that Indians identified themselves according to their caste, language and religion.

Anderson has remarked on 'the "census-makers" passion for completeness and unambiguity. Hence their intolerance of multiple, politically "transvestite," blurred, or changing identifications . . . The fiction of the census is that everyone is in it, and that everyone has one – and only one – extremely clear place. No fractions'.[8] This assumption created categories of difference in India that erased more fluid conceptions of personhood and community. Someone who might speak several languages had to specify one as a mother tongue. It also began to undermine the legitimacy of rulers, whether imperial or local, who did not share language and religion with their subject populations. When coupled with government policies that allocated resources ranging from grants-in-aid for schools to seats in a representative assembly on the basis of numbers rather than status alone, these sharply drawn divisions would spawn new forms of popular political activity. But before analysing these political developments, I will briefly outline the complex interplay of ethnicity, languages and religions in the princely states.

In sparsely populated antique states such as those in Rajputana and the foothills of the Himalayas, there were two fairly distinct population groups. One was the adivasis or tribal groups and the other was the ruling clan and their cohorts. Although the former were readily distinguished from the latter, extensive differentiation exists among the aboriginal groups. Based on research in contemporary Udaipur, Maxine Weisgrau has described the complex variations among one such group, the Bhils. Not only are there social and economic differences within this category, but individual Bhils responded with a variety of names for themselves based on their perceptions of which term was thought most likely to yield desired resources. Thus many Bhils claimed that they were Minas, who are deemed to have a higher social status.[9]

---

[8] Anderson, *Imagined Communities*, p. 166.
[9] Maxine Weisgrau, 'Accounting for Tribal Diversity in Udaipur District', paper presented at Wisconsin Conference on South Asia, 6 November 1993.

Princely rulers had varied relationships with adivasis. In Amber/Jaipur, one aboriginal group, the Minas, was ceremonially incorporated into the state structure. A Mina leader placed the rajatilaka on the forehead of the Jaipur ruler during his installation ceremony, and Minas guarded the private treasure of the princely family. In some states such as Tehri Garhwal in the lower Himalayas, rulers were regarded as protectors of the aboriginals. During the 1960s this role resulted in tragedy in the jungly but mineral-rich state of Bastar in the northern Deccan. Pravir Chandra Bhanj Deo (1929–66), the erstwhile ruler, was considered the priest of Danteshwari Mai, the patron goddess of the adivasis and Bastar state. He provided political leadership for adivasis in their protests against government exploitation of forest and mineral resources and corruption in land settlement and reform programs. Local police responded to their demonstrations with a firing in 1961 that killed thirteen adivasis and another in 1966 when Pravir was shot on the steps of his palace. Nandini Sundar argues that the Pravir 'succeeded in mobilizing people because his movement articulated more than his own personal goals, it took up local issues and latent desires'.[10] There were also tribal groups such as the Meos in Alwar who opposed their ruler during the 1930s because of discriminatory religious and exploitative forest and land policies.[11] Their resistance will be discussed in greater detail below.

In Mughal successor states, of which Hyderabad was the sole example after 1858, the Mughal governor frequently shared few ties with the local population. The nizam was a Muslim, speaking Urdu and using Persian as an official language, in a state whose population in 1901 included only 10 per cent Urdu speakers, 46 per cent Telugu speakers, 26 per cent Marathi speakers, and 14 per cent Kannada speakers. The population was 88.6 per cent Hindu and 10.4 per cent Muslim.[12] In 1918 the nizam established the Urdu-language Osmania University, which fostered the creation of a 'Deccani synthesis' bringing together Hindus and Muslims in a cultural nationalism. This synthesis used Urdu as the linking language and constructed a paternity in which tolerant Muslim rulers fostered local cultural expressions. Unfortunately the education of mainly local Muslims at Osmania University would lead to an intensified conflict between these insider, Hyderabadi Muslims and the outsider, largely Hindu kayasths from northern India, who had monopolised positions in the westernised administration of the state. Anderson has highlighted the key role of the study and analysis of language and of universities in the formation of

---

[10] Sundar, *Subalterns*, p. 231 and ch. 7; Hurtig, *Maharajahs*, pp. 195–8.
[11] Mayaram, *Resisting Regimes*, chs 3–5.   [12] *Imperial Gazetteer. Hyderabad*, pp. 23–4.

European nationalisms. In Hyderabad a university that privileged a language spoken by a minority triggered the development of a Telugu cultural nationalism that ultimately achieved the Andhra Pradesh state in 1956.[13]

In the rebel or warrior states the situation was even more tangled. The princes of the southern Maratha states tended to share the Hindu religion and Marathi language with their subjects, but they were brahman and their subjects were labelled Maratha. Other Maratha rulers, such as those of Gwalior, Indore and Kolhapur, were often considered sudras even though they themselves claimed kshatriya status. Gwalior, Indore and Baroda had few Marathi speakers or Maratha caste members in their populations. In Punjab the maharaja of Patiala was a Sikh, Sidhu Jat, and his state was divided almost equally between Hindus and Muslims, with the Sikhs a minority. But by the 1931 census Sikhs numbered 38.9 per cent with Hindus 38.2 per cent and Muslims 22.4 per cent.[14] The language situation seemed more straightforward since an overwhelming majority of 85 per cent claimed Punjabi as their mother tongue in the 1931 census, and Patiala state would be the core area for the future demand for a Punjabi-speaking state, eventually achieved in 1967.[15]

In Travancore and Cochin there were highly stratified societies with large religious minorities linked by the common language of Malayalam. In the 1941 census Cochin had 45 per cent *avarna* (lower-caste) Hindus, 28 per cent Christians, 19 per cent *savarna* (higher-caste) Hindus, and 8 per cent Muslims; Travancore had 40 per cent avarna, 32 per cent Christian, 21 per cent savarna, and 7 per cent Muslims.[16] In both states there had been a premium on literacy because of a long history of cash-cropping and foreign trade, an ecosystem that allowed the existence of an unusually large leisured class, and higher status for women fostered by the matrilineal system of nayar Hindus and attitudes among Christians. Robin Jeffrey has argued that these cultural and geographical factors made literacy more highly prized than elsewhere, although state policies were also influential. In 1941 Travancore had a literacy rate

---

[13] Leonard, *Social History*, pp. 216–21; Karen Leonard, 'The Deccani Synthesis in Old Hyderabad: An Historiographic Essay', *JPHS* 21 (1973), pp. 205–18; Hyderabad State Committee for History of the Freedom Movements, *Freedom Struggle in Hyderabad*, vol. 4 (Hyderabad, 1966).

[14] A succinct analysis of the increase in Sikhs from 1881 to 1931 in the *Census of India, 1931*, XVII, *Punjab*, Part I, pp. 304–7 has attributed this phenomenon throughout Punjab to a growing denotation of Sikhism as a religion distinct from Hinduism and to a feeling among lower-caste members that there was more prestige in being a Sikh than a Hindu. In the 1911 census the definition of a Sikh was changed from one who wears his or her hair long and refrains from smoking to a definition that allowed each person to register as he or she wished: *Census of India, 1911*, XIV, *Punjab*, Part I, pp. 154–5.

[15] *Census of India, 1931*, XVII, *Punjab*, Part I, p. 284. The next most numerous language was Rajasthani, which 9 per cent of Patialans claimed as their mother tongue.

[16] Quoted from the Census of India, 1941, in Jeffrey, *Politics*, p. 26.

of 47.1 per cent and Cochin had 41 per cent when the all-India rate was 15.1 per cent. Thus although Indian princes might have their power sharply restricted by their colonial overlord, promotion of elementary education by the rulers of Travancore and Cochin in the Malayalam vernacular could make a significant difference in the lives of their subjects.[17] It also eased the integration of these princely states with the adjoining British India district of Malabar into the post-colonial state of Kerala, while the social divisions were a key element in the development of the communist party there.

Although the popular political movements in the princely states are not the same as nationalisms in the European or all-India modes, they were intimately linked to appeals based on class, religious and linguistic commonalities. This situation was very different from what had prevailed during the eighteenth and nineteenth centuries. Then rulers were not expected to share common bonds with their subject populations. According to Hindu political theory enshrined in the concept of rajadharma, rulers were to maintain the military force that enabled them to provide protection and to secure order for their subjects. Some rulers might also have a distinctive religious role as priest or servant of a patron deity of the area. This status tended to be more common in areas on the periphery of major power centres such as in the Himalayan states or coastal ones such as Travancore isolated by geographical features from close interaction with major Indian empires. Consequently, before the late nineteenth century political and economic elites spoke several languages, and rulers imposed a link language such as Persian. In the matter of religion, the most that would be expected is that rulers would be tolerant of the religious practices of their subjects.

By the beginning of the twentieth century, popular political leaders began to demand more. They synthesised traditional and new forms of protest, and rulers responded in equally eclectic modes. What was strikingly different was the increasingly bounded nature of communal categories, such as caste, religion and linguistic groups. British Orientalist constructions of types in Indian society and their manipulation of these categories stimulated much of this demarcation. These fabrications penetrated the Indian states through the instruments of decennial censuses, state gazetteers, religious pamphlets, and newspapers. But the princes themselves contributed to these social constructions through their patronage of caste histories, archaeological projects, and translations of religious texts, as described in Chapter 5. Thus the categories of brahman and non-brahman, kshatriya, Hindu, Muslim and Sikh became new ways of

[17] Ibid., pp. 56–8.

defining oneself and moving from the smaller groups of clan and town identity to larger princely state and pan-Indian categories.

POPULAR POLITICAL ACTIVITY IN PRINCELY STATES

Political activity, by which I simply mean the pursuit of a share of scarce material and ritual resources, in the princely states during the eighteenth and nineteenth centuries has been studied primarily at the elite levels of rulers, their immediate relatives, their clan members, their military allies, and those who controlled land. Frequently all of these were interlinked. Recent scholarship has begun to focus on popular political activity first among literate groups and then among peasant-cultivators and tribal peoples in the princely states. This involvement of larger groups has been labelled political mobilisation. In my analysis I follow Robin Jeffrey's concept that political mobilisation means that there are basic changes in the political attitudes, organisation and goals of these newly involved groups and that their general orientation is to seek some structural adjustments. In the princely states three phases of political mobilisation are discernible.

The first phase of popular political activity centred on specific local grievances such as too many 'foreigners' or outsiders in government offices and a lack of freedom of the press and assembly. Dick Kooiman has also emphasised the ways in which the collection of quantitative data reinforced group consciousness and triggered demands for equity in government employment and social benefits.[18] Urban, literate groups were initially the most vocal in articulating their grievances. In Travancore this stage began in the late nineteenth century, but elsewhere it emerged only during the 1910s and 1920s. Petition was the principal mode of operation, and the organisational structure relied upon informal networks. A second phase commenced in the late 1920s and early 1930s and demanded greater popular representation and the legal right to form autonomous political associations. Although urban-based, literate elites remained dominant, they now entered a more confrontational stance vis-à-vis rulers. Tactics shifted from petitions to public demonstrations.

During the 1930s and 1940s peasant movements constituted a third phase that overlapped temporally but usually not organisationally with the urban-based organisations. In the rural areas middle-caste groups generated the most

---

[18] Dick Kooiman, 'The Strength of Numbers: Enumerating Communities in India's Princely States', *SA* 20, 1 (1997), pp. 81–98.

visible leaders, with relatively few prominent low-caste or scheduled caste and tribal leaders. Peasant movements sought alterations in land relationships, usually to provide greater security for tenant rights. By the 1940s there were demands for the abolition of the jagirdari structure and distribution of land to the cultivators; more equitable land taxes; remission of land revenue in periods of environmental stress; an end to *begar* or forced labour; and adjustments in oppressive conditions resulting from the commercialisation of local economies. During all three phases populist leaders usually reaffirmed the legitimacy of princely rule. To illustrate these phases from the late nineteenth century onward, I will focus on Travancore before exploring more broadly their complex evolution at numerous sites during the twentieth century.

By the 1890s several factors had fostered new organisations and political activity at the state level in Travancore.[19] More influential here than elsewhere, missionary schools, increasingly funded with grants-in-aid from the state, and missionary pronouncements about the theoretical equality of all believers (despite continuing preservation of social distinctions in many missionary establishments) had stimulated group consciousness and rising expectations. Crucial secular factors included an expanded road network that fostered communication and an awareness of the possibility of other lifestyles, as well as a developing state administration that provided wage labour for low-status groups in public works departments and alternative opportunities for educated but economically disadvantaged groups. When more education did not achieve more government positions, nayars, the dominant caste, were the first to organise a new association, the Malayali Sabha, around 1884. Although it projected a non-communal image, nayars were the overwhelming majority in this body that inaugurated petition politics in Travancore. Their Malayali Memorial in 1891 sought a legal definition of who was a native of Travancore and by inference protested against the Tamil brahman preponderance in the state administration. Their demand was similar to the contemporaneous efforts in Hyderabad to define the dividing line between mulki and non-mulki.

Two other major communities in Travancore soon entered petition politics. Dr P. Palpu (1863–50), an early ezhava (avarna) student at Maharaja's College in Trivandrum who was subsequently denied admission to the medical college and government employment in Travancore, organised ezhava petitions to the Travancore Government in 1895–96 asking for entry of ezhavas to all schools and government employment. An ezhava *sannyasi*, Sri Narayana Guru, provided the initial focus for the first caste association in Travancore, the

---

[19] This discussion relies on Jeffrey, *Decline*, Kawashima, *Missionaries*, and Kooiman, 'Strength'.

Sri Narayana Dharma Paripalana Yogam (SNDP Yogam), founded in 1902 'to promote religious and secular education and industrious habits among the Elava [ezhava] community'.[20] In practical politics their goals were the opening of government service and Hindu temples to this low-status caste. Syrian Christians formed a Travancore and Cochin Christian Association that initially sought to end sectarian divisions among Christians and to petition for admission to government service.

The nayars launched several small caste associations that would eventually be superseded by the Nair Service Society (NSS) organised in 1914 to promote caste unity and advancement. Similar to other caste associations in its nurture of educational and welfare institutions, reform of 'controversial or outdated customs' and protection of group political interests, the NSS also wanted reforms of family law. It lobbied for the recognition of liaisons between younger nayar sons and non-nayar women as legal marriages and for the right of nayars to initiate partition of the traditional *tarawad* or joint family holding, thereby creating individual inheritances. Because Travancore was unusual in the close integration of its urban and rural populations and its relatively high rate of literacy, these caste-communal associations bridged the urban/rural divide. Roads and waterways enabled people to move freely, and newspapers spread ideas and programs.

Locally generated and based caste and religious reform organisations similar to those in Travancore may have existed in other princely states during the late 1800s, but scholarly research has made little progress in excavating them. Literary, social and political associations began to proliferate in princely India by the 1920s. R. L. Handa has claimed that there was a growing resentment of princely autocracy, which the British paramount power had allowed after the departure of Curzon in order to use the princes as counterweights to Indian nationalism.[21] Equally important factors were the rise in literacy rates and the consequent growth of indigenous professional elites within princely states; the intensifying hostility against outsiders in princely administrations; the impact of economic changes related to the tightening integration of India into a worldwide commercial economy; and the eruption of political activity during the first non-cooperation movement, which oozed through the porous boundaries between British and princely India. Another issue was the ambivalent relationship between the Indian National Congress and the princely states.

---

[20] As quoted in Jeffrey, *Decline*, p. 210.
[21] R. L. Handa, *History of Freedom Struggle in Princely States* (New Delhi, 1968), pp. 87–8.

THE INDIAN NATIONAL CONGRESS AND THE PRINCELY STATES

After a brief flirtation with the princes as financial benefactors during the 1880s, the Indian National Congress consciously distanced itself from political mobilisation in the princely states. S. K. Patil has bemoaned that '[t]he economic and political demands of the Congress completely neglected the Indian states' before 1920, and Vanaja Rangaswami has claimed that the Congress 'refused to involve itself with the democratic struggle [in the princely states] on its own, at any time'.[22] Both Rangaswami and Urmila Phadnis have defended the Congress strategy of non-interference, of which Mahatma Gandhi was the leading proponent. They argue that it was a conscious policy decision to avoid two fronts because of limited resources, to focus attention on the goal of freedom from the British, and to avoid regional fragmentation.[23] As an all-Indian organisation, the Congress confronted many of the same issues faced by the GOI in its effort to control India with limited resources. In some ways Gandhi's strategy paralleled the British policy of non-interference unless vital interests were threatened. The two all-India rivals concentrated their resources on British Indian provinces and left autocratic princes and their relatively resource-poor subjects to stalemate each other. Once the outcome was decided in the main arena, then both the British and the Congress would attend to princely states.

Several factors besides Gandhi account for Congress ambivalence. Ambitious lawyers dominated the early Congress, and they were concerned about their lack of legal standing in the states, worried about the difficulties of organising in so many disparate units where civil liberties were less protected than in British India, and sympathetic to the princes as sources of legitimation and models of the Indian capacity to govern.[24] On the death of Maharaja Chamarajendra Wadiyar of Mysore, a Congress resolution in 1894 advised Indians that '[h]is constitutional reign was at once a vindication of their political capacity, an example for their active emulation, and their future political liberties'.[25] During the late nineteenth century the social reforms of progressive princes

---

[22] S. K. Patil, *The Congress Party and Princely States* (Bombay, 1981), p. 15; Rangaswami, *Story*, p. 236.

[23] Ibid., pp. 235–46; Urmila Phadnis, 'Gandhi and Indian States – A Probe in Strategy', in S. C. Biswas (ed.), *Gandhi: Theory and Practice, Social Impact and Contemporary Relevance* (Shimla, 1969), pp. 360–74.

[24] Barbara N. Ramusack, 'Congress and the People's Movement in Princely India: Ambivalence in Strategy and Organization', in Richard Sisson and Stanley Wolpert (eds), *Congress and Indian Nationalism: The Pre-Independence Phase* (Berkeley CA, 1988), pp. 378–81.

[25] A. Moin Zaidi and Shaheda Zaidi (eds), *Encyclopaedia of Indian National Congress*, vol. 1, *1885–1890* (New Delhi, 1976), p. 489.

were positive examples of the Indian capacity to rule and sites of Indian resistance to western models.[26] As in the case of Indian women, idealised types of princely rulers and princely states were constructed as part of the dialogue between colonisers and the colonised. Consequently many Congress leaders were equivocal about attacking this part of their heritage.

Since Gandhi's grandfather and father had served in Kathiawadi princely durbars, Gandhi is viewed as being personally sympathetic to the princes. Moreover, he shrewdly calculated the political value of maintaining ties to conservative Indians, whom he labelled trustees. Congressmen, who were professionals, might also have been attracted to the lucrative opportunities for employment as legal counsel as well as administrators in the princely states. Not only did lawyers such as C. P. Ramaswami Aiyar in Travancore serve as 'constitutional advisers' or diwans, but Motilal Nehru and others continued to provide legal services for the princes as late as the early 1930s. More recently, subaltern scholars such as David Hardiman and Ramachandra Guha have emphasised the Congress's suspicion of peasant movements that it did not control.[27] However, much as the stated British preference for non-intervention might be modified in practice in response to local conditions or the viewpoints of particular political officers, so Gandhi as well as other Congress members maintained contacts and occasionally intruded personally in the princely states.

Pleading with the princes to establish *Ramraj*, the ideal rule of Rama, the hero of the epic *Ramayana*, Gandhi articulated a policy of non-intervention in overt political mobilisation within the princely states for almost two decades after his return to India in 1915. Here again there is at least one parallel in the Gandhian strategy for the populations of princely states and Indian women. Both were to concentrate on 'constructive work'.[28] Since the removal of discrimination related to untouchability was a key aspect of 'constructive work', Gandhi felt free to visit Travancore in 1925 to lend support to a *satyagraha* campaign demanding the opening of roads around a Siva temple at Vaikam to low-caste, mainly ezhava, Hindus. As would happen in several Gandhian offensives, this effort ended in a compromise. The government constructed diversionary roads around the temple that all Hindus could traverse. The crusade for the right of all Hindus to enter the temples, nevertheless, continued into the 1930s. When Gandhi returned to Travancore in 1934, he validated a more radical rhetoric including a call for the abolition of caste that brought new

---

[26] Bhagavan, 'Demystifying'.
[27] Hardiman, *Coming*, pp. 206–17; Ramachandra Guha, *The Unquiet Woods: Ecological Change and Peasant Resistance in the Himalaya* (Berkeley, 1989), pp. 83–4.
[28] Madhu Kishwar, 'Gandhi on Women', *EPW* 20 (5 October 1985), pp. 1694–701.

groups of poorer men into the political arena. Eventually Ramaswami Aiyar would have the young maharaja of Travancore proclaim the opening of all the temples on the ruler's birthday of 12 November 1936 to pre-empt the political appeal of the SNDP Yogam. By this time, however, class divisions were emerging within the SNDP Yogam as lower-class ezhavas sought economic amelioration and equality of ritual and social status.[29] A lower-status group in another administratively 'progressive' princely state further north would have similar goals.

David Hardiman has provided a fascinating account of the Devi movement among adivasis and the influence of congressmen and Gandhian injunctions in Gujarat districts spread between the Bombay presidency and Baroda state. Articulating self-purification legitimated by the authority of the goddess Devi, who communicated through possessed individuals, the Devi movement initially promoted temperance, vegetarianism and personal cleanliness among adivasi, who came to call themselves the *raniparaj* or people of the forest. Some goals represented a shift to the lifestyle of clean castes and a higher ritual status, but temperance and the refusal to work for Parsi liquor dealers fused ritual and economic issues. They were also a direct attack on a class who exploited the adivasis as moneylenders and landlords as well as vendors of liquor. During 1922 the Devi, speaking through her human instruments, advocated the burning of foreign cloth, the use of *khadi*, and the boycott of government schools. Shortly thereafter Gandhian lieutenants, notably Vallabhbhai Patel, a Gujarati lawyer and key Congress organiser, began to transform the Devi movement from a religious to a secular one and to try unsuccessfully to mitigate the class struggle against the Parsis. Congress leaders emphasised those aspects that were congruent with the Gandhian program such as temperance and cleanliness. They also endorsed a more disciplined organisational structure with authority coming from resolutions passed by votes rather than messages transmitted during divine possession.

The Baroda authorities responded both more aggressively and more sympathetically than did British administrators, illustrating the personal autocracy possible even in a progressive princely state. In 1923 Manubhai Mehta (1868–1946), the chief minister of Baroda, banned Devi meetings, but the ruling gaekwad lifted the ban as long as the meetings were confined to temperance. In 1925 Gandhi presided at the Third Raniparaj Conference, and many of the adivasis continued to give firm support for a Gandhian program of spinning,

[29] Robin Jeffrey, 'Travancore: Status, Class and the Growth of Radical Politics, 1860–1940', in Jeffrey, *People*, pp. 148–64.

temperance and vegetarianism despite a communal split over these changes in lifestyle.[30]

Although a few individual congressmen from British India were active in princely states during the 1920s, there was little deviation in Congress policy for over a decade. In 1927 political leaders from the princely states made two efforts to establish coordinating organisations and to forge closer ties with the Congress. Representatives from western Indian states dominated an Indian States' People's Conference (ISPC) in Bombay on 17–18 December 1927. An association using the same name but later becoming the South India States' People's Conference convened nine days later in Madras just before the Indian National Congress met there. At their Madras session the Congress responded by declaring that it was 'emphatically of the opinion that in the interests of both the Rulers and the people of Indian States they should establish representative institutions and responsible Governments in their States at an early date'.[31] Individuals from the princely states were allowed to join the Congress, and many participated in the civil disobedience movement of 1930–32. Subsequently they would look for some reciprocal support from the Congress in their struggle for responsible government in the states.

The Indian National Congress as an organisation remained aloof from the states' people's groups until 1938 and 1939 when several Congress leaders, notably Gandhi and Vallabhbhai Patel, became intimately involved in key agitations. Several scholars have argued that the shift in Congress policy was largely for pragmatic political reasons. First, the emerging political organisations and their more confrontational tactics in the states might be an asset to Congress. Second, there was concern about the impact of princely representatives in the federation proposed in the 1935 *Government of India Act*, which will be discussed in Chapter 8. Third, Congress socialists at the national level intensified their demands for a change in the non-intervention policy; they were led by Jayaprakash Narayan and Kamaladevi Chattopadhyaya (1903–90), Congress provincial leaders, especially in Gujarat, and Congress dissidents, most notably Subhas Chandra Bose (1897–1945).[32] According to Ian Copland, some princes were also seeking accommodation with the Congress, perceived after its strong showing in the 1936 elections to be the heir-apparent of their British

---

[30] David Hardiman, 'Adivasi Assertion in South Gujarat: The Devi Movement', in Ranajit Guha (ed.) *Subaltern Studies* III (Delhi, 1984), pp. 196–230; Hardiman, *Coming.*
[31] N. N. Mitra (ed.), *Indian Annual Register*, vol. 2, July–December 1927 (Calcutta, 1927), pp. 411–13.
[32] Bipan Chandra et al., *India's Struggle for Independence 1857–1947* (New Delhi, 1988), pp. 356–74 (Mridula Mukherjee wrote this chapter on the 'The Freedom Struggle in Princely India'); Copland, 'Congress Paternalism', pp. 127–9; Ramusack, 'Congress', pp. 387–9.

patron.[33] On the Congress side, by their active involvement in agitations in Mysore, Travancore and Rajkot, Gandhi and Patel undertook to block their national and provincial rivals from establishing a firm base within a constituency that now appeared to have some potential.

Although it was not the sharp break that some have declared, a compromise resolution passed at the Haripura Congress in 1938 legitimated increased Congress activity in princely India. Initially Gandhi sent emissaries to investigate the situation in the princely states since, like the British, Congress found it difficult at times to comprehend and to control these internal political networks. Because Gandhi wanted these constituencies to conform to his political and social programs and was generally sympathetic to the princes, he used agents who were personally loyal to him and likely to be non-confrontational with durbar officials and popular leaders. Two examples are Rajkumari Amrit Kaur (1889–1964), a member of a branch of the Kapurthala ruling family excluded from succession because of its conversion to Christianity, and Agatha Harrison (1885–1954), a Quaker supporter of Gandhi based in London.[34] Gandhi would also encourage Jawaharlal Nehru, his designated successor, to become more active in princely state politics.

In 1939 Nehru became president of the AISPC (All-India States' People's Conference), which had recently added All to its title, partly to prevent the socialists and Subhas Chandra Bose from capturing this association. Nehru tried to energise the AISPC by appointing Balwantry Mehta as its general secretary and Pattabhi Sitaramayya as editor of a weekly journal, by undertaking some fundraising, and by despatching roving investigators, including Rajkumari Amrit Kaur, who acted as intelligence agents in particularly troubled states. The AISPC also published a few investigative reports and a statistical overview.[35] But Bombay-based leaders continued to dominate, and the AISPC never developed into a national organisation. Thus political mobilisation among princely states' subjects continued to occur at the state level with occasional participation by individual Congress leaders pursuing particular agendas.

Consequently, despite British allegations, outside agitators were not the prime organisers of the subjects within the princely states. The relationship between states' people's groups and the Congress was an anguished one even after the formal prohibition on Congress intervention was modified. This situation would make it difficult for the Congress to solidify its base after 1947 in states that incorporated large blocks of the princely ruled territories. In

[33] Copland, 'Congress Paternalism', p. 132.   [34] Ramusack, 'Congress', p. 390.

[35] During the 1930s the tracts were on Patiala, Orissa, Limbdi, Ratlam, and Bikaner and the overview was *What are the Indian States?*

Mysore and Travancore, however, indigenous leaders established local Congress committees during the 1930s with different results.

POLITICAL MOBILISATION WITHIN THE PRINCELY STATES

During the 1910s urban-based princely state subjects formed *praja mandals* (people's organisations or associations) or *lok parishads* (people's conferences). Generally educated in British India because of the paucity of post-secondary institutions in most princely states, these subjects were based in British India if their target state was actively suppressing the right of association. Princely governments echoed British claims about external agents but few were evident. In this phase during the 1910s and 1920s, the initial demands were for greater recruitment of states' subjects to government employment; the guarantee of civil liberties, particularly the freedoms of press, assembly and association; and in a few instances representative assemblies. Few popular leaders questioned the legitimacy of princely rule or its end. Their epithet for themselves, 'Slaves of Slaves', articulated their assessment that the British had enslaved their rulers. Praja mandals usually attributed political oppression in states not to princes but to authoritarian or corrupt officials, frequently outsiders, or scheming zenana women and their advisers. The Praja Mithra Mandali in 1917 in Mysore might have been the first such state-level association. It was soon joined by others in Baroda, Bhor, Indore, the Kathiawar Rajkiya Parishad in 1921, and the Deccan States Subjects Conference. Similar groups proliferated during the 1920s and 1930s in Kathiawad states such as Bhavnagar, Gondal and Junagadh; in Rajputana including Alwar, Bikaner, Jaipur, Jodhpur and Udaipur; in Orissan states; and in Punjab with the Punjab Riyasti Praja Mandal.[36]

By the late 1920s and into the 1940s the praja mandals entered a second, more activist stage as evinced in public demonstrations and protest marches. Now urban-based praja mandals sought representative and increasingly responsible government that would diminish princely autocracy but not deny princely authority. They asked for the introduction or widening of the franchises for representative assemblies; elected members of legislative councils selected as ministers, particularly after the popularly elected ministries had taken office in British Indian provinces in 1937; privy purses for rulers; and increased funding for social infrastructure, especially educational and medical facilities. They especially coveted formal recognition of the praja mandals as

---

[36] Copland, 'Congress Paternalism', p. 122; Handa, *History*, p. 89.

legitimate political organisations and the release of political prisoners arrested during public protests. Peasant movements developed simultaneously, but contact and collaboration between them and the urban-based praja mandals were limited.

The major challenges for popular political leaders in the states were to broaden their popular base, to use the resources of political groups in British India, and to achieve some leverage with rulers and state administrations.[37] The first and most intricate problems were to bridge the gaps between urban and rural sectors and to overcome the boundaries among caste and religious groups. Mysore, Travancore, Hyderabad, Rajkot, Patiala, Kashmir and states in Rajputana have elicited most of the scholarly attention, so the following overview reflects this coverage. To illustrate the general trends in popular political activity in the princely states, I will focus on three pairs of contrasting states: Mysore-Rajkot, Rajputana-Tehri Garhwal, and Travancore-Patiala. Both the Indian National Congress and individual Congress members interacted with urban-based groups in Mysore and Rajkot. But Mysore was the site of autonomous labour movements that had few parallels in other states. Rajputana and Tehri Garhwal illustrate the ongoing tensions between praja mandals and peasant movements. Associational activities in Travancore and Patiala illuminate the potent appeals of communal and class-based organisations within princely states. Although the Congress was able to lay the groundwork for later dominance in the first two pairs of states, in Travancore and Patiala communist and communal parties were such strong antagonists that they would emerge as major rivals in the post-colonial era. Finally, to delineate the many variants of Muslim political mobilisation within the princely states, I will survey developments in Alwar, Jammu and Kashmir, and Hyderabad.

James Manor has examined how Congress politicians in Mysore were able to integrate three levels of local, state and national politics in a princely state where politics was compartmentalised because of its social structure.[38] Belonging to a kshatriya caste group with fewer than a thousand members in 1881, the Mysore ruling family had no ties to the countryside. Consequently the ruler and his administration had allowed elite land-controllers considerable autonomy at the local level in return for their support of the durbar. During the 1920s and early 1930s, there were two distinct, non-official groupings within elite Mysore politics. Non-brahman but dominant caste leaders, especially the Lingayats, adherents of a devotional reform Hindu sect, and Vokkaligas, an

---

[37] Robert Stern analyses what constituted resources for such politicians in 'An Approach to Politics in the Princely States', in Jeffrey, *People*, pp. 355–71.
[38] Manor, *Political Change*, chs 1–2.

occupational category of cultivators who acquired a base as leaders of district boards, commanded one coalition. They sought more educational facilities and government positions for non-brahmans. Urban-based brahmans who carried the Congress label formed the other bloc and appealed for a responsible, parliamentary style of government. Since they had a small numerical base, the brahmans solicited strength from the political resources offered by Indian nationalism. However, they were relatively ineffective because of the ambivalent policy of the Congress. Neither Mysore group developed an internal mass base during the 1920s and early 1930s. Gradually their mutual experiences with a administratively progressive princely durbar that made only limited political concessions stimulated more radical political demands. Their new aggressiveness in turn occasioned stronger repressive measures.[39]

By 1936 the non-brahman People's Federation agreed to merge with the Mysore Congress. For the non-brahmans the increased attention of the national Congress to states' subjects seemed to promise greater Congress pressure on the British raj, and for the local congressmen the non-brahmans provided needed links to local politics. Gandhi's disapproval of a resolution passed at a meeting of the All-India Congress Committee at Calcutta in 1937 protesting against certain repressive actions of the Mysore administration and calling for support of Mysoreans indicated that Congress patronage was still not unequivocal. Subsequently, from 1936 until 1942 the unified Mysore State Congress worked to break down the isolation between the state and local political arenas,[40] but it faced another formidable challenge from Leftists within and without its organisation over the representation of the interests of industrial labourers.

Because of its program of economic as well as administrative modernisation, Mysore had one of the more sizeable industrial labour forces among the princely states. Janaki Nair has skilfully excavated the development of a working-class culture in Bangalore and the Kolar Gold Fields that generated public protests and private resistance as well as occasional alliances with 'outside' leaders. Workers organised substantial strikes beginning with the compositors at the Mysore Government Press in 1920, to the 18-day strike in the Kolar Gold Fields in 1930, to a 72-day strike at Bangalore textile mills in 1941, to two waves of strikes during the Quit India movement. Within the factory environment workers defied restrictive industrial work routines through tardiness and absenteeism and the appropriation of materials. These actions reveal impressive organisational skills, a consciousness of their own interests, and ultimately

[39] Ibid., chs 4–6.   [40] Ibid., chs 6–7.

a lack of the economic resources necessary to sustain extended strikes. Nair discusses women and the influence of gender ideology in the industrial labour force. Male labour leaders saw themselves as protectors of women, arguing for benefits specific to them such as maternity leave. But they also relegated women to stereotypical female work where the labour was unskilled and the pay was low, such as the winding and reeling sections in textile industries.[41]

From the early 1920s Congress leaders in Mysore sought recognition by the durbar of the representatives of workers as part of their anti-imperialist campaign, while at the same time accepting the durbar's program for capitalist development and social stability.[42] Banning labour unions, the Mysore administration pursued a paternalistic model. Its diwan, Sir Mirza Ismail, served as the supposedly neutral mediator between management and labour but generally favoured the former. Escalating labour militancy and fears of 'uncontrolled' workers prompted the Mysore Government in 1941 to permit labour unions. Despite some effective individual protests, socialists and communists lacked institutional depth for a sustained opposition. Congress became dominant and gained a reputation for 'gentlemanly' trade unionism in Mysore until the late 1970s. Nair has asserted that '[t]he Congress programme was rich with ambiguities: sharing as it did the aspirations of the Mysore bureaucracy, it hoped to transform labour into a "partner" in the capitalist order with limited rights, and unhesitantly used culturally-derived notions of power in order to both initiate mass activity and keep it pegged to safe levels'.[43]

Because of their success in incorporating non-brahman and labour groups, in 1947 Mysore congressmen launched the formidable 'Mysore Chalo' movement that forced the diwan to concede and the maharaja to accept responsible government. After integration with the Indian Union, Congress had a well-forged political organisation in Mysore, albeit, according to Manor, at a level of development that was comparable to those in British Indian provinces during the 1920s.[44] Congress would nevertheless remain dominant in the post-colonial state of Karnataka until the 1970s.

Although Gandhi had withheld active support from agitations in Mysore in 1937, he chose to intervene in Rajkot, where he had lived for several years. John Wood has perceptively analysed the failure of this first attempt to secure constitutional change in a princely state through mass civil disobedience.[45]

[41] Nair, *Miners*, chs 4–8.
[42] Ibid., pp. 163–75, 251–60, 272–86.   [43] Ibid., p. 298.
[44] James Manor, 'Gandhian Politics and the Challenge to Princely Authority in Mysore, 1936–47', in Low, *Congress*, pp. 405–6.
[45] John R. Wood, 'Indian Nationalism in the Princely Context: The Rajkot Satyagraha of 1938–9', in Jeffrey, *People*, pp. 240–74; Chandra, *India's Struggle*, pp. 360–5.

The basis for a political confrontation in Rajkot began when a dissolute son, Dharmendra Sinhji (b. 1910, r. 1931–40), succeeded a sagacious and popular ruler, Thakore Saheb Lakhaji Raj. During the 1930s the young prince and his diwan, Durbar Virawala, restricted the political participation allowed under Lakhaji Raj and granted monopolies of basic products such as sugar, which enriched the administration at the expense of consumers. Popular reaction began with a strike at a state cotton mill to obtain better working conditions. It escalated to a revival of the Kathiawar Rajkiya Parishad, leading to state repression that sparked a *hartal* or general strike in August 1938.

Sardar Patel intervened with demands for new elections to the representative assembly, limits on princely withdrawals from the state treasury, reductions of land revenue, and the cancellation of monopolies. After multilateral negotiations between Patel, the British political agent and the diwan, with Agatha Harrison visiting as Gandhi's envoy, the thakore saheb and Patel concluded a settlement. The tough Gujarati congressman called off the satyagraha campaign in exchange for the ruler agreeing to a privy purse and the appointment of a committee to recommend reforms. Patel was to propose seven of the ten committee members. Alarmed by these concessions, the British indicated that they would support a tougher stance by the Rajkot durbar. The beleaguered administration responded with ordinances banning meetings, arrests, and lathi charges by police patrols. When Patel submitted his nominees, who were either brahmans or *bania*s, the administration adroitly advocated that the committee should be more inclusive of Rajkot subjects, especially Rajputs, Muslims and depressed communities. A shrewd diwan whose method has been labelled intrigue since it relied on surreptitious bargaining checkmated Patel's confrontational style.

In early 1939 Gandhi was facing a serious challenge from Subhas Chandra Bose, who had contested and won the presidency of the Congress for a second term against Gandhi's wishes. To counter the Bengali leader, who argued for Congress support of the political struggle in the princely states, Gandhi proceeded to Rajkot. When the thakore saheb refused to accept Patel's nominees, Gandhi began a fast unto death. The British became worried because of spreading agitations and the viceroy pleaded for arbitration by the British chief justice of India, who basically decided in Patel's favour. But the princely administration still refused to accept Patel's nominees. Their position was reinforced as Rajputs and Muslims in Rajkot threatened to launch their own satyagraha campaigns, and British Indian Muslim and depressed class leaders argued for separate representation on the reform committee. Gandhi admitted defeat on 17 May 1939. Rajkot was a 'priceless laboratory' that vindicated the appropriateness of his pleas for non-intervention. His lack of success also indicated that princely administrations as well as British imperialists and British Indian leaders could manipulate the boundaries between religious and social communities.

Wood has claimed that this episode reflects the divergent political legacies of princely states and British India, especially the commitment to behind-the-scenes negotiations and consensual decisions in the states and the use of public confrontation and compromise by the Congress. It also indicated the strength that the princes derived from the willingness of the British paramount power to back up its clients as counterpoises to the more potent threat from British Indian nationalists. Still the Rajkot satyagraha campaign provided the experience of coordinating goals that would stand Saurashtrian politicians in good stead as they tried to integrate their fragmented political spheres and to promote regional economic and social development after 1947.[46]

Popular political activity occurred decades later in Rajputana than in Travancore and Mysore. Laxman Singh has catalogued the establishment of social reform and political organisations in Jodhpur, Bikaner and Kotah during the early 1920s.[47] Richard Sisson has described how these and earlier social reform groups focused on internal reforms within their communities and is one of the first scholars to mention the importance of fairs and pilgrimage centres such as the Krishna shrine at Nathdwara in Udaipur as nodes of political activity.[48] Leaders of such groups faced expulsion from or arrest in these states if their activities challenged princely authority. Consequently their associations were ephemeral. A more lasting legacy were newspapers such as *Naveen Rajasthan* and *Tarun Rajasthan* in Ajmer, the British Indian enclave within Rajputana, which reported on conditions in the surrounding princely states.

During this early period, peasant protests erupted in Udaipur, arguably the most conservative state in Rajputana, against the jagirdar of Bijolia. Although the details are vague, it appears that *kisan*s, among whom the tribal Bhils were a significant element, had long been discontented with arbitrary taxes, cesses, and the demand for begar. In 1922 the jagirdar, under pressure from the Mewar durbar, instituted panchayats to mediate disputes, but subsequently he reneged on his commitment. The agitation dragged on throughout the 1920s. Directed against a jagirdar rather than a prince, this episode followed

---

[46] John R. Wood, 'British versus Princely Legacies and the Political Integration of Gujarat', *JAS* 44 (1984), pp. 65–99.

[47] Laxman Singh, *Political and Constitutional Developments in the Princely States of Rajasthan (1920–49)* (New Delhi, 1970), pp. 38–53.

[48] Sisson, *Congress Party*, pp. 41–5.

a pattern that persisted in Rajputana and provided organising experience for future political leaders.[49]

Although there was some sympathetic support for the civil disobedience movement of 1930–31 among subjects and a few rulers in Rajputana, the second stage of the formal organisation of praja mandals and more radical demands for structural change started after 1935. The catalysts seem to be the strong success of the Congress in the 1936 elections; more explicit rhetorical support from the Congress; and the emergence of a larger group of educated, ambitious young men within the princely states who sought some share of political resources. This list of factors is not definitive and will be modified by further research. By 1940 praja mandals had been formed in Alwar, Bharatpur, Bikaner, Jaipur, Jodhpur, Kotah, Sirohi and Udaipur.

During this phase of formal organisations with constitutions, elected officers, dues-paying members, and the goal of representative government, some princes attempted to co-opt the praja mandals that increasingly identified with Congress symbols and aspirations. In a striking example, Ganga Singh of Bikaner advised the British chief minister of Jodhpur that Jai Narain Vyas, the principal leader of the Marwar Lok Parishad in Jodhpur and the founder of the *Tarun Rajasthan*, should be given the resources to carry on his political work. In 1937 the prescient Bikaner ruler deemed Narain to be 'thoroughly honest, incorruptible, and true to his conscience and political creed . . . [and] the only man who can wield an elevating influence over thousands of his colleagues and associates who left to themselves will build their thrones upon the ruin of all classes in Rajputana'.[50] An entente between the Jaipur Praja Mandal and the Jaipur durbar existed from 1936 to 1938. It dissolved when the durbar outlawed the Mandal under a new Public Societies Regulation and banned the entry of Seth Jamnalal Bajaj, a devoted Gandhian and long-time treasurer of the Congress whose ancestral home was in Shekhawati, to preside over a Mandal meeting and to assist in famine relief. Similar arrests occurred in other states including Jodhpur, where Parishad leaders were incarcerated in 1940 for protesting against a ban on political meetings.

Although princely rulers in several Rajputana states attempted to conciliate these urban-based popular political leaders with representative assemblies in their capitals and district boards in towns, R. S. Darda has characterised such

---

[49] Laxman Singh, *Political Developments*, p. 40; Sisson, *Congress Party*, p. 44, n. 2, p. 74, n. 2; some documents in Ram Pande, *People's Movement in Rajasthan (Selection from Originals)*, vol. 2 (Jaipur, 1986), pp. ix–xvi, 1–40.

[50] Letter No. 201, P. S. 54–37, Ganga Singh to Sir Donald Field, Prime Minister of Jodhpur, quoted in Sisson, *Congress Party*, p. 52.

institutions as 'toy legislatures and mock local self-governing institutions'.[51] By 1942 the people's groups ended efforts at collaboration and sought to develop independently of state support. They attempted to broaden their base, but in most cases they remained tied to capital cities. Furthermore, educated brahmans, mahajans, Marwaris and kayasths were dominant leaders. Their dilatory efforts to forge links with emerging peasant movements were generally unsuccessful.

In Rajasthan the principal peasant movements developed in specific areas, protested against local grievances, and sought ritual and economic changes that were relevant to their particular conditions.[52] Sisson has described how the *kisan sabhas* evolved within the Jat communities, fought against feudalism, and targeted jagirdars rather than the princes.[53] As discussed in Chapter 6, some rulers had rationalised relations with peasants on khalsa lands to extend their control and ultimately to increase revenues through land settlements with fixed revenue rates. Although these princes were hardly utopian reformers and peasants on khalsa lands still had significant grievances, the conditions of peasants in jagirdari areas could be much worse. Here there were few revenue settlements or defined tenancy rights, and begar was often extracted. Jat political consciousness was raised through contact with Hindu reform societies, especially the Arya Samaj, which sent missionaries into Rajputana from its bases in Delhi and Punjab, with Jat caste associations and Jat religious leaders. A major festival, the Jat Praja Pati Maha-Yagna held in January 1934 in Shekhawati, was a landmark in developing a collective identity.

During the 1930s Jat *kisan sabha*s in Jaipur sought enhancement of their ritual status and economic conditions through public demonstrations and no-rent campaigns. One graphic demand was the right to ride elephants, camels and horses – the prerogative of Rajput jagirdars that symbolised their economic and political dominance. One of most remembered events of the Jat Praja Pati Maha-Yagna occurred when some Jats rode on an elephant, defying the prohibition of the Sikar thikanadar.[54] To complicate the situation, the thikanadars of Jaipur thought that their izzat or honour was being attacked, not just by Jat peasants but by the British. The latter had commissioned the Wills Report, which postulated that thikanadars owed their power to the grant of an ijara

[51] R. S. Darda, *From Feudalism to Democracy: A Study in the Growth of Representative Institutions in Rajasthan, 1908–1948* (New Delhi, 1971), p. 316.
[52] Hira Singh, *Colonial Hegemony and Popular Resistance: Princes, Peasants, and Paramount Power* (Walnut Creek CA, 1998).
[53] Sisson, *Congress Party*, ch. 4.   [54] Ibid., pp. 85–6.

and not to a right based on conquest. Subsequently, Raja Rao Kalyan Singh (succeeded 1922), the thikanadar of Sikar, would be the protagonist in the last stand of a jagirdar against his overlords.[55]

In the summer of 1938 an armed confrontation, subsequently labelled a feudal revolt, erupted in Sikar between small-scale Rajput thakurs and the superior armed forces of the Jaipur durbar. The immediate cause was a protest over British prescriptions for the education of the heir, but the fundamental issues were the British-inspired reforms of the Sikar administration reducing the authority of the *raja rao*. Kalyan Singh lost since the British sided with the durbar. Moreover, the praja mandal, influenced by the Gandhian Bajaj, stayed on the sidelines because the thikanadar and his Rajput allies would not subscribe to non-violent means.

Like the praja mandals in Rajputana, the kisan sabhas represented a crucial organisational development that widened political horizons and emphasised leadership based on achievement rather than ascription. Hira Singh has argued passionately that '[t]he peasant movements in Rajasthan did not "come": they were "made" by the peasants aided by multiple organizations and ideologies, with non-peasant components'.[56] The praja mandals that formed the Rajputana Prantiya Sabha in 1946, which became the Rajputana state unit of the Congress Party in 1948, found it difficult to ally with peasant groups. This inability to forge links between urban and rural-based movements was endemic. Since the Congress had jagirdari abolition as one of its key goals, the kisan sabhas in Rajputana were pre-empted from forming a Rajasthan peasant party and gradually joined the Congress. However, rivalries between urban and rural-based groups and between Rajput and Jat groups continued to exist but now within the organisational framework of an electoral party.[57]

Ecological and cultural factors produced another form of political protest. Ramachandra Guha has argued that '[t]he peasant political ideal, in which the peasantry and the king are the only social forces, came as close as is historically possible to being realized in Tehri Garhwal'.[58] In this sub-Himayalan state of 4500 square miles with a population of 300 000 (1931), the ruler Narendra Shah (b. 1898, r. 1919–49) traced his dynasty back for twelve centuries. His legitimacy was further undergirded by public acceptance of him as a speaking personification of the deity worshipped at Badrinath, one of the holiest Hindu shrines. Before the late nineteenth century the state revenue demand was low,

---

[55] Barnett R. Rubin, *Feudal Revolt and State-Building: The 1938 Sikar Agitation in Jaipur* (New Delhi, 1983).
[56] Hira Singh, *Colonial Hegemony*, p. 248.
[57] Sisson, *Congress Party*, chs 5–6.   [58] Guha, *Unquiet Woods*, p. 62.

and tension between the raja and praja was not evident. By 1900 lumbering in state forests of *deodar* (cedar) for railway sleepers changed this situation. After several decades of exploitation by British concessionaires, the raja resumed control of *chir* (long-needle pine) forests in 1885 and negotiated enhanced revenues from the deodar forests remaining under British management. These forests became the main source of state revenue.

Modern forest management severely restricted peasant access to a resource once held in common. Forests had provided grazing for herds, fertiliser for agricultural fields, and firewood. State forest officials dramatically intervened in the lives of peasants. In response, the peasants resorted to *dhandak* to secure the withdrawal of forest regulations regarded as unjust. Dhandak was a form of customary rebellion that involved individual and collective resistance to oppressive officials, with an accompanying appeal to the raja for justice. A turning point in raja–praja relations occurred during the Rawain dhandak in 1930. The expected response to this protest against further restrictions on the size of herds and the trimming of trees for fuel was for the raja to mediate in person. Unfortunately he was in Europe, so the diwan led a punitive expedition that fired on and looted protesting villagers. His action weakened but did not end respect for the raja.

In 1939 the Tehri Rajya Praja Mandal was founded at Dehradun in British India. Sridev Suman, its principal leader, died in 1941 during a hunger strike demanding legal recognition for the praja mandal. Similar to the situation in Rajputana, the praja mandal initially solicited an alliance with the raja but without incorporating peasant demands. Meanwhile the raja undertook a new land survey and settlement that provoked a peasant *andolan* or movement in 1946. Peasants held meetings; some tore up settlement papers, others marched to the capital, and many were arrested. Congress leaders interceded and secured the legal recognition of the praja mandal but not the release of jailed peasant leaders. Subsequent peasant agitations overthrew local revenue officials and appointed their own representatives as patwaris. Losing control, the raja negotiated with the praja mandal in early 1948 to form a ministry.[59] During the crucial transition to integration with the new state of Uttar Pradesh, the peasant movement and the praja mandal in Tehri Garhwal had collaborated but remained distinct. The peasants did not question the legitimacy of the raja but continued to argue that he did not know of the injustices being done under his authority by oppressive officials.[60] Although the praja mandal was anti-ruler in its rhetoric, it was willing to share power with the raja. It solicited

[59] Ibid., ch. 4.   [60] Ibid., pp. 88–9.

and attained positions in an interim ministry. The Congress achieved an uneasy alliance on the eve of integration.

Contrary to the view that customary rebellion functioned primarily as a safety valve to release pent-up frustrations and thereby maintain the status quo, Ramachandra Guha has argued that it was a shrewd tactic used by peasants to achieve changes in oppressive policies when the dominant authority was judged to be delinquent in dispensing justice.[61] Furthermore, the 1930 dhandak in Tehri Garhwal served as a reference point for peasants in neighbouring British Indian provinces and as prototype for the post-colonial Chipko movement. Chipko leaders focused their protest against forest officials regarded as corrupt because they collaborated with manipulative logging contractors. During the 1970s and 1980s Chipko organisers, whose ascetic self-sacrifice including hunger strikes and non-violent means of protest echoed the earlier peasant leaders, appealed to prime ministers, most notably Indira Gandhi, who claimed to be supportive of environmental protection. In the post-colonial period elected politicians succeeded to the role of fount of justice once held by the raja of Tehri Garhwal.[62] In areas more exposed to external influences, political patterns would be more complex since the populations of these states were more differentiated.

COMMUNAL ASSOCIATIONS AND COMMUNIST ORGANISATIONS

Communal and class appeals were long evident in political activity in Travancore. Various groups had formed political associations as early as the 1890s to lobby for more educational opportunities and government positions. During the 1930s constitutional reforms intensified communal anxieties.[63] The three politically active communities – nayars, ezhavas and Christians – experienced internal divisions yet each tried to create an external united front vis-à-vis other communities. Such aspirations made it difficult for the Congress or local political leaders to build an integrated organisation. The Congress was momentarily successful during the late 1930s, but it confronted challenges from members of the Congress Socialist Party and the Communist Party during the next decade.[64]

---

[61] Ibid., p. 97. [62] Ibid., pp. 172–4.

[63] Dick Kooiman, *Communities and Electorates: A Comparative Discussion of Communalism in Colonial India* (Amsterdam, 1995), pp. 39–49, 63–4.

[64] Ibid.; Jeffrey, 'Sanctified Label' in Low, *Congress*, pp. 435–72; Jeffrey, *Politics*, chs 3–7.

In 1933 a newly formed Joint Political Congress (JPC), not related to the Indian National Congress and known as the Samyuktha Party, composed of Christian, ezhava and Muslim leaders boycotted elections to a new legislature that would be nayar-dominated. The constituents of the JPC sought communal reservations in the legislature and government posts based on population. Under the shrewd direction of Ramaswami Aiyar, the state government undertook reforms to isolate the Christians and accommodate the Hindus. In 1935 it conceded communal reservations in the legislature. In the next year a Temple Entry Proclamation removed the most conspicuous sign of discrimination against non-caste Hindus and attenuated the political opposition of the ezhavas. By 1937 the JPC had won twenty-five out of forty-nine seats in the legislature, but its impetus soon declined as the government fulfilled most of its program. The JPC could not link up with the Indian National Congress since its communally oriented objectives were not congruent with Gandhian standards. A Travancore State Congress had to be at least ostensibly non-communal and able to fuse nationalist goals and symbols with local issues.

Formed in February 1938, the Travancore State Congress (TSC) initially contested the state administration on the issues of freedom of speech and assembly when a nayar lawyer in whose office they had met was arrested for publishing allegedly inflammatory articles. At the next stage the TSC presented a memorial calling for universal franchise, responsible government, and the dismissal and investigation of the foreign diwan, Ramaswami Aiyar. On 26 August 1938, some TSC leaders were arrested as they inaugurated civil disobedience. But the campaign continued and orchestrated the largest public procession ever seen in Travancore on 23 October 1938. Although estimates of the numbers participating range from 2000 to 20 000, the protest was even more remarkable for its challenges to princely authority. First, its leader was a woman, Akkamma Cheriyan (1909–82), a Catholic Syrian school headmistress. Second, the crowd of mixed castes and religions invaded the central 'Fort' area of Trivandrum, the acknowledged preserve of caste Hindus. Eventually the state administration represented to Rajkumari Amrit Kaur, Gandhi's envoy, that the public violence and attacks on Ramaswami Aiyar were evidence of the TSC's lack of commitment to Gandhian tactics of satyagraha, which required non-violence and respect for one's opponent. Once the Travancore Government released Congress political prisoners, the middle-class Congress leaders terminated their civil disobedience campaign. Ramaswami Aiyar proceeded to demonstrate the power of the state to reward its clients and punish its opponents and thereby split the Congress. Nayars won changes in the franchise, and ezhavas left the TSC to achieve similar gains. Christians also fractured, with the Roman Catholics supporting the government in return for protection of its institutions.[65]

During the Second World War the TSC pulled back from agitational activity and organising workers. Students were the only group to mount significant demonstrations during the Quit India movement. Educated, dedicated caste Hindu and Syrian Christian leaders of the Communist Party had an open field in organising urban workers across communal and caste divisions, with ezhavas, Latin Catholics and artisan workers as the intermediary level of leadership. When Ramaswami Aiyar and the maharaja proposed to make Travancore independent of the Indian Union in 1947, the TSC decided against a mass civil disobedience campaign since they feared losing control to the better organised socialist and communist parties. The TSC managed to form the state government from 1951 to 1956, but the strong infrastructure of the Communist Party resulted in the first freely elected communist government in the newly formed state of Kerala in 1957.[66]

Communal appeals and communist organisers were also conspicuous in the Punjab states. The territory of Sikh-ruled states, particularly Patiala, Nabha and Jind, was interspersed through the eastern half of Punjab province. Unlike Baroda and Mysore, they did not enjoy a reputation for progressive reforms. As of 1924 there were no metalled roads in Nabha state, and in 1933 Patiala had 1.24 students per 100 people in schools compared to 4.44 in Punjab province.[67] This latter state, the largest and most populous of the three, with 5932 square miles and a population of almost 1.5 million in 1921, had some elements of administrative modernisation such as a British-style land revenue settlement, canal irrigation schemes, and railway lines. But industrial development was almost non-existent and only 10 per cent of the population was urban-based. Although there were no jagirdars in the rural areas, *biswedars* or land-controllers, who held a sixth of the villages in Patiala, had had their revenue-collecting rights converted into proprietary rights during the land revenue settlement undertaken in the first decade of the twentieth century. This instrument of administrative efficiency had transformed cultivating peasants into *muzara* or occupancy tenants.[68]

---

[65] Ibid., p. 124 and Jeffrey, 'Sanctified Label', in Low, *Congress*, pp. 454–6.
[66] T. J. Nossiter, *Communism in Kerala: A Study in Political Adaptation* (Berkeley CA, 1982).
[67] Romesh Walia, *Praja Mandal Movement in East Punjab States* (Patiala, 1972), pp. 37, 42.
[68] Mohinder Singh, *Peasant Movement*, pp. 13–16.

During the 1910s and 1920s the Akali Sikhs had mounted a major campaign to win control over and reform Sikh gurudwaras throughout Punjab. Ramesh Walia has related how this agitation rather than the freedom movement was the major factor in determining 'the shape, character and dimensions of the praja mandal movement in East Punjab'.[69] The role of maharaja Bhupinder Singh as a patron of moderate leaders in the Sikh gurudwara reform movement has been outlined in Chapter 5. Here it is sufficient to remember that he was an energetic intermediary between his British patron and Akali leaders during the 1920s.[70] The immediate cause for the founding of the Punjab Riyasti Praja Mandal in 1928 was Bhupinder Singh's incarceration of Sewa Singh Thikriwala (c. 1882–1935), a Patiala subject and former state official who had refused to agree, as more moderate Akalis had done, to British conditions during the negotiations over the 1925 *Sikh Gurdwara Reform Act*.[71] As in other states such as Jaipur, the Patiala jail was a convenient repository for political prisoners whom the British found difficult to retain. The intermittent imprisonment and the harsh treatment of Sewa Singh were dramatic evidence of the lack of civil rights in Patiala.

During the first phase of the Punjab Riyasti Praja Mandal from 1928 to 1938, the main focuses were on improving political and economic conditions in Patiala and on persuading the British to depose Maharaja Bhupinder Singh. Their success was limited. Because *Hidayat* (decree) 88, issued in 1932 and in effect until 1946, banned political meetings and restricted the registration of political organisations in the Phulkian states, the leaders of the Punjab Praja Mandal operated from bases in British Punjab. In Patiala the one comparatively safe site for spreading their message was religious *diwan*s or meetings that even the autocratic princely government was reluctant to suppress. Consequently much of the early states' people's movement had a Sikh religious or communal orientation, although in 1931 the Sikh population in Patiala at 38.9 per cent was only the barest of a majority compared to 38.2 per cent for Hindus and 22.4 per cent for Muslims. Moreover the Patiala rulers adroitly blunted Sikh opposition. When Master Tara Singh gained control of the SGPC in 1935, he concluded an agreement with Bhupinder Singh that divided the Akali members of the praja mandal into those who wanted to continue the struggle against the maharaja and those who were willing to turn to other objectives. After Bhupinder Singh died in 1938, his heir, Yadavindra Singh, co-opted one section of the praja mandal when he married Mohinder Kaur, the 15-year-old daughter

---

[69] Walia, *Praja Mandal*, p. 27.   [70] Ramusack, 'Punjab States', in Jeffrey, *People*, pp. 179–91.
[71] Gurbachan Singh Talib, *Sardar Sewa Singh Thikriwala: A Brief Sketch of His Life and Work* (Patiala, 1971).

of its leader Harchand Singh Jeji.[72] As the Akalis neglected peasant issues, the communists found fertile ground for their organising efforts. Mridula Mukherjee has traced communist efforts to organise the occupancy tenants in the biswedari villages during the 1930s and 1940s.[73]

From 1938 to 1947, there were three distinct elements in the freedom struggle: the Akalis, the communists, and the praja mandal. The Akalis were concerned about the position of Sikhs if there were a partition. Some argued for an independent Sikh state and were sympathetic to the Patiala ruler, whose territory might serve as its core. Yadavindra Singh favoured Akali causes, and by the 1941 census the Patiala population was 46.3 per cent Sikh, while Ludhiana, the British Punjab district with the highest percentage of Sikhs, had 41.7 per cent. The increase in the Sikh population of Patiala from the 1901–41 censuses possibly indicates the success of efforts to have Sikhs identify themselves as Sikhs and not Hindus rather than migration or higher birth rates. The communists concentrated on gaining proprietary rights for occupancy tenants, which were eventually achieved in 1952. Mukherjee has pointed out, however, that the political vision of the communist leaders was limited, never linking economic improvement to the end of British rule and of their princely collaborators, namely Yadavindra Singh, and so their efforts had restricted impact.[74]

During the second phase of popular political activity in the Punjab States, urban-based professionals who were mainly Hindu took over the leadership of the praja mandal. They shifted the mandal's focus from Patiala to smaller states such as Nabha and Jind and emphasised different issues such as more employment of educated states' subjects and greater protection of civil rights. The praja mandal was generally silent on peasant demands. After 1947 in the newly created Patiala and East Punjab States Union, the Pradesh Congress experienced the earlier inability of the praja mandal to forge a united front. PEPSU was soon amalgamated into Punjab state in 1956. Seven years later a Punjabi-speaking state was created with Patiala as its geographical centre. The tragic events in Punjab during the 1980s manifested the continuing difficulties of channelling communal appeals based on religion and language into constitutional and electoral arenas.

As seen in Travancore, communal appeals and organisations had existed since at least the early twentieth century. But many British officials such as

[72] Ramusack, 'Punjab States', in Jeffrey, *People*, pp. 187–93. Mohinder Kaur served in the Indian Parliament (Lok Sabha, 1967–1969 and Rajya Sabha, 1964–1967, 1969–71) and was known for her social work interests: Hurtig, *Maharajahs*, pp. 281–94.

[73] Mukherjee, 'Peasant Movement'.

[74] Ibid., pp. 276–83; Mohinder Singh, *Peasant Movement*, chs 2–5 covers the post-1947 campaigns for tenancy legislation.

Michael O'Dwyer, Arthur Lothian and Conrad Corfield and Indian nationalist leaders including G. K. Gokhale had contended that communal activity, by which they usually meant conflicts, ostensibly on religious issues, between Hindus and Muslims, was absent in princely states. O'Dwyer, who had served as resident in Hyderabad (1908–10) and governor of Punjab (1913–20), declared: 'Communal tension was unknown in Hyderabad, and generally in Native States, in those days; for the political agitator who stirs up creed against creed, class against class, and incites his ignorant dupes to defiance of authority, was not tolerated at all, or not to the same extent as in British India.'[75]

But O'Dwyer saw the virus of communal appeals spreading to the princely states during the 1920s. His example occurred in Hyderabad in 1924 when an allegedly Hindu mob murdered a Muslim political officer at Gulbarga. Muslims retaliated by attacking over fifty Hindu temples in the city. Subsequently there was a sharp increase in communal violence between Hindus and Muslims in princely states during the 1930s. Episodes were reported in Alwar, Bahawalpur, Bharatpur, Hyderabad, Jaipur, Jind, Junagadh, Kapurthala, Kashmir, Malerkotla, Ramdurg and Travancore. However, research is fragmentary on most of these incidents and more especially on the possible existence of earlier occurrences.

In this section I will focus on three states – Hyderabad, Alwar and Kashmir – where tensions between Hindus and Muslims reveal the wide variations in communal political activity in princely states. Much of the available research is descriptive rather than analytical, and consequently my account reflects this orientation. Moreover, there has been little attention to how public festivals and institutions such as schools, temples and mosques shaped communal identities in the princely states.

The 1924 episode at Gulbarga was a precursor of a more extended confrontation in Hyderabad during the late 1930s. Several bloody riots throughout the state during 1938 triggered a nine-month satyagraha campaign of civil disobedience that involved the Hyderabad State Congress and indigenous and external groups from the Arya Samaj and the Hindu Mahasabha demanding religious freedom and more popular participation in government. Indian nationalists and their local allies had alleged that the Muslim-ruled state favoured the Muslim minority, which constituted about 11 per cent of the population, at the expense of the Hindu majority, which was about 85 per cent. Thus demands for civil rights and an equitable distribution of public revenues in an autocratic state placed Indians in opposition to an Indian government. Ian Copland has

---

[75] O'Dwyer, *India*, p. 141.

argued that politicisation and proselytisation had created this campaign. The Indian National Congress, the AISPC, the Muslim League and the Hindu Mahasabha had all turned their attention to Hyderabad as it appeared possible that federation might bring this large state into an Indian Union. These political groups attracted the urban proletariat, who had been the object of conversion campaigns by the Arya Samaj encouraging the return of Muslims with Hindu ancestors and by the Ittihad-ul-Muslimeen, a local Muslim society seeking to insulate the Muslim minority position through converts from Hinduism.[76] Copland concludes that communalism was less prevalent in princely states because of their smaller industrial base and their lower level of politicisation until relatively late.[77] But Dick Kooiman claims that in Hyderabad, as in Travancore and Baroda, the spread of official enumeration and earlier rivalries over government employment fostered communal identities that could erupt into communal violence as federation and the prospect of increased popular representation in legislatures raised the stakes.[78] Further north, public protests by Muslim Meos over agrarian and social status issues were coded as communal in the Hindu-ruled state of Alwar.

From the 1910s onward, Maharaja Jai Singh assiduously extended his internal control in Alwar by enhancing demands for land revenue, appropriating natural resources, especially forest products, and exacting forced labour. Simultaneously he contested British paramountcy, projecting himself as a Hindu king and an Indian nationalist through patronage of Hindu organisations, especially the Sanatan Dharma Sabha and the Arya Samaj, and nationalist ventures such as Unity Conferences in 1927 and 1932.[79] These policies adversely affected his subjects. The population of Alwar was 73 per cent Hindu and 27 per cent Muslim. Meos, who were 60 per cent of the Muslim category,[80] were constructed in colonial ethnography as a group of indeterminate social status between tribe and caste, with equally ambiguous religious commitment. The 1901 Census reported the allegation that the Meos 'are ready to observe the feasts of both the Musalman and Hindu religions, the fasts of neither'.[81] In a perceptive analysis based on colonial archives, state propaganda, Meo oral sources and oral interviews, Shail Mayaram has asserted that the Meos claimed 'a bi-genealogical status . . . as inheritors of both Muslim and Rajput traditions'.[82]

---

[76] Ian Copland, '"Communalism" in Princely India: The Case of Hyderabad, 1930–1940', *MAS* 22 (1988), pp. 783–814.

[77] Ibid., pp. 812–14. [78] Kooiman, 'Strength', pp. 92–8.

[79] Mayaram, *Resisting Regimes*, ch. 3; Ramusack, *Princes*, pp. 158–60.

[80] Mayaram, *Resisting Regimes*, p. 164.

[81] *Census of India, 1901*, vol. 25: *Rajputana*, Part I - Report, p. 157.

[82] Mayaram, *Resisting Regimes*, p. 117.

Most accounts of the Meo opposition begin with a no-rent campaign in December 1932. They claim that external Muslim groups, especially the Tabligh movement, had heightened Meo religious identity as Muslims, and interpret the protests as communal, with Muslim Meos attacking a Hindu prince and his Hindu subjects.[83] Mayaram decisively challenges this interpretation. Two Meo texts emphasise that the movement began a month earlier with actions against oppressive revenue collectors; that indigenous Meos were leaders; that the protest was against exorbitant land taxes and demands for forced labour in state properties such as game preserves; that Hindus participated in the protests; and that Hindu banias precipitated Meo attacks when they betrayed their plans to the state.[84] British sources, particularly a report by A. W. Ibbotson, confirm the agrarian character of the movement and discredit charges of looting and property destruction, while revealing that violence against the banias erupted only after Meo leaders were arrested.[85] More recently, Ian Copland agrees that the initial rebellion of Meos in November 1932 was not communal in character at the outset but that the indifference of Hindu groups, the collaboration of external Muslim organisations, and the activities of Alwar officials glossed the rebellion as communal.[86] After requesting British military assistance to regain control, Jai Singh openly orchestrated Hindu support for his regime while defying British pressure for reforms. The British soon ordered him to leave Alwar in 1933. At the same time the Tabligh and other Muslim groups intensified educational and organisational work among the Meos and communal tensions increased, but subsided after the peasant movement. Jai Singh's successor, Tej Singh, exacerbated the situation with continuing support for Hindu communal groups and by appointing N. B. Khare, a strong supporter of the Hindu Mahasabha, as chief minister. Independence brought terror, death and ethnic cleansing to the Meos of Alwar, who were homogenised as Muslims and foreigners.[87]

Far to the north under the shadow of the Himalayas, the Muslim community that constituted 93 per cent of the population in the Kashmir province

---

[83] Partap C. Aggarwal, 'The Meos of Rajasthan and Haryana', in Imtiaz Ahmad (ed.), *Caste and Social Stratification among the Muslims* (New Delhi, 1973), pp. 21–44; Ramusack, *Princes*, pp. 179–80; Majid Siddiqi, 'History and Society in a Popular Rebellion: Mewat 1920–1933', *CSSH* 23 (1986), pp. 442–67.

[84] Mayaram, *Resisting Regimes*, ch. 5.

[85] Ibid., pp. 107–10, 151. The British officer deputed to Alwar stated: 'The immediate cause of the Meo rebellion was the excessive taxation levied on the cultivators': Arthur C. Lothian, *Kingdoms of Yesterday* (London, 1951), p. 124.

[86] Ian Copland, 'The Further Shores of Partition: Ethnic Cleansing in Rajasthan 1947', *PP*, No. 168 (August 1998), pp. 220–5.

[87] Ibid. and Mayaram, *Resisting Regimes*, ch. 6.

of the Jammu and Kashmir state has, until recently, been represented as relatively homogeneous and incorporated with Hindus in Kashmiriyat, a syncretic Kashmiri cultural concord. Tracing the fluctuating bases of Kashmiri identity from the Mughal period to the 1950s, Chitralekha Zutshi argues that regional and national affiliations competed with religious ones in differing formations, with tragic consequences for contemporary Kashmir.[88] During the 1880s material changes such as the deteriorating economic position of shawl merchants and landholders provided the context for contending efforts to define the nature of Islam in Kashmir. Two *mirwaiz*es (head preachers) embodied opposing positions – the mirwaiz Kashmir proclaiming a purified Islam and the need for modern education for Muslims, while the mirwaiz Hamdaani sanctioned prayers to mystical Sufi *pir*s, who were deemed saints. Their campaigns to control Muslim mosques and shrines in the Srinagar Valley and their inability to incorporate rural Muslims hindered the formation of a coherent Kashmiri Muslim community.[89] Efforts during the 1920s would be more successful.

Mass political activity in Kashmir reputedly commenced on 13 July 1931, which was later celebrated as Martyrs Day and a public holiday in the state. Sheikh Muhammad Abdullah, who became known as the 'Lion of Kashmir', was acclaimed as the charismatic leader who orchestrated the political mobilisation. As does Chitralekha Zutshi, Upendra Zutshi has claimed that many long-term developments such as British imperialism, and not just the personality of one man, fostered the agitations in Kashmir during the early 1930s.[90] Both cite British interventions as significant in fostering a political as well as religious communal identity; these included a reformed land revenue system, which granted occupancy rights to most Muslim cultivators, and recognition of Muslim grievances about lack of access to education and government employment.[91] Upendra Zutshi traces how, in articulating their support for the demands of Kashmiri Muslims, informal Muslim groups in Kashmir were joined by Muslim organisations in British India ranging from the Muslim Kashmiri Conference, which began in Lahore around 1911, to the Anjuman-i-Islamia Punjab, to the All-India Muslim League.[92] Thus two decades of petition politics channelled through memorials and resolutions preceded the attention-grabbing outbreak in 1931.

---

[88] Chitralekha Zutshi, *Languages of Belonging: Islam, Regional Identity, and the Making of Kashmir* (New Delhi, forthcoming in 2003).

[89] Chitralekha Zutshi, 'Religion, State, and Community: Contested Identities in the Kashmir Valley, c. 1880–1920', *SA* 23, 1 (2000), pp. 109–28.

[90] U. T. Zutshi, *Emergence*, ch. 1, esp. p. 18.

[91] Chitralekha Zutshi, 'Religion', pp. 114–16.   [92] U. T. Zutshi, *Emergence*, chs 5 and 6.

The Kashmir agitation had three major phases.[93] On 13 July 1931 a crowd gathered to protest against the trial of a Muslim servant arrested for making an allegedly anti-Hindu and seditious speech during a public protest against discriminatory state policies towards Muslims. Police firing into the largely Muslim crowd triggered widespread attacks on Hindu property in Srinagar. During the next few months Sheikh Abdullah (1905–82) emerged as a key leader. He was a 26-year-old graduate of Aligarh Muslim University and a state subject who had recently left the state education department to become a full-time political organiser. But other local and external groups were active. Three Muslim groups from Punjab soon contended as champions of the Kashmiri Muslims: the Ahrars, an urban, middle-class political party anxious to win a rural base for their struggle with the Unionist Party in Punjab; the Ahmadiyya, a heterodox Muslim proselytising sect based at Qadian in Punjab near the Jammu border; and the All-India Kashmir Conference operating from Lahore. Sheikh Abdullah forged political alliances with the Ahmadiyyas and Yusuf Shah, a radical claimant to succeed Rasul Shah as mirwaiz. In the process Kashmiris acquired substantial experience of agitational politics and incarceration in state jails for political activity. When repressive policies failed to quell the public demonstrations, the first phase ended with Maharaja Hari Singh appealing to the British for military force, which was provided in return for a British diwan and a commission of inquiry. As would continue to happen after independence, the GOI became the last resort for an embattled state administration in Kashmir. But British assistance did not terminate the multifaceted political campaign.

The second phase centred on rural grievances in Mirpur and western and southern Jammu, a province with 61 per cent Muslim and 37 per cent Hindu populations in 1941. Muslim peasants initially sought relief from coercive tactics employed to collect land revenue in 1932, but their economic goal acquired communal overtones with subsequent attacks on the property of Hindu shopkeepers and moneylenders. The third phase saw clashes in Srinagar in 1933 between supporters of the rival candidates for mirwaiz. As the popular movement gradually subsided, Abdullah shifted into electoral politics in 1934. In response to British pressure, Maharaja Hari Singh had promised a legislative assembly with thirty-three elected members and forty-three nominated and official members. As in British India, there was a concerted effort to channel

---

[93] This synthesis is based on ibid.; Ian Copland, 'Islam and Political Mobilization in Kashmir, 1931–34', *PA* 54 (1981), pp. 228–59; Barbara N. Ramusack, 'Exotic Imports or Home-Grown Riots: The Muslim Agitations in Kashmir in the Early 1930s', unpublished paper presented at Third Punjab Studies Conference, University of Pennsylvania, 1971.

communal and agitational activity into the electoral arena. Eventually, under the influence of Jawaharlal Nehru and the Indian National Congress, Abdullah Ghulam Abbas, a Muslim leader from Jammu, and Prem Nath Bazaz, a Kashmiri brahman pandit, transformed the Jammu and Kashmir Muslim Conference into the secular Jammu and Kashmir National Conference.[94]

Ian Copland has argued that

religion was an essential factor in the process of mobilization, providing an avenue for organization and propaganda and a sense of communality among Muslims which transcended the formidable barriers of class, education and religion. But the root cause of the revolt was socio-economic – a determination on the part of the Muslims to win for themselves a prominent position in Kashmiri society.[95]

Upendra Zutshi mentions material factors for politicisation such as the completion of the Jhelum Valley Road in 1890, which allowed wheeled traffic to enter Kashmir for the first time, and of the Banihal Cart Road in 1922 linking Jammu to Srinagar.[96] Although he does not explore their implications, these roads might have affected Kashmiri political activity in at least two major ways. First, they facilitated the movement of outside politicians into Kashmir. Second, although Kashmir had been linked to Central Asian and European markets for over a century through the export of shawls,[97] improved roads expanded the Punjabi-dominated trade network between Kashmir and India and tied the state more closely to the world economy. As a result, the dislocations of the First World War and the 1929 depression would be more keenly felt than when the Kashmiri economy was less integrated. Recent but as yet unpublished research of scholars such as Mridu Rai and Chitralekha Zutshi will enhance our understanding of this fateful political mobilisation.

CONCLUSION

Alwar, Hyderabad and Kashmir as well as Mysore, Rajkot, Jaipur, Travancore and Patiala provide a base for reaching tentative conclusions about elite political leadership, non-elite participation and the role of outsiders, the incidence of communal idioms, and the focus of political opposition in the princely states. Because they have left more accessible records, educated urban elites have been portrayed as the path-breakers in associational political activity in the

---

[94] Bazaz, *History*, chs 8–13. [95] Copland, 'Islam', p. 257.
[96] Upendra Zutshi, *Emergence*, p. 129.
[97] Michelle Maskiell, 'Consuming Kashmir: Shawls and Empire, 1500–2000', *JWH* 13, 1 (2002), pp. 27–65.

princely states. Beginning in the late 1910s, these elites first organised around class-oriented issues such as state employment and civil rights. Hampered by repressive measures from princely durbars and ambivalent Congress policies, they found it difficult to develop autonomous organisations. For much of the colonial period, praja mandal leaders sought reforms to broaden their political participation rather than transformations in the political, economic or social structures of the princely states. As did many Congress members, these elites desired social stability and were willing to compromise with princely durbars to gain access to power and economic resources or even more limited goals such as release from jail. Their class interests made it difficult for such leaders to cultivate mass bases. Furthermore, they lacked financial supporters and thus the material resources to undertake full-time political work.

In many princely states, leaders of urban-based praja mandals or rural kisan sabhas began to acquire experience in organising and mobilising their constituencies about forty years later than had British Indian nationalist leaders. Thus the political vanguard in the princely states had only a few decades to establish themselves before independence and integration brought both wider opportunities and stiffer competition from more seasoned politicians. Moreover, the political associations in unions of princely states as in Saurashtra and Rajasthan were fragmented along the borders of the erstwhile princely states. Thus princely state politicians found it difficult to fashion the coalitions necessary to achieve dominance in post-colonial electoral politics. These factors obscure politicians from the princely states in the scholarship on post-colonial Indian politics.

During the 1990s scholars have begun to target peasants, tribal groups and industrial labourers who created autonomous political movements. These political actors sought the revision of government policies that affected them adversely. In Tehri Garhwal peasants demanded the revocation of economically disadvantageous forest policies. In Baroda the Devi movement agitated for improved ritual and economic status for tribal groups. In Mysore urban labourers showed growing political consciousness and impressive organisational skills in a series of strikes from the 1920s onward. Urban elites attempted to incorporate these non-elite groups during the 1930s and 1940s. Although the Congress was relatively persuasive in Mysore, it had less success in encompassing peasant and tribal movements in states such as Patiala. Communists were more effective in Travancore and Cochin.

With a few exceptions, women remain the most veiled of the political actors in princely states. Janaki Nair has recorded the protests of some women workers in Mysore during the strikes in the 1940s, but she has little on other aspects of their lives and political activities. Robin Jeffrey has scrutinised the increasing literacy of women in Travancore and their subsequent entrance to salaried professions, but he selected only four women to illustrate changing roles. Akamma Cheriyan Varkey, who led the 1938 demonstration but then was rejected by the Congress hierarchy after 1948, is the sole example of a woman political activist before 1947.

It is now clear that outsiders from British India were not the primary initiators of popular political activities within many princely states as Indian princes and British officials had claimed. Certainly the borders of princely states were as porous to political ideas as they were to smuggled goods. Although they were influenced by the nationalist project being constructed in British India, local leaders were dominant in the princely states. Only gradually did the Indian National Congress, socialists, communists and communal groups from British India penetrate the princely states. These groups were increasingly eager to broaden their base of support as independence and the high political stakes became more real. After some initial forays during the 1920s, Mahatma Gandhi, Sardar Patel and Jawaharlal Nehru remained disengaged until the late 1930s. Socialists and communists were more aggressive during the 1930s, but they failed to build a strong popular base except in Kerala. During the same decades the Arya Samaj and the Hindu Mahasabha championed the protection of Hindus in the more distant Muslim-ruled states of Bhopal and Hyderabad as well as in Alwar and Bharatpur. Muslim groups ranging from the conservative Muslim League to the more radical Ahrars to the heterodox Ahmadiyyas intervened on behalf of co-religionists in Hyderabad and in Kashmir. The Akali Sikhs had numerous reasons for their deep involvement in Patiala state. But these outsiders rarely achieved firm coalitions with local leaders.

The princely states demonstrate that the forging of communal identities and public, sometimes violent, communal confrontations had complex sources. Although the British exercised considerable formal and informal power over internal affairs, Indian rulers and their governments had significant autonomy in formulating policies that aroused internal opposition, such as employment in expanding state bureaucracies. The Sikhs in Patiala, the Muslims in Kashmir and the Meos in Alwar provide diverse examples of how religious identities and economic grievances fuelled communal political activity.

Princes and urban elites influenced the idioms of political protest in their states. Where a minority of the population shared the ruler's religion and he or she favoured his or her co-religionists with government positions, generous patronage of religious establishments, and protective legislation, popular political activity could quickly become communal in orientation. This process

243

occurred most notably in Kashmir and Hyderabad. In the former a Muslim majority protested against a Hindu ruler who was protecting Brahman pandits and in the latter a Hindu majority challenged a Muslim prince. In Patiala the situation was reversed. Here Akali groups demanded that a Sikh maharaja appoint more Sikh officials including a Sikh chief minister, which Yadavindra Singh eventually did in the 1940s. In Alwar and neighbouring Bharatpur, Hindu rulers transformed their traditional patronage of religious institutions into collaboration with communal political organisations, which had tragic consequences for a liminal minority within their states.

It was quite late in the colonial era before either elite or non-elite politicians endeavoured to alter radically or end princely rule. At least publicly, most viewed princes as benevolent rulers who desired to protect their subjects as a father did his children. Rapacious colonial suzerains, self-seeking ministers, greedy relatives, and perhaps substance abuse deterred rulers from this duty. But princes played multiple roles and increasingly were unable to accommodate their diverse constituencies.

CHAPTER 8

FEDERATION OR INTEGRATION?

By 1929 Indian princes and nationalists were mutually frustrated with British policies. The princes smarted from the refusal of the Indian States Committee to define paramountcy and thereby limit the extent of British intervention in their states. Indian nationalists were angered by the appointment of an Indian Reforms Commission that included no Indian members to investigate the operation of the 1919 reforms. The public demonstrations against the Commission, colloquially known as the Simon Commission after its chair, Sir John Simon, during its tour in India indicated that it would not be business as usual. In a bold move that consigned the Commission's report to the archives, Lord Irwin persuaded Ramsey MacDonald, the Prime Minister, to convene a Round Table Conference in London in 1930. Representatives of all British and Indian parties would be invited to discuss the future constitutional relationship between Britain and India. For the first time, representatives of the Indian princes would participate in such deliberations. Although the prime goal of the British was to channel elite Indian opposition into constitutional debates away from mass protests, the Round Table Conference also put the final nail in the coffin of the British policy of isolating the princes from each other and from British Indian leaders.

Princely participation in the Round Table Conference shows that neither the British nor the Indian nationalists considered the princes to be political ciphers or puppets. Although the British wanted the princes to counter the Indian nationalists, they did not pull the strings that triggered princely support for or later opposition to federation with British Indian provinces. Both British officials and Indian nationalists pursued princely allies, but the princes, for better or worse, exercised significant autonomy throughout the protracted constitutional negotiations, inaugurated in 1927 and finally suspended in 1939. This process was the first instalment in the integration of the princely states into a post-colonial government. It reveals the difficulties that the princes encountered in any effort to present a united front, as well as the multiple constituencies in Britain with conflicting agendas in India.

Although formal constitutional proposals during the Second World War were limited to the Cripps Mission in 1942, the princes, like other political leaders, worked to enhance their bargaining positions. Congress politicians

broadened their mass appeal; socialists and communists organised urban industrial workers and peasant unions (kisan sabhas); Muslim League leaders
undertook a mass contact campaign. Simultaneously the Muslim League and
many Indian princes sustained their beleaguered patron during crucial internal
challenges such as the Quit India Movement of 1942.

By mid-1943 most British officials and Indian politicians understood that
substantial devolution of power would occur whenever the war ended. By
May 1945, when victory was declared in Europe, the British accelerated the
process known as decolonisation. Much of the historiography on this topic has
focused on whether the British withdrew from India primarily on their own
initiative or whether the Indian nationalists pushed them out. Historians have
tended to a middle position. H. V. Brasted and Carl Bridge have argued for 'an
approach which coordinates all of the existing contextual strands'[1] and suggest
that first, the '"high political" story has still not been satisfactorily told as
regards Congress and British strategies'; second, 'more detailed psephological
analysis of the 1937 and 1945–46 elections is needed'; third, 'the "history from
below" studies must be integrated into the main account – Did the subalterns
force Congress, the League, and the British, to solve the constitutional problem
quickly in order to head off an impending social "revolution"?'; and fourth,
'since decolonisation was the product of changes at the metropolitan, colonial
and international levels, it is likely that it can only be explained in terms of
changes at all of those levels'.[2]

These same trends should also be applied to the analysis of the last two
decades of the princely states. Expanding in breadth and depth upon earlier studies by Steven Ashton, Urmila Phadnis and myself, Robin Moore and
more recently Ian Copland have detailed the high political story of British
and princely strategies and personalities during the devolution of power.[3]
John McLeod has surveyed the merger of small princely states in the attachment scheme in western India,[4] and Lucien Benichou and Michael Witmer
have analysed the integration of Hyderabad in the context of international
diplomacy as well as Indian regional and national politics.[5] Consequently our

---

[1] H. V. Brasted and Carl Bridge, 'The Transfer of Power in South Asia: An Historiographical Review',
SA 17, 1 (1994), p. 94.
[2] Ibid., p. 114.
[3] Ashton, *British Policy*; Urmila Phadnis, *Towards the Integration of Indian States, 1919–1947* (London,
1968); Ramusack, *Princes*; R. J. Moore, *Escape from Empire: The Attlee Government and the Indian
Problem* (Oxford, 1983); Ian Copland, *Princes*.
[4] McLeod, 'Agency', and *Sovereignty*.
[5] Benichou, *Autocracy*; Michael D. Witmer, The 1947–1948 India–Hyderabad Conflict: Realpolitik
and the Formation of the Modern Indian State, PhD thesis, Temple University, 1995.

understanding is slowly being refined; certain aspects become more sharply defined while others remain indistinct.

Several human and structural factors were responsible for the unexpectedly smooth and quick integration of most princely states into independent India and Pakistan. First, the princes, who did not have decades of experience in collective negotiations, found it difficult to decide on their mutual best interests and then to unite and stay united in a common campaign, both during the 1930s and the more intense bargaining from 1945 to 1948. Second, the British had made promises that they lacked the material resources and the ideological resolve to fulfil. Third, the official British hierarchy had long encompassed conflicting opinions about the princely states and these differences sharpened during this unprecedented crisis. In the face of such divisions, authority gravitated to those who were politically secure and prepared to exercise power. In 1946, Lord Mountbatten had the political support at home and the personal rapport with Jawaharlal Nehru to impose a policy of accession of the princely states to independent states despite stout resistance from key British political officers. Fourth, Congress leaders had equally ambivalent views of the princes and employed threats, equivocation and British collaboration to secure integration after the British departed. Here again, individuals who were prepared to act decisively at a crucial juncture were pivotal. Sardar Vallabhbhai Patel, with extensive experience in the states' people's politics of Gujarat, and V. P. Menon, his administrative deputy, secured integration with skill, determination, and Mountbatten's active collaboration. Integration was not a foregone conclusion but once the process began it was carried through with extraordinary rapidity.

PREPARATIONS FOR CONSTITUTIONAL NEGOTIATIONS

Disgruntled by the refusal of the Butler Report to define paramountcy, the princes saw the Round Table Conference in London as a venue to negotiate directly with British authorities in the metropole to restrict British intervention in their internal affairs. Although the support of the princes for federation at the Round Table Conference in November 1930 was a dramatic formal gesture, it was not without precedent. Neither were the process of negotiations or the factors that influenced their course. There were at least five areas of continuity.

First, some princes renewed informal deliberations with British Indian politicians, who still saw them as useful allies or players who had to be accommodated. Second, ministers employed by the princes, either individually or jointly, were influential intermediaries in the consultations. Third, the Standing Committee of the Chamber of Princes became a battleground for control of the Indian States Delegation to London and its agenda. Fourth, internal rivalries among the princes were now projected into a larger arena and amplified as the stakes were perceived as larger. Fifth, conflicting attitudes towards the princes within the British imperial establishment continued to influence, usually covertly, the strategies of individual princes as well as the negotiations.

Once the Congress and Gandhi declined to attend the Round Table Conference and decided to launch a civil disobedience movement, moderate nationalists, most notably Tej Bahadur Sapru, and communalists such as Muhammad Ali and M. M. Malaviya dominated the negotiations prior to the Conference. Meanwhile prominent princes within the Chamber, mainly Ganga Singh of Bikaner, Hamidullah of Bhopal and Hari Singh of Kashmir, were meeting with British Indian leaders during 1929. They sought to generate a constitution that would be acceptable to all major political groups in India.[6] Such consultations became more crucial as British officials hinted that it might be possible to go beyond the recommendations of the Simon Report. However, the princes and nationalists, ranging from congressmen such as Motilal Nehru, to Hindu Mahasahbites such as Malaviya and B. S. Moonje, to Muslim Leaguers such as Muhammad Ali and M. A. Jinnah, reached no concrete agreements at a series of teas and dinners during 1930. On 29 March 1930, British Indian leaders assured the princes that a dominion government would be far more cooperative than the existing GOI. Moreover, Malaviya promised them that they would not be forced to adopt any prescribed form of government.[7] These remarks were clearly sweet music to the ears of the princes. However, as fewer Indian nationalists were willing to attend such sessions, Liberal and communal leaders were more prominent.

Collaboration between princes and British Indian politicians sympathetic to federation also occurred on the faultline of Muslim politics. On the princely side, Hamidullah of Bhopal was friendly with many Muslim politicians since his student days at Aligarh.[8] Before the first Round Table Conference, Hamidullah hosted a series of talks in London between moderates such as Sapru, Sastri and Setalvad and Muslims leaders including the Aga Khan, Jinnah, and Muhammad Shafi from Punjab. Later in 1931, Bhopal, with the

---

[6] Ramusack, *Princes*, pp. 188–91. Other significant sources are Ashton, Copland and Phadnis.
[7] Meeting of March 29, 1930, PSAP, CS, Supplementary Index, Case No. V, File No. 14 of 1930.
[8] Ramusack, *Princes*, pp. 54–5 and passim.

blessing of Gandhi, would try unsuccessfully to fashion a compromise on the issue of separate electorates for Muslims in a federation.[9]

From the late 1920s onward, the ministers and legal advisers of the princes played a more conspicuous role as surrogates for their employers. Indeed Ian Copland has argued that the princes agreed to a rapprochement with the nationalists in 1928 mainly because of the 'artfully deceitful pen' of K. M. Panikkar.[10] This assertion ignores the extended contacts that Chamber members had with moderate, pro-federation British Indian politicians in their professional capacity as lawyers and in cultural and religious institutions. At the same time, it highlights the changing roles of ministers. Princes had long used talented British Indians as bureaucrats within their states to consolidate princely control at the expense of their indigenous nobilities. Now rulers engaged resourceful, ambitious British Indians externally as diplomatic agents and internally as administrators. They used ministers to produce position papers and speeches on complex issues and to serve as contemporary vakils in Westminster and New Delhi. Increasingly, these ministers shaped the agendas as well as the strategy and tactics of the princes in their constitutional negotiations with the British, Indian nationalists, and other princes.

Kailash N. Haksar (1878–1953), a Kashmiri brahman, and K. M. Panikkar (1894–1963), an Oxford-educated nayar from Travancore, were the two most active intermediaries during the 1930s. A member of the minority government in Gwalior, Haksar undertook several assignments for the Chamber of Princes. Panikkar looked to Haksar as a mentor and worked in the Chamber Secretariat and later in Patiala and Bikaner.[11] Other significant ministers were Sir Manubhai Mehta (1868–1946), then at Baroda; Sir Abkar Hydari (1869–1941), the finance minister at Hyderabad; Sir Mirza Ismail, the diwan at Mysore; and Mir Maqbool Mahmud and Sir Liaqat Hayat Khan at Patiala. Although only a few ministers such as Mir Maqbool Mahmud moved freely between political careers in princely states and British India,[12] many of these

---

[9] Ibid., p. 204, notes 74 and 75; R. J. Moore, *The Crisis of Indian Unity, 1917–1940* (Oxford, 1974), pp. 126–7, 144, 158–63.

[10] Copland, *Princes*, p. 75.

[11] K. M. Panikkar, *An Autobiography*, translated from the Malayalam by K. Kirshnamurthy (Madras, 1977), pp. 73–146.

[12] Unlike most of the ministers in princely states, Mahmud and Liaqat also participated in British Indian politics. Elected to the Punjab Legislative Council in 1923 and 1926 (as a member of the Swaraj Party) and to the Punjab Legislative Assembly in 1937 (as a member of the Unionist Party), Mir Maqbool Mahmud was a close political associate and relative of Sir Sikandar Hayat Khan, the Unionist leader and chief minister (1937) of Punjab. Two of his sisters were married to Sikandar and a daughter married Shaukat Hayat Khan, Sikandar's son. Liaqat Hayat Khan was the brother of Sikandar: Syed Nur Ahmad, *From Martial Law to Martial Law: Politics in the Punjab, 1919–1958*,

men were concerned about the future shape of the Indian nation.[13] However, there has been no significant study of their contribution to the ideology or construction of Indian nationalism.

The participation of these ministers in the negotiations over federation has long been known, but their influence is not sharply etched. Moreover, moderate and communal British Indian politicians were significant collaborators with them. One prime example is the relationship between two Kashmiri brahmans, Haksar and Tej Bahadur Sapru.[14] A Liberal party leader and highly successful lawyer based in Allahabad with many princes as professional clients, Sapru had written the chapter on the Indian princes in the 1928 report of the All-Parties Conference that formulated principles for a future Indian constitution. This document argued for federation, that treaty rights and obligations of the princes should transfer from the British Crown to an Indian successor government, and that any dispute on treaty provisions should be referred to a supreme court.[15] Haksar, a close personal and political friend of Sapru, was an enthusiastic advocate of federation. These two men lobbied intensively with the princes for this goal. In 1927 Haksar had approached Panikkar to accept employment in Kashmir state and subsequently used the latter's research and journalist skills as an employee of the Chamber of Princes to fashion pro-federation propaganda.

During the summer of 1930, preparations for what was to be the first of three Round Table Conferences were in high gear. Appointed as secretary of the India States delegation, Panikkar produced the draft for a book, *Federal India*, which advocated ministries responsible to elected legislatures in British India with full internal autonomy for the princely states.[16] More specifically, federation might accomplish three princely goals. First, the ability of the British to intervene in princely durbars because of paramountcy might be reduced. Second, a federation might lead to the dissolution of the political department in the GOI since federating units would have full responsibility for their internal affairs and a federation would have no need for political officers. Malcolm

---

edited by Craig Baxter from a translation from the Urdu by Mahmud Ali (Boulder CO, 1985), pp. 53, 61, 113, 152, 186. Another example is Dr Jivraj Narayan Mehta, the son-in-law of Manubhai Mehta, who served as Prime Minister of Baroda in 1948 and then was Chief Minister of Gujarat from 1960 to 1963.

[13] Panikkar, *Autobiography*, p. 138 and passim mentions his commitment to federation and Indian nationalism.

[14] Mohan Kumar, *Sir Tej Bahadur Sapru: A Political Biography* (Gwalior, 1981); Sender, *Kashmiri Pandits*, pp. 262–6.

[15] Ramusack, *Princes*, pp. 190–1.

[16] Panikkar presented an insider's view of the extended negotiations over federation in his *Autobiography*, pp. 82–110 and claimed that Haksar's name was added to the book as an author to obtain greater credibility for his arguments: ibid., pp. 83–4.

Hailey, a distinguished former governor of Punjab and the United Provinces, remarked after the First Round Table Conference that 'the princes seem to be out for the extinction of the Political department, rather than the creation of a Federal constitution'.[17] Third, the princes might enhance their reputation for statesmanship by agreeing to federation that would trigger political advances in British India.[18] Other ministers generated additional schemes, notably Hydari in Hyderabad and Ismail in Mysore, who possibly hoped for a reduction of the large Mysore subsidy. Their efforts disclose how ministers served not only as intermediaries but also attempted to shape the policies of the Indian princes.

Princely responses reveal the diversity and difficulty of the rulers operating as a coherent order. Bikaner and Bhopal were early and energetic advocates of federation. However, Bhupinder Singh of Patiala, who as Chancellor of the Chamber of Princes was the nominal supervisor of Haksar and Panikkar, initially supported federation but then vacillated. His inconstancy forecast how challenging it would be to secure and retain princely support for federation, the multiplicity of factors that influenced princes, and, most significant, how for many advocates of federation it was an instrument for achieving other goals rather an end in itself.

Patiala's primary objective was the diminution of paramountcy and not of his own authority, now besieged from many sides. In 1930 Sikh groups and the Punjab Riyasti Praja Mandal, the local states' people's group, assailed his sexual habits, his financial extravagance and alleged mismanagement, and his political despotism. As mentioned earlier, an official inquiry headed by Fitzpatrick, the local political officer, had exonerated him. Although there is no surviving documentation of what was said in meetings between Fitzpatrick and Patiala, Copland suggests that Patiala's wavering support for federation might indicate that Fitzpatrick, who was 'a "Diehard" before the term had gained . . . notoriety', had pressured him to resist federation and cooperation with Indian nationalists.[19]

In the lengthy negotiations over the composition of the Indian States Delegation to London, there were two key issues. First, the states' people's groups were seeking representation. Princes were adamantly opposed. British officials and moderate Indian politicians such as B. L. Mitter and Chimanlal Setalvad supported the princes. W. Wedgwood Benn, the Labour Secretary of State, reasoned that '[o]ur prime objective is to make the Conference a success. Merely on the grounds of tactics, therefore . . . it would be fatal to alienate

---

[17] Hailey to Irwin, 19 November 1930, OIOC, MSS Eur E 220/34.
[18] Kailas N. Haksar and K. M. Panikkar, *Federal India* (London, 1930).
[19] Copland, *Princes*, p. 82.

the princes'.[20] The second issue was more critical: which princes should be invited. On the one hand Patiala sought to limit the composition to members of the Standing Committee of the Chamber (whom the resident at Hyderabad said people in the Deccan called a phalanx of Rolls Royce rajas) and others who were generally not supportive of federation. The nizam of Hyderabad was miffed since he thought that his state lacked appropriate representation. Therefore Akbar Hydari, his chief minister; Ismail from Mysore, who also felt slighted; and Ganga Singh of Bikaner, Patiala's long-term rival, collaborated to influence the viceroy to pressure Patiala to revise his list. The result was an enlarged delegation that included Hamidullah of Bhopal and Sayajai Rao of Baroda, strong advocates of federation, as well as such pro-federation ministers as Haksar, Ismail and eventually Hydari, who became a firm supporter of federation during the voyage out from India.[21]

THE FEDERATION DRAMA

Once most of the delegates reached London in October, informal meetings proliferated. Acting as the secretary-general of the Indian States delegation, Haksar continued to lobby for princely commitments to federation, but he faced powerful countervailing factors. First, Maharaja Gulab Singh of Rewa, representing conservative princes, feared that federation would bring democracy to the states. Second, some officials at the India Office were rumoured to be against federation. Third, the ministers who supported federation were divided by personal ambition and conflicting strategies about how to realise this goal. But Haksar persisted and with Sapru and M. R. Jayakar as intermediaries between the Indian States and the British Indian delegations, they set the stage.

On 12 November 1930, George V opened the Round Table Conference with words of welcome spoken into a silver and gold microphone that represented a new era of communication in imperial politics.

After an adjournment to study the official despatch from India on the Simon Report, the first plenary session opened five days later. Then Sapru, the liberal constitutionalist, asked the princes to join an all-India federation, and Ganga Singh of Bikaner dramatically assented. The Simon Report was consigned to the archives. The conference quickly divided into several committees to devise concrete formulas for a federation. The Minorities Committee chaired

[20] W. Wedgwood Benn to Lord Irwin, 12 December 1929, NAI, GOI, F&P, 1929, Reforms Branch, File No. 193-R.
[21] Copland, *Princes*, pp. 83–6.

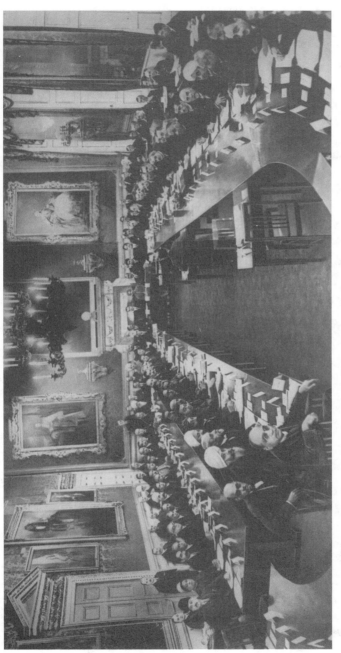

Plenary session of the first Round Table Conference, with Bhupinder Singh of Patiala in a western suit at the far end of the table.

Sir Tej Bahadur Sapru, Maharaja Jai Singh of Alwar and Prime Minister Ramsey MacDonald at the first Round Table Conference.

by Ramsey MacDonald and the Federal Structure Committee headed by Lord Sankey, the lord chancellor, were the most significant groups.

After the British delegation recovered from its initial surprise, Labour Party members, the Liberals under the guidance of Lord Reading, the former viceroy, and moderate Conservatives pondered the possibility of limited responsible government at the centre. In a federal central government, the princes could act as a counterweight to the nationalists. Thus all three parties – the princes, moderate Indian politicians, and British officials – considered federation principally as a means rather than as a primary goal. Although some indications of future sticking points emerged, most crucially in regard to communal representation and the federal structure, the first Round Table Conference ended optimistically.[22]

After their laudatory treatment as political innovators in London, the members of the Indian States delegation received a much cooler reception in India. Many princes were lukewarm towards, afraid of, or even hostile to federation. After reluctant acquiescence in London, Bhupinder Singh of Patiala became ambivalent towards federation. He was concerned about the princes' ability to compete effectively in a parliamentary system, the financial consequences, and the ongoing lack of definition of paramountcy. Personal pique was also a factor since Hamidullah defeated Patiala for the chancellorship of the Chamber in a close election in March 1931. Lord Irwin remarked that he would '[n]ever feel quite certain that the future would not see Patiala putting spokes in the Federation wheel that Bhopal would be pushing around'.[23] The situation was not more encouraging among large states in the south, whose cooperation was crucial. The nizam of Hyderabad was more concerned about reclaiming his sovereignty over Berar than about all-India goals, and the maharaja of Mysore did not speak out. Their pro-federation ministers, Hydari and Ismail, aroused personal jealously among their colleagues, who then attacked them by opposition to federation. But the shock troops of the anti-federation movement were conservative princes who were against any changes that might possibly open their states to democratic reforms.

Even more immediately, perhaps as many as 300 princes who ruled smaller states feared that they would not survive as independent polities. Most of these states did not enjoy full sovereign rights such as their own high courts or the ability to impose the death penalty; they did not have direct treaty relations with the British, and were not directly represented in the Chamber of

<hr />

[22] Ibid., pp. 87–91; Ramusack, *Princes*, pp. 202–3.
[23] Irwin to Wedgwood Benn, 23 March 1931, OIOC, MSS Eur C152/6.

Princes. As rumours circulated that the upper house of the federal legislature, in which the princes would have a greater proportion than in the more popular lower house, would have around a hundred members, even those lesser princes who were members of the Chamber worried about their future existence. Bhupinder Singh of Patiala assumed the leadership of this constituency with the publication in June 1931 of a pamphlet in which he proposed a Union of States based on a Chamber of Princes enlarged to include more small states.[24]

When the princes and their ministers met at Bombay in late June 1931, they debated vigorously about the potential impact of federation and their position at the second Round Table Conference. Several rulers opposed federation, including those from Bahawalpur, Kutch, Rampur, Sachin and Sangli, and ministers such as Bapna of Indore and Pattani of Bhavnagar. Bikaner and Bhopal remained advocates. They claimed that federation would restrict British encroachment and that representatives in the federal assembly were more likely to split on regional than on British India/princely lines. Although the pro-federation princes won at the Bombay session, Patiala retained a firm base among the smaller states.

In early August 1931 Bhupinder Singh and Udaibhan Singh (b. 1893, s. 1911, d. 1954) of Dholpur, his cousin, further refined the alternative to federation. All states presently members of the Chamber and collective representatives of the smaller states would form a federation that would then join British India in a confederation. This government would have restricted functions and consequently limited expenditures and need for income. The federation of states would also form an electoral college to select representatives of the states to a federal legislature with British India. On 28 August 1931, Patiala was able to attract twenty-nine princes favourable to confederation to Bombay and asked the viceroy that Dholpur should present their scheme to the second Round Table Conference. Meanwhile Bhupinder Singh confronted major financial difficulties since he was unable to obtain loans to satisfy his many creditors. Therefore, claiming that he wished to remain in India to work for confederation, he secured the appointment of Liaqat Hayat Khan to the Indian States delegation. Sending a minister rather than a ruler was far less expensive and perhaps more effective.

Besides the division within princely ranks, there was opposition to federation in British India. Jawaharlal Nehru was opposed because Indians would

---

[24] 'Federation and the Indian States', PSAP, CS, File No. III (c) 36 of 1931, and *Tribune*, 18 June 1931, p. 1.

not control the army or the salaries of the services; princes and landlords whom he viewed as reactionary were to be included; and there were too many concessions in the area of finance. States' people's groups sought a guarantee of fundamental rights for all citizens and the election of states' representatives to any federal legislature. More ominously, groups sometimes sympathetic to the princes were also negative. Liberal British Indians, especially those associated with the Servants of India Society in Poona, protested at the lack of both democratisation in the princely states before federation and adequate provision for election of states' representatives. With a few exceptions such as Terence Keyes in Hyderabad, British political officers deprecated federation. Their reasons ranged from a fear that the princes would be no match for British Indian politicians to a concern about their future employment. So the initial euphoria over federation had significantly subsided less than a year after it had first appeared.[25]

From September to December 1931 during the second Round Table Conference, the Federal Structure Committee, under the able guidance of Lord Sankey, worked to make the outline of the future federation more concrete. The details made many princes apprehensive. A list of fundamental federal rights was proposed and subjects allotted to the federal government opened areas for intervention such as jurisdiction over railways. Although the princes had agreed not to raise the issue of paramountcy in London, they now worried that they would have to rely on the Crown and the viceroy as the Crown's agent for protection of their sovereignty and therefore face renewed British intervention. Another issue was the composition of the federal legislature, where the princes desired parity, namely half the seats in a large upper house and weighage in the lower house. The Sankey Report called for an upper house of 200 with the states allotted 40 per cent. Finally, the princes were distressed about the fiscal consequences of federation. They optimistically wished to get redress from fiscal burdens including subsidies, customs duties, and excise taxes on items such as salt. At the very least they did not want to increase their financial contributions to a central, federal government. There were signs of princely disaffection in London. A former political officer and now member of the India Council, Reginald Glancy, commented that since housing for the princes was insufficient at the beginning of the Second Round Table Conference, many left early and '[t]here is not one genuine friend of federation left among the Princes'.[26] Still, Sir Samuel Hoare, the secretary of state for India, advised Lord

---

[25] Copland, *Princes*, pp. 113–21; Ramusack, *Princes*, pp. 208–14.
[26] Reginald I. R. Glancy, Supplementary Memorandum, 29 October 1931, T. C. 2A quoted in Moore, *Crisis*, p. 231.

Willingdon, who had replaced Irwin as viceroy, that '[t]he Government and I are pledged at every turn to the All-India Federation'.[27]

By early 1932 major states including Jaipur, Jodhpur, Udaipur and Kolhapur had openly defected from the federation camp. Patiala continued his propaganda campaign for confederation and attracted several princes from Kathiawar including Ranjitsinhji of Nawanagar. Perhaps suspicious that Willingdon did not share his commitment to federation, Hoare urged the viceroy to prevent the princes from abandoning federation. In March 1932 Willingdon responded with a supportive speech at the annual meeting of the Chamber of Princes on the advantages to the princes of federation; he also informally canvassed key princes. At the same time Hoare had urged the members of the Federal Finance Committee chaired by J. C. Davidson, which was to tour India in early 1932, to lobby with the princes for federation.

The Federal Finance Committee was one of three expert committees who were to supply data that Hoare could use to construct a reform bill. Davidson promoted federation but also avowed that there was a lack of strong support in India for federation among both princes and British officials. He advised Hoare that he did not 'think Willingdon is capable, certainly the Political Department is not, of getting the scheme across, especially when it is not their own, and they are unsympathetic in principle to the whole idea of federation'.[28] Lord Lothian (Philip Kerr), the chair of the Franchise Committee, also thought that 'official Delhi' was not sympathetic to federation since it was not its initiative.[29] Meanwhile, Davidson relayed that both M. R. Jayakar and Lothian urged Hoare or the Prime Minister to make a clear statement that the British Government was firmly in favour of federation and that princely hesitation would delay it.[30] Although Lord Hastings, another member of the Finance Committee, thought that a lack of civility by Willingdon towards Davidson had made the latter take a negative view of Willingdon's support for federation, Davidson continued to argue that London should impose a scheme upon the princes since they could never agree among themselves.[31] He was proposing what the British would do in 1947 when they advised the princes to

[27] Hoare to Willingdon, 28 January 1932, OIOC, MSS Eur E240/1.
[28] Davidson in Bombay to Hoare, 24 April 1932, OIOC, MSS Eur E240/14(a).
[29] Lothian in New Delhi to Hoare, 27 March 1932, OIOC, MSS Eur E 240/14(b).
[30] Davidson to Hoare, 12 March 1932, ibid., and Lothian to Hoare, OIOC, Templewood Collection, MSS Eur E240/14(b). Jayakar thought that the GOI was indirectly assaulting federation by stressing the difficulties associated with it for the princes.
[31] Hastings in Viceroy's House in New Delhi to Hoare, 16 April 1932, and Davidson in Simla to Hoare, 15 April 1932, OIOC, Templewood Collection, MSS Eur E240/14(a). Relationships between members of the Finance Committee must have been tense. Davidson advised that 'Although

accede to successor governments or to face the consequences without British support.

On the princely side, the volatile but astute Bhupinder Singh realised the need for compromise since he was unable to expand his supporters to include the largest states, especially Hyderabad and Mysore, whose adherence was crucial for success. The pro-federation princes, notably Ganga Singh and Hamidullah, were worried because the prime minister had warned that he would make an arbitrary award of seats to the princes if they did not produce their own plan. Once again ministers, especially Prabhashankar Pattani from Bhavnagar and Mir Maqbool Mahmud, then serving at Alwar, were delegated to fashion a format that would reconcile confederation with the proposals of the Federal Structure Committee. After a year of not talking to each other, Ganga Singh, Hamidullah and Bhupinder Singh met on 11 March 1932, in New Delhi. Personal animosities were resolved as all three agreed to support a supposedly neutral Ranjitsinhji of Nawanagar for the chancellorship in 1932, and subsequently Bhopal and Bikaner would campaign for Patiala in the 1933 election. Meanwhile C. P. Ramaswami Aiyar was to chair another committee of ministers to devise safeguards that reconciled confederation with the Sankey Report. Their proposition allowed states to federate either individually or collectively and became the basis of the so-called Delhi Pact submitted for approval to the Chamber of Princes.

The March 1932 session of the Chamber was the longest (it lasted for ten days), the liveliest, and the best attended (sixty were present) of such meetings. Rulers from the smaller states came in force and were not enthusiastic about the Aiyar plan. But Patiala made a forceful speech and Willingdon and Davidson lobbied informally. On 1 April 1932, a majority of the princes voted to federate. However, the proposed federal structure was encircled with two categories of safeguards. One focused on protecting princely prerogatives such as individual seats for members of the Chamber in an upper house and the preservation of treaty rights. The other asked for safeguards from intervention by the federal government in the internal affairs of a state. However, the demands from middle-sized princes for limits on British intervention in internal affairs of the states was inconsistent with the concern of small states for a commitment from the paramount power to guarantee their existence. British officials in London and in India took small comfort in the princely

Hastings is inclined to be thoughtless and brusque he gets away with it for reasons which you know as well as I do' and that Major-General Hutchinson, another member, was lazy and disgruntled that he had not been chosen as chair: Davidson to Hoare, 7 March 1932, ibid.

assent and as Reginald Glancy remarked, 'We are none of us, I should imagine, convinced that [federation] . . . will work, but we . . . are pledged to try the experiment'.[32]

While Samuel Hoare was a strong supporter of federation, other members of his party were not. They were eager to exploit the ambivalence of the princes. During the early 1930s Winston Churchill emerged as the leader of the Diehard faction. They would be implacably opposed to any constitutional reforms in India, including federation and its complement of limited responsible government at the centre. Although Churchill enjoyed qualified support among Conservative MPs, some allies commanded attention because of their administrative experience in India, and key newspapers – the *Morning Post* and its editor H. T. Gwynne, the *Daily Express* of Lord Beaverbrook, and the *Daily Mail* of Lord Rothermere – were sympathetic.[33] In their effort to derail constitutional advance, the Diehard faction reasoned that if the princes did not federate then the train of central responsibility would be stalled. So the princes were the key to frustrating constitutional reforms.

The Diehards focused on Ranjitsinhji, the chancellor of the Chamber in 1932, and recruited L. F. Rushbrook Williams, then his foreign minister, to influence him. Since Nawanager was irate towards the British because of economic and symbolic issues and fearful of the penetration of popular politicians from British India into the princely states, he was amenable to anti-federation proposals. Delhi had refused any concessions in a customs arrangement that drastically reduced the customs revenue at Bedi port which the jam sahib had developed with state funds; and it had not increased his 13-gun salute, which was lower than that of many of his Chamber peers.[34] The jam sahib considered both issues to be serious infringements on his sovereignty. The Diehards were initially successful. While Ranjitsinhji was in England for health reasons during the summer of 1932, he issued two circulars claiming the princes would not federate until paramountcy was defined. However,

---

[32] Quoted as Richard Glancy to Sir F. Stewart, 29 February 1932, in Copland, *Princes*, p. 111. It must have been Reginald Glancy who was then serving on the Indian States Enquiry Committee that Lord Eustace Percy chaired.

[33] Ibid., pp. 113–15.

[34] In 1934 Ranjitsinhji's successor accepted Delhi's offer of arbitration by Lord Dunedin, who ordered Willingdon to work out a settlement. By its terms Nawanagar was allowed to retain Rs 5 lakhs collected as duty on goods consumed in British India and all of the duty on goods consumed within Nawanagar: McLeod, *Sovereignty*, pp. 105–8.

Nawanager proved no match for the stout resistance of the reconciled duo of Bikaner and Patiala and the articulate skills of Panikkar, now secretary of the Chamber. By September Nawanagar reluctantly agreed to support the resolution of the Standing Committee and the Chamber favouring federation. But the Diehards opened another front with Bhupinder Singh, who succeeded Nawanagar as chancellor in 1933 and benefited from an unlikely ally in India.

In mid-July 1932 the report of the Federal Finance Committee provided incentives for the princes to federate. It recommended the phasing out of tributes paid by some states to the Crown and some concessions such as allowing coastal states in Kutch and Kathiawar to manufacture salt for local consumption. Most states would benefit, but a few, notably Cochin and some Kathiawar states, would lose revenue from customs that they presently collected. At the same time Willingdon undertook a strategy that impeded federation despite its proclaimed support for that goal.[35]

Acting on a suggestion from Sir Maurice Gwyer, a legal adviser to the India Office, the viceroy now decided that a more reliable means of achieving federation would be to court six of the largest states – Hyderabad, Mysore, Travancore, Gwalior, Baroda and Indore – at the expense of the middle-sized Chamber group dominated by Bikaner and Patiala. His premise was that if larger states obtained multiple seats in a small upper house, then only a smaller number of states would have to accede to achieve federation. Supported by Hydari and other ministers from the so-called Big Six states, Willingdon called a meeting at Simla in September 1932. Here he divided the states with his proposal for multiple seats based on historical importance, salute rank, and population. Ministers of large and small states were amenable to a strong paramount power as an ally vis-à-vis nationalist interference. Their position was an affront to the Bikaner-Bhopal demand for safeguards to prevent the paramount power from interference in the internal affairs of states. By the end of the meeting an angry Hamidullah reiterated that the Standing Committee would not federate without the resolution of paramountcy, a position similar to that of the jam sahib. Willingdon had unconsciously furthered the objective of the Diehards against the often-stated policy of Hoare, his superior in London.[36]

The omens for success at the third Round Table Conference in late 1932 were not positive. Willingdon invited rulers of twelve states to attend or to send their ministers, and thereby excluded Haksar. Once again Bhupinder Singh could

[35] Copland, *Princes*, pp. 114–18.   [37] Ibid., pp. 118–21.

not attend for financial reasons, and he was able to persuade Bikaner and Bhopal that their attendance would be an affront to his honour.[37] Consequently, with the exception of the raja of Sarila, the Indian States delegation included only ministers who could not make binding decisions on behalf of the princes. Since the Congress refused to join the British India delegation, the five-week session in London resolved few issues.

Disunity prevailed among the princes. The states delegation remained divided on representation in the federal legislature and the basis for allocating it. They reluctantly had to accept a proposal for 40 per cent of the seats in an upper house instead of their demand for parity. They also could not agree on a timetable for the accession to federation by their employers, with the consequence that the princes appeared to control the inauguration of federation and responsible government at the centre. Meanwhile, in London on a private visit, the jam sahib, in contact with the Diehards, once again threw a spanner in the works by diverting attention to paramountcy. He eventually claimed that the princes should stay out of federation to prevent democratisation. The Bikaner-Patiala group was now concerned about Nawanagar's possible appeal to smaller states.

Robin Moore argues that the third Round Table Conference retreated from a 'self-governing conference' to a 'Simonesque procedure for the preparation of an official scheme, its embodiment in a state document, and its consideration by a joint committee, assisted by witnesses or assessors, prior to its presentation to parliament'.[38] If the princes and Indian politicians could not draw up an acceptable blueprint, then the British would. A White Paper was published on 18 March 1933. A Joint Select Committee of Parliament (chaired by Lord Linlithgow, who would succeed Willingdon as viceroy) deliberated on its contents from April 1933 to October 1934, and its report was the basis for a *Government of India Act* that received royal assent in August 1935.

Still dedicated to federation, Hoare gained some concessions for the princes in the White Paper. Their seats in the upper house of 260 were increased from ninety to a hundred and references to fundamental rights were removed. Although Liaqat Hayat Khan and Manubhai Mehta recommended that the Chamber endorse the White Paper at their March 1933 annual meeting in

---

[37] Patiala's finances remained precarious and were the main reason why the viceroy did not want the ruler to go to London to give evidence before the Joint Select Committee: Willingdon to Hoare, 23 May 1933, OIOC, MSS Eur E240/12 (a).

[38] Moore, *Crisis*, pp. 296–7.

Delhi, Ranjitsinhji protested that 'the constitution as it has emerged from the White Paper will inevitably work as to destroy the very principle of Indian Kingship'.[39] Willingdon ruled the chancellor out of order. Many princes, including Patiala, obliquely rallied to Nawanagar's defence by demanding more safeguards. The Chamber ended up passing two contradictory resolutions – one made the accession of the princely states to federation conditional on safeguards, and the other, from Nawanagar, linked accession to a resolution of paramountcy. Suffering from ill health that brought his death ten days later, the jam sahib did not stand for the chancellorship and Bhupinder Singh easily won.

Now the Diehards opened another front with the Patiala ruler, whom Delhi had rebuffed on several issues. The GOI had denied Patiala's request to appoint Fitzpatrick as his prime minister and then imposed Sir Frederick Gauntlett as his finance minister and a schedule of reduced expenditures to stem possible bankruptcy. Moreover, personal relations between Bhupinder Singh and the viceroy were strained and the new resident, Harold Wilberforce-Bell, was far less sympathetic than the departing Fitzpatrick. As agents, the Diehards used N. Madhava Rao, an Indian correspondent for the *Morning Post*, who allegedly had evidence suitable for political blackmail of Bhupinder Singh, and Mir Maqbool Mahmud, now the secretary of the Chamber. Madhava Rao urged Gwynne, his editor at the *Morning Post*, to orchestrate a delegation of Diehard MPs to lobby with Patiala and other princes during 1934 as the Joint Select Committee in London was hearing testimony on a proposed Government of India Bill. Lymington from the Lords and Jack Courtauld from the Commons found receptive listeners among the numerous princes, including Patiala, who still judged British intervention more troublesome than that of British Indian politicians or popular political opponents and were uncertain about the benefits of federation. Consequently the envoys were able to secure the signatures of five out of ten members of the Standing Committee of the Chamber to a letter stating that they might not accede to federation unless there were significant changes in the White Paper. These middle-sized and smaller rulers were apprehensive because of reports from London that the final form of the GOI bill might not be as favourable to them as hoped. They were also alarmed by popular agitations in Kashmir and Alwar and the deposition of Jai Singh of Alwar. Although the erratic Alwar ruler had few close personal friends among the princes, his fate was disconcerting.

---

[39] Speech of 24 March 1933 quoted in Copland, *Princes*, p. 124.

After a second delegation of Diehards returned from India and reported positively on princely opposition to federation, in late July 1934 Winston Churchill and other Conservatives promised publicly that they would support the princes 'against any attempt to encroach upon their rights and privileges'. However, the Diehard strategy began to unravel in the autumn. Ministers such as Liaqat, Panikkar and Akbar Hydari stiffened princely support for federation. In Delhi, Willingdon made some timely concessions, most notably on Berar to Hyderabad, on the possible retrocession of the Bangalore cantonment to Mysore, and on the customs dispute with Nawanagar, as well as some covert threats to Bhupinder Singh. Meanwhile in Bristol at the annual meeting of the Conservative Party, the Diehards lost by seventeen votes on an amendment to repudiate Hoare's policy on India. Although that margin was small, the House of Commons subsequently endorsed the report of the Joint Select Committee by a vote of two to one.[40]

The final scene in the constitutional saga that began in 1927 transpired in January 1935 with the annual session of the Chamber of Princes. In his opening speech Bhupinder Singh, still the chancellor, equivocated, asking his colleagues

to consider whether we should put ourselves in the position in which practically every important body of opinion in British India considers us unwelcome partners and looks upon our entry into Federation with suspicion. The benefits of a Federal Scheme to the Indian States are . . . not so overwhelming that, whatever the opinion of British India, it would be in our best interest to join it.[41]

Both Willingdon and Patiala's colleagues on the Standing Committee applied immediate pressure that seemed to have an effect. By the next day the Sikh ruler retracted some of his comments. When Ganga Singh moved a resolution of endorsement for the Joint Select Committee report, it passed with no word from Patiala. Although the Diehards by now understood that Patiala's support was like the motion of a weathervane, they continued to apply pressure through Madhava Rao.

When the princes and their ministers next met at Bombay in March 1935 to decide their response to the GOI bill, their highly conditional acceptance encouraged the Diehards. The princes continued to bargain for better terms, especially on the issue of paramountcy, but London and Delhi decided to stand

---

[40] Ibid., pp. 121–43.
[41] Speech of 22 January 1935, quoted in Kavalam M. Panikkar, *The Indian Princes in Council: A Record of the Chancellorship of His Highness the Maharaja of Patiala, 1926–1931 & 1933–1936* (London, 1936), pp. 118–20.

firm.[42] Willingdon threatened Patiala with possible deposition for maladministration and Hoare reported that the king-emperor himself gave the ruler 'a proper dressing down . . . saying that it was an outrageous affair for a great Indian Prince to intrigue with conspirators here and [with] a miserable correspondent of the *Morning Post* in India'.[43] Hoare also engineered a directive that the princes would not be invited to the silver jubilee celebrations of George V in 1936. Nevertheless he tried to be conciliatory and made concessions in the bill in response to princely concerns about the power of the federal legislature to make laws for the states and the obligations of the Crown to the states in the non-federal areas. In June 1935 the bill passed and became law with royal assent on 2 August 1935.[44]

ACCESSION IS DEFERRED

Desultory negotiations between the British and the Indian princes ensued from 1935 to 1939. Although they were ultimately suspended upon the outbreak of the Second World War, this result should not be read backwards into the historical narrative. In the late 1930s many British officials and Indian princes still considered federation to be possible even if the initial euphoria had evaporated during the realpolitik of extended negotiations. Moreover, personnel shifts and political events slowed the pace of negotiations so that their suspension in 1939 did not alarm anyone.

First, there was a reversal in the respective attitudes towards federation of Delhi and London. Earlier, Hoare in London had persistently pushed Willingdon in India to motivate the princes to support federation proposals more vocally. Even when the viceroy acted, some Britons questioned his commitment. In June 1935 the marquess of Zetland, who as Lord Ronaldshay had served as governor of Bengal, replaced Hoare. Then in April 1936, Lord Linlithgow succeeded Willingdon. Both men endorsed federation with the princes as a goal, but they differed over procedures and timing. Now the viceroy in India acted with a sense of urgency, planning to inaugurate federation by 1 April 1938,[45] while his superior in London urged caution. In August 1936, four months after his arrival in India, Linlithgow appointed three political officers, Courtenay Latimer, Arthur C. Lothian and Francis Wylie, as his special

---

[42] Copland, *Princes*, pp. 138–40.
[43] Hoare to Willingdon, 31 May 1935, OIOC, MSS Eur E240/4.
[44] Copland, *Princes*, pp. 138–43.
[45] Linlithgow to Wylie, 18 August 1936, OIOC, L/P&S/13/613 in Copland, *Princes*, p. 145.

emissaries to the princes to probe their positions on federation. But in late September the secretary of state advised the viceroy:

It does, however, occur to me that there may be a point in the negotiations with the Princes beyond which the application of more haste might result in the achievement of less speed . . . Let me add that I shall have to keep a sharp eye on Parliament in all matters connected with the establishment of the Federation.[46]

Although no one found the princes enthusiastically investigating the opportunities that federation might present, the British envoys had differing perceptions of the princely response. Lothian, who toured in central and south India, claimed 'that, if one or two of the bigger states could be persuaded, "even at the sacrifice of principle, financial or otherwise", to join the Federation, the rest of the States would "tumble over each other to follow"'.[47] Thus the princes apparently continued to bargain for concessions on longstanding grievances as the price for accession. In later recollections a more pessimistic and perhaps cynical Wylie asserted that most princes did not understand the implications of federation and were confused by high-priced lawyers. He added that the largest ones, especially Hyderabad, did not want to federate, whatever they might say, and that others such as Hari Singh of Kashmir were bored by discussions over federation. Wylie, who adopted a demanding policy towards the princes when he was political adviser during the early 1940s, concluded that

if left to their own devices, there was never the slightest chance of getting rulers representing fifty percent of the population of the princely states to sign instruments of accession before the second world war broke out in September 1939. The only way, so far as the British government were concerned, if they genuinely wanted to expedite the creation of federation, would have been to take the princes by the neck and compel them to come. This is what Patel and V. P. Menon did later on.[48]

An Instrument of Accession acceptable to the princes was never achieved, and most scholars share Wylie's perception of the negative role of lawyers in this process. But the lawyers acted on behalf of combatants who had longstanding enmities. Within the Chamber, Patiala, who was now publicly supportive of federation, sponsored W. H. Wadhams (1891–1970), a retired American judge, as the Chamber's advocate. When Dholpur, who had remained committed to

---

[46] Zetland to Linlithgow, 25 September 1936, OIOC, MSS Eur F 125/3.
[47] Quoted from NAI, F&P, No. 20, Federation Secret, 1941 in Phadnis, *Integration*, p. 104.
[48] Sir Francis Wylie, 'Federal Negotiations in India 1935–9, and After', in C. H. Philips and Mary Doreen Wainwright (eds), *The Partition of India: Policies and Perspectives 1935–1947* (Cambridge, MA, 1970), p. 521.

confederation and was resolutely anti-federation, unexpectedly succeeded his cousin as chancellor in early 1936, he employed John H. Morgan, the legal adviser to the Diehard *Morning Post*. Although a compromise was reached with both lawyers representing the Chamber, the two were not united in their negotiations with the India Office during 1936 over the Instrument of Accession. Meanwhile the nizam of Hyderabad employed Sir Walter Monckton (1891–1965), who served as his legal adviser until 1947.

However, as Ian Copland has argued, many factors other than lawyers were at work. Some were personal. Ganga Singh of Bikaner was angered by what he perceived as a lack of appropriate recognition in London at the king-emperor's silver jubilee celebration and the number of seats allocated to his state in the federal legislature. Hydari did not calculate any benefits for Hyderabad since the Berar issue was settled and internal demonstrations seemed more threatening. Other states also experienced intensifying popular agitations. By 1938 Congress leaders, including Gandhi, for varying reasons intervened more publicly in oppositional politics in the states, especially in Rajkot, Travancore and Mysore. Although the ultimate failure of Gandhi to secure his objectives in Rajkot in 1939 demonstrated the difficulties of sustained political protest in the princely states, the Rajkot satyagraha was indicative of future cooperation across borders. As home-grown state politicians were emboldened to organise public rallies, princely attention swerved from constitutional negotiations to the containment of local opposition. These autocrats became more fearful of the contagion of political hostility spreading from British India to their states. So when Linlithgow announced that negotiations over federation were suspended because of the need to focus on wartime demands, the princes were not perturbed.

PRINCES, THE BRITISH, AND THE SECOND WORLD WAR

When, without consultation of the elected Indian officials at the centre or in the provinces, Linlithgow declared that India was at war, the Congress ministries, at the direction of their party executive, resigned in protest. The British therefore were most appreciative of Indians who continued to collaborate, especially the Muslim League and the Indian princes. Many rulers were quick to provide military aid, much as they or their predecessors had done in 1914. Stalwarts such as Ganga Singh, who had first served during the Boxer Rebellion, were active in planning and coordination. Younger men such as the future maharao raja of Bundi personally served in Burma, while many more rulers made significant donations of cash and war materiel. More crucially, the princes opened their borders to recruiters for the British India Army and their subjects enlisted at a higher rate than in any British Indian province with the exception of Punjab. On the home front princes reaffirmed their personal loyalty to the British Crown and acted to control political dissent within and along their borders, especially during the 1942 Quit India movement.[49]

In turn the British patron acknowledged the assistance of these faithful allies with positions on government boards and on the Governor-General's Executive Council for Indians associated with the princely states, most notably C. P. Ramaswami Aiyar from Travancore. These appointments followed the pattern developed when the maharaja of Patiala and a minister from Gwalior had been appointed to the Governor-General's Legislative Council as rewards for support in 1857. Moreover, the British moderated their lobbying for internal structural reforms such as civil lists, legislative assemblies, and protection of fundamental rights within the princely states. For example, before his departure in 1943, Linlithgow lamented that most princes had yet to establish civil lists, a reform that Lord Irwin had urged in 1927. However, British oversight of the princes might diminish, but it did not wither.

In 1942 Sir Stafford Cripps, then Lord Privy Seal and a member of the War Cabinet, attempted a constitutional resolution. He did little to satisfy the princes. His draft declaration provided for membership of the princely states in a constitution-making body but added that 'whether or not an Indian State elects to adhere to the Constitution, it will be necessary to negotiate a revision of its Treaty arrangements, so far as it may be required in the new situation'.[50] When members of the Standing Committee of the Chamber sought reassurance about their future in a meeting with Cripps on 28 March 1942, the Labour MP pledged:

So far as the undertaking of our obligations of defence of the States was concerned . . . there was no insuperable difficulty from the naval point of view so long as we held Ceylon, or from the air point of view so long as we had the aerodromes which were necessary in one or other of the states . . . [S]umming it all up, we should stand by our treaties with the States unless they asked us to revoke them.[51]

Later Cripps tried to dilute this promise, but the Cabinet at home reiterated their protection of the princes. His words must have reinforced the princely

---

[49] Copland, *Princes*, pp. 183–9.
[50] Quoted from Reginald Coupland, *The Cripps Mission* (Bombay, 1942), p. 29 in Phadnis, *Integration*, p. 136.
[51] Quoted in Copland, *Princes*, p. 188.

perception that the British would continue to shield them and that drastic reforms were not yet necessary.

By 1943, however, British support in India for continuing guarantees of princely rule became more ambiguous. Two factors were crucial. One related to personnel changes at the top of the official hierarchy. First, in August 1943 Francis Wylie had become political adviser to the viceroy (who was known as the crown representative in his relations with the Indian princes after 1937). In October Lord Wavell succeeded Linlithgow as viceroy. Liberal and blunt, as indicated in the earlier quotation on princes and federation, Wylie was committed to demanding internal reforms within the states. Wavell, who had served in the Middle East and was formerly commander-in-chief in India, had little knowledge of the princes and allowed Wylie significant initiative. At the same time Allied victories in 1943 indicated that there was likely to be a successful end to the war, however high the human and material costs. Consequently the British now must begin to plan for the devolution of power after the war.

Among the princes there were also significant personnel changes. Key ministers such as Hydari died in 1942 or fell out of favour, for example Ismail, who moved from Mysore to Jaipur. Among the Chamber stalwarts, Ranjitsinhji of Nawanagar and Bhupinder Singh of Patiala had passed away in the 1930s. Then in February 1943 Ganga Singh of Bikaner died. Their successors lacked the political experience and shrewdness of their fathers. Hamidullah of Bhopal remained, but he withdrew from active participation in the Chamber until he became chancellor in 1944. There were a few energetic, committed princes in the Chamber, but they had to operate without a supportive network of equally dedicated colleagues. Contrary to some expectations, Digvijaysinhji of Nawanagar, who became chancellor upon the death of Patiala in 1938, had revived the Chamber with a circumspect expansion of membership and the regularisation of its finances so that it might lobby more effectively for princely interests. Unfortunately, the administrative reorganisation and increased attendance at annual sessions did not produce any meaningful political or constitutional reforms within the states. The princes remained naively unaware of how they might institute painful changes from the top to preclude demands for more radical reforms from their British patron, their Congress rivals, or their own subjects.

During the early 1940s the princes did not face consistent opposition from either the Congress or states' people's groups. The former was hamstrung by massive arrests after the Quit India campaign of 1942, and the latter were diverted by leadership struggles and conflicts between urban/professional and rural/peasant factions.[52] However, the British continued to challenge princely sovereignty in two key areas. One was the Attachment Scheme of small non-salute states in western India. The other was the implementation of industrial policies that seemed to constrict the economic boom stimulated by war demands in some states.[53] John McLeod has traced the origin of the Attachment Scheme to a proposal that Sayaji Rao of Baroda made in 1920 for annexation of states that paid tribute to him in western India. His not so disguised objective was to augment and consolidate his territorially fragmented state. Three times the British rejected his request because their assent would appear to renege on the promise made in 1858 that there would be no further annexations of princely states. By April 1939, however, the viceroy advised his superior in London that the merger of smaller states into larger ones for administrative purposes was needed even if pressure was required.[54] The British argued that a merger that was given the supposedly more benign name of attachment was required to bring these small units into the federation through the accession of the attaching states and to improve conditions within these revenue-poor states. Despite considerable opposition from the princes, the British finalised the Attachment Scheme in 1943 and thereby reduced around 435 states in western India to sixteen. McLeod has argued that the British hoped that by eliminating petty units which could not provide basic government services, they might fortify the enhanced states against Congress criticisms and ensure their survival.[55] Furthermore, both McLeod and Copland claim that the British support of the Attachment Scheme indicated that the British were less concerned about princely sensitivities than administrative rationalisation and Congress opposition.[56] From their side, several princes were troubled about the implications of the Attachment Scheme for their sovereignty. When the British refused to reassure them, Hamidullah of Bhopal and the Standing Committee of the Chamber resigned in late 1944.

By June 1945 Hamidullah and the Standing Committee had returned to office, and the chancellor launched a program to protect princely interests during the momentous postwar changes. His plan was fivefold: to rebuild the Chamber; to press for internal reforms; to preserve the British relationship;

---

[52] Sisson, *Congress Party*, ch 4, esp. pp. 89–96 provides one example.

[53] A general overview of these constraints is in Copland, *Princes*, pp. 201–4. In 'Emergence of Labor Politics', Janaki Nair argues that the Second World War stimulated several new ventures in Mysore but a lack of indigenous capital along with restrictive colonial policies hampered industrialisation in Mysore: pp. 89–99.

[54] Linlithgow to Zetland, 5 April 1939, OIOC, L/P&S/13/971 quoted in McLeod, *Sovereignty*, p. 128.

[55] Ibid., p. 136.

[56] Ibid., pp. 129–41; Copland, *Princes*, pp. 198–200.

to explore the possible benefits of an alliance with the Muslim League; and to achieve some kind of understanding with Congress. If time had been on their side, which it was not, the princes might have achieved some notable successes. At a meeting in Bombay in May 1945, attending princes pledged to reform their administrations 'along democratic lines in preparation for the part which the Indian States expect to play in the event of a national government in India'.[57] Subsequently elected legislative assemblies and at least partly responsible executive councils began to pop up in the states like mushrooms after a spring rain. Some princes, most notably in Orissa, Punjab, Rajputana and the Deccan, took the lead in proposing regional confederations in order to create more viable bargaining units for the forthcoming constitutional negotiations. Meanwhile Bhopal remained in close contact with Muslim politicians, and assorted princes and their ministers renewed communications with Congress leaders including Nehru. Continuing the pattern established from 1927 to 1935, these conversations demonstrate that the Congress, as had their British predecessors, were prepared to use the princes as best suited their goals.

THE DENOUEMENT OF INTEGRATION

During the tumultuous years from 1945 to 1947, British policies towards the princes reflected a combination of expediency, nostalgia, and the desire to be seen as honourable and perhaps even doing the honourable thing. On the one hand the replacement of an astute but unsympathetic Wylie by Sir Conrad Corfield (1893–1980) as political adviser to the crown representative in June 1945 meant a sympathetic mediator in the British hierarchy. Corfield had long seen princely India as the real India and wanted to broker a principled transition for the princes from British paramountcy to Indian self-government. His tactics offended Mountbatten, and his memoirs tried to justify the integrity of his position. However, the new Labour Government in London decided that British pledges of protection to the princes had to be sacrificed in the process of decolonisation. The problem was to evolve a scheme by which the British could disengage themselves without outright repudiation of their legal obligations to the princes.

In 1946 the Cabinet Mission came to India for one final round of constitutional negotiations that aimed to transfer power to a united Indian dominion. The princes were clearly subordinated to this goal but were still a concern. The British assuaged their legal consciences by promising that independence would

---

[57] Quoted in ibid., p. 212.

mean the end of their treaties with the princes and that paramountcy could not be transferred to a third party. While they asserted that the states would have much to gain from acceding to the new Indian state, the British would not coerce the princes to accede. The initial princely response was positive since the Cabinet Mission Plan terminated the hated paramountcy and seemed to grant independence. However, the British also called for a Constituent Assembly and the establishment of an interim government of Indian leaders to manage internal affairs until independence.

As the princes had haggled over the composition of their delegations to the Round Table Conferences, they now debated their participation in the Constituent Assembly. Bhopal sought to be the chief negotiator for the Chamber of Princes in the Assembly and briefly tried to ally the princes with the Muslims to counter Congress dominance.[58] K. M. Panikkar takes credit for derailing this proposal,[59] but C. P. Ramaswami Aiyar, on behalf of Travancore, was the first to desist from a single princely negotiator. Eventually the representatives of sixteen states joined the Constituent Assembly, but the fate of the princes would be handled by individual, personal negotiations as well as group debate. The princes could not stand together and therefore they would be integrated individually.

Communal allegiance became a heightened source of identity and commitment for princes as well as their subjects. The motivation for Bhopal's political pilgrimage that eventually led to his resignation from the Chamber is clouded. Panikkar is vitriolic in his memoirs in depicting Bhopal as a scheming communalist who was anxious to join with the nizam of Hyderabad in forming a Muslim third column in the heart of an independent India.[60] Copland, however, takes a more measured view of Bhopal's conversion to the cause of Pakistan. In any case Bhopal was not the only prince to increase his overt or covert support for communal organisations. The maharajas of Alwar and Bharatpur, among others, were financial and political supporters of the Hindu Mahasabha and the RSS,[61] and Yadavindra Singh of Patiala was sympathetic to Sikh groups. Just when the princes needed a united front, a division on communal lines was added to long-existing ones related to size, region, and memories of past rivalries.

When Mountbatten arrived as the last British governor-general, viceroy and crown representative, he sought to accelerate the British withdrawal and to create a united Indian dominion. He later claimed that 'nothing had been said

---

[58] Ibid., pp. 223–4, 235, 240–6, 266–7.
[59] Panikkar, *Autobiography*, pp. 153–7. [60] Ibid., pp. 138–64.
[61] Mayaram, *Resisting Regimes*, pp. 171–2 and Copland, 'Further Shores', pp. 228–39.

in London to prepare him for the gravity and magnitude of the problem of the states'.[62] After five weeks of personal exposure and extensive conversations with Nehru and Jinnah, Mountbatten was convinced of the inevitability of a quick partition and transfer of power. Nehru reluctantly accepted partition and agreed to dominion status with the understanding that the princes would be integrated into the new dominions. The princes held out for the right not to accede to either dominion, to remain independent, or to form a union of states. To retain Nehru's support, Mountbatten was willing to serve as the enforcer with the princes.[63] Meanwhile Nehru also protested at the proposed dissolution of the political department in the face of the end of paramountcy.

Mountbatten therefore agreed to the creation of a states department headed by Vallabhbhai Patel to handle relations between the interim government and the princes, and then accepted the concept of a Standstill Agreement. This instrument confirmed that the independent states of India and Pakistan would continue the agreements and administrative arrangements that existed between the British and the princes. The crucial document was the Instrument of Accession by which rulers ceded to the legislatures of India or Pakistan control over defence, external affairs, and communications. In return for these concessions, the princes were to be guaranteed a privy purse in perpetuity and certain financial and symbolic privileges such as exemption from customs duties, the use of their titles, the right to fly their state flags on their cars, and to have police protection. Between 2 and 14 August 1947, 114 states acceded to India and none to Pakistan. Only a few such states as Hyderabad, Mysore and Kashmir were to remain autonomous for the present. By December 1947 Patel began to pressure the princes into signing Merger Agreements that integrated their states into adjacent British Indian provinces, soon to be called states or new units of erstwhile princely states, most notably Rajasthan, Patiala and East Punjab States Union, and Matsya Union (Alwar, Bharatpur, Dholpur and Karauli). The integration of princely states into Pakistan proceeded more slowly and has attracted little scholarly attention.[64]

The three-step process that led to the integration of most princely states into the Indian Union as well as the initial refusal of four – Hyderabad, Jammu and Kashmir, Junagadh and Travancore – to sign Standstill Agreements is better documented than most aspects of the history of the princes. V. P. Menon's account has been extraordinarily influential in shaping the historiography that generally portrays Menon as the low-key, sensitive negotiator who offered the

[62] Moore, *Escape*, p. 290.   [63] Ibid., pp. 290–314.
[64] Wayne Ayres Wilcox, *Pakistan: The Consolidation of a Nation* (New York, 1963) remains the basic source.

carrots of income guarantees and political privilege and Patel as the hard-headed dictator who threatened deposition and physical force. In subsequent years other participants such as H. V. Hodson, Conrad Corfield and K. M. Panikkar have produced their memoirs. Significant British official papers are available in the monumental *Transfer of Power* series and selected papers of Nehru and Patel have been published. Unfortunately for them, the princes involved did not write memoirs and they have not been well served by biographers. Thus their voices are muted. However, it appears that many princes belatedly realised that the British left them no alternative but to accede and gain whatever concessions the Congress were willing to make. It probably worked to the princely advantage that the Congress leaders were confronting partition, communal riots, and an unimagined transfer of population while Menon was negotiating accession and then integration. It was in the best interests of the Congress to entice as many princes as possible with sweet gifts and to take a hard line with the few who refused their offers. Most princes acceded for a variety of reasons including patriotism, the advice of their ministers, the pressure of popular political leaders in their states, and a sense of abandonment.

EPILOGUE

Just as the British did not create the native/Indian princes, the accession and integration of the princely states into the independent states of India and Pakistan did not cause their rulers to disappear from Indian and Pakistani politics and culture. The most striking example of the long-term impact of princely states is the contested status of Jammu and Kashmir. Domestically, the current militant movement in Kashmir impugns the national identities of India as a secular state and Pakistan as an Islamic state. Materially, it has caused both countries to allocate extensive resources to defence and to several wars and military confrontations that have drastically reduced the funds available for internal development projects. Internationally, it has occasioned concern about the dangers of a nuclear confrontation between India and Pakistan. The British colonial policy of indirect rule imposed and helped to legitimate the rule of a Hindu prince in the Muslim-majority areas of Jammu and Kashmir. But policies of the rulers of Jammu and Kashmir were factors in fostering tensions between Muslim peasants and Hindu landlords, Muslim subjects and Hindu officials. Communal groups in British India, the policies of state and national governments in India and Pakistan, as well as groups indigenous to Jammu and Kashmir are also responsible for the present, difficult situation of this erstwhile princely state.

Although in the decades immediately after 1948 scholars claimed that the integration of the princely states into independent India and Pakistan ended the political power of their rulers, princes have continued to play numerous roles in politics and popular culture. Since there is so little research on the princes in Pakistan, this brief survey will focus on princes in independent India. From the late 1940s onward, the princes have served in appointed positions where political ritual and symbolism were prominent. During the negotiations over the integration of the princely states into India, several princes were installed as *rajpramukh* and *uprajpramukh*, governor and deputy governor respectively, of unions of princely states or even of their erstwhile state.[1] Rajpramukhs included Yadavindra Singh of Patiala in PEPSU, Man Singh of

---

[1] Much of this discussion is based on Hurtig, *Maharajahs*; Menon, *Story*; William L. Richter, 'Traditional Rulers in Post-Traditional Societies: The Princes of India and Pakistan', in Jeffrey, *People*, pp. 329–54.

Jaipur in Rajasthan, Jivaji Rao Scindia of Gwalior in Madhya Bharat (the core of the present state of Madhya Pradesh), and Rama Varma of Travancore in Travancore-Cochin. To accommodate princely izzat, senior and junior upra-jpramukhs were instituted. In Rajasthan, the rulers of Jodhpur and Kotah were the senior, those of Bundi and Dungarpur were the junior, and the maharana of Udaipur had his premier position among Rajput rulers recognised with the ceremonial title of *maharajpramukh* for life.[2] Maharaja Jaya Chamarajendra Wadiyar became the governor of Mysore, one of the two princely states (the other being Hyderabad) that remained distinct political units until the creation of Karnataka and Andhra Pradesh, which are Kannada and Telugu-speaking states, in 1956. Reflecting the special status of Jammu and Kashmir, Karan Singh became Sadar-I-Riyasat (governor) in 1952 upon the abdication of his father. He retained this post until 1967. The GOI also appointed a few princes to be governors of states that were not unions of princely territory. The first was Maharaja Krishna Kumarsinhji of Bhavnagar, who became governor of Madras in 1948.

After the posts of rajpramukh and uprajpramukh were abolished with the reorganisation of states and the integration of princely unions into larger states in 1956, some princes accepted diplomatic postings. Yadavindra Singh of Patiala was a member of the Indian delegation to the United Nations and to its Food and Agriculture Organisation, and later was ambassador first to Italy and then the Netherlands, where he died in 1974. Man Singh of Jaipur was ambassador to Spain and was later elected to the Rajya Sabha of the Indian Parliament.

Electoral politics were more risky but potentially provided more power than appointed positions. The princes who chose to contest elections, either at state or national level, had three options. They could form loose coalitions or join parties in opposition to the Congress party, stand as independent candidates, or run on the Congress ticket. Maharaja Hanwant Singh of Jodhpur (1923–52) followed the first path when he contested the 1952 elections for seats in both the Rajasthan legislature and the Lok Sabha. Tragically, he died in an airplane accident on the day of his victory in both constituencies.[3] His coalition won a majority of the seats in the territory of Marwar but did not develop into an effective force. Running on the ticket of the Swatantra party, which opposed the socialist policies of Jawaharlal Nehru, in 1962 Maharani Gayatri Devi won a seat in the Lok Sabha with a plurality of 175 000 votes

[2] Menon, *Story*, pp. 256–68.
[3] Dhananajaya Singh, *The House of Marwar* (New Delhi, 1994), pp. 186–99.

over the next candidate.[4] As independents, Maharaja Karni Singh of Bikaner won several terms in the Lok Sabha, and Maharaja Yadavindra Singh won a seat in the Punjab Legislative Assembly in 1967. The Congress party recruited many princes including Karan Singh of Jammu and Kashmir or their close relatives to run on its party ticket in areas where the Congress did not have a strong base, mainly in the territories of princely states. Openly pursuing his father's informal allegiance to the Congress party, Amarindar Singh of Patiala became the chief minister of Punjab in 2001 when Congress achieved victory.

The former ruling family of Gwalior has one of the more complicated patterns of involvement in electoral politics. In 1957 Maharani (rajmata after the death of her husband in 1961) Vijayaraje Scindia, running on a Congress ticket, won a seat in the Lok Sabha with a plurality of 60 000 over her opponent from the Hindu Mahasabha, an ironic victory considering her later affiliation with the BJP.[5] In 1967 the rajmata won a parliamentary seat on the Swatantra party ticket and one in the Madhya Pradesh state assembly on the Jana Sangh ticket. Accepting the assembly seat, she was a power-broker from 1967 to 1969 in state politics and formally joined the Jana Sangh, the precursor of the BJP. After imprisonment (which she shared with Gayatri Devi) during the Emergency in 1975–76, Vijayaraje Scindia joined the BJP and was elected its vice-president.[6] Soon estranged personally and politically from her only son, Madhavrao Scindia (1945–2001), who became a leading member of the Congress and Minister of Railways in Rajiv Gandhi's government during the late 1980s, she died in January 2001.[7] Her will, which left nothing to Madhavrao and sought to deny him the traditional right of a son to light her funeral pyre, revealed the depth of her antipathy. Tragically Madhavrao, sometimes mentioned as a future prime minister of India, died in a plane crash in October 2001 at the age of 56. His death left a major gap in the leadership of the Congress party. Meanwhile his sister, Vasundhara Raje (b. 1953), had joined her mother in the BJP. In early 2003 Vasundhara Raje became the leader

---

[4] Gayatri Devi, *Princess*, pp. 251–75; Hurtig, *Maharajahs*, pp. 172–7.

[5] Scindia, *Princess*, pp. 169–80; Hurtig, *Maharajahs*, pp. 198–215.

[6] Basu, 'Feminism Inverted', pp. 25–36.

[7] In June 2001, Prince Dipendra of Nepal killed most of his immediate family, supposedly because of his mother's refusal to permit his marriage to Devyani Rana, the child of Vijayaraje's second daughter Usha Raje. It was alleged that Queen Aishwarya opposed Devyani on two counts. Her father was from a different branch of the Rana's family than hers, and her grandfather was a Maratha, which the queen deemed subordinate to Rajputs: *The Independent*, 4 June 2001, p. 3. Ironically, the rajmata's maternal rana grandparents went from Nepal into exile in India in the 1880s after her grandfather's involvement in the murder of the ruling maharaja and two other rana relatives in December 1885: Scindia, *Princess*, pp. 3–23.

of the BJP unit in Rajasthan and was touted as a chief minister-in-waiting if her party would win the next state elections.

William Richter has highlighted four major factors that are characteristic of rulers who entered electoral politics. First, they were primarily from regions with sizeable concentrations of princely state territories and political leaders sympathetic to the princes such as Orissa and Chhattisgarh in Madhya Pradesh. Second, size was significant since politically active princes needed sizeable resources to contest elections. Those from larger states sought seats in the national Parliament while those from smaller states focused on state legislatures. Third, gun salutes as status symbols under the British were another factor. As was true of participation in the Chamber of Princes, princes from what Richter labels upper-middle-level families (I would assert from thirteen to seventeen guns) were the most active. The former ruling families of Hyderabad, Indore, Mysore, Travancore and Udaipur, having twenty-one or nineteen guns, have not been attracted to electoral politics. Finally, family ties could be important although they did not ensure political alliances, as the Scindia family of Gwalior illustrates. The relatives of Sayaji Rao of Baroda are a counter-example since five had held elective office as of 1978 and four were members of the Congress party.[8]

Through a constitutional amendment passed in 1971, Indira Gandhi stripped the princes of the titles, privy purses and regal privileges which her father's government had granted. Even so in the popular imagination and media, the former rulers remain symbols of regional identity and rajadharma. One example occurred in 1989 in Maharashtra. A major controversy erupted over a new Marathi language edition of the Kolhapur District Gazetteer, which published letters from Maharaja Shahu Chhatrapati II to the British which appeared to tarnish his reputation as a nationalist and reformer. Rallies and newspaper articles soon demanded the withdrawal of the Gazetteer from print because it was interpretive and not what was deemed an official record. Protests included a public burning of copies of the offending publication, a *bandh* 'in protest against the distorted gazetteer accounts of beloved Shahu Maharaja',[9] heated debates in the Maharashtra Legislative Council and Assembly, and a series of scholarly lectures over Shahu's role as a social reformer and a nationalist and the function of gazetteers as official documents that report and not histories that interpret. Véronique Bénéï concludes: 'Plainly, the history of Shahu

---

[8] Richter, 'Rulers', pp. 335–9.

[9] Véronique Bénéï, 'Reappropriating Colonial Documents in Kolhapur (Maharashtra): Variations on a Nationalist Theme', *MAS*, 33(4) (1999), p. 916. The quotation was the subtitle of an article in *Sakal*, a statewide newspaper, on 24 October 1990.

Maharaj nowadays functions as a "myth" in Kolhapur'. She adds: 'In the local context, Shahu embodies Kolhapuri identity both in general, and more particularly for the Marathas, Other Backward Castes and Dalits'.[10] Those three groups had particularly benefited from Shahu's social reforms, which included the reservation of 50 per cent of state posts for non-brahmans as well as free and compulsory primary education. Their interpretation of Shahu's policies motivated local leaders and political parties to assert guardianship of Shahu's image against brahman attempts to undermine his reputation with the collusion of the Maharashtrian Government.[11] Bénéï claims that a unifying bond exists between Kolhapuris and the person of the king that cuts across caste and time and is renewed by the annual celebration of Shahu's birth anniversary and rituals which his descendants perform during the Dasera festival in the autumn.[12]

In a more mundane mode, in the 2003 List of the fifty most powerful people in India published in *India Today*, Gaj Singh (b. 1948) of Jodhpur is number 45 'Because he's the king of royalty. Because none else in the blue-blooded pantheon straddles the feudal and the modern with such aplomb', 'Because he once had Finance Minister Jaswant Singh as private secretary. Because he's tourism's regal face'.[13] The last accolade refers to the romantic allure of princely culture for international and domestic tourists.

The princes of India offer fantasy for post-modern consumption. Faced with escalating maintenance costs and declining sources of income, princely entrepreneurs transformed palaces into hotels where tourists could experience an idealised, pampered lifestyle of royalty during a democratic era. In 1954 Karan Singh of Jammu and Kashmir leased his main palace in Srinagar to the Oberoi chain; it seems appropriate that he became minister for tourism and civil aviation in 1967 in Indira Gandhi's government.[14] In 1958 the Rambagh Palace Hotel opened in Jaipur followed by the much photographed Lake Palace Hotel in Udaipur in the early 1960s. In recent decades nobles and merchants in the former princely states have joined princes in opening palaces, *havelis*, forts and hunting lodges, from Mysore city in the south to the foothills of the Himalayas, to tourists. Rajasthan has the largest concentration of such establishments, many of which stage programs of Indian folk dance and music to entertain tourists. Palaces-on-wheels, which originally were renovated railway cars commissioned by the princes and now are replications of such luxurious cars, connect major sites. Other attractions include museums, which

---

[10] Ibid., p. 919.   [11] Ibid., pp. 927–30.   [12] Ibid., p. 926.
[13] *India Today International*, 3 February 2003, p. 46.
[14] Karan Singh, *Sadar-I-Riyasat: An Autobiography* (Delhi, 1985), vol. 2, pp. 12, 158–62.

display princely material culture to those who cannot not afford role-playing in palace hotels and palaces-on-wheels while preserving historical artefacts.[15]

In the past few years the glamour of princely jewellery and clothing has appealed to new audiences. A museum exhibit of designs by the Paris-based Cartier showcased the dramatic designs produced for the princes, frequently with gemstones supplied from princely treasure houses, during the 1920s and 1930s.[16] That exhibit also documented how the princes influenced the evolution of Indian-inspired designs of multicoloured gemstones, labelled tutti-frutti, and bracelets and necklaces of simply polished gemstones, called barbaric since the stones were not cut or faceted.[17] During December 2002 Cartier exhibited a recreation with cubic zirconium stones replacing diamonds in the original platinum chains of an extravagant bib necklace that Bhupinder Singh had commissioned using diamonds from his treasury. The *New York Times* reported that it was one of the highlights of the Christmas season in New York, drawing large crowds to Cartier's holiday window displays on Fifth Avenue.[18]

The princes of India and their states were and remain a significant aspect of the South Asia cultural, economic, and political landscape. Although the British ensured the continued existence of the princes and the states, the princes, their officials and their governments were agents who influenced the daily lives of their subjects and were a factor in imperial and nationalist politics beyond their borders. The princes played diverse roles as religious and cultural patrons, symbols of Indian abilities to govern other Indians for good or ill, and imperial politicians in military and civilian arenas. It is unfortunate that we yet know relatively little about their lives, their states, and their subjects.

---

[15] Ramusack, 'Fantasy', pp. 66–89; Ramusack, 'Tourism', pp. 235–55.

[16] Judy Rudoe, *Cartier, 1900–1939* (New York, 1997), pp. 31–6. This exhibit appeared in London, New York, and Chicago. Katherine Prior and John Adamson's *Maharaja's Jewels* (Ahmedabad, 2001) provides a broad survey from the medieval period to the present and of many western jewellers beyond Cartier.

[17] Rudoe, *Cartier*, pp. 156–87.

[18] Wendy Moonan, 'An Heirloom Is Resurrected at Cartier', *New York Times National*, 29 November 2002, p. B 39; Bill Cunningham, 'On the Street', *New York Times*, 22 December 2002, Sunday Styles section, p. 4.

BIBLIOGRAPHICAL ESSAY

Although there is a voluminous historiography on the princely states, it is uneven in its coverage, readability and scholarship. Consequently the secondary sources cited are those that I have found most useful or distinctive in their interpretations. Where authors have first published on their topics in journals and then substantially incorporated their articles into a monograph, I have cited only the titles of books, which are usually more developed statements of their research. Moreover, in my footnotes I have cited dissertations and unpublished papers but not included them here since they are more difficult to obtain. Since primary sources are the building blocks for the edifices of historians, I have included a few major collections of key documents, influential histories by British officials, and memoirs of British officials and Indian princes. Finally, all works are cited only once even where they are relevant to the topics of more than one chapter.

1 Princely States prior to 1800

Thought-provoking analyses of the underpinnings of kingship in India are J. Gonda's *Ancient Indian Kingship from the Religious Point of* View (Leiden, 1969); J. C. Heesterman's *The Inner Conflict of Tradition: Essays in Indian Ritual, Kingship, and Society* (Chicago, 1985); and Ronald Inden's 'Ritual, Authority, and Cyclic Time in Hindu Kingship', in J. F. Richards (ed.), *Kingship and Authority in South Asia* (Madison WI, 1978), pp. 28–73. Bernard Cohn developed an influential structural model that elegantly categorises differing levels of state formation in 'Political Systems in Eighteenth Century India: The Banaras Region', *JAOS* 82 (1962), pp. 313–20.

Rajput-ruled states have long attracted the attention of British officials, Indian and international historians, travellers and tourists who recorded their views and interpreted Rajput history and culture. James Tod's *Annals and Antiquities of Rajast'han*, 2 vols. (New Delhi, 1971, reprint of 1914 edn), which glorifies Mewar-Udaipur and disparages Amber-Jaipur, has dramatically shaped the historiography of Rajasthan to the present. Two very different studies challenge those historians influenced by Tod. Jadunath Sarkar's *A History of Jaipur c. 1503–1938*, revised and edited by Raghubir Singh (Delhi, 1984) defends the prudence of Jaipur's politics and its claim to pre-eminent Rajput status. Dirk H. A. Kolff's *Naukar, Rajput and Sepoy: The Ethnohistory of the Military Labour Market in Hindustan, 1450–1850* (Cambridge, 1990) incisively contends that military employment and not genealogy originally fostered Rajput identity. Based on painstaking research, Satya Prakash Gupta's *The Agrarian System of Eastern Rajasthan (c. 1650–c. 1750)* (Delhi, 1986) emphasises the relative prosperity in Amber that was accompanied by increasing economic stratification in the rural area. Karine Schomer and colleagues' *The Idea of Rajasthan*, 2 vols (New Delhi, 1994) exemplifies the diverse scholarship on Rajput states and Rajasthan during the 1970s and 1980s and includes many essays cited in my footnotes. Norman P. Ziegler's Action, Power and Service in Rajasthani Culture: A Social History of the Rajputs of Middle Period Rajasthan, a PhD thesis at the University of Chicago (1973), is a goldmine of data. His essays, 'Some Notes on Rajput Loyalties during the Mughal Period', in Richards' *Kingship* and 'Evolution of the Rathor State of Marvar: Horses, Structural Change and Warfare', in Schomer's *Ideas*, vol. 2, exemplify the depth of his scholarship. Norbert Peabody's 'In Whose Turban Does the Lord Reside? The Objectification of Charisma and the Fetishism of Objects in the Hindu Kingdom of Kota', *CSSH* 33 (1991), pp. 726–54 and his *Hindu Kingship and Polity in Pre-Colonial India* (Cambridge, 2003) delineate the dynamic, interactive relationships among brahman priests, kings and merchants in the legitimation of kingly authority in Kotah. *Gods, Kings and Tigers: The Art of Kotah* edited by Stuart Cary Welch (Munich, 1997) beautifully records how paintings both illuminated and legitimated secular and sacred power in Kotah. Karni Singh, the last maharaja of Bikaner and a former member of Parliament, provides a broad overview of the changing fortunes of a desert outpost in *The Relations of the House of Bikaner with the Central Powers 1465–1949* (New Delhi, 1974). In *Polygamy and Purdah: Women and Society among Rajputs* (Jaipur, 1995), Varsha Joshi explores the lives and political influence of royal women in Rajputana. The essays in N. K. Singhi and Rajendra Joshi (eds) *Religion, Ritual and Royalty* (Jaipur, 1999) combine textual research with oral histories in their exploration of Rajasthan history and contemporary life. Daniel Gold highlights how Maharaja Man Singh II of Jodhpur manipulated his religious and kingly identities to consolidate political power in 'The Instability of the King: Magical Insanity and the Yogis' Power in the Politics of Jodhpur, 1803–1843', in David N. Lorenzen (ed.) *Bhakti Religion in North India: Community Identity and Political Action* (Albany NY, 1995).

The princely states of south India continue to attract scholarship. In *Nizam–British Relations 1724–1857* (Hyderabad, 1963), Sarojini Regani outlines the tortured relationships of the nizams of Hyderabad with external powers. Sunil Chander's From a Pre-Colonial Order to a Princely State: Hyderabad in Transition, *c.* 1748–1865, PhD thesis at the University of Cambridge (1987), provides a more finely grained analysis of the complexities of Hyderabadi politics. For Mysore, Kate Brittlebank's *Tipu Sultan's Search for Legitimacy: Islam and Kingship in a Hindu Domain* (Delhi, 1997) imaginatively considers how Tipu Sultan creatively used multiple sources of legitimation. K. M. Panikkar's *A History of Kerala 1498–1801* (Annamalainagar, 1960) and A. Sreedhara Menon's *A Survey of Kerala History* (Kottayam, 1967) are basic overviews. In 'Hindu Kingship and the Origins of Community: Religion, State and Society in Kerala, 1750–1850', *MAS* 18 (1984), pp. 186–202, Susan Bayly explores the construction of the sophisticated military and civil administration in the Kerala states. Her highly influential *Saints, Goddesses and Kings: Muslims and Christians in South Indian Society 1700–1900* (Cambridge, 1989) elaborates on how ecumenical religious patronage legitimated Indian kingship. Nicholas Dirks' *The Hollow Crown: Ethnohistory of an Indian Kingdom* (Cambridge, 1987) provocatively explores the complex relationships among caste groups, kingly patronage and colonialism. Pamela Price effectively challenges his thesis about the destructive impact of colonial interventions on royal symbols and power in *Kingship and Political Practice in Colonial India* (Cambridge, 1996).

Although not focused primarily on the Marathas, Sir John Malcolm's *A Memoir of Central India*, 2 vols (New Delhi, 2001, first published in 1823) is a foundational source for British officials and many historians on the Maratha rulers of Indore and Gwalior as well as the Afghan rulers of Bhopal. André Wink's *Land and Sovereignty in India: Agrarian Society and Politics Under the Eighteenth-century Maratha Svarajya* (Cambridge, 1986) is a bold, controversial analysis of how rebellion was an integral aspect of Maratha state formation. In *The Puars of Dewas Senior* (Bombay, 1963) Manohar Malgonkar, probably best known for his novels, provides a detailed introduction to a state that would later fascinate another novelist E. M. Forster. R. K. Saxena's *Maratha Relations with the Major States of Rajputana (1761–1818 A.D.)* (New Delhi, 1973) and S. C. Misra's *Sindhia–Holkar Rivalry in Rajasthan* (Delhi, 1981) are empirical accounts of Maratha external and internal antagonists. Stewart Gordon has a more nuanced overview in *The Marathas 1600–1818* (Cambridge, 1993) in this series and his thought-provoking essays on specific aspects of the Maratha politics are collected in *Marathas, Marauders, and State Formation in Eighteenth-Century India* (Delhi, 1994). A direct descendant of the last begum and a career diplomat of Pakistan, Shaharyar M. Khan provides a welcome political history of five determined women in *The Begums of Bhopal: A Dynasty of Women Rulers in Raj India* (London, 2000).

For the princely states in Punjab that survived after 1858, Lepel Griffin's *The Rajas of the Punjab* (Patiala, 1970, reprint of 1870 edn) and J. Hutchison and J. Vogel's *History of the Panjab Hill States*, 2 vols (Lahore, 1933) remain the basic sources. In 'Ala Singh: The Founder of Patiala State', in Harbans Singh and N. Gerald Barrier (eds) *Punjab Past and Present: Essay in Honor of Dr. Ganda Singh* (Patiala, 1976), Indu Banga argues convincingly that political expediency and secondarily religious commitment guided Ala Singh's largely successful policies.

2 The British Construction of a System of Indirect Rule

Secondary sources on British indirect rule in India focus on three broad topics: the policies of individual governors-general and political officials; the intermediaries between the British and the princes, especially residents and other political officers; and the relations between the British and individual states or regional groups of them. Although the British initiative implied in its title is overstated, Edward Thompson's *The Making of the Indian Princes* remains the paradigmatic history of the policies of governors-general from Lord Wellesley to Lord Hastings, especially towards the Maratha-ruled states. Other studies in the first category are B. B. Srivastava's *Sir John Shore's Policy Towards the Indian States* (Allahabad, 1981); Edward Thompson's *Life of Lord Metcalfe* (London, 1937); Mohan Sinha Mehta's *Lord Hastings and the India States: Being a Study of the Relations of the British Government of India with the Indian States, 1813–1823* (Bombay, 1930); William Lee-Warner's *The Life of the Marquis of Dalhousie K. T.*, 2 vols (Shannon, Ireland, 1972, first published 1904); S. N. Prasad's *Paramountcy under*

Dalhousie (Delhi, 1963); Muhammad Abdur Rahim's *Lord Dalhousie's Administration of the Conquered and Annexed States* (Delhi, 1963); Bhupen Qanungo's 'A Study of British Relations with the Native States of India, 1858–62', *JAS* 26 (1967), pp. 251–65; Ajit K. Neogy's *The Paramount Power and the Princely States of India, 1858–1881* (Calcutta, 1979); Mihir Kumar Ray's *Princely States and the Paramount Power, 1858–1876: A Study of the Nature of Political Relations between the British Government and the Indian States* (New Delhi, 1981); and Urmila Walia's *Changing British Attitudes Towards the Indian States, 1823–1835* (New Delhi, 1985). Polemical or partisan works about the relationships between the British GOI and the princes, which appeared when princes were protesting against British interventions based on its doctrine of paramountcy, are A. P. Nicholson's *Scraps of Paper: India's Broken Treaties, her Princes, and the Problem* (London, 1930) and K. M. Panikkar's three briefs: *An Introduction to the Study of the Relations of the Indian States with the Government of India* (London, 1927), which rejected British claims related to paramountcy; *The Evolution of British Policy towards Indian States 1774–1858* (Calcutta, 1929); and *Indian States and the Government of India* (London, 1930).

The early development of the residency system and its officials is delineated in K. N. Panikkar's *British Diplomacy in North India: A Study of the Delhi Residency 1803–1857* (New Delhi, 1968) and Robin Jeffrey's 'The Politics of "Indirect Rule": Types of Relationships among Rulers, Minister and Residents in a "Native State"', *JCCP* 13 (1975), pp. 62–81. Prodigiously documented, Michael Fisher's *Indirect Rule in India: Residents and the Residency System, 1764–1858* (Delhi, 1991) analyses the activities and perspectives of British officials and their Indian employees who operated within the states.

Reflecting their size and claim on the imagination of historians, studies of British relations with princely states concentrate on Rajput and Maratha rulers as well as those of Hyderabad, Mysore, and Jammu and Kashmir. A representative sample includes Anil Chandra Banerjee's *The Rajput States and British Paramountcy* (New Delhi, 1980); Sukumar Bhattacharyya, *The Rajput States and the East India company from the Close of the 18th Century to 1820* (New Delhi, 1972); R. J. Bingle, 'Changing Attitudes to the Indian States, 1820–1850: A Study of Oudh, Hyderabad and Jaipur', in C. H. Philips and M. Doreen Wainwright (eds) *Indian Society and the Beginnings of Modernization, c. 1830–1850* (London, 1976): R. M. Mathur's *Rajput States and the East India Company* (Delhi, 1979); Peter Wood's Vassal State in the Shadow of Empire: Palmer's Hyderabad, 1799–1867, PhD thesis, University of Wisconsin-Madison (1981); and Zubaida Yazdani's *Hyderabad During the Residency of Henry Russell, 1811–1820: A Case Study in the Subsidiary Alliance System* (Oxford, 1976).

States in western India are treated in Mani Kamerkar's *British Paramountcy: British–Baroda Relations 1818–1848* (Bombay, 1980) and Ian Copland's *The British Raj and the Indian Princes: Paramountcy in Western India, 1857–1930* (Bombay, 1982). The latter is a keen analysis of the evolution of imperial policies with a detailed description of their implementation in a specific region. Mian Bashir Ahmed Farooqui's *British Relations with the Cis-Sutlej States, 1809–1823* (Lahore, 1971) provides a basic overview.

3 The Theory and the Experience of Indirect Rule in Colonial India

Several seminal works have shaped historical debate over the nature and operation of British rule in India over the past few decades. They include Bernard S. Cohn's essays, which are most accessible in *An Anthropologist among the Historians and other Essays* (New Delhi, 1987) and *Colonialism and Its Forms of Knowledge: The British in India* (Princeton, 1996); Ronald Inden's *Imagining India* (Oxford, 1990); C. A. Bayly's *Indian Society and the Making of the British Empire* (Cambridge, 1988). The scholarly fascination with imperial rituals that affirmed relations between the British and the princes has a genealogy that includes Bernard S. Cohn, 'Representing Authority in Victorian India', in Eric Hobsbawn and Terence Ranger (eds) *The Invention of Tradition* (Cambridge, 1983) on the Imperial Assemblage of 1877; many articles on the alleged Baroda scoff at the Imperial Durbar of 1911: Charles W. Nuckolls, 'The Durbar Incident', *MAS* 4 (1990), pp. 529–59; Stephen Bottomore, '"Have You Seen the Gaekwar Bob?": Filming the 1911 Delhi Durbar', *HJFRT* 17 (1997), pp. 309–45; and most recently, David Cannadine's *Ornamentalism: How the British Saw Their Empire* (Oxford, 2001). Tony McClenaghan's *Indian Princely Medals: A Record of the Orders, Decorations and Medals of the Indian Princely States* (New Delhi, 1996) documents the ways in which princes instituted their own systems of honours. In *The Raja's Magic Clothes: Re-Visioning Kingship and Divinity in England's India* (University Park, PA, 1994), Joanne Punzo Waghorne provides the perspective of an historian of religion on the interaction between British overlords, bureaucrats and scholars and Indian princes and pandits in Pudukkottai to create a synthesis of divine and secular sources of legitimacy for their respective authority.

The core primary source on the legal framework of indirect rule is C. U. Aitchison (comp.), *A Collection of Treaties, Engagements and Sanads relating to India and Neighbouring Countries*, 13 vols (Nendlem, Liechtenstein, 1973, reprint of 1931 edn); J. Sutherland's *Sketches of the Relations Subsisting between the British Government in India and the Different Native States* (Calcutta, 1837) provides an early interpretation from the field, while Adrian Sever (ed.) *Documents and Speeches on the Indian Princely States*, 2 vols (Delhi, 1985) is a useful compendium of influential primary sources. Authoritative British official interpretations of basic principles underlying indirect rule are Charles Lewis Tupper's *Our Indian Protectorate: An Introduction to the Study of the Relations between the British Government and Its Indian Feudatories* (London, 1893) and *Indian Political Practice: A Collection of the Decisions of the Government of India in Political Cases*, 4 vols (Delhi, 1974, reprint of 1895 original edn); William Lee-Warner, *The Protected States of India* (London, 1899) and a revised edition entitled *The Native States of India* (London, 1910). Since British political officers applied abstract principles in their daily decisions, scholars seeking to understand the experience of indirect rule must consult sources on these men, their ideas and their careers. Terence Creagh Coen (1903–70), an ICS officer who began his service in the princely states in 1935, wrote a descriptive, insider's history in *The Indian Political Service: A Study in Indirect Rule* (London, 1971). More analytical accounts are Ian Copland's 'The Other Guardians: Ideology and Performance in the Indian Political Service', in Jeffrey, *People*, and W. Murray Hogben, 'An Imperial Dilemma: The Reluctant Indianization of the Indian Political Service,' *MAS* 15 (1981), pp. 751–69 and The Foreign and Political

Department of India, 1876–1919: A Study in Imperial Careers and Attitudes, PhD thesis, University of Toronto (1973). After their careers ended with Indian independence, British political officers produced memoirs that vary in introspection and detail. A representative sample includes Conrad Corfield's (b. 1893) *The Princely India I Knew: From Reading to Mountbatten* (Madras, 1975); Kenneth Fitze's (b. 1887) *Twilight of the Maharajas* (London, 1956); and Edward Wakefield's (1903–69) *Past Imperative: My Life in India, 1927–1947* (London, 1966).

Scholarly analyses of the impact of indirect rule investigate specific states or incidents. Perceptive articles include Ian Copland's 'The Baroda Crisis of 1873–77: A Study in Governmental Rivalry', *MAS* 2 (1968), pp. 97–123 and his 'The Hyderabad (Berar) Agreement of 1933: A Case Study in Anglo-Indian Diplomacy', *JICH* 6 (1978), pp. 281–99; Edward Haynes' 'The British Alteration of the Political System of Alwar State: Lineage Patrimonialism, Indirect Rule, and the Rajput Jagir System in an Indian "Princely" State, 1775–1920', *SH* 5, new series (1989), pp. 27–71; Vasant Kumar Bawa's *The Nizam between Mughals and British: Hyderabad under Salar Jang I* (New Delhi, 1986); Bharati Ray's *Hyderabad and British Paramountcy 1858–1883* (Delhi, 1988); and Tara Sethia's British Imperial Interests and the Indian Princely States, PhD thesis, University of California at Los Angeles (1986), which focuses on railway development in Hyderabad. S. R. Ashton's *British Policy towards the Indian States 1905–1939* (London, 1982) and my *The Princes of India in the Twilight of Empire: The Dissolution of a Patron–Client System, 1914–1939* (Columbus OH, 1978) provide broader overviews of changing British attitudes and policies during the early twentieth century.

4 Princes as Men, Women, Rulers, Patrons, and Oriental Stereotypes

The princes are the subject of a diverse range of books: biographies ranging from authorised to sensational, adulatory to vituperative, empirical to post-modern, collections of essays, lavishly illustrated volumes designed for coffee tables, and perceptive scholarly articles and monographs. Perhaps because of his persona as the first Indian to play cricket for England, Maharaja Ranjitsinhji of Nawanagar is the focus of multiple biographies and a fictional account, Ian Buruma's *Playing the Game* (New York, 1991), which speculates about the person behind the mask of cricketer and prince. Ronald Wild's *The Biography of Colonel His Highness Shri Sir Ranjitsinhji* (London, 1934) is a hagiographic official biography that projected how the subject wished to be represented to an English-reading audience. Satadru Sen takes a different approach in *The Loyal Insurgency: Empire, Identity and K. S. Ranjitsinhji* (Manchester, forthcoming in 2004) where he examines how this prince moulded himself first to be a socially acceptable black/brown cricketer/prince in England and later a prince/politician who challenged the imperial establishment in India. This bold, thematically organised study uses the life of an individual prince to illuminate broader themes of imperial history – image, identity and migration. Although not an official biography, K. M. Panikkar's *His Highness The Maharaja of Bikaner: A Biography* (London, 1937), produced on the occasion of Ganga Singh's golden jubilee on the gaddi, is a sympathetic portrayal of a domineering personality. Similar descriptive and generally favourable biographies are

H. M. Bull and K. N. Haksar's *Madhav Rao Scindia of Gwalior 1876–1925* (Lashkar, Gwalior, 1926); Stanley Rice's *Life of Sayaji Rao III: Maharaja of Baroda*, 2 vols (London, 1931); and more recently, Quentin Crewe's *The Last Maharaja: A Biography of Sawai Man Singh II Maharaja of Jaipur* (London, 1985). Two biographies by family members are *Sayajirao of Baroda: The Prince and the Man* (Bombay, 1989) by Fatesinghrao P. Gaekwar, the great-grandson of Sayajirao, and *The Magnificent Maharaja: The Life and Times of Maharaja Bhupindar Singh of Patiala, 1891–1938* (New Delhi, 1998) by K. Natwar-Singh, the grandson-in-law of Bhupinder Singh. V. K. Bawa, the former director of the Andhra Pradesh State Archives, portrays the idiosyncratic ruler once reputed to be the world's wealthiest man in *The Last Nizam: The Life and Times of Mir Osman Ali Khan* (New Delhi, 1992).

Several princes and princesses have produced their memoirs, often with the assistance of novelists. They include Gayatri Devi of Jaipur and Santha Rama Rao, *A Princess Remembers: The Memoirs of the Maharani of Jaipur* (Philadelphia, 1976); Karan Singh's *Heir Apparent: An Autobiography* (Delhi, 1982); and Vijayaraje Scindia with Manohar Malgonkar, *Princess: The Autobiography of the Dowager Maharani of Gwalior* (London, 1985). A historical complement to these women's representations of their marriage is Frances Taft Plunkett's 'Royal Marriages in Rajasthan', *CIS*, n.s. 6 (1972), pp. 64–80. Although not a formal autobiography, Sultan Jahan Begam's *The Story of a Pilgrimage to Hijaz* (Calcutta, 1909) recounts her preparations for the governance of Bhopal in her absence and her experiences while on her haj to Mecca. Charles Allen and Sharada Dwivedi have recorded the reminiscences of the last generation of princes who actually ruled and their children in *Lives of the Indian Princes* (London, 1984). *Reversing the Gaze: Amar Singh's Diary, A Colonial Subject's Narrative of Imperial India*, with editing and commentary by Susanne Hoeber Rudolph and Lloyd I. Rudolph with Mohan Singh Kanota (New Delhi, 2000), provides a truly extraordinary insider's view of Rajput princely life and politics as well as British imperial institutions. The discerning scholarship of the Rudolphs reflects a lifetime of dedication to the study of India and particularly to an understanding of Rajput culture and politics.

In 'Perceptions of Princely Rule: Perspectives from a Biography', pp. 127–54 in T. N. Madan (ed.) *Way of Life: King, Householder, Renouncer: Essays in Honour of Louis Dumont* (New Delhi, 1982), Adrian Mayer recounted how Maharaja Chhatrapati Shahaji II of Kolhapur (b. 1910, r. Kolhapur 1947–49) interpreted classical concepts to legitimate his rule. Mayer elaborated on how other princes in central India conceptualised and claimed legitimacy in 'The King's Two Thrones', *Man* 20, new series (1985), pp. 205–21 and 'Rulership and Divinity: The Case of the Modern Hindu Prince and Beyond', *MAS* 25 (1991), pp. 765–90. Princely patronage of religious rituals and institutions are detailed in Philip Lutgendorf's 'Ram's Story in Shiva's City: Public Arenas and Private Patronage', in Sandia B. Freitag (ed.), *Culture and Power in Banaras: Community, Performance, and Environment, 1899–1980* (Berkeley CA, 1989), pp. 34–61 and Barbara N. Ramusack's 'Punjab States: Maharajas and Gurdwaras: Patiala and the Sikh Community', in Jeffrey, *Princes*, pp. 170–204. Other areas of princely patronage are delineated in Joan L. Erdman's *Patrons and Performers in Rajasthan: The Subtle Tradition* (Delhi, 1985) and Edward S. Haynes' 'Patronage for the Arts and the Rise of Alwar State', in Schomer, *Idea*, vol. 2, pp. 265–89.

287

Physically oversize books that graphically represent those aspects of princely life encapsulated in Orientalist images are legion. Some of the more thoughtful are *Princely India: Photographs by Raja Lala Deen Dayal, Court Photographer (1884–1910) to the Premier Prince of India*, edited and with a historical text by Clark Worswick (New York, 1980); Maharaja of Baroda (Fateh Singh Rao Gaekwad), *Palaces of India* (New York, 1980); Naveen Patnaik, *A Desert Kingdom: The Rajputs of Bikaner* (London, 1990); and Ritu Kumar, *Costumes and Textiles of Royal India* (London, 1999).

5 Princely States: Administrative and Economic Structures

In the area of administration and economy, a few large states and those in Rajputana again dominate the scholarship. For Hyderabad, Karen Leonard's 'The Hyderabad Political System and Its Participants', *JAS* 30 (1971), pp. 569–82; 'Banking Firms in Nineteenth-Century Hyderabad Politics', *MAS* 15 (1981), pp. 177–201; and *Social History of an Indian Caste: The Kayasths of Hyderabad* (Berkeley CA, 1978) are fundamental. Benjamin B. Cohen explores three Hindu kingdoms or *samasthan*s in Hindu Rulers in a Muslim State: Hyderabad, 1850–1949, PhD thesis, University of Wisconsin at Madison (2002). The quartet of 'progressive' princely states is reasonably well served. Donald R. Gustafson's Mysore 1881–1902: The Making of a Model State, PhD thesis, University of Wisconsin at Madison (1968) argues for the agency of Indian administrators as opposed to British officials in the modernisation of the state administration. Janaki Nair's 'Prohibited Marriage: State Protection and the Child Wife', in Patricia Uberoi (ed.), *Social Reform, Sexuality and the State* (New Delhi, 1996) is more critical of the label of progressive and makes a strong case that Mysore state implemented social reforms to extend state control into local society. Influenced by development theories, Bjørn Hettne's *The Political Economy of Indirect Rule: Mysore 1881–1947* (London, 1978) traces the relationship between political autonomy and economic development, while Janaki Nair's *Miners and Millhands: Work, Culture and Politics in Princely Mysore* (Walnut Creek CA, 1998) explores industrial development from the perspective of the workers. David Hardiman's 'Baroda', in Jeffrey, *People*, is a perceptive overview of the mutually beneficial alliance between the Baroda rulers and elite peasant-cultivators and emerging industrialists. More data on the latter are in Howard L. Erdman's *Political Attitudes of Indian Industry: A Case Study of the Baroda Business Elite* (London, 1971).

A sample of the seminal work of Susanne Hoeber Rudolph and Lloyd I. Rudolph on the history, administration and culture of Rajput states, princes and nobility is readily available in *Essays on Rajputana* (New Delhi, 1984). Richard Sisson's *The Congress Party in Rajasthan: Political Integration and Institution-building in an Indian State* (Berkeley CA, 1972) perceptively tracks the impact of princely administrative structures and internal politics on post-independent Rajasthani political institutions. Robert W. Stern's *The Cat and the Lion: Jaipur State in the British Raj* (Leiden, 1988) skilfully integrates Jaipuri internal politics with British–Jaipur relations from the early 1800s to 1948.

G. S. L. Devra's 'A Rethinking on the Politics of Commercial Society in Pre-Colonial India: Transition from Mutsaddi to Marwari', Occasional Papers on History and Society No. 38, NMML (New Delhi, 1987); Madhavi Bajekal's 'The State and the Rural Grain Market in Eighteenth Century East Rajasthan', in Sanjay Subrahmanyan (ed.),

Merchants, Markets and the State in Early Modern India (Delhi, 1990); Dilbagh Singh's *The State, Landlords and Peasants: Rajasthan in the 18th Century* (Columbia MO, 1990) provide solid evidence of a vibrant economy and aggressive efforts by the state to expand its control over the wealth generated. For the late nineteenth and early twentieth centuries, John Hurd II's two articles set the terms of the debates, 'The Economic Consequences of Indirect Rule in India', *IESHR* 12 (1975), pp. 169–81 and 'The Influence of British Policy on Industrial Development in the Princely States, 1890–1933', *IESHR* 12 (1975), pp. 490–524. C. P. Simmons and B. R. Satyanarayana, 'The Economic Consequences of Indirect Rule in India: A Reappraisal', *IESHR* 15 (1979), pp. 185–206 dispute Hurd's assessment. However, Edward S. Haynes provides supporting evidence for Hurd's arguments in 'Comparative Industrial Development in 19th and 20th Century India: Alwar State and Gurgaon District', *SA*, 3(2) new series (1980), pp. 25–42. In *Violence and Truth: A Rajasthani Kingdom Confronts Colonial Authority* (Delhi, 1997), Denis Vidal emphasises how Sirohi state's geographical location on a major trade route led to the interdependence of warriors and merchants. Equally innovative is his analysis of how threats of and actual violence were employed to adjust political and economic relations within Sirohi and were distorted when the British criminalised traditional forms of resistance. Hira Singh's contentious *Colonial Hegemony and Popular Resistance: Princes, Peasants, and Paramount Power* (Walnut Creek CA, 1998) is significant for its focus on the economic conditions and political resistance of peasants in Rajputana.

Ministers, both foreigners/outsiders and indigenous/insiders, were crucial to princely efforts to centralise their administrations and develop their economies. Although Henny Sender's *The Kashmiri Pandits: A Study of Cultural Choice in North India* (Delhi, 1988) does not focus primarily on Kashmiris who served in the princely states, it provides a cultural context for those who did. Significant memoirs and autobiographies by peripatetic ministers include Mirza Mahomed Ismail's *My Public Life* (London, 1954); K. M. Panikkar's *An Autobiography*, translated from the Malayalam by K. Krishnamurthy (Madras, 1977); and M. A. Sreenivasan's *Of the Raj, Maharajas and Me* (Delhi, 1991) on his service in Mysore, London and Gwalior.

6 Princely States: Society and Politics

Memoirs abound of life in the princely states, from British travellers, officials and employees of the princes. Two of the most perceptive or unusual focus on Maharaja Tukoji Rao II of Dewas Senior State: J. R. Ackerly's *Hindoo Holiday: An Indian Journal* (New York, 1960, first published in 1932), which a son of Tej Bahadur Sapru who was married to a daughter of K. N. Haksar once advised me to read for an authentic view of life in the princely states; and E. M. Forster's *A Hill of Devi* (Harmondsworth, Middlesex, 1965, first published 1953) on his service in Dewas Senior State, which provided material for his most famous novel, *A Passage to India*.

Historical scholarship on the relationship between political activity and social movements within the princely states from the late nineteenth century to 1947 is more extended than on other topics. Informative samples are the essays in Robin Jeffrey (ed.) *People, Princes and Paramount Power: Society and Politics in the Indian*

Princely States (Delhi, 1978) and a special issue of the *Indo-British Review* 15(2) (December 1988) on the theme of 'Princely India and the Raj'. I have grouped subsequent books and articles according to the states or groups of states analysed. For south India, Hyderabad is the focus of Lucien D. Benichou's *From Autocracy to Integration: Political Developments in Hyderabad State (1938–1948)* (Chennai, 2000); Margrit Pernau's *The Passing of Patrimonialism: Politics and Political Culture in Hyderabad 1911–1948* (New Delhi, 2000); and Michael D. Witmer's The 1947–1948 India–Hyderabad Conflict: Realpolitik and the Formation of the Modern Indian India, PhD thesis, Temple University, 1995. Mysore is the focus of James Manor's *Political Change in an Indian State: Mysore 1917–1955* (New Delhi, 1977) and his 'Gandhian Politics and the Challenge to Princely Authority in Mysore, 1936–47', in D. A. Low (ed.) *Congress and the Raj: Facets of the Indian Struggle 1917–47* (London, 1977); Vanaja Rangaswami's *The Story of Integration: A New Interpretation in the Context of the Democratic Movements in the Princely States of Mysore, Travancore and Cochin 1900–1947* (Delhi, 1981); and Manu Bhagavan's *Sovereign Spheres: Princes, Education and Empire in Colonial India* (Delhi, 2003), which compares educational reform in Mysore and Baroda. For Travancore there is Robin Jeffrey's *The Decline of Nayar Dominance* (London, 1976) and his *Politics, Women and Well-Being: How Kerala Became 'a Model'* (Houndmills, Hampshire, 1992); Koji Kawashima's *Missionaries and a Hindu State: Travancore 1858–1936* (London, 1998); James Chiriyankandath, '"Communities at the Polls": Electoral Politics and the Mobilization of Communal Groups in Travancore', *MAS* 27 (1993), pp. 643–55; and the first-person narrative of Louise Ouwerkerk, a former professor at the Maharaja's Women's College and the University of Travancore from 1929 to 1939, *No Elephants for the Maharaja: Social and Political Change in the Princely State of Travancore (1921–1947)*, edited with an introduction by Dick Kooiman (New Delhi, 1994). Encompassing both Madras Presidency and the southern princely states, S. Chandrashekar's *Colonialism, Conflict and Nationalism: South India: 1857–1947* (New Delhi, 1995) is an effective overview.

Further north, John R. Wood's 'Indian Nationalism in the Princely Context: The Rajkot Satyagraha of 1938–9', in Jeffrey, *People*, pp. 40–74, and his 'British versus Princely Legacies and the Political Integration of Gujarat', *JAS* 44 (1984), pp. 65–99; John McLeod's *Sovereignty, Power, Control: Politics in the States of Western India, 1916–1947* (Leiden, 1999); and Harald Tambs-Hyche, *Power, Profit and Poetry: Traditional Society in Kathiawar, Western India* (New Delhi, 1997) are perceptive on states in western India. Kamla Mittal's *History of Bhopal State: Development of Constitution, Administration and National Awakening 1901–1949* (New Delhi, 1990) and Siobhan Lambert-Hurley's Contesting Seclusion: The Political Emergence of Muslim Women in Bhopal, 1901–1930, PhD thesis, University of London, 1998 and her 'Princes, Paramountcy and the Politics of Muslim Identity: The Begam of Bhopal on the Indian National Stage, 1901–1926', *SA* 26 (forthcoming in August 2003) provide new insights on a key Muslim-ruled state in central India. For the great swath of Rajput states there are the foundational essays of Susanne Hoeber Rudolph and Lloyd Rudolph; Laxman Singh's *Political and Constitutional Development in the Princely States of Rajasthan (1920–49)* (New Delhi, 1970); Richard Sisson's *The Congress Party in Rajasthan: Political Integration and Institution-Building in an Indian State* (Berkeley CA, 1972); K. L.

Kamal and Robert W. Stern, 'Jaipur's Freedom Struggle and the Bourgeois Revolution', *JCPS* 11 (1973), pp. 231–50; Barnett R. Rubin's *Feudal Revolt and State-Building: The 1938 Sikar Agitation in Jaipur State* (New Delhi, 1983); Majid Siddiqi, 'History and Society in a Popular Rebellion: Mewat 1920–1933', *CSSH* 23 (1986), pp. 442–67; and Ian Copland's 'Islam and the "Moral Economy": The Alwar Revolt of 1932', *SA* 22 (1999), pp. 109–32. For Punjab there is Romesh Walia's *Praja Mandal Movement in East Punjab States* (Patiala, 1972); Mridula Mukherjee's 'Peasant Movement in Patiala State', *SH* 1 (1979), pp. 215–83 and her 'Communists and Peasants in Punjab: A Focus on the Muzara Movement in Patiala, 1937–53', *SH* (1981); Barbara N. Ramusack's 'Incident at Nabha: Interaction between Indian States and British Indian Politics', *JAS* 28 (1969), pp. 563–77 and her 'Maharajas and Gurdwaras: Patiala and the Sikh Community', in Jeffrey, *Princes*; and Mohinder Singh's *Peasant Movement in PEPSU Punjab* (New Delhi, 1991). Ian Copland's 'Congress Paternalism: The "High Command" and the Struggle for Freedom in Princely India', *SA* 8 (1985), pp. 121–40 and Barbara N. Ramusack's 'Congress and the People's Movement in Princely India: Ambivalence in Strategy and Organization', in Richard Sisson and Stanley Wolpert (eds) *Congress and Indian Nationalism* (Berkeley, 1988), pp. 377–403 demonstrate that Congress support for political activity in the princely states was sporadic at best.

While research has become increasingly difficult, there are several informative and challenging works on politics in Jammu and Kashmir. They range from the first-person account of Prem Nath Bazaz in *The History of Struggle for Freedom in Kashmir* (New Delhi, 1954) to U. K. Zutshi's *Emergence of Political Awakening in Kashmir* (New Delhi, 1986); Santosh Kaul's detailed *Freedom Struggle in Jammu and Kashmir* (New Delhi, 1990); Chitralekha Zutshi's *Languages of Belonging: Islam, Regional Identity, and the Making of Kashmir* (New Delhi, forthcoming in 2003); and Mirdu Rai's *Kashmir: Hindu Rulers, Muslim Subjects* (New York, forthcoming in 2003).

Princely states in tribal areas benefit from the multidisciplinary approach of Nandini Sundar's *Subalterns and Sovereigns: An Anthropological History of Bastar, 1854–1996* (New Delhi, 1997) and Biswamoy Pati's 'Light in the "Dark Zones"?: The Congress, the States' People and the Princes of Orissa, 1936–1939', in Biswamoy Pati (ed.), *Issues in Modern Indian History: For Sumit Sarkar* (Mumbai, 2000), pp. 198–230.

In recent years there has been renewed concern about the incidence of communalism in the princely states, the ways in which princely patronage exercised as rajadharma helped to foster the growth of communalism in certain areas of India, and the role of the princes during the terrible years surrounding independence and partition. These studies have centred on a few key areas: on Alwar, Shail Mayaram, *Resisting Regimes: Myth, Memory and the Shaping of a Muslim Identity* (Delhi, 1997) and Ian Copland, 'The Further Shores of Partition: Ethnic Cleansing in Rajasthan 1947', *PP*, no. 168 (August 1998), pp. 203–39; for Hyderabad, Ian Copland, '"Communalism" in Princely India: The Case of Hyderabad, 1930–1940', *MAS* 22 (1988), pp. 783–814; for Kashmir, Ian Copland, 'Islam and Political Mobilization in Kashmir, 1933–43', *PA* 54 (1981), pp. 228–59 and Christopher Snedden, 'What Happened to Muslims in Jammu? Local Identity, "The Massacre" of 1947 and the Roots of the "Kashmir Problem"', *SA* 24, (2001), pp. 111–34; on Patiala, Ian Copland, 'The Master and the Maharajas: The Sikh Princes and the East Punjab Massacres of 1947', *MAS* 36 (2002), pp. 657–704 delineates a grim scenario. Dick Kooiman has taken a broader approach in *Communities and Electorates: A Comparative Discussion of Communalism in Colonial India* (Amsterdam, 1995), which focuses on Baroda and Travancore; 'The Strength of Numbers: Enumerating Communities in India's Princely States', *SA* 20 (1997), pp. 81–98; and his more extended analysis in *Communalism and Indian Princely States: Travancore, Baroda and Hyderabad in the 1930s* (New Delhi, 2003).

7 Federation or Integration?

A few key works have shaped the existing historiography on the last decade of princely rule in India. The most significant primary sources are Nicholas Mansergh, E. W. R. Lumby and Sir Penderel Moon (eds), *Constitutional Relations Between Britain and India: The Transfer of Power, 1942–7*, 12 vols (London, 1970–83); V. P. Menon, *The Story of the Integration of the Indian States* (London, 1956); and Penderel Moon, *Divide and Quit* (London, 1961), an acerbic, incisive account of the human cost of the British decision to partition in the princely state of Bahawalpur, which would eventually accede to Pakistan. Early informative studies are R. J. Moore, *Escape from Empire: The Attlee Government and the Indian Problem* (Oxford, 1983); Urmila Phadnis, *Towards the Integration of Indian States, 1919–1947* (London, 1968); and Wayne Ayres Wilcox, *Pakistan: The Consolidation of a Nation* (New York, 1963). H. V. Brasted and Carl Bridge's 'The Transfer of Power in South Asia: An Historiographical Review', *SA* 17, 1 (1994), pp. 93–114 highlights the limited scope of the historiography on the British withdrawal. A trenchant, perceptive political history, Ian Copland's *The Princes of India in the Endgame of Empire, 1917–1947* (Cambridge, 1997) is indispensable on negotiations among the princes and between the princes and various British groups in the final years of empire. Recent consideration of the ways in which individual Indians experienced the trauma of partition and migration gives little notice to the subjects of princely states. In *Resisting Regimes: Myth, Memory and the Shaping of a Muslim Identity* (Delhi, 1997), Shail Mayaram demonstrates the dramatic possibilities of recouping the lived experience of one liminal group, the Meos, as a result of sensitive ethnography, keen analysis of texts in multiple languages, and assiduous archival research.

Epilogue

Several works that analyse political activity from the colonial into the independence era are mentioned above such as V. P. Menon's *Story of Integration*. A few articles look more specifically at how the princes are remembered and used for various political, economic and cultural activities after integration. William L. Richter, 'Traditional Rulers in Post-Traditional Societies: The Princes of India and Pakistan', in Jeffrey, *People*, pp. 329–54 and William L. Richter and Barbara N. Ramusack, 'The Chamber and the Consultation: Changing Forms of Princely Association in India', *JAS* 34 (1975), pp. 755–76 are early analyses of the political activities of the princes in independent India and Pakistan. In *Maharajahs*, cited earlier, Christiane Hurtig provides a more extended analysis of the impact of the 1971 Derecognition constitutional amendment and the subsequent involvement of princes in electoral politics. Karan Singh, *Sadar-I-*

Riyasat: An Autobiography vol. 2 (Delhi, 1985) is useful for its perspective on internal Kashmiri politics and for the attitudes of a ruler sympathetic to the Congress party. Véronique Bénéï's 'Reappropriating Colonial Documents in Kolhapur (Maharashtra): Variations on a Nationalist Theme', *MAS* 33 (1999), pp. 913–50 reveals the continuing resonance of princely icons in contemporary politics. Barbara Ramusack describes the relationship of the princes to contemporary tourism in 'Tourism and Icons: The Packaging of the Princely States of Rajasthan', in Catherine B. Asher and Thomas R. Metcalf (eds) *Perceptions of South Asia's Visual Past* (New Delhi, 1994), pp. 235–55 and 'The Indian Princes as Fantasy: Palace Hotels, Palace Museums, and Palace-on-Wheels', in Carol A. Breckenridge (ed.) *Consuming Modernity: Public Culture in a South Asian World* (Minneapolis, 1995), pp. 66–89. Judy Rudoe, *Cartier 1900–1939* (New York, 1997), with beautiful illustrations and an informative text, is a useful complement to the more comprehensive Katherine Prior and John Adamson, *Maharajas' Jewels* (Ahmedabad, 2001), Janaki Nair's 'Past Perfect: Architecture and Public Life in Bangalore', *JAS* 61 (2002), pp. 1205–36 is a pioneering contribution to the history of urban sites in the erstwhile princely states.

GLOSSARY

Note: In India it is common to refer to a ruler by the name of his state, for example Patiala may be used when referring to Maharaja Bhupinder Singh of Patiala.

Abhiskheka	Affusion, the pouring of consecrated substances such as water, milk or ghee (clarified butter) over a person or the image of a deity.
Adivasi	Aboriginal inhabitant.
Akhbar	Newsletter or newspaper.
Akhara	Training pit for Indian wrestlers.
Amildar	Lowest level of revenue officers, similar to tahsildar.
Andolan	Movement or struggle.
Anjuman	Cultural, educational or political association among Muslims.
Avarna	Lower-status caste groups in Cochin and Travancore.
Bania	Moneylending caste group; some are also associated with industrial development.
Bandh	A general strike, involving closing of all businesses in protest.
Begar	Forced labour.
Bhadralok	Respectable people, generally brahmans and kayasths, in Bengal.
Bharatnatayam	Classical Indian dance form, originally associated with rituals in Hindu temples.
Bhayad	Brotherhood. Among Rajput and Kathi rulers in western India, younger sons who had limited rights to revenue and to distribute criminal justice.
Bhonsle	Family name of Marathas who formed the state of Nagpur.
Biswedar	Land-controller, principally in Punjab.
Brahman	Highest ranking *varna* of priests in Hindu society.
Charan	Bard who composed celebratory poems and genealogies of Rajput warrior-rulers.
Chaudhuriyat	The right to collect land revenue in a designated area, held by the *chaudhuri*.
Chauth	Tax of one-fourth of land revenue that Marathas collected for military protection or as tribute.
Chir	Long-needle pine tree.
Chubdar	Ritual stick that is a symbol of danda.
Danda	Stick used to inflict punishment, symbol of sovereignty.
Dargah	Muslim tomb, frequently of a Sufi saint and thus a site of pilgrimage.
Darshan	The auspiciousness of seeing and being seen by a superior being.
Dasa	Servants.

Deshmukh	Marathas leaders, frequently with martial skills, who achieve control over land and people, mainly through colonisation of abandoned or waste lands.
Dhandak	A form of customary rebellion when the ruled perceived a breach of the covenant between ruler and ruled; used mainly in the sub-Himalayan region.
Dharma	Duty or obligations of an individual or social group.
Diwan	Senior revenue official in Mughal administration.
Doab	Land between two rivers.
Durbar	The court of a ruler. By extension, the administration of a state or the ceremonies associated with major life events of a ruler.
Ezhava	Lower caste groups in Kerala associated with cultivation and products of coconut palm. Also transliterated as *irava* or *izhava*.
Farman	Imperial order or edict.
Fitna	A strategy combining conciliation and competition.
Gaddi	Cotton-stuffed cushion. Here used to mean a *rajgaddi*, the ensemble of a cushion and low chair that is the Hindu version of a throne.
Garuda	Bird who serves as the vehicle of the Hindu preserver god, Vishnu.
Gaekwad	Surname of Maratha family who formed the state of Baroda in Gujarat.
Gharana	School or style of Hindustani music.
Ghats	May refer to coastal mountains, as in Kerala but it also commonly means steps on the banks of rivers or steps leading down into tanks of water adjacent to Hindu temples where ritual bathing is done.
Girasias	Literally mouthfuls (singular *giras*). In Kathiawar *girassia* meant petty chiefs who controlled resources sufficient to produce a mouthful of food.
Gunijankhana	Royal department of musicians.
Gurudwara	Repository of Guru Granth Sahib, the Sikh holy scripture.
Hartal	General strike.
Hidayat	Decree.
Holkar	Surname of Maratha family who formed the state of Indore in central India.
Ijara	Tax-farming contract.
Imam	Gift of land or assignment of revenue from land to secular subordinates, intellectuals, religious leaders or institutions.
Izzat	Honor, prestige, reputation.
Jagirdar	Holder of *jagir*, the right to collect revenue from designated tract of land granted by a superior power in return for service or acknowledgment of suzerainty.
Jam Sahib	Title of the ruler of Nawanagar in Gujarat.
Jamabandi	Day or period when land revenue was collected, especially in Mysore.
Jama'dar	Military jobber-commander

Jatha	Military group among the Sikhs based on personal, kinship, or regional bonds.
Jauhar	The Rajput practice, when confronted with military defeat, to consign women and children to a fiery death and men to die fighting to maintain honour.
Kala pani	Literally black water, and by extension seas and oceans.
Kalari	System of martial training in Travancore; teachers were known as *panikkars*, now a surname among nayars.
Kallar	Warrior-pastoralist group in south India, sometimes translated as thief.
Kayasth	Literate, kshatriya caste group with tradition of bureaucratic employment, frequently in a link language such as Persian or English.
Keddah	Round-up of wild elephants in Mysore.
Khadi	Hand-spun and hand-woven cloth.
Khalsa	Lands from which king directly collected revenue. In Sikhism, the community of the pure who are baptised by taking *amrit* or sugared water.
Khutba	Prayers offered on Friday in the principal mosque which acknowledge the legitimate Muslim ruler.
Khilat	Robe of honour sanctified by being touched to the body of a patron and then presented to a client.
Kisan	Peasant-cultivator.
Kisan Sabha	Peasant political or economic organisation.
Kshatriya	Second-ranking varna of kings and warriors in Hindu society.
Kumkum	Red powder used in the *tilak* ceremony.
Lingayat	Devotional Hindu reform sect in south India, particularly prominent in Mysore.
Lok Parishad	People's conference in princely states.
Madrasa	Muslim school usually attached to a mosque.
Mahant	A Hindu priest who assumed control of the Sikh gurudwara when Sikhs were persecuted, mainly during the eighteenth century.
Mahajan	Merchant or moneylender.
Maharaja	Great ruler. Variants include maharana and maharao.
Mansabdari	Imperial Mughal administrative system. A *mansabdar* is the holder of a *mansab* or rank in this system. A mansabdar could have both civilian and military duties.
Mirwaiz	Hereditary leader of Muslim reform movement in Srinagar.
Misldar	Leader of *misl*, an intermediate Sikh political unit that incorporated *jathas*.
Mulki	Indigenous or son of the soil in distinction to non-mulki or outsider.
Mulkgiri	Annual military operation to collect tribute in Kathiawar.
Muzara	Occupancy peasant tenants in Punjab.
Nambudiri	Brahman group in Travancore.

Nawab	Literally the plural of *na'ib*, the deputy or first minister of a ruler; by extension, the ruler of a Muslim state.
Nayar	Caste group in Kerala with martial and matrilineal descent traditions.
Nazar	Gold coin given by client to patron.
Nizam	Title of the Muslim ruler of Hyderabad.
Panchayat	Literally a council of five. Generally a caste or village council that decided disputes relating to personal law.
Pargana	District.
Patel or Patil	Village headman.
Patidar	Peasant cultivators in Gujarat.
Patwari	Village accountant.
Peshkash	Valuable object presented by client to patron.
Peshwa	Initially the title of the chief minister of the Marathas, later head of the Marathas.
Pindari	Martial groups who frequently support themselves by plundering. Loosely associated with Marathas.
Pir	Sufi saint.
Poligar	Warrior little king in south India.
Praja mandal	Popular people's association in the princely states.
Raja	Ruler.
Rajadharma	Duties of a king.
Rajaputra	Son of a *raja*.
Rajmata	Mother of a ruling prince.
Rajpramukh	Governor of unions of princely states in independent India; *uprajpramukh* is deputy governor; *maharajpramukh* might be translated as 'great governor'.
Ramayana	Great Indian epic of Ram, the ideal warrior-king
Ramraj	Rule of Ram and thus an idealised Hindu ruler and his government.
Rana	Title of minor Hindu prince. Also surname of family that served as prime ministers in Nepal.
Raniparaj	Literally people of the forest, term used by Gandhians for aboriginal people in south Gujarat.
Ryotwari	Land revenue settlement made directly with *ryot* or peasant-cultivator.
Sahukar	Local banker, used in Hyderabad and Gujarat.
Sakti	Life force.
Samasthan	Kingdom.
Sanad	Letter, decree or contract. By extension British certificate offering protection to or recognition of succession to a Indian prince.
Sannayasi	Holy man. Nominally the fourth stage of life for a Hindu man when he detaches himself from material concerns and seeks spiritual enlightenment.
Sardar	Honorific title of a leader. In Punjab a Sikh landholder.

Sardeshmukhi	Assessment of 10 per cent of land revenue to support the *sardeshmukh*, the overlord of several deshmukhs in Maratha-controlled territory.
Sarkar	District. By extension may also mean government. Transliterated as 'circars' in designation of districts in eastern India ceded to the British before 1765.
Satyagraha	Grasping the truth, basis for non-violent resistance to evil.
Savarna	Higher-status caste group in Cochin and Travancore.
Scheduled castes	Groups outside the *varna* system. Pejoratively known as 'untouchables' because considered to be ritually polluting.
Scindia	Surname of Maratha family who formed the state of Gwalior in northern India.
Shaikh	Sufi mysical holy man.
Shikar	Hunting for animals.
Subahdar	Governor of a Mughal *subah* or province.
Sudra	Lowest ranking of the four *varna*, generally peasants and some artisans.
Swadeshi	Use of indigenous products, particularly during the independence movement.
Tahsildar	Collector of revenue in *tahsil*, subdivision of a district
Taluqdar	Leader of a *taluqa* or area controlled by a lineage related through the males, generally found in Awadh.
Tarawad	Joint family with a matrilineal household dwelling and commonly held lands in Travancore.
Thakur	Lord, common title among elite Rajputs.
Thikanadar	Ruler of a little kingdom, especially in Rajputana.
Tikka Sahib	Heir to a gaddi.
Tilak	Auspicious, vertical mark on forehead made with *kumkum*, a red powder, but sometimes with blood. A *rajatilaka* was the tilak made on the forehead of a ruler during an installation ceremony.
Vakil	Agent or intermediary between rulers.
Vam	Mythological unit of inclusiveness among Rajputs.
Varna	Literally colour. The four major social ranks or divisions within Hindu society: *brahman, kshatriya, vaishya, sudra*.
Vokkaliga	Occupational category of cultivators in Mysore.
Wazir	Chief minister of a state.
Yuvraj	Heir to a raja or a princely gaddi.
Zamindar	Holder of *zamin* or land who acquired a right to a share of the produce of the land for services such as fostering cultivation. Also a petty chief who offered protection.
Zenana	Women's quarters.

INDEX

THE NEW CAMBRIDGE HISTORY OF INDIA

I The Mughals and Their Contemporaries

*M. N. PEARSON, *The Portuguese in India*
*BURTON STEIN, *Vijayanagara*
*MILO CLEVELAND BEACH, *Mughal and Rajput painting*
*CATHERINE ASHER, *Architecture of Mughal India*
†*JOHN F. RICHARDS, *The Mughal Empire*
*GEORGE MICHELL, *Architecture and art of Southern India*
*GEORGE MICHELL and MARK ZEBROWSKI, *Architecture and art of the Deccan Sultanates*
RICHARD M. EATON, *Social history of the Deccan*

II Indian States and the Transition to Colonialism

†*C. A. BAYLY, *Indian society and the making of the British Empire*
*P. J. MARSHALL, *Bengal: the British bridgehead: eastern India 1740–1828*
†*J. S. GREWAL, *The Sikhs of the Punjab: revised edition*
*STEWART GORDON, *The Marathas 1600–1818*
*OM PRAKASH, *European Commercial Enterprise in Pre-Colonial India*

III The Indian Empire and the Beginnings of Modern Society

*KENNETH W. JONES, *Social and religious reform movements in British India*
*SUGATA BOSE, *Peasant labour and colonial capital: rural Bengal since 1770*
†*B. R. TOMLINSON, *The economy of modern India, 1860–1970*
†*THOMAS R. METCALF, *Ideologies of the Raj*
*DAVID ARNOLD, *Science, technology and medicine, c. 1750–1947*
*DAVID LUDDEN, *Agriculture in Indian history*
*BARBARA N. RAMUSACK, *The Indian princes and their states*
GORDON JOHNSON, *Government and politics in India*

IV The Evolution of Contemporary South Asia

†*PAUL R. BRASS, *The politics of India since Independence: second edition*
†*GERALDINE FORBES, *Women in modern India*
†*SUSAN BAYLY, *Caste, society and politics in India from the eighteenth century to the modern age*
RAJNARAYAN CHANDAVARKAR, *The urban working classes*
FRANCIS ROBINSON, *Islam in South Asia*
ANIL SEAL, *The transfer of power and the partition of India*

*Already published
†In paperback